HISTORY
OF RUSSIA

Sergei Mikhailovich Soloviev

The Academic International Press Edition of Sergei M. Soloviev's History of Russia From Earliest Times. *Peter von Wahlde, General Editor.*

Contributing Editors:

HUGH F. GRAHAM

JOHN D. WINDHAUSEN

ALEXANDER V. MULLER

K. A. PAPMEHL

RICHARD HANTULA

WALTER J. GLEASON, JR.

WILLIAM H. HILL

G. EDWARD ORCHARD

LINDSEY A.J. HUGHES

SERGEI M. SOLOVIEV

History of Russia

Volume 25

Rebellion and Reform

Fedor and Sophia, 1682–1689

Edited, Translated and With an
Introduction by

Lindsey A.J. Hughes

Academic International Press

1989

The Academic International Press Edition of S.M. Soloviev's
History of Russia from Earliest Times in fifty volumes.

Volume 25. *Rebellion and Reform. Fedor and Sophia, 1682-1689.*
Unabridged translation of the text of Volume 13, Chapters 2-3, and
Volume 14, Chapter 1, of S.M. Soloviev's *Istoriia Rossii s
drevneishikh vremen* as found in Volume VII of this work published
in Moscow in 1962, with added annotation by Lindsey A.J. Hughes.

Library of Congress Card Number:
ISBN: 0-87569-108-0

Composition by Barbara Knoelke

Printed in the United States of America

A list of Academic International Press publications is found at the
end of this volume.

ACADEMIC INTERNATIONAL PRESS
Box 1111 Gulf Breeze FL 32562

CONTENTS

Reforming Activities of Tsar Alexis's Successors—Tsar Alexis's Family—News of Fedor's Accession—Banishment of Matveev—Exile of Andrei Savinov—Nikon's Sentence Amended—The Tsar's Favorites: Yazykov and Likhachev—Prince Vasily Golitsyn—The Doroshenko Affair—Roslavets, Adamovich, Doroshenko—Doroshenko in Moscow—Yury Khmelnitsky's Manifesto—Moscow Negotiates with Samoilovich—The First Chigirin Campaign—Zaporozhian Affairs—Porosukov's Embassy to Turkey—The Second Chigirin Campaign—Relations with Poland—Peace Talks with Turkey—Truce with the Sultan and the Khan—Doroshenko Becomes Governor of Viatka—Death of Serko—Swedish, Danish and Austrian Affairs—Kalmyks and Cossacks—Disturbances Among the Bashkir—Siberian Peoples and the Government—The Silk Trade—Trade with the Greeks—Revision of Penalties for Capital Offenses—The Schism—The Church Council of 1681—Measures to Convert Tatars—Local Government Measures—Fiscal Measures—Abolition of the Code of Precedence—Proposed Separation of Civil and Military Offices—Project for an Academy—Death of Tsaritsa Agafia and Tsarevich Ilia—Fedor's Second Marriage and Death—Death of Nikon—Improvement of Matveev's Situation

Peter and Ivan—Ivan's Supporters—Scenes at Tsar Fedor's Funeral—Disturbances Among Musketeers and Soldiers—Government Weakness and Rebellious Musketeers—Miloslavsky's

Plot—Arrival of Matveev—Musketeers Rebel—Sophia's Regency Begins—The Musketeers' Dilemma—The Column on Red Square—Activities of the Old Believers—Khovansky and the Musketeer Dissenters—The Dissenters Rebel—Musketeers Desert the Dissenters—The Disturbances Continue—The Court Departs Moscow—Execution of the Khovanskys—The Service Gentry Summoned—Musketeers and Soldiers Beg Forgiveness—Conditions of Pardon—The Musketeers Admit Their Guilt—Shaklovity Commands the Musketeers—Measures Against Rebellion—Disturbances in the Ukraine and on the Don

Polish Plans for Rebellion in the Ukraine—Prince Vasily Golitsyn and His Policies—The Holy League against Turkey—Russia Invited to Join the Holy League—Peace with Poland and Entry into the Holy League—Ecclesiastical Subordination of Kiev to Moscow—Consultations with Hetman Ivan Samoilovich—Chetvertinsky Becomes Metropolitan of Kiev—Consultations with the Eastern Patriarchs—First Crimean Campaign—Sophia Sends Shaklovity to Visit the Troops—Overthrow of Samoilovich and Election of Mazepa—Lazar Baranovich—Turkish Christians Urge Russia to War—Second Crimean Campaign—Relations with Europe and Asia—The Treaty of Nerchinsk—Domestic Affairs

WEIGHTS AND MEASURES

Linear Measure

Verst: 500 sazhen, 1166 yards and 2 feet, .663 miles, 1.0668 km.
Sazhen: 3 arshins, 7 feet, 2.133 m
Arshin: 16 vershoks, 28in. (diuims) 72.12 cm
Chetvert: 1/4 arshin
Fut: 12 diuims, 1 foot, 30.48 cm
Vershok: 1.75 in., 4.445 cm, 1/16 arshin
Diuim: 1 inch, 2.54 cm
Desiatina: 2400 square sazhens, 2.7 acres, 1.0925 hectare
Chetvert (quarter): 1/2 desiatine, 1.35 acre (sometimes 1.5 desiatinas or ca. 4.1 acres)

Liquid Measure

Stof: Kruzhka (cup), 1/10 vedro, ca. 1.3 quarts, 1.23 liters
Kufa: 30 stofy
Vedro (paid): 3.25 gallons, 12.3 liters, 10 stofy
Bochka (barrel): 40 vedros, 121 gallons, 492 liters
Chetvert (quarter): 1.4 bochka, 32.5 gallons

Weights

Berkovets: 361 olbs., 10 puds
Pud: 40 funts, 36,113 lbs. (US), 40 lbs. (Russian), 16.38 kg
Funt: 96 zolotniks, .903 lb., 14.4 ozs., 408.24 grams
Grivenka: 205 grams
Korob (basket): 7 puds, 252 lbs.
Rad: 14 puds, 505.58 lbs
Chetvert (grain measure): 1/4 rad, 3.5 puds, 126.39 lbs., ca. 8 bushels
Chetverik (grain measure dating from 16th century): 1/8 chetvert, 15.8 lbs.
Zolotnik: 1/96 lb., 4.26 grams

Money

Chervonets (chervonny): A gold coin minted in the first half of the 18th century worth
  about 3 rubles
Muscovite Denga: 200 equals 1 ruble
Novgorod Denga: 100 equals 1 ruble
Ruble: 100 copecks, 200 dengas
Altyn: 6 Muscovite dengas, 3 copecks
Grivna: 20 Muscovite dengas, 100 grivnas equals 1 ruble, 10 copecks
Poltina (Poltinnik): 50 copecks, 100 dengas
Polupoltina (-nik): 25 copecks, 50 dengas
Poltora: 1 1/2 rubles
Peniaz: 10 equals one grosh (Lithuania)
Kopa grosh: 60 groshas, one Muscovite poltina
Chetvertak: silver coin equal to 25 copecks or 1/4 rubles (18-19th centuries)
Copeck: two Muscovite dengas
Foreign Denominations: 1 efimok or 1 thaler (Joachimsthaler)-about 1 ruble, 1 chervonets
  or chervonnyi—a ducat, about 3 rubles
Levok—Dutch silver lion dollar

Note: Weights and measures often changed values over time and sometimes held more than
  one value at the same time. For details consult Sergei G. Pushkarev, *Dictionary of
  Russian Historical Terms from the Eleventh Century to 1917* (Yale, 1970).

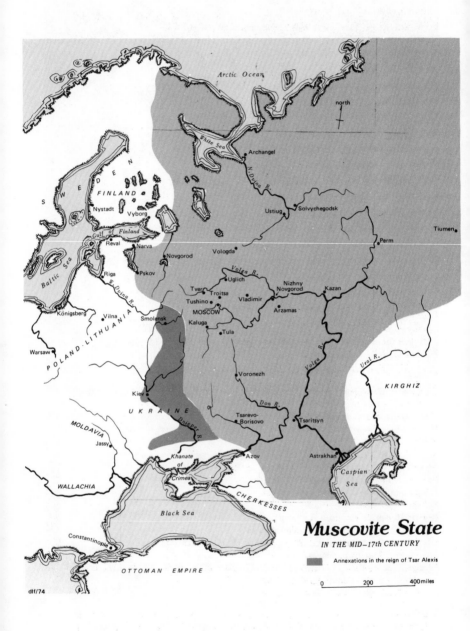

Arctic Ocean

north

White Sea

Archangel

S W E D E N

FINLAND

Nystadt

Vyborg

Gulf of Finland

Reval

Narva

Baltic Sea

Riga

Pskov

Königsberg

Vilna

Warsaw

POLAND-LITHUANIA

Smolensk

N. Dvina R.

Ustiug

Solvychegodsk

Tiumen

Perm

Vologda

Novgorod

Volga R.

Tver

Uglich

Troitsa

Tushino

Vladimir

MOSCOW

Kaluga

Tula

Nizhny
Novgorod

Kazan

Arzamas

W. Dvina R.

KIRGHIZ

Voronezh

Don R.

Volga R.

Ural R.

Kiev

UKRAINE

Dnieper R.

Tsarevo-
Borisovo

Tsaritsyn

MOLDAVIA

Jassy

Khanate
of
Crimea

Azov

Astrakhan

Caspian
Sea

WALLACHIA

CHERKESSES

Black Sea

Constantinople

OTTOMAN EMPIRE

Muscovite State

IN THE MID-17th CENTURY

Annexations in the reign of Tsar Alexis

0   200   400miles

dlf/74

Tsarevna Sophia Alekseevna

Engraved by Abraham Bloteling, Amsterdam c. 1689, from an original by
Leonty Tarasevich.

Prince V.V. Golitsyn

Engraved by Leonty Tarasevich, 1689

Tsars Ivan and Peter

Engraved by Larmessen, Paris, c. 1687

PREFACE

This book is an unabridged translation of Volume 13, Chapters 2-3, and Volume 14, Chapter 1, which are pp. 179-302 and 365-437 in Volume VII of the multi-volume edition of Soloviev's *Istoriia Rossii s drevneishikh vremen* (History of Russia From Earliest Times, 29 vols., St. Petersburg, 1851-1879) published from 1962 through 1966 in Moscow.

The present translation endeavors to render the text and Soloviev's thought as accurately as possible. No attempt has been made to reproduce his style and text word for word for this would have yielded a bizarre Russianized text. The main consideration has been to make his history as readable as possible consistent with accuracy, while retaining at least something of the flavor of the language of the era. An effort has been made to find English-language equivalents for all technical terms Soloviev employs (ranks, offices, titles, legal, administrative and so forth) in the belief that English is no less rich in such terms than other languages. This is intended to smooth the flow of the narrative for the reader and to avoid marring the pages with annoying untranslated words. The exception involves Russian words which have become common in English—boyar, tsar, cossack. In all of this the translator remains painfully aware of the inevitable shortcomings that may remain.

Soloviev's pages are featureless and interminable, one long and complex sentence marching after the last. To make the text easier to follow for today's readers, long paragraphs and sentences have been broken into shorter ones. Most of the subtitles are based on the descriptive topic headings clustered at the beginnings of the chapters in the Russian edition. These headings have been moved into the body of the text as subtitles to mark and ease for the reader the transition from one subject to another. In some cases, to even the frequency of breaks in the text or to show topics not listed by Soloviev at the beginning of chapters, new subtitles have been added. Soloviev's arrangement of the material has been followed strictly.

Brief explanatory or interpretive materials have been inserted into the text enclosed in brackets, or added as footnotes to each chapter at the end of the book. All material enclosed in brackets has been added by the present editor and all material in parentheses is the author's. Emphasized words or phrases in italics are the author's.

The general policy followed in annotating has been to identify prominent personalities at first mention, and to give explanation and elucidations of less common or obscure terms and passages, assuming the typical reader to have relatively little familiarity with Russian history. If brief, these have been included in the text in brackets; otherwise they appear as numbered footnotes at the back of the book by chapters. Most of the author's own notes are not included because their highly specialized archival, documentary and bibliographic nature is of value solely to specialists who, in any case, will prefer to consult the original Russian text. In addition, most of the notes added by the editors of the edition published in the Soviet Union which also are technical in nature—fuller bibliographic citations than those in Soloviev's notes—have not been included. When the author's notes and those of the Soviet editors are included, they are so designated. All other notes are those of the present editor.

Russian personal names are preserved in their Russian form except for Alexander, Alexis, Michael, Nicholas, Catherine and Peter, which English usage has made familiar with respect to Russian historical figures, and for important ecclesiastics whose names have been recast into Latin or Greek equivalents, especially for the earlier period of Russian history. This applies to prominent individuals; Russian forms usually are used for the less prominent. Certain other names and terms have been anglicized for the sake of clarity and because they are used widely— Casimir, Sophia, Danzig, boyar, rubles, versts, Dnieper river, and others.

The editors of the edition published in the USSR frequently have added patronymics and other names, and these have been retained without brackets; patronymics appearing in the original edition have also been included. Plural forms for names and terms which might be confusing have been anglicized—Vologdians rather than Vologzhane, Voguls and not Vogulichi, the Dolgorukys not Dolgorukie, and so forth. Even so, in a few cases the Russian plural form is used when this form is common. Most Slavic surnames show gender, and this has been preserved. Since an "a" at the word end usually signifies a female, Golovkin would have a wife or daughter Golovkina. The final "iia" in feminine personal names has been shortened to "ia"—"Maria" and "Evdokia" instead of "Mariia" and "Evdokiia".

Non-Russian names, locations, terms, ranks and so on are spelled according to the language native to the person or particular to the city, region or culture when this can be determined. Confusion arises at times because the text is not clear about nationalities. An excruciating example is Lithuania where at least three languages intermingle. In such cases the context is the guide used and as a last resort the Russian spelling in the text is accepted. Individuals whose names were once non-Russian but had been in Russian service for generations are named by the original spelling of the family name. Turkish, Tatar, Persian and other names and terms are spelled in the original according to accepted forms in scholarly books. In some instances, if not otherwise ascertainable they are translated from the Russian as given by Soloviev. The names of geographical locations conform to commonly accepted English usage—Podolia, Moscow, Copenhagen, Saxony and so forth.

Finally, with respect to transliteration, this translation follows a modified Library of Congress system omitting diacritical marks and ligatures, and rendering the initial "ia" and "iu" as "ya" and "yu" ("Yasnaia" and "Yury"), the suffixes "ii", "skii", "skaia" and "skoe" as "Dmitry Poliansky", "Polianskaia", "Polianskoe", and the form "oi" has been replaced by "oy" ("Donskoy" not "Donskoi") for certain family names familiar in this form in English. In some cases "i" has been inserted in place of hard and soft signs, or apostrophes indicating these signs. Hence Soloviev, not Solov'ev. The soft sign is not indicated by an apostrophe, as in some transliteration systems, but is dropped completely.

All dates, as in the original, except where otherwise specified, are according to the Julian calendar ("Old Style"); that is, for the seventeenth century, ten days and for the eighteenth century eleven days behind the Gregorian used in the West. A table of weights and measures is included at the front of this volume for the convenience of the reader.

This volume has been prepared for publication in two distinct stages, the first some ten years ago, when the text was translated and some of the footnotes written, and the second more recently, when I had the opportunity to check, update and augment my material and utilize some of the expertise acquired whilst researching into the 1680s in the intervening years. In the earlier stage I received welcome advice from colleagues in the Queen's University of Belfast and the University of Reading and, in particular, from Patrick O'Meara of Trinity College, Dublin, whose own labors on a Soloviev volume made him especially sympathetic to the problems involved. The revision was supervised by Professor G. Edward Orchard, another member of the Soloviev team. Not only has he subjected my text and notes to rigorous and expert scrutiny, but he also arranged for their transfer into computer format, with the help of Mrs Diane Bland, secretary to the Department of History, University of Lethbridge. Peter von Wahlde put the finishing touches. I am most grateful to all of them. Any errors that remain are, of course, my own. Final thanks are due to Jim Cutshall. This volume is dedicated to him.

Lindsey A.J. Hughes

INTRODUCTION

Volumes 13 and 14 of Soloviev's *History of Russia* were published in 1863-64, two years after Alexander II abolished serfdom and embarked on a major program of reform. The date of their appearance is not without its significance, for Soloviev's treatment of the administrations of Tsar Fedor (1676-1682) and Tsarevna Sophia (regent 1682-1689) forms an essential preliminary to his account of the reign of that greatest of tsar-reformers, Peter I, the early years of which are covered in the last chapter of Volume 14.

In Soloviev's historical scheme the late seventeenth century formed the "border between the two major divisions of Russia's historical development" (A.M. Sakharov, Commentary to Volumes 13 and 14 of Soloviev's *History*, Moscow, 1962, p. 667). In his subsequent analysis of Peter's reign, Soloviev decisively rejected the Slavophile notion that Peter's reforms had diverted Russia from its natural path; on the contrary, he emphasized their "lawfulness, the regularity of their flow from the preceding conditions of Russian society" (*Notes of S.M. Soloviev*, Petrograd, 1914) or, as he wrote in the foreword to the first volume of his *History* in 1851: "In our history the seventeenth century is closely linked to the first half of the eighteenth; the two cannot be separated."

Soloviev also believed that Russia followed, albeit belatedly, the same rules of historical development as other European nations. In a critique of the Slavophile view of history he wrote: "We are Europeans and nothing European can be alien to us." ("Schlözer and the Antihistorical Trend", *Russkii vestnik*, 1857, no. 8.) For Soloviev, basically a Westernizer in all but his Orthodox religious convictions, the "new Russia" of Peter's time and beyond was synonymous with a westernized Russia. The task that faced Peter and his immediate predecessors and successors was to bring Russia onto a level with its European neighbors in order to allow the country to take its rightful place in the European community. Russian rulers and their governments were crucial to this process for, as Soloviev indicates on more than one occasion in this volume, individual initiative and responsibility were poorly developed; the people sensed the need for change, but the driving force could come "only from above, from the great sovereign himself." Fedor, underaged and chronically sick, and Sophia, hampered by her sex, could not provide the same vigorous leadership as their brother Peter was later to give, but in Soloviev's scheme they were marked out as reformers nonetheless.

Soloviev's Soviet critics have rebuked the historian for attempting to "explain" Russia's domestic and foreign affairs purely in terms of the activity of rulers and their immediate advisers, but in Soloviev's defense it should be noted that he believed, in theory at least, that "great men" never acted in splendid isolation from lesser mortals. "The great man is a child of his age, of his people; he is divested of his supernatural significance, his actions lose their fortuitous and arbitrary nature and he is raised up as a representative of his people at a given time, the bearer and expresser of the people's ideas" (P.V. Bezobrazov, *S.M. Soloviev. His Life and Scholarly and Literary Work*, St. Petersburg, 1894, p. 67).

In the present volume, as in others, the ordinary people are very much in the background for, as Soloviev wrote in his later *Observations on the Historical Life of Nations* (1868-1876), he believed that the historian's task is to focus not on the masses and their daily life but on their representatives, the government, "the very best indicator and sounding-board of that life." Soloviev felt this principle of history-writing to be especially applicable to Russia, whose geographical peculiarities and vulnerability to attack made the role of government a vital one. He viewed the Russian government as impartial and "classless", an arbiter in disputes between different elements of the community; government as the selfish representative of ruling class interests had no place in Soloviev's scheme.

Even the Soviet commentator A.M. Sakharov is obliged to admit that Soloviev's account of the late seventeenth century provides "a wealth of factual material on the events of one of the most vivid and interesting periods of our history." At the time these volumes appeared comparatively little had been written on the Russian seventeenth century. None of the major general histories to his time went beyond the beginning of the century. V.N. Tatishchev's pioneering *History of Russia* (published 1768-1784) ended with the reign of Ivan IV. Prince M.M. Shcherbatov's *History* (1770-1791) reached the year 1610, and N.M. Karamzin's *History of the Russian State* (1816-1829) ended with 1611. N.A. Polevoi's six-volume *History of the Russian People* (1830-1833) stopped in the year

1598. Tatishchev and G.F. Müller (1705-1783) produced short sketches of the reign of Fedor, both known to Soloviev, but neither had been published. The only full-length work on the subject was V. Berkh's *The Reign of Tsar Fedor Alekseevich* (1835), which was described later by E.E. Zamystovsky as "Little more than a collection of facts, very clumsily compiled" (E.E. Zamplovsky, *The Reign of Fedor Alekseevich*, I, St. Petersburg, 1871, p. 4). Soloviev makes only one reference to Berkh's work, and then only to query the dating of one of the documents quoted.

Sophia had attracted more attention, if only for the reason that her regency found a place at the beginning of works on Peter the Great. The eulogistic nature of most eighteenth-century works on Peter generally condemned her to hostile treatment. A notable example was Ivan Golikov's *Deeds of Peter the Great*, first published in 1788-1789. Karamzin, in an article of 1820, offered a rare favorable assessment, calling her "one of the greatest women that Russia ever produced," but criticizing her for love of power. In 1856 the first separate account of her administration, P. Shchebalsky's *The Regency of Tsarevna Sophia*, appeared. Like Soloviev, whose views on late seventeenth-century Russia he doubtless knew, Shchebalsky termed the period "the dividing line between pre-Petrine and new Russia." He stressed the importance of Sophia's regency for correcting the view that Peter created the "new Russia" out of nothing, but went further than Soloviev in his evaluation of the regent's personal leadership: "The unanimous testimony of contemporaries leaves us in no doubt that the greater part of government activity...was initiated by the tsarevna herself and that she was the main inspiration behind the government of the period."

An altogether more hostile assessment of Sophia's regency appeared in 1858 in the first volume of N. Ustrialov's *History of the Reign of Peter the Great*, which covered the years 1672-89. A more detailed and scholarly account than Shchebalsky's, but a product of the Petrine cult encouraged by Nicholas I's doctrine of official nationality, it found in Sophia's seven-year administration "nothing of significance for either the nation's general welfare, the development of its industrial forces or for its education." Ustrialov viewed most of Sophia's enactments as defensive measures for restoring and maintaining order after the revolt of 1682; he also criticized her for the loss of the Amur region in 1689, for her undertaking and direction of the Crimean campaigns of 1687 and 1689, and for her harsh treatment of the Old Believers. Sophia, he believed, was "willing to sacrifice anything in her lust for power." Soloviev was to make use of a number of the documents published for the first time in Ustrialov's *History.*

Soloviev, then, had no serious rival in his detailed treatment of Fedor's reign, and provided new perspectives on Sophia's regency, the subject of two recent publications. He was the first historian to examine the period as a part of comprehensive study of the seventeenth century.

Fedor, the eldest surviving son of Tsar Alexis (1645-1676), makes a poor subject for biography. Only fourteen at the time of his accession, he was weak and ailing, like all the male offspring of Alexis and his first wife, Maria Miloslavskaia. But Soloviev does not share Michael Florinsky's view that Fedor "left no personal imprint on the course of Russian history," as expressed in his *Russia. A History and an Interpretation* (Vol. 1, New York, 1953, p. 253). Fedor's education, his knowledge of Latin and Polish and his penchant for things Polish (especially after his marriage to a girl of Polish origin) fitted him, in Soloviev's view, for the role of reformer, if only from the confines of his bedchamber. To what extent Fedor *personally* ruled remains unclear; obviously he was unsuited, both by constitution and upbringing, for active participation in the military affairs that dominated his reign and probably merely put the royal seal of approval to the plans for the abolition of the Code of Precedence, presented by Prince Vasily Golitsyn and his associates in 1682. The tsar's opening gambits with respect to the Charter of the Academy, on the other hand, are doubtless a true reflection of Fedor's concern for improving his country's educational standards. The Jesuit Georgius David, in Moscow from 1686 to 1689, mentioned Fedor's plans to found schools and colleges. But Soloviev overstates the case when he suggests, in his anxiety to focus upon the crown, that "the young tsar seemed to have a premonition of his imminent death and hastened to deal with all crucial measures." In his accounts of the reign Soloviev is in fact obliged to concentrate more on the tsar's officials than on Fedor himself.

Fedor's sister Sophia (1657-1704) is a more interesting subject if only for the reason that she was the first woman effectively to rule Russia. She remains a controversial figure. A more recent study of her reign, C.B. O'Brien's *Russia under Two Tsars, 1682-89* (1952), described her policies as "both vigorous and enlightened", an assessment which pales in comparison with the eulogy in verse and inscriptions which accompanied an engraved portrait, c. 1687, attributing to her the seven virtues of wisdom, chastity, love of truth, piety, generosity, magnanimity and eloquence. Ustrialov, on the other hand, described her as "glib, crafty and ingratiating, with humble piety in her expression but indomitable passions in her breast." Even her appearance is the subject of debate. Some writers remarked upon her beauty whilst others, like the Frenchman Foy de la Neuville, claimed in his *Relation curieuse et nouvelle de Moscovie* (1698), that she was "of a monstrous size, with a head as big as a bushel, growths on her legs and at least forty years old." Apart from the obvious objection that Sophia was only thirty-two in 1689 when de la Neuville visited Russia, and the fact that he probably never saw her, his comments provide a good idea of how Sophia's reputation was distorted after her downfall in 1689, and after Peter I emerged onto the European stage. De la Neuville's work was one of several published in the wake of the tsar's visit to the West in 1697-1698. After Sophia was implicated in the musketeer rebellion of 1698 (dealt with by Soloviev in Chapter 3 of Volume 14 of his *History*) her reputation underwent a further decline. By the time of Peter's death in 1725 she was well and truly in his shadow. Soloviev attempts to steer a middle course between the images of saint and sinner, treating Sophia as a reformer in her own right rather than a mere "precursor" of Peter, and offering an objective view of personal and political motives.

In Old Russia the daughters of the tsar, the *tsarevny*, were condemned to lives of seclusion in the upper chambers of the palace, devoting themselves to needlework and prayer. In the seventeenth century they remained unmarried, a practice which may have served to simplify succession claims and also to minimize the patronage networks to which the tsars were obligated. But in the reign of Alexis, writes Soloviev, "the doors of the tsarvenas' *terem*, or upper chamber had opened and the captives had glimpsed the light of day." He viewed the gradual emergence of royal women into the public gaze as yet another sign of the changing times. Describing the confrontation between Old Believers and church authorities in July 1682, he remarks: "The maiden tsarevnas openly were showing themselves to the people and one of them was in charge of the proceedings, but the dissenters failed to see this novelty as a sign of the times."

Soloviev sees the prime motive of Sophia's bid for power as her desire to frustrate the attempts of the Naryshkins, relatives of the "hated stepmother" Natalia, Alexis's second wife, to rule after Fedor's death. Sophia, with her sense of outraged sisterly loyalty, emerged as the "only member of the royal family who had any desire to govern." During her regency the joint tsars Peter, still a minor, and Ivan, "mentally and physically degenerate," could play no part in government affairs and so she was assured of at least temporary ascendancy. In this section Soloviev makes no mention of the fact that after the "eternal" peace with Poland in 1686 Sophia tried to legitimize her position by adding her name to those of her brothers in official rescripts and assuming the title of autocrat (see L.A.J. Hughes, "Sophia, 'Autocrat of All the Russias'," *Canadian Slavonic Papers*, XXVIII (1986), pp. 265- 86), nor does he attempt to specify the nature of her relationship with Vasily Golitsyn, her leading minister, a topic which has attracted the attention of lesser writers.

Unable to attribute all initiative in government business to Fedor and Sophia, Soloviev moves one step outwards to their immediate advisers. "When considering the political affairs of that very young and ailing tsar, Fedor Alekseevich," he writes, "it is essential not to lose sight of the people around him." Sophia's administration was "reported to be quite strong, thanks to the men from whom she drew her support." In Fedor's reign the servitors Ivan Yazykov and Alexis Likhachev enjoyed the position of personal advisers, providing a counterbalance to the influence of the Miloslavskys. By the end of the reign Yazykov had risen to the rank of boyar and Likhachev had succeeded him as lord of the bedchamber. Both were to fall from favor (and Yazykov to meet his death) after Fedor's reign ended.

The most prominent courtier of both reign and regency was Prince Vasily Golitsyn (1643-1714), whom Soloviev considered "indubitably more impressive and talented than any of his aristocratic contemporaries." During Fedor's reign he headed the commission which abolished the Code of Precedence, whilst under Sophia he was "guardian of the great royal seal and the state's great ambassadorial affairs," commander-in-chief of the army and prime minister in all but name. Soloviev does not overlook the enigma of Golitsyn's character. Despite his erudition and culture and his lofty desire to transform Russia—"to colonize the desert, enrich beggars, make savages into men, turn cowards into heroes and herdsmen's huts into stone palaces," to quote de la Neuville's eulogy—he proved inept in dealing with the petty realities of court intrigue and wasted his talents by joining what turned out to be the wrong side. In my *Russia and the West. The Life of a Seventeenth-Century Westernizer, Prince Vasily Vasilievich Golitsyn* (1984). I have termed him a "man of vision who remained too briefly in office to accomplish any of his far-sighted schemes, an ardent adherent of the West, who was ruined and banished by the greatest Westernizer of all."

Much of this volume is devoted to an examination of the intrigues of favorites and factions which, on the death of the twice-married Tsar Alexis, resulted in an open clash between the Miloslavskys and the Naryshkins, the exile of Alexis's minister A.S. Matveev, hated by the former for his Naryshkin connections (he was Natalia Naryshkina's guardian) and, after Fedor's death in 1682, the musketeer rebellion. As Soloviev writes, "The clash of interests and hatred thus engendered were terrible indeed." Soloviev's account of clan rivalries can be read usefully in conjunction with recent studies of kinship and marriage networks and promotion patterns, for example R.O. Crummey's *Aristocrats and Servitors. The Boyar Elite in Russia, 1613-1689* (1984).

The musketeers' rebellion of 1682 is seen by Soloviev as a continuation of the factionalism encouraged by the accession of weak and underaged rulers. Soviet critics have been displeased by an approach which characterizes the revolt in terms of manipulation from above and not as a popular "anti-feudal, anti-government" movement, an approach epitomized by the work of V.I. Buganov, the leading Soviet specialist on the "popular rebellions of the late seventeenth century." Soloviev does, in fact, refer on more than one occasion to the class interests involved in the rebellion as, for example, in his citation from the musketeers' petition to the crown in May-June 1682 in which they joined with soldiers, artillerymen, stockade guards, merchants, tradesmen, artisans and post drivers in appealing for absolution from guilt. The musketeers were well aware of the weakness of their position in relation to the "bosses."

Soloviev is more interested in musketeer psychology than in class feelings. His account of the revolt provides a masterly study of mob rule, underlining the musketeers' insecurity, superstitiousness and fickleness. He shows how their grievances against their officers made them vulnerable to manipulation, bribery and suggestion, first at the hands of the Miloslavskys, then by the Old Believers and Prince Ivan Khovansky. The musketeers' interests could be no more closely identified with the Miloslavskys than with the Naryshkins, but it was the former who realized the usefulness of musketeer support and acted accordingly, whilst the latter remained strangely inactive, despite the fact that Peter's claim to the throne was backed by most of the boyars and the patriarch. Insensitive behavior by the Naryshkins, including the rapid promotion of several younger members of the clan, gave rise to rumors that they were exploiting the underaged ruler Peter and had plans for settling scores with the musketeers. The latter easily were induced to march on the palace by the rumor of Tsarevich Ivan's murder, to massacre officials of the Naryshkin faction and later to voice the wishes of Sophia's party for the subordination of Peter to Ivan as "senior tsar" and the appointment of Sophia herself as regent.

Soloviev allocated Sophia a prominent role in the organization of the uprising, but as I have argued elsewhere ("Sofiya Alekseyevna and the Moscow Rebellion of 1681," *Slavonic and East European Review*, LXIII (1985), pp. 518-39), a careful examination of contemporary sources suggests that Sophia's reputation for intrigue owes much to later, frequently hostile accounts. In fact, the evidence used by Soloviev is consistent with the theory that the rebellion of 1682 had its roots in Fedor's reign and gathered a momentum of its own. Sophia was a beneficiary of the direction taken by events. For a time the influence of Prince Ivan Khovansky, "a fervent adherent of the old ways," threatened to divert musketeer support away from Sophia, but Soloviev's analysis makes it clear that the musketeers, like other sections of Muscovite society, were "as weak and helpless as children," an anarchic force, deeply resentful of abuses committed by their officers but lacking the leadership and understanding to turn their revolt into a truly anti-government rebellion. In the end Sophia's strategic withdrawal of the court from Moscow, the execution of Khovansky and most important of all, the threat of attack by the service gentry formations were enough to bring the rebels to heel. Those who supposedly had rendered the crown a great service were forced, like "guilty slaves," to humble themselves and admit their guilt. One is reminded of the more terrible retribution that awaited the same militia at the hands of Peter in 1698.

Moving away from life in the capital, much of Soloviev's narrative is devoted to foreign affairs, notably Russia's relations with Poland and Turkey. Russia's struggle with Poland over the lands of Western Russia, as Soloviev calls the Ukraine and Belorussia, had come to a head in 1654 with the annexation of the Ukraine to Moscow under the terms of the Treaty of Pereiaslavl. After thirteen years of war, the Truce of Andrusovo (1667) had divided the region into two, Left Bank Ukraine going to Russia and Right Bank to Poland. Soloviev pays considerable attention to subsequent disputes, centering on Moscow's attempts to retain Kiev, won on a temporary basis in 1667, and Poland's efforts to draw Russia into an alliance against the Turks. Not only did the Muscovite government have to contend with Polish intervention in the Ukraine but also with internal hostilities and subversion in the area. On numerous occasions Moscow was obliged to intervene in personal quarrels between the Left Bank hetman, Ivan Samoilovich, and the Zaporozhian ataman, Ivan Serko, commander of the Cossack stronghold on the Dnieper. In the summer of 1676 the government had to deal with the alleged plot of Colonel Peter Roslavets of Starodub to remove Samoilovich from power and later, during the Crimean campaign of 1687, had to remove Samoilovich himself from office when local opinion had turned against him.

Soloviev was one of the first Russian historians to pay attention to Ukrainian domestic politics, but he offered little insight into Ukrainian nationalistic feelings. The traditional freedoms of the cossacks made them unreliable subjects and the period saw the further whittling away of their liberties as Moscow strove to ensure the allegiance of the vacillating population. A decree of July 1687 admonished the new hetman, Mazepa, and his officers "to do their utmost to unite the Ukrainian and the Russian people" and "unanimously to proclaim the autocratic rule of their majesties the tsars." In Ukrainian history the period is known as "the ruin."

In foreign affairs as elsewhere, personalities are to the fore. In Chapter I Soloviev relates the last stand of Peter Doroshenko, hetman of Right Bank Ukraine. Even more prominent is the Left Bank hetman, Ivan Samoilovich, who receives the lion's share of the narrative. Samoilovich is quoted at great length as the chief mouthpiece of the Ukrainian point of view. As an educated and influential "man on the spot" his pronouncements on relations with Poland and Turkey and Ukrainian domestic affairs are of great interest, but it is doubtful whether he merits the detailed attention that Soloviev devotes to his family problems and his fall from power. Soloviev's treatment of Samoilovich highlights some of the shortcomings of his self-confessed method of concentrating upon leaders at the expense of broader, less personalized analysis. Soviet commentators accordingly have criticized Soloviev for "trivializing" Ukrainian affairs by focussing upon the activities and personal foibles of leaders such as Samoilovich, Doroshenko and Serko whilst ignoring the aspirations of the cossack population.

In the period under consideration Russia's relations with Turkey were linked inextricably to the Ukrainian problem. The Turks were the third party in the disputed region, ever threatening to expand their borders at the expense of both Russia and Poland, and a number of cossack leaders, including Doroshenko and Serko, preferred, at least temporarily, allegiance to Turkey to rule by either Russia or Poland. Religion also played a part; Soloviev cites rescripts from civil and church leaders in the Ottoman empire calling upon the Orthodox tsars to liberate their fellow Christians from the Muslim yoke. However, the policy of religious guardianship, in the seventeenth century as later, was nearly always subordinate to considerations of defense and territorial expansion. The religious problem was complicated by the fact that the Catholic Poles also were considered to be "the eternal enemies of God's Church", as Ambassador Vasily Tiapkin argued in 1678, and the choice between Romans and infidels was not a simple one. A third factor in the Turkish question were the Crimean Tatars, who still exacted tribute as the last heirs of Russia's Mongol overlords, but who were themselves subjects of the sultan of Turkey.

In 1676 Peter Doroshenko's overtures to the Turks were nipped in the bud when Samoilovich forced him to relinquish his hetmanship and claimed the Right Bank capital of Chigirin for the tsar. The Turks responded by proclaiming their captive Yury Khmelnitsky hetman in Doroshenko's stead. In the summer of 1677 a Turkish and Tatar force unsuccessfully besieged Chigirin, but a second attack in August 1678 forced the Russians to abandon the town.

As Soloviev reports, the Poles were highly displeased by what they saw as Muscovite encroachment upon their territory, and dismissed Ambassador Tiapkin's claim that the Russians merely had liberated Chigirin and other Right Bank towns from the Muslim yoke. Moscow suspected the Poles of trying to reach a separate agreement with the Turks, whilst the Poles were, in fact, eager to form an alliance with Moscow; their efforts grew more insistent after the Treaty of Zórawno in 1676, by which Poland had to cede Kamieniec and Podolia to Turkey. Russia, at this stage, preferred to deal peaceably with the Turks and Tatars. The government undoubtedly was swayed by Hetman Samoilovich, who could see no benefit in a Polish alliance and was deeply suspicious of Polish intentions. As he later remarked in 1684: "They are a deceitful and unreliable crowd, the inveterate enemies of the Muscovite and cossack peoples."

In 1681 Muscovite envoys Tiapkin and Zotov negotiated a twenty-year truce with the sultan and khan. "The Muscovites were relieved to be rid of a major and dangerous war for the price of a stretch of barren steppe," that is, the Right Bank Ukraine, but the peace was to last for little more than five years. In a lengthy analysis of the origins of the balance of power system in Europe, Soloviev shows how Russia was about to gain a more prominent role in Continental affairs, paving the way for Peter's active involvement in European politics. Turkey's interference in Austria's Hungarian domains and the sultan's unsuccessful siege of Vienna in 1683 forced Russia to make a final choice. Neither a Turkish victory over Poland and Austria nor Poland's individual ascendancy in a war against Turkey were thought to be to Russia's advantage. Samoilovich's objections were overridden and in 1686 a treaty of permanent peace was signed between Russia and Poland, drawing Russia into the Holy League with Poland, Austria and the Venetian Republic against the Turks for the reward of permanent possession of Kiev, which Golitsyn succeeded in extracting from the Poles after lengthy negotiations. Sophia's claim that "the peace with Poland was more glorious and more profitable than anything her ancestors had known" was, in the words of L.R. Lewitter, "no vain boast." ("The Russo-Polish Treaty of 1686 and its Antecedents," *The Polish Review*, IX (1964), p. 30.)

Moscow's part in the campaign was to wage war in the Crimea and Soloviev suggests that, apart from the prize of Kiev, one of the chief motives for joining the alliance was "Moscow's growing sensitivity about its national pride and ever increasing intercourse with civilized countries." The "intolerable affronts and degradations" which payment of tribute to the Tatars entailed were mentioned in the proclamation of the campaign in the fall of 1686. In a rescript to ex-Patriarch Dionisius of Constantinople and the hospodar of Wallachia on the eve of the second campaign in 1688, the government claimed that it was "unfailing solicitude for all Orthodox Christians living under the infidel yoke" which had prompted their renewed attack. In this context it is interesting to note the visit of Archimandrite Isaiah from Athos to Moscow in September 1688 with messages from Orthodox leaders in the Turkish empire. Their admonitions reveal that they feared the "Romans" as much as the Turks and were convinced that an Austro-Polish victory would result in a "yet more dreadful servitude" and the eradication of Orthodoxy. Russia was invited to widen its campaign by attacking Bessarabia, the lands across the Danube and even Constantinople itself in order to preempt the Austrians and the Poles, but the necessary preliminary to such an ambitious scheme, the subjugation of the Crimea, was not achieved.

The campaigns in the Crimea were a failure in the short term, despite Sophia's attempts to suggest otherwise by showering rewards upon the "victors." Golitsyn and his armies were beaten back, first by fire on the steppe then by the barrenness and aridity of the terrain. As Soloviev says, the campaigns "did divert the Khan's attention and prevented him from aiding the Turks elsewhere," thus helping Russia's allies, but they were a failure in the eyes of Muscovite society and struck a decisive blow against Sophia's administration and the "guardian's" personal reputation. The conquest of the Crimea was not accomplished until the reign of Catherine the Great.

In the period 1676-1689 Russia's direct links with Western Europe were overshadowed by Polish and Turkish affairs. The peace was maintained with Sweden, and trade with Holland and the German states continued. As Soloviev indicates, Russia's diplomatic service was still in its infancy; during an abortive mission to France and Spain in 1687 the Muscovite ambassadors Dolgoruky and Myshetsky were instructed to invite the king of France to enter an alliance with his arch-enemy the emperor of Austria and to obtain a loan from poverty-stricken Spain. Yet the presence of Russian ambassadors abroad on such an international errand was in itself of significance. The 1680s saw Russian envoys dispatched all over Europe: to London, Copenhagen, Vienna, Berlin, Stockholm, Florence, the Hague.

In the east the Treaty of Nerchinsk (1689) was a landmark in Russo-Chinese relations. Soloviev records the negotiations between Ambassador Fedor Golovin and the Chinese over the disputed Amur region at some length and includes the Russian version of the resultant treaty, but fails to provide a satisfactory analysis of Russia's position in the Far East. How, for example, did Muscovite contemporaries view the treaty? News of the agreement (signed on August 17, 1689) must have reached Moscow some time after Sophia's downfall and could have played no part in the unpopularity of her regime if, indeed, the terms were viewed unfavorably at the time. Here, as elsewhere in the narrative, the modern reader no doubt would be willing to sacrifice detail for explanation and analysis.

The negotiations at Nerchinsk were complicated for the Russians by the defection of a number of their tribute-paying natives to the Chinese. Russia's expansion eastwards and subjugation of native tribes is one of the outstanding features of its history, although many historians have regarded it as a "back door" activity and accorded it scant attention. Soloviev considered the urge eastwards to be an integral part of Russian history and devotes some attention to Siberian affairs in his narrative. Characteristically, Soloviev concentrates on the role of government, although the remoteness of the Siberian towns from the seat of legislation allowed more personal initiative, even rugged individualism, than in central Russia. Golovin, for example, took three years to reach Nerchinsk; in view of such time-lags local servitors often were obliged to make their own arrangements.

In cases where the government was required to intervene directly, Soloviev lays stress upon its benevolent efforts to curb both the excesses of its agents and the barbarism of the natives. In 1677, for example, a clash between Don Cossacks and Kalmyks ended, despite provocative raids by the natives, in the cossacks being ordered to return to their settlements and to cease their attacks upon the "servants of the great sovereign." Later in Fedor's reign Baltuga, the leader of a Yakut rebellion, was pardoned and released on bail despite the pleas of officials that "the Yakut and Tungus are robbing us, your orphans, setting fire to us and killing us like pigs." The crown's chief concern was undoubtedly the regular and peaceful payment of tribute by the natives. It was aware that its agents often disrupted this process by taking advantage of both the natives and their own underlings, as in the case of the Okhotsk tribute-collector Yury Kryzhanovsky, who inflamed tempers by exacting excess tribute, or the crown official Shulgin, who was removed from his office in Nerchinsk by local servitors whom he had flogged and abused.

Compared with the space devoted to foreign and frontier affairs, domestic matters are fairly cursorily treated here. In Soloviev's view, the crown stood apart from the main groupings of Muscovite society, performing a civilizing and conciliatory role. In a "young society which was yet to impose restraints upon the strong," the government was obliged to deal as best it could with powerful offenders: peasants of out-of-favor boyars were assaulted and killed by the servants of more privileged nobles, lesser nobles by their wealthier fellows, priests by their parishioners, land surveyors by landowners. Soloviev viewed such incidents as examples of abuse of the weak by the strong, which he also considered to be the basic principle underlying the institution of serfdom. In relations between masters and their serfs and bondsmen national demands rarely allowed the crown to favor the weak. Sophia's decree of 1684 which confirmed the right of domicile for peasants who had fled to town settlements, and forbade their restoration to their former owners, was an exception. In general, landlords' rights were confirmed. A decree of 1683, for example, prescribed merciless flogging for those unfortunate slaves who had been persuaded by the musketeers to claim their freedom. In 1682 twenty-seven serfs from the Belgorod district, who had been tricked into rebelling by an unscrupulous townsman, were flogged severely. The legislation of the period contains no hint of Vasily Golitsyn's much-quoted plan, for which de la Neuville is the only source, to emancipate the serfs.

Soloviev's picture of the tsarist administration as a civilizing force is not entirely convincing. During Fedor's reign penalties of mutilation for criminal offences were commuted, but in Sophia's regency the removal of ears was substituted for the amputation of fingers! In 1677 and 1682 incidents were recorded of women who had murdered their husbands being dug from the ground (interment was the penalty for such crimes) and sent to convents; in 1689 the penalty was replaced by decapitation. Some provisions were made for social welfare after the Church Council of 1681 had recognized the problem of beggars, and during Sophia's regency attempts were made to improve social behavior by issuing decrees to curb the use of whips and firearms in towns and the unruliness of courtiers and their servants in the precincts of the palace, but in general achievements seem to have been small. Indeed, Sophia's regency saw the consistent implementation of savage penalties for religious dissidence, including burning at the stake.

The most important measure of the period was the abolition of the Code of Precedence in 1682, to which Soloviev gives detailed consideration. The abolition readily was accommodated into his scheme of historical progress. In Soloviev's view, this detrimental practice "tottered and collapsed as a result of the general instability of the whole ancient order" as it came into conflict with the crown's need for military reform. The Code, which regulated government appointments on the basis of the appointee's aristocratic status and former family service, was an obvious impediment to efficient administration of both domestic and military affairs, as former tsars had recognized by waiving the Code during major campaigns. In his account of the abolition proceedings Soloviev attributes the initiative firmly to influence from above; what he fails to clarify is the benefit which the service gentry gained from the Code's removal. Modern historians generally have seen abolition as a further step in the consolidation of the power of the gentry at the expense of the hereditary aristocracy, although N. Shields Kollmann (*Slavic Review*, XLV (1986), pp. 501-502) has argued that the "fundamental changes in Muscovite society and values" signalled by the removal of the Code require much closer analysis, particularly in the context of the changing views of the Muscovite establishment. The confirmation of appointments on the basis of merit rather than birthright foreshadowed Peter the Great's Table of Ranks of 1722.

The perennial problem of tax collection, especially acute in wartime, also is given attention. In 1681, after instituting a number of piecemeal measures, delegates were summoned from each town in an attempt to regularize tax and service obligations. This, like a number of Fedor's projects which Soloviev regarded as progressive, such as the scheme for the Academy and for the separation of military and civil posts, had no immediate results.

Some of the domestic matters mentioned by Soloviev give a tantalizing but incomplete glimpse of the period. The decree of 1679 abolishing a number of local posts and transferring their duties to the governors was ostensibly for the purpose of relieving the people of excessive subsistence payments; but to what extent did it accord with a definite policy of administrative centralization? What are we to understand by the list of wages paid to secretaries and clerks in the Chancellery of Musketeers in 1683? Soloviev has a penchant for such lists but often neglects to clarify their significance.

Soloviev attached considerable importance to the historical role of the Russian Orthodox church and gives extensive treatment to religious affairs in this volume. By 1676 the schism, whereby a large element of the faithful had rejected the reforms of books and rituals instituted by Patriarch Nikon in the 1650s, had become a fact of national life and government measures were often ineffectual in the face of Old Believer resistance. Soloviev records the last years and death, in August 1681, of ex-Patriarch Nikon. His chief Old Believer opponent, Archpriest Avvakum, who died at the stake in 1682, is dealt with in an earlier volume. Nikon's pride and tenacity to the last emerge vividly from his own letters and the reports of jailers and informers.

Despite his own strongly-held Orthodox convictions, Soloviev displays admirable restraint when chronicling the activities of the dissenters. The period saw the establishment of many Old Believer communities in remote regions of Siberia and the Don, which attracted not only religious but also political malcontents who expressed their dissatisfaction in religious dissent. Some of these communities committed mass suicide by burning. A decree of 1685 which prescribed the stake for those who incited people to self-immolation simply led to a further outbreak of such incidents. Others clung tenaciously to this world. In 1688-1689 the dissenter settlement of Kuzmin held out for eight months against a cossack siege. As Soloviev indicates, the enmity between the Old Believers and the established church involved more than disagreement about ritual detail, such as the number of fingers to be used in making the sign of the Cross. The dissenters were true conservatives, stubborn adherents of an old way of life yet, ironically, their persecutors, in particular Patriarch Joachim, were themselves far behind the new times in their own resistance to foreign innovations. In the end, the split in the church's ranks was merely to facilitate Peter's task in sweeping away the power of the church in cultural and intellectual life. This aspect of the problem Soloviev barely touches upon here.

Soloviev does not gloss over the often low standards of religious life in seventeenth-century Russia. Intrigues and squabbles amongst church leaders, such as Patriarch Joachim's quarrel with Tsar Alexis's confessor Andrei Savinov (accused of drunkenness and fornication) and Archbishop Lazar Baranovich's disputes with Archpriest Simeon Adamovich and Metropolitan Gedeon of Kiev present an unedifying picture. The resolutions of the Church Council of 1681 revealed that many monks and nuns were deserting their communities for lives of dissipation in the towns and that certain priests even administered the sacraments whilst inebriated.

In the 1680s the church was weakened further by the more insidious threat from so-called "Latinists" within its own priesthood. In the reign of Tsar Alexis the church had turned to clerics in the Orthodox Ukraine and Belorussia to obtain the learning which its own clergy lacked, but such a policy had its dangers, for many of these scholars had come into contact with Catholic ideas radiating from Poland. The Belorussian monk Simeon Polotsky, for example, tutor to Tsar Alexis's children, had studied at the Jesuit college in Wilno (Vila) and later was described by Patriarch Joachim, an ardent opponent of "Latinism" and foreign influences in general, as having been "trained by the Jesuits and subverted by them." As Soloviev shows, Polotsky's views of transubstantiation were indeed more akin to Catholic than to Orthodox belief. This was a time of religious confusion, when even the prelates of the church sometimes were ignorant of important issues; Patriarch Joachim was obliged to apply to Metropolitan Gedeon of Kiev for information about the important Council of

Florence of 1439. To add to the confusion, a number of schismatic statements recorded by Soloviev accused the established church authorities of deviation. The laborer Martynka Kuzmin of Pskov, for example, claimed that the patriarch himself had been "infected with the Latin heresy." Small wonder that at the time of the musketeer rebellion ordinary people clamored to "know the truth."

Soloviev's account of developments in the Ukrainian church is concerned as much with politics as with religion, for the unification of the Ukrainian and Muscovite churches was a "natural corollary to political unification," an attempt to remove outside interference by either Constantinople or Warsaw. Kiev's defection from the authority of the patriarch of Constantinople was facilitated by Turkey's desire to appease the tsars, whilst the appointment of Gedeon Chetvertinsky in July 1685 was a personal triumph for Hetman Samoilovich.

Perhaps the question of education is best considered within the context of church affairs. For Soloviev education was a prerequisite for the fashioning of the new Russia and, like other commodities of modern European life, it initially had to be borrowed. Under Fedor and Sophia education still was tied firmly to the needs of the church. In quotations from the Charter of the Academy relating to the projected Slavic-Greek-Latin. Academy Soloviev illustrates this firmness: extensive testimonials were required of prospective teachers, guaranteeing their Orthodoxy; the curriculum was strictly controlled; the rector and teachers had special authority to regulate not only the school but also access to foreign books, the behavior of converts to Orthodoxy, and potential enemies of the church. "Much more than a school," writes Soloviev, "it was a frightful tribunal of inquisition."

Despite its narrowness the Academy, finally established in 1687, was a landmark in the history of Russian education. Pupils from various social backgrounds were taught grammar, rhetoric, poetics, logic and physics. The provision in the charter that, except for aristocrats, only graduates of the Academy might aspire to government office, foreshadowed Peter's education policy. The Academy's ascendancy was shortlived for, as Soloviev argues at the beginning of his discussion, only teachers from Western Europe could supply the answers to economic, technical and military problems.

Of culture Soloviev says scarcely anything at all here, although reference is made in other contexts to the poets Simeon Polotsky, Silvester

Medvedev and Karion Istomin, generally regarded as the first exponents of literary verse in Russia. The inventory of Golitsyn's books and furnishings gives some indication of the broadening cultural horizon of the elite in this age of transition.

Imported secular titles on literature, history, geography, architecture and science began to appear alongside the standard religious fare in seventeenth-century Russian libraries, even though Moscow's sole press, which was controlled by the patriarchate, printed almost nothing but religious books. Aristocrats began to brighten their dwellings with the paraphernalia of Western comfort—clocks, armchairs, prints, mirrors. The first theatrical performance occurred in Moscow in 1672, although the practice seems to have been discontinued temporarily under Fedor and Sophia, and several of the people who appear in Soloviev's narrative, including Sophia, Golitsyn, A.S. Matveev, Tsaritsa Natalia and Patriarch Nikon, had their portraits painted or engraved, a genre almost unknown in Russia before the end of the seventeenth century. Soloviev's failure to mention the distinctive Moscow Baroque style of art and architecture which dates from Sophia's regency is understandable, as it was not seriously examined until the end of the nineteenth century, but is is worth noting that a number of buildings commissioned by Sophia and Golitsyn, amongst others, were decorated lavishly with renaissance and baroque motifs. Cultural evidence further confirms Soloviev's assertion that "the old Russia was coming to an end and the new was beginning." The reforms of Peter I were not such an unheralded nor such a revolutionary break with an uneducated and inward-looking past as has sometimes been suggested.

A few words need to be said about Soloviev's sources. In an introductory article to the first volume of the Soviet edition of Soloviev's *History*, L.V. Cherepnin comments: "It would be impossible to name one scholar amongst Soloviev's predecessors who put such a wealth of new sources and facts into scholarly usage." Soloviev's pioneering services were especially valuable in the study of the seventeenth and eighteenth centuries. The first half of the nineteenth century saw the appearance of a number of collections of documents, such as the Archeographical Commission's publications *Acts Collected in Libraries and Archives of the Russian Empire* (4 vols., 1836) and *Historical Acts* (5 vols., 1841-42; *Supplements*, 12 vols., 1846-72), the *Complete Collection of Laws of the Russian*

Empire (134 vols., 1831-1916) and the *Collection of State Papers and Treaties* (4 vols., 1813-23), and Soloviev drew liberally upon these official sources, which reflected his concern with government activities. He also delved extensively into unpublished materials, for example in the archives of the Ministries of Foreign Affairs and Justice, for his examination of relations with Europe, Turkey, the Crimea and Ukrainian affairs, and the archive of the Holy Synod for church affairs. Throughout this volume he refers to and quotes from letters, ambassadors' reports, legal documents and travelogues, many of them unpublished.

To give but one illustration of Soloviev's use of source materials, in his study of the musketeer rebellion he uses, in addition to official papers, the accounts of a number of eyewitnesses of different persuasions—Sophia's adherent, the monk Silvester Medvedev; the dissenter Savva Romanov; an unknown Polish observer; A.S. Matveev's son Andrei and the Danish diplomat Butenant von Rosenbusch—welding their evidence into a coherent whole.

Despite the fact that Soloviev's study appeared more than a hundred years ago, it still provides one of the fullest treatments available of the reign of Fedor and the regency of Sophia. It was followed by specialist and general studies of the 1670s and 1680s by Russian historians such as N. Aristov, M. Pogodin, E. Shmurlo and V.O. Kliuchevsky in the latter part of the nineteenth century, but Soloviev was not superseded. Since 1917 Soviet scholars have illuminated the period further, for example V.I. Buganov, who has published and analyzed much primary material, and more recently A.P. Bogdanov's studies of literary monuments, but a Soviet monograph on either Fedor or Sophia has yet to appear. In the West this is perhaps one of the least studied periods of Russian history. The era has received some attention at the beginning of monographs on Peter I (e.g. R.K. Massie, *Peter the Great*, New York, 1980) and there is one worthy but outdated historical study (C.B. O'Brien, quoted earlier) and several popular and somewhat unreliable ones—R. Nisbet-Bain, *The First Romanovs, 1613-1725* (London, 1905), Z. Shakovskoy, *The Fall of Eagles. Precursors of Peter the Great* (New York, 1964) and others. New sources have been discovered and published since Soloviev wrote his work, but the modern reader may still turn to him with confidence for a reliable analysis and vivid evocation of the major personalities and issues of late seventeenth-century Russia.

History of Russia

Volume 25

Rebellion and Reform

Fedor and Sophia, 1682 – 1689

I

THE REIGN OF FEDOR

The Russian land was in turmoil and confusion. After eight centuries of looking to the east, the Russian people had made an abrupt turn westwards, forced to change direction and seek a new path by the economic and moral bankruptcy of national life. There was much talk of the need to find remedies to make the nation strong, win the respect of other countries, bring increased prosperity and raise moral standards. People spoke of the need for education, and teachers arrived from foreign lands. Some came from Greece and from Western Russia,[1] monks and nobles who had been schooled in Poland. Others came from the distant West, men of foreign race and creed, "Germans,"[2] to give instruction in the military arts and other practical subjects. These new teachers clashed with the old, and strife and division ensued. In their alarm at these changes people began to clamor about the end of the world, the Second Coming and the reign of Antichrist. And in some senses they were right to do so, for the old Russia was coming to an end and the new was beginning.

But how was the transformation to be accomplished, in view of the insolvency of the old ways and the demands of the new? The central pivot of Muscovite society was, of course, the tsar, the great sovereign. This state of affairs arose from the weakness and insignificance of individual communities; they were separated one from the other, split by inner differences which came to the fore whenever forces were united or common action was undertaken. In a word, they were as weak and helpless as children.

In the palace there was complete freedom of action. Each petition on some new official matter was received and dealt with as the authorities saw fit. If a dispute arose, with a clash of demands, there certainly was no question of the crown consulting and bowing to the wishes of the majority. Childlike helplessness has been mentioned, and in this context the following examples are instructive: all the tax-paying common people referred to themselves as the sovereign's "orphans." These were the peasants, the lowly toiling population, but what of the upper classes, the warriors and freemen, how did they refer to themselves? They called themselves the sovereign's "slaves"![3] Helpless orphans and slaves obviously could not be expected to be strong and independent and have their own personal opinions. Both elements of the community sensed the inadequacy of the old ways and understood the need for change, but because they were uneducated they were unable clearly to picture what lay ahead and were incapable of taking the initiative. This could only come from above, from the great sovereign himself.

REFORMING ACTIVITIES OF TSAR ALEXIS'S SUCCESSORS

It fell to Alexis's successors[4] to undertake the business of transformation or reform. The way in which they set off along the path which the people were already treading was to depend upon their character and upbringing. Acknowledgement of the need for education brought a new species of teacher to Moscow. Invitations were extended to teachers from the Orthodox clergy of Greece and Western Russia in an attempt to protect the ancient faith from the new learning. These men brought scholastic learning to Moscow and with it the demand for the establishment of schools. The Western Russian scholars were able to set up schools like those in their own area, which were themselves based upon the Polish model. Because of the close ties between their homeland and Poland, the scholars from Western Russia generally were raised in an atmosphere of Polish influence. There was no Western Russian literary language. They wrote in either so-called Church Slavonic, or in Latin or Polish. They were also well versed in Polish literature. This habitual usage of Polish language and literature they brought with them to Moscow. Here Polish influence was further strengthened by Russia's own direct links with Poland, both in wartime, when peace talks were always in progress, and in peacetime, when alliances were formed and negotiations continually held to discuss closer co-operation or the election of the Muscovite tsar or his son to the Polish throne.[5]

Polonisms began to enter the Russian language. One need look no further than the letters and dispatches of Vasily Tiapkin, the Russian ambassador in Warsaw, for a convincing illustration of how strongly Polish influenced Russian, quite independently of the conscious desire of the Russian speaker. Tiapkin, who will appear again in the narrative, was a pure-blooded Russian who died in Poland pining for his native land. He never got on with the Poles and always saw their worst side, yet this man began to write in a mixture of Polish and Russian and sent his son to a Polish school. He spoke to the king in the most up-to-date language of the day, half Polish and half Latin.

The teachers from Western Russia imported Polish influence into Muscovy. They introduced grammar, rhetoric, philosophy and theology. During the reign of Tsar Alexis they discussed the establishment of schools to teach these subjects, and under Alexis's successors they achieved this goal.

Yet there was one very urgent and obvious need which these particular teachers could not satisfy. The first priority was to put an end to economic insolvency, to strengthen the country and increase its prosperity. If this new prosperity was to be brought about by trade and industry, the first essential was a foothold on the sea, but this could be achieved only by force of arms. Old scores also remained to be settled, like the abolition of the tribute which still was being paid to the Crimean Tatars under the guise of gifts. In other words, military skills had to be acquired. The Russians had to learn how to construct ships and how to sail in them, and how to build fortresses. If levels of trade and prosperity were to be raised they must become proficient in the making of roads, the building of canals and in many other practical skills. None of these things could be learned from Greek or Western Russian monks or from the polonized petty nobles from Western Russia whom the Russian high court dignitaries employed as tutors for their children. No, for this Germans were needed. The required teachers must be sought not in Kiev or Warsaw, but further afield, in the German maritime states of Western Europe.

Tsar Alexis's successors, then, had at their disposal two varieties of teacher to meet the urgent demand for education: Orthodox Western Russians and Greeks, and Germans. The influence which these teachers inevitably exercised over their pupils was of two varieties: Polish and German. Tsar Alexis's successors vacillated between these teachers and their influences according to their own individual characters and upbringing.

TSAR ALEXIS'S FAMILY

Tsar Alexis's large family was an interesting phenomenon. His first wife Maria Miloslavskaia (1625-69)[6] bore him eight daughters and five sons. Of these, the six surviving daughters were robust with strong constitutions. One of them, Sophia, also had a remarkably lively mind. As one of her enemies remarked, "She was highly intelligent and astute, endowed with an intellect more manly than feminine."[7] The sons, on the other hand, were weak and sickly. Three died while their father was still alive and, of the two survivors, the elder, Fedor, suffered from chronic scurvy whilst the younger, Ivan, was both physically and mentally deficient. Then Tsar Alexis's second wife Natalia Naryshkina bore him a veritable Hercules[8] of a son, strong in body and mind like his sister Sophia.[9] The weak and ailing Fedor[10] could not be expected to participate actively in those essential reforms which Russia needed so badly. It was not he who would create a new army and lead it to victory, build a fleet and fortresses, cut canals and urge along progress by his own personal example. Fedor was a reformer only insofar as this was possible from the confines of his own chambers and bedroom.

These circumstances were in keeping with his upbringing. His tutor was the Belorussian monk Simeon Polotsky[11] who naturally introduced a strong religious element into Fedor's education, as well as Polish influence. Fedor was proficient in Polish. Lazar Baranovich,[12] who in 1672 dedicated his books *The Lives of the Holy Fathers* to Tsarevich Fedor and *Spiritual Strings* to Tsarevich Ivan, wrote to the tsar: "I have published these books in Polish because I wrote them at a time when the Poles had intentions of electing your royal majesty to the throne of Poland in order to consolidate the union of peaceful co-operation. I have published them in Polish because I know that Tsarevich Fedor reads books not only in our native tongue but also in Polish. I have dedicated my book *Spiritual Strings* to the faithful Lord Tsarevich Ivan Alekseevich and published it in Polish because I am aware that even your illustrious majesty's council does not disdain this language. They also read books of Polish history with enjoyment." Fedor also is reputed to have known Latin, although not as well as his brother, the late Tsarevich Alexis. Polotsky also taught Fedor to compose syllabic verse. It is even suggested that the translations of Psalms 132 and 145 in Polotsky's *Psalter in Verse* (1680) can be attributed to Fedor.[13]

Fedor's reign was followed by the regency of Sophia. She too had been raised under Polotsky's guidance and, like her brother, read Baranovich's *Lives of the Holy Fathers* in Polish. When Polotsky presented her a copy of his book *The Crown of Faith* (1670), he wrote the following verse: "O most noble Tsarevna Sophia, you always seek heavenly wisdom. You lead your life in keeping with your name—wise in word and deed. You are accustomed to reading the church books and to seeking wisdom in the calendar of the Holy Fathers. When you learned that a new book entitled *The Crown of Faith* was being written, you wished to see it for yourself and read it assiduously while it was still in draft. Recognizing it to be spiritually useful, you ordered that a fresh copy be made."

Because she was a woman, Sophia's sphere was limited to the confines of the palace. As a consequence it was the influence of Western Russian teachers which predominated under Fedor and Sophia and this influence was reflected in the establishment of the Slavic-Greek-Latin Academy.[14] The suspicions of the patriarch were immediately aroused by the apparently un-Orthodox tendencies introduced into Muscovy by Polotsky and he hastened to lend his support to Greek teachers. A fierce struggle ensued from which the patriarch emerged victorious, thanks to the overthrow of Sophia and her adherent Silvester Medvedev,[15] the patriarch's chief adversary and a pupil of Polotsky. Polish influence was at an end. Catholic propaganda was halted and the Jesuits were expelled.[16]

Tsar Alexis's youngest son Peter differed from his elder brother in both character and upbringing. The strength of this unprecedented Hercules oppressed him like a heavy burden. He wanted to know the why and wherefore of everything, to try out everything for himself. He felt constricted in the ancient Kremlin palace, deprived of space in which to stretch his Herculean frame, with no one to answer his questions. And so he took to the streets and ended up in the Foreign Quarter.[17] From then on the work of reform took a new direction. The great sovereign was no less avid a reader than his brothers, Polotsky's pupils, but he was no student of rhetoric—he was a ship's carpenter and a bargeman. As a result the Slavic-Greek-Latin Academy faded into the background and was replaced by other schools with new teachers of mainly German Protestant origin. Just as Patriarchs Joachim and Adrian once deemed it necessary to combat Catholicism, the guardian of the vacant patriarchal throne, Stefan Yavorsky,[18] now was obliged to do battle with Protestant tendencies and propaganda.

Tsar Alexis died unexpectedly and prematurely, leaving his domestic affairs in sad disarray as far as the country was concerned. His death was to herald serious disturbances at a time when the realm already had many weighty problems to contend with, when everything trembled on the brink of an upheaval and a major war with the powerful Turks threatened a country still utterly exhausted by previous conflicts.

The eldest son, who solemnly had been pronounced heir to the throne during his father's lifetime, was a sickly lad of fourteen. The late tsar's closest and most trusted agent had been A.S. Matveev.[19] This man justifiably enjoyed the tsar's confidence and intimacy, for he was remarkably erudite for his time, a great patron of education and learned men, a consummate writer and skilled statesman with long experience in the management of foreign affairs. Matveev would have been the obvious person to advise and support the young tsar but unfortunately a great gulf had opened up between Fedor and his father's favorite. Fedor's stepmother, Natalia Naryshkina, had been Matveev's ward and in those days the word stepmother held terrible connotations. Never before had the Russian royal family suffered the misfortune of dissension between the offspring of different mothers.[20] Worse still, this lamentable state of affairs occurred at a particularly crucial moment: reform was at hand and the reformer was being raised, but the first sentiment that he met with in his own family was one of enmity.

Even though we do not know all the details, it is not hard to imagine the effect that Tsar Alexis's second marriage must have had upon relations at court, given the large number of children from his first marriage. There was no preventing this marriage. Anonymous letters were scattered in the corridors and hallways of the palace, accusing Matveev of practising sorcery, but to no effect: Matveev cleared himself and the sovereign married his ward.

It must have been irksome for the tsar's daughters, especially the prominent Sophia, to curtsey before the young tsaritsa and to be on daughterly terms with a young woman who was mother only in name, possessing full maternal rights untempered by maternal feelings. All this took place as if by design at a time when new customs and ideas were penetrating the palace. The doors of the tsarevnas' *terem*, or upper chamber,[21] had opened and the captives had glimpsed the light of day. The strongest amongst them had grasped the possibility of crossing the threshold, spreading their wings and seeing, thinking and feeling things which previously were out of reach, of acquiring new ideas and experiencing new sensations. The strength of these aspirations was in direct proportion to the former restraint. Naturally the captives of the upper chamber desired as much room as possible in which to live and try out their strength. But suddenly they were thwarted. It was not that the new tsaritsa was actively hostile towards her stepdaughters or that she persecuted them and drove them back into seclusion.

Tsar Fedor Alekseevich

Painting by I. Saltanov (1685). Above the tsar is Simon Ushakov's renowned
icon "The Savior's Face Imprinted on the Veil of King Abgar of Edessa (1673).

No, it was the moral objection that engendered antagonism and hostility, the mere fact that someone had appeared who albeit involuntarily stood between them and their father, between them and those around them, who were all obliged to turn towards the new sun.

The tsarevnas and the Amazonian Sophia Alekseevna can be left aside for the moment. Alexis's marriage to his first wife was a long one and he had grown attached to her. As a result relations at court took on a stable and well-established pattern. The Miloslavskys and their kinsfolk, cronies and devotees consolidated their influence. They were talented, energetic people who knew how to gain influence and how to use it to full advantage. They were unprincipled and unscrupulous in their methods. Then suddenly the tsar remarried and it seemed that the cozy nest which they and their friends had built for themselves in the palace was about to be torn apart. There was a new tsaritsa with her own family and close advisers. Matveev ruled the roost at court. The clash of interests and hatred thus engendered was terrible indeed.[22]

NEWS OF FEDOR'S ACCESSION

With the death of Tsar Alexis and the accession of Fedor, Miloslavskaia's son, to the throne, the situation changed. The hatred which the tsarevnas, the Miloslavskys and their friends had amassed for Natalia Naryshkina boded ill for the tsaritsa, her children and Matveev. But, one inevitably asks, surely Matveev must have anticipated such a situation? If so, why had he not attempted to make some provision for himself and his relatives in the event of a change of sovereign? Leaving aside for a moment moral scruples, which Tsar Alexis, if not Matveev, held very strongly, it can be argued that Tsar Alexis was still in the prime of life and it seemed likely that his ailing sons would not survive him, and would follow their brothers to the grave. Peter then would succeed to the throne. The tsar's sudden death put things in a different light. Foreign accounts tell of Matveev's efforts on Peter's behalf at this moment of crisis. The most detailed, written by an [anonymous] Polish author in his interesting account of the musketeers' rebellion,[23] records the following: "When the tsar's first wife Maria Miloslavskaia died, she left two sons and six daughters who suffered much from Matveev. They had to endure even worse ill-treatment when Matveev succeeded in obtaining the tsar's marriage to his kinswoman, the daughter of Kirill Naryshkin, a captain from Smolensk."

On his death-bed Alexis designated Fedor, his son by Miloslavskaia, as his heir. The boy was ill in bed at the time and Prince Yury Dolgoruky[24] was appointed his guardian. Artamon concealed the news of the tsar's death and won over the musketeers to Peter's side by bribes. Not until nightfall did he inform the boyars of the sovereign's demise. While they were assembling he placed the child Peter upon the throne and urged them to recognize him unconditionally as their sovereign since Fedor was all swollen up on his sick-bed and unlikely to recover. The boyars, however, awaited the arrival of Prince Dolgoruky, for the patriarch had told them of the tsar's dying wish that Fedor should succeed him and that Dolgoruky be made guardian. Dolgoruky finally made his entrance into the palace, roaring like a bull in his grief for the tsar. He questioned the patriarch directly: "Who is the sovereign's appointed heir?" "Fedor," the patriarch replied. Thereupon Dolgoruky and the boyars, deaf to Matveev's appeals that they elect Peter, headed for Fedor's chamber. They found it locked and Dolgoruky ordered the doors be broken down. The boyars lifted up Fedor, who was unable to stand unaided because of the swelling in his legs, carried him to the throne and seated him upon it. They approached him one by one and congratulated him upon his accession. Peter's mother and Artamon went into hiding for they realized that they were powerless against Dolgoruky and all the boyars."[25]

It would be wrong to give too much credence to this report for later, when Matveev's downfall was being engineered and all manner of wild accusations were employed to convict him, not one word of reproach was uttered by those high court dignitaries whom Matveev is alleged to have urged to bypass the sick Fedor and swear allegiance to the child Peter.

Be that as it may, Fedor came to the throne peacefully and there were no changes. Matveev retained his powerful position as guardian of the great sovereign's ambassadorial affairs. But his enemies had won power at court and had no intention of leaving him in peace. The sick Fedor was tended by his aunts and six sisters, and the stepmother was sent away. Especially strident in her denunciation of the tsaritsa was Anna Petrovna Khitrovo, a lady-in-waiting and a strict observer of fasts who wielded considerable influence.[26] Her criticisms of the dowager tsaritsa, Natalia, were extended to Matveev, for the two could not be separated. Khitrovo found male supporters for her campaign, not themselves strict observers of fasting but powerful men, like the boyar Ivan Mikhailovich Miloslavsky.[27]

The latter bore a grudge against Matveev whom he blamed for arranging his removal to the governorship of Astrakhan during Tsar Alexis's reign.

Miloslavsky was joined by another powerful boyar, the majordomo Bogdan Matveevich Khitrovo.[28] Khitrovo was of fairly humble origin, from a family of provincial service gentry hailing from Aleksin. He had been introduced into society by Morozov.[29] But he had no love for the other new men whose talents far outshone his own, Ordin-Nashchokin[30] and Matveev included, especially when he discovered or came to suspect that the latter had informed Tsar Alexis of certain abuses committed by him and his nephew Alexander Savostianovich Khitrovo during their directorship of the Chancellery of the Royal Household. Matveev alleged that "the Khitrovos continually stocked their own estates with produce from the royal villages and domains and built mills. They quite blatantly made fat profits by inordinate embezzlement, shamelessly plundering the beverage, fodder and grain stores. They also got rich on huge bribes received from the palace contractors."[31]

Miloslavsky's and Khitrovo's chief weapon was Lord-in-waiting Vasily Semenovich Volynsky, who had long envied Matveev. Volynsky was a man of limited ability, badly educated even for those days, but he was also a loud-mouth who knew how to ingratiate himself with the powerful. It is said that he first came to public notice thanks to his wife, who kept excellent seamstresses and took in orders from all the aristocracy.

BANISHMENT OF MATVEEV

Matveev's fate was sealed. He was removed from his post in the Pharmacy on grounds that such a suspicious individual should not be left in charge when the sovereign was sick. Then the Danish diplomat Mons Gioe,[32] who was about to leave Moscow, lodged a complaint against Matveev, claiming payment of five hundred rubles for Rhine wine which he had delivered to Matveev's house. He alleged that the Chancellery of Foreign Affairs had responded to his demands for payment by sending him a counterfeit contract. Matveev was ordered to pay the five hundred rubles and the occasion was used to dismiss him from the directorship of the Chancellery of Foreign Affairs and banish him from Moscow.

When Matveev arrived at the palace as usual, Boyar Rodion Streshnev brought the decree from the chamber to the entrance hall and informed him that the great sovereign had appointed him to the governorship of Verkhoturie. The Chancellery of Foreign Affairs was handed over to

Crown Secretary Larion Ivanov. And so Matveev set off with his son and relatives for honorific exile, taking with them a monk, a priest, the son's tutor—a Polish nobleman by the name of Poborski—and a large retinue of domestic servants. They also took along two cannon for protection.

In Laishev Matveev was stopped by Luzhin, a lieutenant colonel of the Moscow musketeers, who demanded that Matveev hand over a certain medical primer containing inscriptions in code. He also demanded two of Matveev's servants, Ivan the Jew and Zakhar the dwarf. Matveev denied all knowledge of the primer but gave up the two servants.

One night about a month after his arrival in Laishev Matveev was awakened by Crown Councillor Sokovin and Crown Secretary Semenov who had come from Moscow. They ordered him to hand over the wife of Ivan the Jew and his own papers and property for inspection. They also demanded that he give up his relatives, the monk, the priest and all his servants. Matveev immediately obeyed. Sokovin and Semenov then went to the local government office, ordering Matveev to attend them there directly. The boyar arrived on foot. They interrogated his relatives and servants about the aforementioned medical primer and took written statements from all of them. From Matveev they elicited a statement about how he had prepared and administered drugs to the sick tsar. Matveev told them that the drugs were made up by the doctors Costerius and Stefan Simon from prescriptions kept in the Pharmacy. Each preparation was tasted first by one of the doctors, then by Matveev himself, and then by the sovereign's personal attendants, Prince Fedor Fedorovich Kurakin and Ivan Bogdanovich Khitrovo. After the drug had been administered Matveev himself drained the glass before the sovereign's eyes.

Sokovin and Semenov were joined in Laishev by a servitor with an order for Matveev's transfer to Kazan. Here he was placed under guard by the governor, Ivan Bogdanovich Miloslavsky. Before long a royal decree arrived ordering that Matveev's servants disperse to their villages and the others be released. One night a crown secretary named Gorokhov came to order Matveev to hand over his belongings. To this Matveev retorted: "None of my property has been acquired as a result of theft, brigandage, robbery, treachery or any other foul means. I received everything from my father and mother and their parents and some by God's grace and the sovereign's benevolence in recognition of my services at the Chancellery of Foreign Affairs and in the military field, for all the great toil and effort of sixty-nine years of service. But if the hour of my destruction has come, innocent though I am of any crime, and the great sovereign has commanded that an innocent man be stripped of his possessions, may God's and the sovereign's will be done."

The next to arrive was Table Attendant Tukhachevsky, who had been appointed as Matveev's warder. He demanded that Matveev hand over guns, powder, lead, armor, helmets and manacles. Matveev replied: "I have always tried to put a stop to all kinds of crime. I have never engaged in it myself." Then a messenger, a colonel of the musketeers, came from the governor to escort Matveev, his son and his servants with their wives and children to the government office. They went on foot, exposed to the scorn of the crowd. In the office the charges against Matveev were read out. In the statement he made in Laishev he had claimed that he always drained the last drops of medicine after it had been administered to the sovereign, but the tsar's attendants Kurakin and Khitrovo refuted this claim. The apothecary David Berlov reported that he had gone once to Matveev's house to treat his servant Zakhar the dwarf and was told by the latter that his injuries had resulted from a beating by his master. It appeared that the dwarf had fallen asleep behind the stove in a room where Matveev and Doctor Stefan were reading from a book on black magic. As they read a host of evil spirits appeared and warned them that there was a third person in the room. At this Matveev leapt up and, discovering Zakhar behind the stove, tore off his fur coat, lifted him up, threw him to the ground, trampled on him and hurled him from the room in a dead faint.

Berlov had added that he himself once had seen Matveev with Doctor Stefan and the Greek translator Spafarius[33] reading a book of black magic behind closed doors. Spafarius used to instruct Matveev and his son Andrei from this book. Matveev tried to object but Secretary Gorokhov told him to listen and hold his tongue. Matveev was deprived of the rank of boyar and stripped of his entire possessions. He was given just a thousand rubles and he and his son were exiled to Pustozersk.[34]

Matveev was horrified at these deprivations. He sent three petitions: one to the tsar protesting his innocence, one to the patriarch, and one to the privy boyars begging them to intercede on his behalf. The old man may have been experienced in affairs of state but he was little acquainted with the adversities of life. He could not deny himself the consolation of submitting petitions, confident that they would have some effect, oblivious to the fact that the charges against him were absurd, his conviction illegal, and that this in itself removed all hope of acquittal or mitigation of his plight as long as the adolescent tsar was surrounded by the Miloslavskys, Khitrovos and their followers.

He wrote to the sovereign: "I, your slave, beg to disagree with David the apothecary and my servant Zakhar the dwarf. Under interrogation by torture Zakhar told your boyars that he was asleep and snoring behind the stove while I was reading a book with Doctor Stefan and Spafarius. According to him, I heard his snores, grabbed him by the hair and threw him out. But he made no mention under torture of any evil spirits: that obviously was fabricated by that rogue David. Even if Zakhar did claim to have seen evil spirits there is no reason to believe him. He should be asked how he could possibly have seen evil spirits: what did they look like and how did he recognize them? As for that rogue David, why did he not mention exactly what we were reading from the book and repeat the actual words and formulas which he heard? And what did Spafarius teach my son and me?

"Zakhar did have two broken ribs but he was injured through playing with Ivan Solvtsov, not as a result of my beatings. The evil spirits are supposed to have spoken of a 'third person' in the room, namely Zakhar, but Zakhar said that there were three of us reading from the book—Doctor Stefan, Spafarius and myself. Who got it wrong and mistook four men for three—the damned and infernal spirits or those scoundrels David and the dwarf? Zakhar claimed to be asleep behind the stove but it is impossible for anyone to sleep behind the stove in that particular room. The stove has two free sides, the third is attached to the wall with no space behind, and the fourth contains the door of the stove. Zakhar also said that he was snoring in his sleep but how can a sleeping man overhear a conversation, never mind his own snores!

"Spafarius never gave me any kind of instruction and certainly none of a sacrilegious nature. He did teach my son a little basic Latin and Greek but what time did I have for lessons with your royal affairs to attend to? I read and collected in my humble dwelling only those books which were edifying to the soul and pleasing to God. And in the service of the great sovereigns I and my assistants, crown officials and translators in the Chancellery of Foreign Affairs, compiled books which were previously unattainable and which now can be seen there as a testimonial to our combined efforts.[35] Informers claim that I took many bribes and treated your servants badly, forcing them to sell their patrimonies. But no one from any of the towns and districts under my jurisdiction in the chancelleries ever lodged a complaint against me nor will they do so in the future. When I traveled through some of these places on my way into exile the people treated me kindly and gave me gifts of food, as they are accustomed to do with the wretched and downfallen. But I heard not one word of rebuke.

"I served your grandfather and your father on military expeditions. When the army was retreating from Lwów the situation became desperate.[36] Father raged against son, brother against brother; cold and hunger set in. Soldiers, musketeers and servitors deserted the guns, left all the supplies on the steppe and fled. The boyar Buturlin set off on a forced march, leaving me on the steppe with the abandoned guns and supplies. And with the help of those who remained, I harnessed myself to the guns and we got back fifty-nine guns and the supplies to Belaia Tserkov and then to Moscow. When your majesty's troops suffered a set-back at the battle of Konotop and the commanding officers retreated to Putivl, it was I, your slave, who organized the building of trenches, the transport, the plan and the route and got them back to Putivl in safety.[37] And when the soldiers refused to obey Prince Alexis Trubetskoy's orders to march on the cossack towns, mutinied and tied up the boyar in his cloak, it was I and the musketeers who rescued him.

"Before the capture of Astrakhan I wrote to your father urging him not to allow the rogue Stenka Razin to leave Astrakhan because of all the dastardly crimes he committed when he first took to the sea.[38] I made the Austrian envoys agree to address the great sovereign as your majesty rather than your highness and I persuaded the Polish and Swedish ambassadors to agree to remove their headgear when seated in the sovereign's presence. During my term of office in the chancelleries I made great profits. I reopened the Pharmacy and the state liquor trade and with the proceeds I had stone premises erected for the Foreign Affairs and Greek chancelleries and shops built.

Before I took over the Chancellery for Little Russia,[39] it was the practice to send food supplies to the troops in Kiev and other towns by boat from Briansk. The boats were made there in Briansk and a *chetvert*[40] of grain cost seven rubles or more. But when I began to organize the sale of grain, a *chetvert* never cost more than a ruble. After the death of your father I was able to show you a balance of 182,000 rubles of gold, silver and copper coin. The mint stood empty for fifteen years, without silver for the production of coin.[41] It was I who ordered the resumption of minting with the result that the treasury has shown a profit ever since.

"And for all my humble services I was rewarded with your royal favor. I was raised to the rank of boyar and granted hereditary and service estates. I earned your royal favor in the performance of my duties in military service, on missions and diplomatic errands and on your royal business and now everything has been unjustly taken from me. Great sovereign, there are those who have lived in the homes of strangers, worn other people's clothing and eaten their bread, people who during the reigns of your father and grandfather earned as much or more than I who rendered such services. Yet I alone am hated and reputed to have great wealth, gold and possessions. You now know the true extent of my meager effects and that they are not what they have been made out to be. From the inheritance left to me by my father and my own wretched belongings I received the sum of one thousand rubles and I do not know whether to spend your endowment on food for myself or leave it as a legacy for my wretched worms of dependents.

"Why should anyone believe that drunken rogue of a Dane who spent his whole time in Moscow earning a reputation for being carried home drunk lolled over the saddle of a horse or with his legs sticking out of a cart, and the lads running after him yelling: 'Drunkard! Drunkard! Get back to the Kukui!'[42] The tippler cut Peter Marselis's throat with a glass and killed him.[43] Why was I not allowed a confrontation with him? Why was the rogue not brought back? Stenka Razin was interrogated in front of all the boyars in a formal process at the police headquarters but I, a boyar, was convicted without trial! We, your slaves, entreat you to have mercy on us, in the midst of our bitter tears, great sovereign. We are starving, unable to buy a portion of meat. Even a copeck's-worth of ordinary bread is not to be had, not to mention meat or fancy loaves. The well-off folk here eat roots and a handful of rye flour, and the poor eat only roots. And even roots don't grow in Pustozersk—they have to be brought from Izhma. People are leaving on account of the food shortages, and those who remain will soon follow them."

Matveev sent three letters to the patriarch. He also wrote to the tsar's confessor, Archpriest Nikita Vasilievich, to Prince Yury Dolgoruky, Prince Mikhail Dolgoruky, Prince Nikita Odoevsky, Prince Yakov Odoevsky and Boyar Rodion Streshnev, begging them to intercede with him. He even petitioned his enemies, the agents of his misfortune Ivan Miloslavsky and Bogdan Khitrovo. He swore to Miloslavsky that he had not been responsible for his dispatch to the governorship of Kazan. To Khitrovo he wrote: "One more special favor I ask of you: please beg my lady the gracious boyarina, Anna Petrovna, to bestow her mercy and favor upon me. I would have her and you speak to the great sovereign on my behalf, which surely she will do when she sees the misery of an innocent man, the bitter and unceasing tears shed for my children and my infinite ruin. She shall be recompensed by heavenly blessings in the eternal kingdom."

In his ignorance of the turn of events at court Matveev even wrote to Kirill Naryshkin, Tsaritsa Natalia's father, with a request that the tsaritsa and Tsarevich Peter intercede for him. Matveev was unaware that the tsaritsa was unable to defend even her own brother Ivan Naryshkin from the denunciations of that same Doctor Berlov. On the basis of information divulged by the latter, Naryshkin was summoned to the Kremlin and surrounded by musketeers and their lieutenant in front of the Palace of Facets. Prince Yury Dolgoruky came out, accompanied by a crown secretary who read out the charges: "You, Ivan, spoke about his royal majesty with your retainer Ivan Orel on the Sparrow Hills[44] and in other places where you were observed by Doctor Berlov. You said: 'You are an old eagle, but there is a young eagle flying over the creek.[45] You should shoot him with your gun and when you have done so the sovereign lady Natalia Kirillovna will bestow great favors upon you and God will reward you in ways you cannot even imagine.' Ivan replied: 'I would do it, but it's impossible. The wood is flimsy but the fence is high.' This testimony was extracted from David under repeated torture with fire and tongs. He repeated it before the sovereign, the patriarch and the boyars and confessed it to his priest. He insists that you, Ivan, incited Ivan Orel to murder the pious tsar. Thus the great sovereign has decreed and the boyars resolved that for your fearful crime and treachery you are sentenced to be flogged, burnt with fire and tongs and put to death. But the great sovereign in his mercy has commuted your death sentence and decrees that you be exiled to the town of Riazhsk near Riazan and there imprisoned for the rest of your days." Ivan's brother Afanasy was exiled with him.

EXILE OF ANDREI SAVINOV

Whilst Miloslavsky and Khitrovo were dealing with Matveev, Patriarch Joachim[46] was settling his own score with two clergymen who had lost their only protector when Tsar Alexis died. Joachim had made one attack already on Andrei Savinov, the tsar's confessor, accusing him of immoral conduct and lack of respect for him, the patriarch. Tsar Alexis had begged the patriarch to forgive Savinov. On the very day of the tsar's funeral, however, the old enmity between the two flared up more strongly than ever. During the funeral service the confessor flew into a rage because he believed the patriarch had usurped his right by placing a valedictory charter in the hands of the deceased tsar. After the funeral he went into the palace to the room where the royal family was assembled and shouted: "The late tsar did not receive a fitting farewell for the patriarch prevented me from handing him the valedictory charter. Give me two thousand armed men and I shall pursue the patriarch and kill him. Kill my enemy the patriarch with weapons or poison. If you won't put him to death I shall curse you and deal with him myself. I have already hired five hundred troops to kill him." Official sources record somewhat naively that the tsar, tsaritsa and tsarevnas "did not assent" to Savinov's demands. They handed over the enraged priest to the patriarch.

Joachim convoked a church council and on March 14, 1676 sentence was passed. As well as the outrageous behavior in the palace, the following offences were listed: (1) When this evil priest took over the management of spiritual affairs in the royal household at the tsar's request, he quite illegally and wrongfully overstepped his authority and referred to himself as archpriest without obtaining the blessing of the patriarch or receiving an official charter. (2) Instead of interceding for the wretched, he caused much torment and injury to a number of people who had written letters justly accusing him of fornicating with a married woman. He should have repented of his sin: instead he avenged himself upon his accusers and subjected them to ill-treatment. Many were tortured and sent off into exile on his account. (3) He got drunk in the company of disreputable people, delighted in lewd songs and engaged in various rowdy pastimes. (4) He built himself a church without the patriarch's permission. He continued to celebrate mass even while under patriarchal interdict, and without being authorized in any way to do so. (5) He set the tsar against the patriarch in an attempt to evade the latter's well-founded charges against him. In the end the tsar stopped going to the cathedral to receive the patriarch's blessing. (6) He abducted the wife of a living man and forced her to marry another. He ordered a priest on his estate to marry the couple against his will and then took the woman away from her second husband, committed adultery with her then had her innocent first husband sent far away into exile and thrown into jail in chains.

Savinov was duly defrocked and exiled to the Kozheozero monastery.

NIKON'S SENTENCE AMENDED

Two months after sentence had been passed on Savinov the Church Council amended the sentence of that old prisoner Nikon.[47] It appeared that he had been on friendly terms with the convicted confessor. Nikon had been very upset by the news of Tsar Alexis's unexpected death, which had been brought to the Ferapont monastery by Fedor Lopukhin. His eyes brimmed with tears but he expressed his predominant feelings by declaring harshly: "He and I shall stand together at the terrible Day of Judgement." To Lopukhin's request that he send a letter of farewell to the deceased, Nikon replied: "In imitation of Our Lord Jesus Christ, who taught us to forgive the sins of our fellow men, may God forgive the late tsar, but I refuse to send a letter of farewell because he did not release me from captivity during his lifetime."

It did not occur to Nikon that, now that Alexis was dead, an even greater misfortune awaited him than his continued imprisonment during the tsar's lifetime, a misfortune for which he had only himself to blame. On April 13 Nikon's jailer Prince Shaisupov reported that Nikon was demanding the dispatch to Moscow of Ignaty Bashkovsky and his serving woman Kilikeika. It seemed that Bashkovsky knew of some grave and terrible matter concerning the great sovereign. In his letter Nikon signed himself patriarch, which in itself was sufficient to infuriate the incumbent patriarch, but Nikon in addition had sent his own informer to Moscow at the very moment when evidence against him was eagerly being sought. Bashkovsky reported that a sick peasant from the Ferapont monastery, whom Nikon had been treating, had died as a result of drugs administered to him by the ex-patriarch. He also reported that Nikon had been shooting from his cell with an arquebus and had brought down a cormorant. He had been visited by a number of his relatives from Kurmysh.

At this time Nikon's jailer Shaisupov was relieved of his duties and came to Moscow. He too had much to report about Nikon. He had been consistently disobedient and ordered others to act likewise. He commanded people to address him as his holiness the patriarch and demanded that the same title be used in letters. On crosses along the lake and roadside he had the following inscription carved: "This cross was erected by the humble Nikon, patriarch by the grace of God, at the time of his imprisonment for defending the Word of God and the Holy Church." He shot and wounded a cormorant and ordered that its wings, head and feet be cut off as a punishment for eating his fish. Anyone who made Nikon angry was beaten with sticks and lashes by musketeers and lay brethren. The ex-patriarch used to boast to Shaisupov that he had foretold to Rodion Streshnev the devastation caused by the Stenka Razin rebellion. When Lopukhin visited from Moscow he told him that he had four relatives, crown agents, in Turkey to whom he sent money and that the patriarch of Constantinople cursed the patriarchs who had convicted him and referred to them as scoundrels. After Tsar Alexis's death he drank heavily throughout Lent and in his inebriated state tormented everyone quite needlessly. On his orders Elder Pafnuty was flogged for a whole week during Lent. A lay brother called Obrosimov died as a result of a beating which Nikon personally administered. Lavrenty the elder was beaten with sticks and also died after Nikon had forced him to take a large draught of liquor. On feast days Nikon would receive the abbot, monks and lay brethren seated in an armchair and they were obliged to kiss his hand. He set up his own chancellery and court. Once a young woman of twenty and her small brother came to him for medical treatment and Nikon killed her by giving her too much to drink.

When the new jailer, Adadurov, arrived at the monastery he reported to the authorities that Nikon was not living under a prison regime. He had built twenty-five cells, with exits and entrances and large windows overlooking the monastery compound and the outside world. These cells were inhabited by about ten people of various ranks.

A new informer appeared in the shape of Nikon's steward, Brother Jonas, one of his closest friends. He reported that Nikon rarely went to church, did not pray for the sovereign and the patriarch and that he forbade the monks to do so. He allowed no one to enter the church when he was there, and celebrated communion at the altar jointly with the officiating cleric. He had not been to confession for four years. During the liturgical responses he referred to himself as patriarch of Moscow. He treated the allowance sent to him by the sovereign disparagingly, trampling it underfoot and furiously uttering all manner of abuse against the great sovereign.

Jonas gave the following testimony:[48] "He also said that all parts of the body should be annointed with holy oil and that a demon occupied that secret member which is not guarded by the life-giving cross or annointed with oil. He gives medical treatment to people of both sexes in his cell, says prayers over them and annoints them with oil. Women and girls come to him, allegedly for treatment, and he stays alone with them and makes them strip naked so that he can diagnose their ailments. He calls maidens and young women his 'daughters' and betroths them in his cell; then after the wedding they come to him and he gets them drunk and they stay in his cell until midnight. He forced a woman in advanced pregnancy to marry against her will. The groom did not wish to marry her so Nikon beat him with lashes and forced him to obey. The monastic servant Nikita Nikitin used to bring his own wife to Nikon's cell at night. The sexton Isakov used to bring in a woman by night. The lay brother Isaev saw Nikon in the sanctuary with a woman. On feast days he organizes private banquets for women from the neighboring settlement. He gets them drunk and then has them taken back to the settlement, dead drunk, in the monastery carts. He forced the maiden Marfutka to take the veil and he paid a donation to the convent for her. He dispenses alms to maidens and young women to the sum of twenty *altyns* each but to the old women he gives only a *denga*. Women and maidens visit him at unseemly times and stay in his room at night."

The accusations gave Joachim and the council grounds for revising Nikon's sentence. Zheliabuzhsky, a state councillor,[49] and Archimandrite Paul were sent to the Ferapont monastery to inform Nikon of the sovereign's decree that he be transferred to the monastery of St. Cyril, a few miles to the southwest.[50] He was to be attended there by two experienced and trustworthy elders who would render him the respect befitting his station, but other monks and laymen were not to be admitted, nor was he to be given paper or ink or allowed to receive any gifts.

The envoys received their instructions on May 16, 1676 and arrived at the Ferapont monastery in June. At the end of mass they read out the decree and charges to Nikon. Nikon listened meekly to the decree; as for the charges against him, some he rejected outright, others he disputed. He argued, for example: "Ivan Krivozuba, who informed against me, was caught thieving and was beaten by me, the abbot and a priest. I forced no one to kiss my hand, but simply offered my hand to be kissed by those who visited me. I did not set up my own court; the abbot and I jointly tried the Krivozuba case. The cells were built by order of Tsar Alexis. I pray ceaselessly for the great sovereign and the ecumenical patriarchs, but I refuse to pray for Patriarch Joachim. For one thing, the archbishop of Vologda sent a letter to the monastery of St. Cyril ordering that prayers be said for himself but not for the patriarch and, besides, Joachim has treated me badly and is now seeking to destroy me. But I do not stop the priests from praying for Patriarch Joachim. I did celebrate the communion at the altar with the officiating priest Varlaam, but I have not been to confession for about three years because my confessor, the archimandrite of the monastery of St. Cyril, has not been to visit me. In the liturgical responses the priests and deacons refer to me as they wish: I have given them no special instructions. Nor have I issued any order that I be addressed as patriarch of Moscow or compelled anyone thus to address me. The envoys sent by Tsar Alexis always addressed me as great and holy father. During the period that Prince Shaisupov was my warder, people were always applying to me for medical treatment, but the prince made no attempt to put a stop to it. I would have admitted no one if the prince had so ordered, and I obeyed the new jailer Adadurov when he banned such visits."

Zheliabuzhsky and Paul tried everything to persuade Nikon to pray for his holiness the patriarch in the cathedral and to refrain from abusing him, but on his way out of the church Nikon said: "I shall pray for the great sovereign and for the ecumenical patriarchs, but I refuse to pray for the patriarch of Moscow, or even refer to him as such."

That same day Nikon was transferred to the monastery of St. Cyril. Now that he was being moved to hostile surroundings, where he no longer could enjoy the authority that was his at the Ferapont monastery, Nikon was obliged to change his tune. He was also alarmed to hear that two of his most intimate and trusted servants, the priest Varlaam and the deacon Mardary, were to be taken from him and sent to the monastery of the Cross, situated on the White Sea. Just before his departure Archimandrite Paul made one final attempt to persuade Nikon to pray for the patriarch. Nikon's reply was: "If his holiness the patriarch is merciful to me and spares me from a wrongful and distressing death, I shall pray for him and address him as patriarch. When I was interrogated about my retirement to the Resurrection monastery during Tsar Alexis's reign[51] I advised the sovereign to appoint Joachim as patriarch because of his humility."

With tears in his eyes Nikon begged Paul to appeal to the sovereign and the patriarch that Varlaam and Mardary be allowed to remain with him and not be sent to the monastery of the Cross, for they were accustomed to his company and he to theirs. At their interrogation these men had testified to Nikon's innocence of the charges against him, but Mardary had let slip the information that he had delivered letters and appeals from Nikon to the great sovereign in Moscow. These he had handed over to the tsar's confessor, Savinov, and to Poliansky, a secretary in the Privy

Chancellery, and they had delivered them to the sovereign. He had taken the confessor a number of gifts from Nikon—wooden dishes, wine bowls, glasses, spoons and fish; Poliansky had received only fish. The news that the hated Savinov had mediated between Nikon and the tsar naturally hardened Joachim's attitude towards Nikon.

Savinov was exiled to the Kozheozero monastery and Nikon was transferred to the monastery of St. Cyril, but Simeon Polotsky, the tsar's tutor, was more powerfully placed than either, and continued to publish his sermons without the patriarch's blessing. Both the fact that he was close to the tsar and that, unlike Savinov, he had done nothing to incriminate himself, kept Polotsky safe from Joachim's strictures.

THE TSAR'S FAVORITES: YAZYKOV AND LIKHACHEV

The addresses on Matveev's letters give some indications of those who enjoyed most intimacy and influence with the tsar. They were joined shortly by yet another Miloslavsky, Boyar Ivan Bogdanovich, who had been governor of Kazan at the time of Matveev's exile. Ivan Bogdanovich was the most energetic of the Miloslavskys, Ivan Mikhailovich being adept only at underhand dealings. On his return from Kazan, Ivan Bogdanovich took charge, but there was an immediate flood of complaints against him, and he was estranged from the young tsar. Fedor already had two favorites—the gentleman of the bedchamber, Ivan Yazykov, and the personal table attendant, Alexis Likhachev, former tutor to Tsarevich Alexis. Yazykov's intimacy with the tsar is easily explained by the nature of his duties. The same important post had been held by Adashev during the reign of Ivan IV, and by Rtishchev under Tsar Alexis.[52] It was rumored also that Yazykov and Likhachev were promoted purposefully to their positions by the two old boyars, Dolgoruky and Khitrovo, who wished to counterbalance the influence of the Miloslavskys, since they were unable to compete with the latter by constantly attending the tsar. Surviving accounts suggest that Yazykov was an extraordinarily adroit courtier; he is described as "a man of great acumen who had become a great expert first on the relationships among courtiers and then on the inner workings of the palace." Likhachev is described as "a man of conscience, highly intelligent and devout." His brother Michael enjoyed a similar reputation.

The problem that most concerned all these people was naturally that of the tsar's marriage. A young tsaritsa could eclipse or weaken the power of the tsarevnas, the tsar's sisters and aunts, and consequently the power of the Miloslavskys. She would be able to introduce her own relatives into the court. The story goes that one day during a religious procession Fedor caught sight of a girl who took his fancy. Yazykov was entrusted with the task of finding out about her; he reported that her name was Agafia Semenovna Grushetskaia and that she lived with her aunt, the wife of Crown Secretary Zaborovsky. The secretary was informed that he should not betroth his niece to another pending a decree from the palace. Miloslavsky attributed the tsar's intention to marry Grushetskaia to the intrigues of Likhachev and Yazykov, and tried to blacken the reputations of Grushetskaia and her mother, but Yazykov exposed the scandalous nature of his imputations.

The tsar and Grushetskaia were married in July 1680 and Miloslavsky was banished from the court; thus his influence was at an end, despite the tender-hearted young tsaritsa's pleas on his behalf. In 1678 Yazykov received the title of *conciliar* gentleman of the bedchamber, and in 1680 he was raised to the rank of lord-in-waiting and given the post of armorer.[53] He was promptly succeeded as gentleman of the bedchamber by Likhachev. At the end of Tsar Fedor's reign Yazykov was made a boyar. Yazykov and Likhachev, then, both young newcomers, were the tsar's closest advisers and wielded considerable influence in affairs of state.

PRINCE VASILY GOLITSYN

There was another man who, although he did not enjoy the same intimacy with the tsar, was a force to be reckoned with in national life. This was Prince Vasily Vasilievich Golitsyn, a member of one of Russia's most ancient aristocratic clans, but himself still quite a young man.[54] He had much in common with his famous ancestor and namesake, who was renowned for his steadfastness during the Time of Troubles.[55] Golitsyn was indubitably more impressive and talented than any of his aristocratic contemporaries. He was, moreover, unusually well educated for his time and this endowed him with a certain broadness of vision and the ability to discard harmful old customs, despite the fact that he himself had as much to gain from the old ways as anyone.

So, when considering the political affairs of the reign of that very young and ailing tsar Fedor Alekseevich, it is essential not to lose sight of the people around him, beginning with Miloslavsky and, from 1680 onwards, Yazykov, Likhachev and Golitsyn, although lack of more detailed information obviously prevents us from defining more precisely what each contributed to the running of the country.

THE DOROSHENKO AFFAIR

In the sphere of foreign affairs Fedor inherited three complex problems from his father: the settlement of the Doroshenko affair,[56] the rejection of Poland's demand for the literal fulfillment of the Truce of Andrusovo[57] and the war with Turkey.

In January 1676, shortly before Tsar Alexis's death, Doroshenko had informed Prince Grigory Romodanovsky[58] that he had already sworn an oath of allegiance to the great sovereign in the presence of the Zaporozhian Host[59] cossacks and had no intention of repeating his oath, either before the boyar and the hetman, or before his royal majesty in person. He said that a journey to Moscow was out of the question, for he expected the Turks and Tatars to stage an attack on Chigirin at any moment. He also refused to send the mace.[60] This had been bestowed upon him by the Host, and it was up to them to take it away from him—mace and commander were inseparable. For many years, he argued, Chigirin had been ruled by the mace and not once had the town been without its hetman. It had been confirmed by royal charter that he and his relatives might live wherever they wished and he chose to live in Chigirin, where he had been born and raised. Doroshenko later relented and began demanding that the sovereign send a high-ranking official before whom he could repeat his oath of allegiance.

A story was circulating in Chigirin that as Metropolitan Joseph Tukalsky of Kiev lay dying, Doroshenko paid him frequent visits. The dying man begged the hetman in God's name to leave the service of the sultan of Turkey and subject himself to the authority of the great sovereign: if he failed to do so he would be ruined. Joseph's request angered Doroshenko, who did not visit him again before his death.

In March the new sovereign sent a table attendant named Derementov to Chigirin with a letter for Doroshenko. Before long, Derementov returned with the news that Hetman Samoilovich[61] had not allowed him to proceed from Baturin to Chigirin. Samoilovich justified his action in a letter to the sovereign in which he wrote that Doroshenko was as devious as ever, and had no intention of carrying out the late tsar's demands. Derementov's mission had proved, moreover, that the sovereign had revoked the decision decreed by Tsar Alexis, whereby all negotiations with Doroshenko were to be carried out by Prince Romodanovsky and himself. Samoilovich wrote in conclusion that the sovereign should send Doroshenko a charter of assurance, omitting his patronymic Dorofeevich and any reference to his rank; he should send in addition special charters of privileges and assurance to the common people of Chigirin, forbidding them to address Doroshenko as hetman, warning them not to trust him, and commanding them to switch their allegiance to him, Ivan Samoilovich. In his reply the sovereign declared that he was making no change to his father's decrees and that Derementov's mission was supposed to be subject to the scrutiny of Romodanovsky and the hetman, as the Lord God moved them. Romodanovsky decided that there was no point in detaining Doroshenko's father-in-law, Yanenko Khmelnitsky, and allowed him to go to Chigirin with Goriainov, a cavalry adjutant.

Over dinner, in Goriainov's presence, Doroshenko poured some wine and said: "I drink a toast that I may not be obliged to relinquish the mace to Ivan Samoilovich, and that he will not take it from me by force." "We shall never give up the mace," said the officers. "If that son of a priest tries to snatch it from us, we'll put up a fight." "God is Hetman Ivan Samoilovich's judge," Doroshenko continued. "The town of Chigirin is no mean defense for Little Russia against the Turks. It's he who should send the insignia of office to Chigirin: instead he takes them away and stops grain being sold to us and writes to me in a tone which I wouldn't adopt even to my serving lad."

Six Zaporozhians were seated at the table. They had been sent to bring Doroshenko to their camp with the insignia of office and the mace. Doroshenko drained his glass and addressed them: "Don't do as the cossacks did to Stenka Razin and betray me. The Don Cossacks may have done so, but don't you follow their example!" "We shan't betray you," the Zaporozhians replied.

Samoilovich, meanwhile, went into action in the hope of putting a swift end to the trying affair. He dispatched an army to the Dnieper under the command of seven colonels. Vasily Burkovsky from Chernigov crossed the river with a detachment of men selected from all the regiments, and on March 18 came within sight of Chigirin. Doroshenko came out of the town with a retinue of infantry and sent a messenger to enquire how the troops were there, and on whose orders. "The sovereign demands and the cossack army implores that you take the oath of allegiance and resign from your command," Burkovsky replied. At this Doroshenko returned to the town, sending a messenger to inform the colonel that he would do nothing without the consent of the ordinary people of the Zaporozhian Host.

He then sent Burkovsky a letter for Samoilovich. It was addressed to the hetman of the Zaporozhian Host, but the words "of both sides of the Dnieper" were omitted. He wrote: "I have always desired to be your confederate and brother and to enjoy your friendship, since we are both sons of the Ukraine. Even before I swore allegiance to his majesty the tsar, when a rift had opened between us, sinners that we are, I always treated you with love and friendship and sent you secret warning of the approach of enemies. This month, when the Host warned me of the schemes of the Turks and Tatars, I let the boyar and your grace know of this, and now you have sent the colonel from Chernigov and his troops to defend our small territory and this side of the Dnieper. I thank you for your assistance to our poor locality and I wish your forces victory over our common foe.

"One thing only surprises me. Your Grace has sent the troops in secret to engage the enemy without first informing me, and you have been trying to win over the towns and even the soldiers with promises of food and provisions. To the townsmen you have promised a peaceful and inoffensive occupation by foreign troops. But how can you speak of defensive action when you lure our men over to your side, and of a peaceful occupation when you destroy territories that are not your own?

"You write that you have sent your forces to the Dnieper in order to ensure our safe conduct when we leave our city, homes, wives and children and come to take the oath of allegiance to the new sovereign with the insignia of office and the commanding officers, and lay down the command. But I have already explained why I am unable to come. Since it is the insignia of office which most concern your grace, let me remind you, innocent as I am of any crime, that I have no fear of travelling to see you or even to the capital itself, but I should never make so bold as to relinquish, at my own whim, the insignia which the Host has entrusted to me on numerous occasions during the past ten years, certainly not without an assembly of the entire service and ordinary cossacks.

"What thanks would I receive, what glory and honor would I bring to my descendants? Reflect, use your wits and drop this matter. God in His abundance has granted your grace full authority from his majesty the tsar. No one covets your position or troubles you. You write that if I ignore your advice and refuse to come to you, the colonel from Chernigov has been instructed to attack us. A fine thing—to stir up internecine strife for the sake of temporary honor and out of caprice! Will God bless us for it? And how the enemy will laugh at us! We shall surely be condemned, for we already have enough innocent blood on our hands, enough innocent captives to answer for, and yet we hope to prosper on worse! In my innocence I wish ill to no man, and am ready to respond to every request."

One of Doroshenko's colonels, a man called Petrikovsky, came to see Burkovsky and warned him: "For God's sake, don't trust Doroshenko. He is fooling everybody. He has long since sent word to the Crimean Horde and is staking everything upon his former agreement with Serko[62] and the Zaporozhians."

Samoilovich had to content himself with making threats, for a decree arrived from the tsar instructing him to reassure Doroshenko of his royal favor and to attempt to win him over by all means at his disposal. He should not offer any provocation unless Dorosheko himself acted in an aggressive manner. The hetman had no choice but to order Burkovsky and his men to withdraw from Chigirin and dismiss the troops.

Samoilovich was also being harrassed by Serko, who wrote: "We have sworn allegiance to the new sovereign, but if you continue to exclude us from the sovereign's favor, it will be you who will suffer. We have put up with enough from you already." Serko was angry because Samoilovich had not sent him the insignia of office which had been confiscated from Khanenko.[63] He also had failed to send grain supplies to the Zaporozhian Camp (Sech) and had ordered that Zaporozhians be ejected from the towns. He had not handed over the royal subsidy, the Perevolochna ford or the township of Kereberda, nor had he allowed the Zaporozhian herds to winter at Poltava. At the cossack assembly the hetman's messenger heard the rank and file complaining bitterly and vociferously about the hetman.

The following day Serko got drunk and summoned the messenger. He grabbed him by the shirt-front and called for a saber. "How would you like me to cut off your head!" he cried. "When the hetman learns that I have gone past Starodub, then fighting will break out there. I have sworn to serve the great sovereign tsar, but I shall not desert the monarch of my forefathers, the king of Poland. If Ivan Samoilovich comes to Zaporozhie and bows before the Cossacks, let him be hetman, but if he fails to do so and Doroshenko comes, let Doroshenko be hetman."

In Moscow the choice already had been made between the hitherto established hetman and the persistently unreliable cossack. All Serko's complaints were submitted to the hetman, who was told on no account to delay the provision of food to the Zaporozhian Camp for fear that the Zaporozhians would feel banished from the tsar's favor.

It was rumored that Doroshenko was preparing to leave for Zaporozhie. In fact he intended to keep to his decision and remain in Chigirin where he had been born and raised. Samoilovich continued to keep the authorities informed of his behavior. "He sends important officials not only to the pashas, but also to the sultan and the khan themselves," he wrote. "He is also in communication with the Poles. Your majesty should not be deceived by the fact that he sends you Turkish sanjaks.[64] It has long been his practice to give verbal avowals of submission to all monarchs, especially Christian ones, but in actual fact the Turkish sultan is the only one who enjoys his true loyalty. It is the sultan who allowed him to send the sanjaks in the event of some Christian monarch making a serious attack upon him. He has no intention whatsoever, nor did he ever have, of coming over to this side or of resigning from his command. The boyar and I find it a dishonorable duty to send him letters all the time. He merely has a laugh at our expense and spreads all kinds of fantastic tales amongst the Little Russian people." Samoilovich begged leave to stage an attack upon Doroshenko before the Turks and Tatars could come to his aid.

While the hetman was trying unsuccessfully to deal with Doroshenko and Serko, Archbishop Lazar Baranovich was quarrelling with Archpriest Simeon Adamovich. The quarrel had arisen because the archpriest owned a large amount of property, whilst the diocese of Chernigov was badly off. "The archdiocese needs more money," wrote Baranovich, "for the embellishment of churches, for the monasteries and other necessities, while the archpriest has only his own domestic needs to see to. I recently reinstituted two archimandrites in Chernigov and Novgorod Seversk." The hetman and his officers supported the archbishop. They told the archpriest that his villages and one hamlet with mills had been transferred to the archbishop. Adamovich complained to the authorities in Moscow that the archbishop had confiscated his property forcibly. When Baranovich heard about the complaint, he ordered that charges be brought against Adamovich by the archimandrite and archpriests, but Adamovich did not see fit to appear at the trial, and left for Moscow.

Baranovich appealed to the sovereign: "If he dares to spread false calumny, I humbly beseech your illustrious majesty to give no credence to his lies. Just as the mouth speaking untruth shall be closed, so should his impudence be utterly discredited." The hetman also wrote to the tsar on the archbishop's behalf, explaining that as hetman, and with the approval of his officers, he was entitled to confiscate the archpriest's property and transfer it to the archbishop, who was in greater need of funds. The matter finally was resolved in the Chancellery for Little Russia in Moscow, with Adamovich withdrawing his claim to the disputed property. The sovereign informed Baranovich in a letter that the archpriest had appealed to him and tearfully begged forgivenness for having angered his pastor. He said that it was fear, not guile, which had made him disobedient. The tsar asked the archbishop, in God's mercy, to pardon the archpriest for his artless misdemeanor and to receive him back into his flock.

ROSLAVETS, ADAMOVICH, DOROSHENKO

No sooner was one problem solved than another arose. On August 4 Colonel Peter Roslavets from Starodub filed a complaint at the Chancellery for Little Russia: "After the Easter festival Ivan Samoilovich sent about five hundred cossacks, who had come over to his side from the right bank of the Dnieper, to my regiment in Starodub. I billetted them in various villages and hamlets and ordered that they and their horses receive food and drink, and allotted five rubles per week to battallion commanders, nine altyns to atamans, two grivnas to the rank and file, and one quart of oil and two quarts of wine per man. But this didn't satisfy the cossacks; they began to make unauthorized collections of money and provisions from the local people. Then on July 9 the archbishop of Chernigov sent a directive forbidding priests to officiate in church or perform any religious rites. No prayers are said for your majesty's health, many people have died without making their confession, babes are unbaptized and women lie in childbirth without prayers. The hetman's envoys make exorbitant requisitions; they are ruining the local people and cossacks, and undermining my authority."

Roslavets requested that the regiment in Starodub be placed directly under the sovereign's control, with Prince Romodanovsky in command, to conform with the regiments in Sumy, Rybensk, Akhtyrka and Kharkov. He pointed out that the towns of Starodub, Novgorod Seversk, Pochep, Pogar and Mglin were all the sovereign's ancestral property and always had been Muscovite towns. Roslavets finally asked that the regimental church in Starodub be administered by the patriarch of Moscow.

That same day, August 4, a letter arrived by courier from Hetman Samoilovich reporting that Roslavets was urging the soldiers in Starodub to reject the hetman's authority; the soldiers had told the hetman of this and begged leave to elect a new colonel. The hetman gave his permission, and Roslavets fled to Moscow. Here the colonel received a reprimand on the tsar's behalf for having flouted the conventions of the Host by failing to render the necessary obedience to the hetman and appealing to Moscow without the latter's permission. It was his duty to curb unruliness in others, yet he himself had behaved in an unruly fashion!

Table Attendant Almazov was sent to the Ukraine to settle the dispute. He was ordered to hold extensive talks with the hetman and to do all that he could to ensure that he was not offended. He was to prevent discord between the two and to win over the hetman by promising him that the colonel would treat him with deference. He was also to make sure that the officers were not annoyed; he should observe them and find out their views on the matter. All these inquiries were to be conducted in secret, with the aim of restoring peace between them and the Host, and arresting the spread of the trouble.

As soon as Almazov mentioned reconciliation, the hetman replied: "Even had Roslavets offended me more than he has done, I would forgive him, but matters cannot rest there. Roslavets said that many people conspired with him in this recent affair, and that I, the hetman, am disliked on this side of the Dnieper. Therefore he must be tried by the commanding officers according to the conventions of the Host: he must be made to disclose the names of his accomplices and of those people who dislike me. It is not only here in Little Russia that you'll find scoundrels and unruly elements, but in Great Russia too, and in other countries. You will find criminals even in places where people are living in fear, but here in Little Russia we live in freedom. If I did not enjoy the sovereign's favor there would be ten new hetmans every year."

Almazov returned to Moscow and reported that all the officers were cursing Roslavets, but nobody had a bad word to say against the hetman. The archbishop had forbidden the Starodub clergy to officiate because Roslavets had assaulted a priest. Finally Samoilovich sent word that Roslavets had acted in collusion with Simeon Adamovich. Almazov hurried back to Baturin and brought Roslavets to trial before a cossack tribunal; the tsar, meanwhile, wrote to the hetman asking him to forgive the offender, who had repented of his crime.

Throughout the spring and summer there were rumors that the Turks were about to attack Kiev. Prince Vasily Golitsyn marched to Putivl with reinforcements for Romodanovsky and Samoilovich, who were instructed to repulse the enemy, but if the Turks and Tatars failed to make a raid on

Kiev or the Left Bank, they were to proceed to the Dnieper, cross the river and launch an attack against Doroshenko in Chigirin, in accordance with Tsar Alexis's previous decrees and with an eye to the local situation. There was no sign of the Turks or Tatars, and so Romodanovsky and Samoilovich made for the Dnieper. When they came within about a hundred versts of the river an advance party was sent on, composed of about fifteen thousand Muscovite troops under the command of Table Attendant Grigory Kosogov and four regiments under Standardbearer Leonty Polubotok. At the approach of the tsar's army the inhabitants of the riverside settlements near Chigirin began to surrender. Kosogov and Polubotok skirmished with local cossacks in the approaches to Chigirin, and after this negotiations commenced. Kosogov sent a letter of admonition from the sovereign to Doroshenko, who this time was left with no alternative but to comply with the tsar's demands. Priests bearing crosses, the commanding officers and the ordinary people of Chigirin came out to the supply train of the besieging forces on the small Yanychara river about three versts from the town, where they took the oath of allegiance.

Doroshenko sent his cousin Kondrat Tarasenko and a secretary, Voekhevich, to request that the assurances he had received concerning his wellbeing and property be honored. The commander and the hetman reassured him on that score, and he came out to meet them with a retinue of two thousand men, and laid before them his insignia of office—the mace, the banner and the horsetail standard. Chigirin, "a town of vital importance to the great sovereign and the whole Ukraine," had been captured by the tsar's troops, half Muscovite and half Ukrainian.

Samoilovich returned from the Dnieper in triumph. In Pereiaslavl he found Almazov with Roslavets. When he heard that the tsar was seeking a pardon for the offender, he said: "I shall not punish Roslavets without the tsar's permission, but new information has come to light. Doroshenko's former chief secretary, Voekhevich, has given me a signed testimony claiming that Simeon Adamov, the archpriest from Nezhin, sent a cossack called Dubrovsky to Doroshenko, claiming that everyone wanted him to be hetman, and that Colonel Peter Roslavets from Starodub, Colonel Lazar Gorlenko from Prilutsk, Dmitry Raicha and former secretary Karp Mokriev all supported him. He also told Doroshenko that not only commanding officers, but also the sovereign himself wanted to get rid of me. They agreed to deal with me as Doroshenko ordered, to kill me if he so wished, or to send me to Moscow like a criminal. The archpriest swore a solemn oath on the cross and sent the cross itself to Doroshenko, who gave it to me."

On October 3 Roslavets was brought before the hetman and officers. Samoilovich said: "I had hoped that you were my good friend, Peter, but you forgot God and your oath, and repaid my kindness by trying to kill me, only the Lord God did not assist you." "I never conspired with the archpriest," Roslavets protested, "and I know nothing of his schemes. I am guilty of one thing only—I went to see his majesty the tsar without your knowledge or leave, for fear that the assembly of the common people would kill me." With that Roslavets fell prostrate before the hetman and lay there for a long time. On October 27 the great sovereign decreed and the boyars resolved in the antechamber that Roslavets and his accomplices be tried under the regulations of the Host. The trial was fixed for January 1677.

More urgent than Roslavets's case was the problem of what to do with Doroshenko, and where he was to live. Initially Romodanovsky and Samoilovich accommodated him in Sosnitsa in the Chernigov regimental district, but in November Table Attendant Prince Ivan Volkonsky sent orders to Baturin that the hetman send Doroshenko to Moscow to affirm his oath. In order to reassure Samoilovich, Volkonsky told him that Doroshenko was being summoned to Moscow out of consideration for Samoilovich's loyal service. Doroshenko had long been the hetman's enemy, and now that he was on Samoilovich's territory he might well return to his old ways and harrass the hetman by fomenting unrest and crime amongst men who had no desire for peace.

Volkonsky arrived in Baturin at the beginning of December and went to discuss the Doroshenko affair with Samoilovich for four hours before dawn. "Doroshenko cannot be sent to Moscow immediately," said the hetman. "He has arrived only recently on this side of the Dnieper and hasn't yet set up house, and many of his belongings are yet to arrive. The trial of the archpriest from Nezhin and Roslavets cannot take place without Doroshenko, since he is the chief accuser. Besides, we promised Doroshenko at the time of the attack on Chigirin that he would be at liberty to live wherever he chose, and that his former crimes would not be held against him. I have granted the Chigirin officers' request to settle on this side of the Dnieper, but if Doroshenko is sent to Moscow now, they will be discouraged and refuse to come over. Besides, Doroshenko has many friends on both sides of the Dnieper, and they will think that he is being exiled to Siberia. I have no reason to fear him; even when he was not the great sovereign's subject and not living under my jurisdiction I knew of all his schemes, and from now on I shall be all the better informed."

Finally the hetman declared that he could make no decision until he had conferred with his officers. After the conference Volkonsky again was informed that Doroshenko could not be sent to Moscow, for the reasons already given. It was decided that the hetman should send a letter of explanation to the tsar, and that Volkonsky should await further instructions in Baturin. The instructions arrived: Doroshenko was to remain in the Ukraine.

In January 1677, on the third day after Epiphany, the trial of Adamovich and Roslavets began in Baturin. Archbishop Baranovich was represented by Archimandrite Ioanniky Goliatovsky of the Elets monastery in Chernigov, Abbot Melety Dzik of the St. Cyril monastery in Kiev, and three archpriests. After the witnesses had given their evidence, the judge sentenced Adamovich and Roslavets to death. Their accomplice, former Chief Secretary Karp Mokriev, was banished from the Ukraine, and former colonels Dmitry Raicha from Pereiaslavl and Lazar Gorlenko from Prilutsky were obliged to swear that they had taken no part in the nefarious scheme of Adamovich and Roslavets.

The very next day, however, the hetman presented letters in which the sovereign alluded to a pardon for the offenders. These were considered by the religious authorities and the cossack officers, who announced that Adamovich might take monastic vows instead of being executed. Adamovich himself requested that he be allowed to become a monk, as he said he had desired to do earlier, but had never carried out his intention. No doubt God now was humbling him for his omission. The archpriest was sentenced to take monastic vows, and Roslavets to several years' imprisonment. Adamovich, escorted by Standardbearer Leonty Polubotok, was sent to Archbishop Baranovich in Chernigov to take his vows, but on arrival he revoked his decision. "I do not wish to become a monk," he said. "The last shall not be more bitter than the first." On hearing this, Baranovich had him defrocked and handed over to Polubutok as a layman, subject to secular law. Polubotok ordered him placed in "close confinement" whereupon Adamovich, unable to endure the discomfort, offered to give detailed evidence of his plans and accomplices.

Polubotok summoned a number of ecclesiastical and lay figures, before whom Adamovich gave the following testimony: "Dmitrashka

Raicha said that he would shoot the hetman with a pistol from amongst the Host. On another occasion he said that he was going to Zaporozhie to raise rebellion. Karp Mokriev twice said that he would accompany Dmitrashka to Zaporozhie to raise rebellion against the hetman. I advised Doroshenko to hasten to this side with the Zaporozhian Host and his own men, and promised him that he would be made hetman. Roslavets told me: 'We shall take care of the health of the lord hetman because he acts ungraciously towards me.' Once again, when I met him in the village of Semenovskoe—I on my way back from Moscow, he on his way there— he told me to go to the Ukraine to raise rebellion amongst the Zaporozhians and with Doroshenko in order to further our plans. Dmitrashka said that we should kill the chief justice and the standardbearer along with the hetman. It was decided that once the hetman was dead we would not serve the tsar, but become subjects of the khan." Adamovich signed this statement.

DOROSHENKO IN MOSCOW

The authorities in Moscow were still convinced that the old hetman of Chigirin would be less of a threat in the capital than in the Ukraine. In February Table Attendant Semen Almazov, with whom we are acquainted, returned to Baturin to demand that Doroshenko be sent to Moscow. Samoilovich told him: "We shall have to consult the officers, because they are mistrustful folk. When they hear that Doroshenko is being sent away to Moscow they will begin to gossip, and the rumors eventually will reach Serko's ears. He will add to the rumors, and may God preserve us from the evil which may result! Doroshenko's presence on this side of the Dnieper causes the Poles great anxiety. They are afraid that Doroshenko and I will make a truce with the Turks and declare war on them. They have no idea how unstable the situation is: it takes just one man to say the word, and everyone will join him. But may the Lord God chastise me body and soul if I have any wicked intentions; may he destroy my wife, my children and my home. I shall keep my children in Moscow as a mark of loyalty, and if there is any trouble in the Ukraine I shall leave everything immediately and come to Moscow. Let it be as his majesty the tsar wills, but better that Doroshenko remain in Moscow. My envoys and Serko's can visit him there to confirm that he enjoys the tsar's favor. I shall allow him to go with you, but don't tell anybody. It would be well were his brother Grigory be allowed to leave Moscow, to return to Little

Russia. When their relatives observe his majesty's benevolence, they will be glad and reassured of the tsar's favor. Their mother has written to me many times from Chigirin about Grigory's release."

The hetman ordered Chief Justice Ivan Demontov to accompany Almazov to Sosnitsa. He carried a letter for Doroshenko explaining that he need have no misgivings about going to Moscow; there had been an earlier royal decree about his transfer, but he might not depart until he had been interrogated. The sole reason for visiting Moscow now was to take part in talks on Turkish and Crimean affairs. Nevertheless, Doroshenko was highly agitated at Almazov's unexpected arrival. "When a man is condemned to death, he is given advance warning," he said. "May God judge the hetman for not telling me." But he had no choice but to leave.

On March 20 Doroshenko had an audience with the sovereign. A crown secretary delivered a speech declaring that his crimes had been pardoned and never would be referred to again. The sovereign decreed that he was to live in Moscow as a favored subject, where he would assist with military preparations against an assault on the Ukraine by the Turks and Tatars. As a token of the sovereign's favor and at Hetman Samoilovich's request, his majesty the tsar had ordered the release of Doroshenko's brother Grigory. The latter was to have been taken under guard to the hetman's son, Semen, but now, again at the hetman's request, he was to be allowed to return to the Ukraine.

Doroshenko appealed to the sovereign to allow his wife and daughter to come to Moscow. When the clerk Yudin went to fetch them, however, he was told by Doroshenko's brother Andrei: "My brother wrote and asked me to send his wife to Moscow only if she has been behaving herself as she promised when he released her from the convent; if she was misbehaving I was to write and keep nothing from him. I have told the hetman of her behavior, and now I am telling you and writing to my brother. My brother Peter made her take the veil because of her wrongdoing, but when he saw his little daughter without a mother he relented and took the miscreant back to be his wife; she promised that never again would she touch intoxicating liquor till the end of her days. But as soon as my brother left for Moscow she again took to intemperate drinking, and went around getting up to mischief without my knowledge. When I told her to get ready to leave for Moscow she screamed, in the presence of her father Yanenko, 'If you force me to go to Moscow, your brother Peter is not long for this world.'"

This story struck Yudin as suspicious, especially since the hetman had shown him a letter from Doroshenko, begging Samoilovich to intercede with the tsar for his return to the Ukraine. In it he recalled the promise he had received about living wherever he chose. "I know that I am not needed here in Moscow," wrote Doroshenko, "and that there is also no need for my wife to come here. But I shall have no choice but to do as the authorities command." The hetman did not send Doroshenko's wife to Moscow.

YURY KHMELNITSKY'S MANIFESTO

Throughout the spring the customary preparations were made in the Ukraine for an engagement with the Turks and Tatars. The sultan had proclaimed his captive Yury Khmelnitsky[65] hetman and prince of Little Russia in Doroshenko's stead. On April 5 Khmelnitsky sent a rescript to Zaporozhie: "For our Savior all is possible; he makes the beggar to sit down with princes, he raises up the humble, and the mighty he casts down. Wicked men prevented me from living in my beloved fatherland. After I had fled from them I suffered many misfortunes and fell into servitude. But God touched the heart of the most illustrious Turkish emperor, ruler of three quarters of the world, who pardons more sinners than he condemns (as I myself can vouch). The emperor granted me my freedom, bestowed his favor upon me, and made me prince of Little Russia. When I was in Zaporozhie you promised to treat me with love and goodwill, and have me as your leader. The time now has come to keep your promise: send your envoys to Kazykermen for negotiations with me." It was signed: "Georgy Gedeon Venzhik Khmelnitsky, prince of Little Russia and commander of the Zaporozhian Host."

This letter made an impression in Zaporozhie. When Crown Agent Perkhurov arrived there on May 15 to deliver the royal allowance and, as was customary, to read the tsar's rescript to the assembly, a cry went up from the warriors: "They've sent us too little cloth! How can it be divided up? There's only enough for one sleeve each! We have served the tsar and his father before him faithfully, we carry out endless military operations against the Muslims, but they send us an inadequate allowance. All the same, we promise to serve faithfully in the future." Serko said: "The Host refuses to obey me because I do not have the royal allowance, the banner and the mace. The cossacks would become obedient if the banner and mace were sent to me." The cossacks continued to shout:

"Hetman Samoilovich confiscated our crossing-place at Perevolochna. He refuses to allow us free transport and doesn't send our supplies. If the Turks attack our camp, we shall burn the Zaporozhian Camp and make our way along the islands in the river. There is no point in staying here, because we have run out of provisions."

MOSCOW NEGOTIATES WITH SAMOILOVICH

Samoilovich resumed the dispatch of reports on Serko to Moscow. He claimed that Serko had agreed to a truce with the Crimean khan and was in regular communication with Khmelnitsky, to whom he now had yielded completely. In July the sovereign sent Table Attendant Karandeev to Baturin with gifts of sables and satins for the hetman and his officers in recognition of their loyal service. He had been instructed to confer with Samoilovich about Serko, Doroshenko and the as yet unresolved Roslavets-Adamovich affair. Karandeev demanded that the hetman "send a high-ranking official to Zaporozhie and that he do his utmost to prevent Serko from making a truce with the khan. He should send his own troops to besiege Kodak[66] in order to stop the Turks from capturing it. If he failed to do so, hardship and ruin would befall the people of the Zaporozhian Host, and the enemy would have free access to the towns of Little Russia. The Zaporozhians would be reassured by the dispatch of Ukrainian troops to Kodak."

"I cannot send troops to Kodak," the hetman replied, "because the town is under Serko's control. It would anger the Zaporozhians if I were to send troops without consulting them." Karandeev then turned to the subject of Doroshenko's wife; her husband was still requesting that she be sent to Moscow. "I have no objections to her going," said the hetman. "Then why, hetman, are you trying to have Doroshenko sent back to the Ukraine? What are you afraid of? It was for your sake and for the safety of Little Russia that he was sent to Moscow, to prevent him from causing trouble in the Ukraine." "I have no intention of petitioning for Doroshenko's return to the Ukraine," the hetman replied. "With war threatening, Doroshenko's presence here would be undesirable." Finally conversation turned to the Roslavets-Adamovich affair. "I shall send the archpriest and Roslavets to Moscow with special messengers," said the hetman. "I shall appeal to the sovereign to send them into life-long exile in far-off Siberia as a warning to others."

THE FIRST CHIGIRIN CAMPAIGN

Roslavets and Adamovich were brought to Moscow on August 11. The next day a decree was issued condemning them to exile in Siberia. The authorities were eager to resolve the affair quickly in order to appease the hetman, who was already advancing on the Dnieper with an army twenty thousand strong. Since August 4 Ibrahim Pasha and Khmelnitsky had been stationed outside Chigirin awaiting the arrival of the khan. Referring to himself as prince of Sarmatia, Khmelnitsky sent a demand that the capital surrender to him now that Doroshenko had forfeited the right of command. The governor of Chigirin was Major General Trauernicht. On the night of August 7 he made a successful sortie and captured eleven prisoners for interrogation. The Turks had begun to dig a mine to the upper fortress, but had to stop when they hit solid rock. Meanwhile, on August 10, Samoilovich joined up with Romodanovsky, and on August 17 they sent a detachment of cossack infantry and a thousand dragoons to Chigirin from Sniatin, ordering them to march throughout the day and night. They did as they were ordered, crossed to the right bank of the Dnieper and stole past the enemy divisions by night. Their appearance at Chigirin was greeted with indescribable joy by the besieged inhabitants. The latter were exhausted and dispirited, for they had received no news of their own troops, but had witnessed the khan and his horde joining up with the Turks.

On August 25 Prince Romodanovsky and Samoilovich appeared at the Buzhin landing stage on the bank of the Dnieper opposite Chigirin. The khan and his Tatars and part of the Turkish forces had taken up position on the other bank. The enemy occupied an island in the middle of the river to prevent the Russians from crossing, but they were dislodged. The Russians crossed from the island to the right bank, and on August 28 engaged the enemy, defeated them and drove them back to a position five versts from the river. The next day the terrified Turks and Tatars retreated from Chigirin, abandoning their supplies and guns, and leaving four thousand janissaries dead outside the town. Ibrahim Pasha blamed the defeat upon the khan, who had arrived on the left bank too late and failed to inform him of the approach of the Muscovite and cossack forces.

The following men showed outstanding bravery during this memorable victory; Lieutenant Colonel Semen Voeikov of Major General Agey Shepelev's select regiment, the infantry colonel, Samuil Vestov, Table Attendant and Colonel Grigory Kosogov and, from the Ukrainian divisions, Colonel Levenets of Poltava and Colonel Barsuk of Nezhin.

Romodanovsky and Samoilovich remained in Chigirin until September 9; when they heard that the Turks were fleeing for the frontier they started back across the Dnieper. Their departure was hastened also by the fact that all horse fodder had been destroyed by the enemy, and the troops were short of provisions.

Samoilovich returned in triumph, for it was he who had persuaded the Muscovite government to defend Chigirin. The hetman now insisted that the sovereign order Chigirin to be fortified, posted with troops and stocked with provisions, just as Kiev was. He suggested that the sovereign send a boyar to the town with government troops, as he himself did not have enough men to defend Chigirin unaided and could not rely on his own troops without Muscovite support. Chigirin must not be abandoned, he said, for it provided fine protection and defense for the entire Ukraine, located as it was on the Tiasma river, where the Horde had no crossings or fords. The Chigirin campaign also provided Samoilovich with the opportunity to discredit Serko. He wrote to the tsar: "The cossack leader is badly disposed towards your illustrious majesty's sovereign power and towards me because he made a truce with the khan and the Turks before the Chigirin campaign; he gave us no help during the battle, and when the khan swam across the Dnieper with his men he did not attack them, but ordered his cossacks to ferry the Tatars across in their canoes."

The dispute between the hetman and the illustrious warrior of the steppe aroused great displeasure in Moscow. The boyars resolved that Serko and the hetman should be reconciled. "Serko will answer for his wicked deeds at the Day of Judgement," the sovereign wrote to Samoilovich, "but we, being a merciful Christian monarch, have no desire to commit him to eternal ruin in the name of Christianity. We await his conversion and forgive his crimes and offenses if he exculpates them by loyal service and is well-disposed towards you as were previous hetmans."

Table Attendant Colonel Tiapkin was sent to the Ukraine to convey the tsar's heartfelt gratitude to Romodanovsky and the hetman for their victory at Chigirin. He was instructed to question Romodanovsky about his plans for Chigirin: could the town be defended, or should it be destroyed? What advantages were to be gained from defending it? How many Muscovite troops and cossack regiments were needed there? Where were they to obtain supplies of food and arms for Chigirin, and how were reinforcements to be sent to the garrison across the great expanse of the Dnieper river? Romodanovsky's view was that Chigirin should not be destroyed: "Such a step would be ignominious, and we would be in fear of the enemy. Not only would it be to the disadvantage of the Ukraine, it also could have grave consequences for Kiev itself. I shall deal with each of the remaining questions when I have consulted the hetman."

Tiapkin put the same questions to Samoilovich in Baturin. The hetman replied: "If we destroy Chigirin or abandon it to the enemy, before destroying it or abandoning it, we may as well tell the whole Ukrainian people that the sovereign has no further need of them. It is the firm belief of the cossack nation that whoever holds Kiev and Chigirin must be our lord forever. If Yury Khmelnitsky establishes himself in Chigirin with his rebels, all those people who have come across to this side of the Dnieper will return to join Yury. If the Turks occupy the town the sultan will not send supplies from his own country, but will plunder towns and villages on this side of the Dnieper. The Turks will have free access to Putivl and Sevsk because the Dnieper and the lands beyond will be in their possession." With this the hetman looked at the icon of the Savior, burst into tears, and exclaimed: "Let us pray that the Lord God and the great sovereign will deliver us and our descendants from the heavy burden of the Muslim yoke!" On the subject of Serko, Samoilovich told Tiapkin quite openly that the cossack leader had become a subject of the sultan. "The sultan sent the bey of Kazykermen thirty thousand gold *chervonnye* as a bribe to win over Serko and the cossacks. The bey is a Tatar from the Polish regions; he is an educated man and knows several languages. He and Serko met on the steppes, walked between the bushes arm in arm, and the cossack then swore allegiance to the sultan."

ZAPOROZHIAN AFFAIRS

In December Clerk Shestakov was sent to Zaporozhie to deal with the problem. He was accompanied by the hetman's envoy and deputy Artemy Zolotar. At the cossack assembly Shestakov reprimanded the Zaporozhians for failing to come to the assistance of the government troops at Chigirin. He asked why they had not attacked the Tatars as they fled from the town across the Dnieper. Serko replied: "We did not march on Chigirin because there were too few warriors in the camp, and because the Turks and Tatars wanted to attack the Zaporozhian Camp first, then Chigirin. We forestalled their nefarious scheme by making peace with the khan in the hope that the Tatars then would ransom some prisoners from us, because the warriors were starving; we had no booty, and the provisions were running out. Another reason we made peace with the khan is that, although we repeatedly wrote to Hetman Samoilovich, asking him to urge his majesty the tsar to send troops to defend us, as Tsar Alexis used to do, and to send us some of his own service cossacks, the hetman failed to send either troops or supplies, and the cossacks had nothing to eat but fish.

"The truce with the khan allowed us to win a large ransom for the Tatars and to go to the sea to collect salt. Had we not made a truce with the khan, the host would have died of starvation. We did not attack the Turks and Crimeans when they fled from Chigirin because we did not have enough men in the Sech. Everyone was banking upon a truce with the khan, and had gone off to ply their various trades. There remain a few cossacks at the Camp, but only because they still are able to work their businesses. May the sovereign grant our request and send us his troops, and command the hetman to send the Poltava regiment. Then, in the spring, as soon as the troops and provisions have arrived, we shall break our truce with the khan and wage war on the Crimea." Serko told the hetman's envoy in confidence that he had not betrayed the tsar; he had made the truce with the Turks and Tatars merely to lure Khmelnitsky into his hands, capture him and send him to Moscow. To confirm this, Serko took a cross from his bosom and kissed it.

None of this succeeded in dispelling Samoilovich's hostility towards the Zaporozhian commander. Serko soon aroused the hetman's wrath even more by advising the sovereign to destroy and abandon Chigirin. Samoilovich wrote: "He is recommending this solely so that he can carry out the wicked plan that he is devising with the vile Khmelnitsky. Once they get their hands on Chigirin they will fortify it, even if it has been destroyed. Khmelnitsky will make it the capital of his principality and Serko the headquarters of his territory. Why, even now Serko addresses Khmelnitsky as prince of Little Russia, and Khmelnitsky refers to Serko as commander and hetman of the Zaporozhian Host." A list of the terms agreed between Serko and Khmelnitsky reached Kiev from Turkish territory. They were: (1) The Orthodox faith should not be subjected to persecution. (2) There should be no payment of taxes or taking of prisoners. (3) The liberties of the Zaporozhian Host must not be violated. (4) Turkish and Tatar officers and troops must not enter Ukrainian towns. News arrived from Constantinople itself that Serko was sending to the sultan all communications from the tsar and letters from the hetman.

POROSUKOV'S EMBASSY TO TURKEY

It was now essential to prepare for a major war on several fronts. Throughout the winter and spring of 1678 news continued to arrive of huge Turkish forces massing outside Chigirin in readiness for a final assault on the town. Table Attendant Porosukov was in Constantinople at the time; he had been sent there to deliver a letter from the tsar in an attempt to avert a major and perilous war or, at the very least, to obtain more information about Turkish plans. To this latter end, Porosukov sought out the patriarch. The patriarch told him that he wished the great sovereign well, just as he himself hoped to enter the Kingdom of Heaven, and he spoke of the plans of the enemies of Christ's cross. He said that the sultan of Turkey, insatiable in his Muslim lust for power, was planning that summer to launch an offensive with his infidel armies in the hope of wresting the domains of Peter Doroshenko from his majesty the tsar's control, and subsequently winning the entire Ukraine. The Turks had prophesied clearly that they would be defeated by the tsar at some time as yet unknown and, fearing this prophesy, the sultan would go no further than Baba, but would send his vizier to attack Chigirin.

Porosukov asked whether Yury Khmelnitsky had revoked his monastic vows with the patriarch's blessing. The patriarch replied: "Khmelnitsky revoked his vows of his own free will, seeking release from bondage as much as a principality or a hetmanship. On several occasions at Khmelnitsky's insistence I was threatened and entreated by the vizier's messenger to release him from his vows and consecrate him prince of Little Russia and hetman of the Zaporozhian Host; but I succeeded in escaping their coercion by presenting gifts and refusing to receive Yury. Yesterday," the patriarch continued, "the letter which you brought from the tsar was read to the sultan. He ordered that you be released, but a letter will be sent to his majesty the tsar that Chigirin and Doroshenko's domains along the Dnieper be surrendered to Turkey. I beseech his majesty, for the sake of God's churches and the Christian faith, not to surrender Chigirin and the Ukraine to the sultan. If he does, not only Little Russia but the Muscovite realm itself will suffer at the hands of the enemy."

THE SECOND CHIGIRIN CAMPAIGN

The sovereign agreed with Samoilovich, Romodanovsky and the patriarch of Constantinople on the necessity of defending Chigirin, fortifying it and posting a garrison there. Lord-in-waiting Ivan Ivanovich Rzhevsky was appointed to govern Chigirin; he was well known for his organizational ability, and had demonstrated his skill in keeping on good terms with the Ukrainians during his time as governor of Nezhin. Rzhevsky was to collect food supplies in Kiev, and the hetman was to supply him with transport. He would be joined by the Ukrainian regiments assigned to occupy Chigirin, and a division of Romodanovsky's men. None of these arrangements materialized, however, and on March 17 Rzhevsky entered Chigirin alone. He had no food supplies because the hetman had failed to send transport, and there was no news of the troops for Chigirin. On arrival in the town Rzhevsky found that the walls had been destroyed and the granaries were empty; he had heard accounts of incessant Tatar raids. When news of this reached Moscow in April, Table Attendant Almazov swiftly was dispatched to visit Romodanovsky in Kursk and Samoilovich in Baturin, to find out what they were up to. Romodanovsky replied that he would set off at once for the Dnieper and organize the defense of Chigirin. The hetman explained that his troops were not mobilized, and that he would go alone to have talks with Romodanovsky. He assured Almazov that there was no cause for concern: the troops and provisions would reach Chigirin in good time, despite the dreadfully high cost of transport. It cost four or five rubles to hire a cart, and there was no telling whether half would ever return.

The reinforcements and supplies did reach Chigirin in time, for Vizier Mustafa did not arrive to besiege the town until July 9. Romodanovsky and Samoilovich had stationed their troops by the Dnieper at the Buzhin landing stage at the beginning of July, and on July 6 began to transfer their men to the right bank. The crossing was a slow process and the majority of the troops were still on the left bank when, on July 10, the Tatars stealthily crossed the river at Krylov and ambushed the Russian supply train; but they were repelled with heavy losses. An enemy attack on July 11 on the Russian advance forces on the right bank also ended in failure. By July 12 the entire Russian army had been drawn up on the right bank in the Buzhin fields, and the next day they had a successful engagement with five Turkish pashas and the Crimean khan. The battle raged ceaselessly from that time onwards. The Turks, who had come from Chigirin by way of Krylov, stationed their supply trains about seven versts from the Russians, and frequently raided the Russian camps. On July 29 Prince Kaspulat Mutsalovich Cherkassky came to the assistance of the Russians with a division of Kalmyks and Tatars, and played an active part in the fighting.

On August 3-4, after a fierce struggle, the Russians captured the strategically vital Strelnikov Hill; they drew near to Chigirin and established contact with the town. They learned that Governor Rzhevsky had been killed. On August 3 he had climbed onto the walls and rejoiced at the sight of the advancing Russian regiments, but at that very moment a grenade was tossed from the enemy camp and struck him down.

Chigirin did not hold out long after Rzhevsky's death. The Turks dug three mines beneath the lower part of the main town, and on August 11 they broke through by the Tiasma river. Nearby houses were set alight and, at the sight of the fire, the besieged inhabitants fled across the Moscow bridge towards the Russian supply trains. The Turks set fire to the bridge, which collapsed, killing many Russians, including Colonel Krinitsky of Gadiach. Many cossacks also perished as a result of the mines. As well as burning the lower part of the town, the Turks succeeded in burning the new upper section recently constructed by Rzhevsky. The Russians ensconced themselves in the old district of the upper town and engaged the enemy until nightfall, twice driving the Turks from the town. That night an order came from Romodanovsky and Samoilovich, instructing them to set fire to the town and come out to the supply trains. They carried out this order, and at dawn Romodanovsky and the hetman marched towards the Dnieper, leaving behind forever the smouldering ruins of Khmelnitsky's ill-fated capital. The enemy pursued the retreating forces without success, and by August 20 the Turks, too, had left the area.

The vizier's retreat from Chigirin did not mark the end of hostilities. Khmelnitsky and his Tatar forces remained on the west bank, capturing Nemirov, Korsun and other towns. From there they staged an attack on the east bank. This alarming situation prevailed throughout that fall and winter, and in the summer the people of the Ukraine again awaited the arrival of the sultan himself. In March 1679 one of the hetman's leading aides, Ivan Stepanovich Mazepa,[67] arrived in Moscow, where he had the following interesting conversation with Crown Secretary Larion Lopukhin: "It is essential," said Mazepa, "that a large army be sent to defend Kiev and the whole Ukraine. The army should be under the command of a small number of boyars and officers and the troops should obey them: there should be one commander-in-chief. If there are a lot of boyars and commanders in charge of different regiments, they will dispute amongst themselves about precedence,[68] and no one will entrust his own soldiers to anyone else. Each will keep control of his own men, and there will be

discord." "The appointment of boyars and commanders has been recorded
in royal charters," Lopukhin told him. "The organization of the operation
will depend on the local situation and the advice of the hetman; these things
cannot be known in advance. We must act as the military situation dictates.
The boyars and commanders will be on equal footing; there is no reason
for any disputes to arise between them."

"May the great sovereign's will be done," continued Mazepa, "but in
the last war Prince Romodanovsky had a large army under his command,
but when they were on the other side of the Dnieper and went to relieve
Chigirin and captured the hill from the enemy and withdrew from Chigirin,
very few of the sovereign's troops were engaged in the action. There were
only the infantry regiment and the musketeer units, and only about three
hundred musketeers were actively engaged; the rest were behind the lines
by the supply trains. As for the cavalry and the provincial servitors, they
did little more than shout. The colonels and the lieutenants kept appealing
to the hetman for reinforcements, and he sent them his own troops, leaving himself with only a personal bodyguard and the regiment of dragoons
which the sovereign had ordered to stay by him in battle." Lopukhin
replied: "The cossack divisions had their lieutenants, and the cavalry their
colonels and officers. What were they up to? Why did they not send their
men into battle? That is their job." Mazepa responded: "No one had time
to give orders; it was every man for himself!"

The second, unsuccessful Chigirin campaign marked the end of Prince
Romodanovsky's long military career. He was recalled to Moscow. Hetman Samoilovich was left alone to carry out reconnaissance raids along
the right bank. He informed the sovereign that he had sent a force under
the command of his son, Semen, to the Right Bank. At the sight of the
government troops the inhabitants of Rzhishchev, Kanev, Korsun, Cherkasy and other towns renounced the sultan's authority and swore allegiance to his majesty the tsar. The hetman's son burned all the towns,
townships, villages and hamlets along the right bank in order to deprive
the enemy of future refuge.

RELATIONS WITH POLAND

What was the Polish view of events along the right bank of the Dnieper,
an area to which they still laid claim under the articles of the Treaty of
Andrusovo? At the beginning of Fedor's reign Tiapkin was still the
Russian diplomatic resident in Poland and continued to complain to

Moscow about the wretchedness of his position. He grumbled that he received no money from Moscow, and that the Poles provided him with no subsistence either. "I cannot get to Cracow for the coronation," he wrote from Lwów. "I shan't be able to get a loan without a pledge. I did have a gilded sable tunic, but that has been pawned to a merchant in Warsaw, and I have no money to redeem it. Much against my will, I shan't be able to attend the coronation unless I obtain the money to get there. I used to have a decent horse for attending the king's court and visiting the nobility, but now it has died; I've no way of visiting people, and very likely soon I myself shall give up the ghost from poverty. My old wounds trouble me all the time. Things are very different here from what they are in Muscovy, where one monarch and sovereign shines over the universe like the bright sun in the heavens; he alone shines everywhere, his sovereign rule is like the rays of the sun. We obey, fear and serve a single ruler. He alone gives and takes away the power invested in him from on high. Here in Poland it's the nobles who rule the roost. They don't even fear the Creator, never mind their own elected sovereign. It's impossible to know to whom to apply in order to do business. The Poles are concerned with nothing but their own gratification." Finally Tiapkin found two kind people from whom he borrowed some money, leaving his last few wretched belongings as a pledge, and set off for Moscow.

King Sobieski[69] was astonished when Tiapkin told him of Doroshenko's defection. The resident could tell by his expression that the news caused his majesty some displeasure. Amongst themselves the nobles were saying: "So that's how the tsar shows his friendship and aid, by robbing us of the whole Ukraine!" Others consoled themselves with the thought that the wrath of the sultan and the khan now would be directed against Moscow, and the tsar would be forced into closer alliance with Poland. There were continual reports that the sultan was mobilizing his troops, and on March 4, 1676 the Lithuanian chancellor, Christofor Pats, demanded that Tiapkin immediately seek plenipotentiary powers from his government to allow him to put his signature to the following terms: that the tsar order his troops to unite with the Poles and attack the Turks under a joint command, while the king would send part of his army to link up with the Russians for a campaign against the Crimea. This resolution should be implemented at once, and not be confined to vacuous promises and excuses. "Will you agree to a thirteen-year extension of the truce?" asked Tiapkin. "We can agree to half," Pats replied. The Moldavian envoy,

Cantacuzene, however, on the eve of his departure, had told Tiapkin in confidence that the king secretly had sent the nobleman Carbowski as a diplomatic agent to Moldavia with orders to conduct peace talks with the Turks, using the hospodar of Moldavia as mediator. Cantacuzene promised to keep Tiapkin informed of Carbowski's negotiations through Bishop Anthony Winnicki. He added that the peace talks between the Poles and the Turks had been initiated through the mediation of the Crimean khan.

At the first opportunity Tiapkin let the Lithuanian nobles know that rumors of the secret peace talks with Turkey had reached his ears, and that this constituted a breach of the Andrusovo and Moscow treaties. At first the nobles tried to identify Tiapkin's informant, but when Tiapkin refused adamantly to reveal it, they insisted that no peace had yet been concluded with the Turks. Envoys had been sent to Transylvania and Moldavia solely in an attempt to prevent the Turks from attacking Poland until agreement finally was reached about joining forces with the tsar. "It should come as no surprise to you that our envoys and couriers are so active," said the nobles. "A drowning man will clutch at a straw. We have received many promises from his majesty the tsar, but so far we have seen no results, and the Commonwealth is suffering greatly as a consequence." Hetman Michael Pats spoke: "In order to allay his majesty's suspicions about joining forces with us, the king is ready to give any guarantee. Why, he would even send his own son to Moscow as a hostage, if only his majesty the tsar would order unification of our forces without suspicion or misgiving. Should the Turkish sultan show willingness for peace, his majesty the king and the Commonwealth will inform you immediately." "On what terms would you agree to a truce with the sultan?" asked Tiapkin. "We should demand the return of Kamieniec and all conquered territories," replied Pats. "But what if the sultan rejects those terms?" asked Tiapkin. "Then we should have no alternative but to relinquish everything in order to save the Commonwealth from destruction," the chancellor replied.

On March 16 a courier arrived from the Polish resident in Transylvania with the terms the vizier had sent to the prince of Transylvania. Poland was to cede Kamieniec, Podolia, Volhynia and the whole of the Right and Left Bank Ukraine to the Turks in perpetuity, and not hamper the Turkish conquest of the Russian-occupied towns of the Ukraine. For his part, the sultan would drop all claims to the tribute promised by King Michael.[70]

The Poles were required immediately to send commissioners to draw up a peace treaty before the sultan and vizier crossed the Polish frontier with their armies, for once they had entered Poland they would not agree to peace even on these terms. Both Chancellor Pats and the hetman told Tiapkin bluntly that these terms would have to be accepted. "God will punish those neighboring rulers who fail to come to Poland's aid," they said to the resident. "Write to Artamon Sergeevich Matveev and ask all the boyars, lords-in-waiting and clergy to appeal to the tsar and beg him to join forces with us."

The reports which they were receiving from Tiapkin did not encourage the Muscovite authorities to consent to Polish demands. "Wallachians and Moldavians," wrote Tiapkin, "prominent officials, come to me and advise me, from their superiors and on their own behalf, that the great sovereign without fail should command his armies to make a bold assault on the Crimea. When, with God's blessing, the Crimea is captured, all Christian lands will subject themselves to his majesty's lofty rule, not only the Ukraine, Volhynia and Podolia, but also the Wallachians, the Moldavians and the Serbs. Huge Turkish forces are at this moment being mobilized, and there is no telling whether they are aiming to attack Poland or Kiev. But if there were some secret agreement between the Turks and the Poles, the Turks very likely will attack Kiev. That is why the hospodars of Moldavia and Wallachia bid the Muscovite realm take all reasonable precautions. The Poles are sending a continuous stream of secret messengers to Turkey, the Crimea, Moldavia and Wallachia, all seeking some means of making peace with Turkey; if they are successful, this could have grave consequences for neighboring countries. The Poles are very much opposed to the Crimea and the other lands I have mentioned coming under the control of the great sovereign, for then the domains of the Roman Catholic church would be encircled by the Orthodox faith. The Poles are the inveterate enemies of God's church. They worship Jewish idols, treat the Jews as their brothers, and would much rather associate with a Jew than with an Orthodox Ruthenian. Their clergymen persecute and abhor the church of God. They dare not destroy the prayerhouses of the Lutherans and Calvinists in the same way as they devastate and annihilate Orthodox churches, for the prayerhouses are protected by the king of Sweden and the elector of Brandenburg, who have made treaties to this effect. The Orthodox Christians of these countries therefore entreat the great sovereign to insert a clause safeguarding them from Catholic persecution into his treaties with the Polish realm."

The Poles discovered (apparently by unsealing the resident's dispatches) that Tiapkin was ill-disposed towards them and was writing to Moscow about "threats to the Muscovite state from various hostile alliances and factions." When the king saw him, he angrily scolded and threatened him. Waving his cane, Sobieski shouted: "Thanks to your fanciful dispatches we still have not succeeded in concluding a treaty with his majesty the tsar and obtaining his assistance." Tiapkin was told that he would not be recognized as resident until a charter was received from the new tsar confirming his status. He was sent away from Cracow to Warsaw, and there were even rumors of a threat to send Tiapkin to Marienburg[71] and imprison him there. Tiapkin replied to the senators: "Your sovereign is wrong to be angry with me and to suspect me of stirring up hostility between him and the tsar. Not just I, but the whole world knows that his majesty the king and you, lord senators, have contravened and continue to contravene the peace treaties. It is well known that you have been communicating quite openly with the Turks and Tatars, making no secret of it, but without informing the great sovereign either through your own ambassadors or through me. I cannot act as though I am deaf, dumb and blind; I write about everything I see and hear, and shall continue to write the whole truth to my sovereign and keep him fully informed."

Tiapkin was true to his word and continued to keep the sovereign informed of the "wild schemes of the French faction."[72] He wrote that the king of France was anxious for peace between Poland and Turkey so that French and Polish forces might make a combined attack upon the emperor of Austria and the king of Prussia. Once they had conquered the Austrians and Prussians they would unite with the Swedes and attack Muscovy. After the defeat of Muscovy all the Catholic rulers would attack Turkey, without the Orthodox state as an ally, in order to convert the Greek Orthodox peoples to Catholicism. If they allowed Muscovite troops to invade Turkish territory, the Greeks, Wallachians, Serbs, Moldavians and Ukrainian cossacks would unite with them and gain the upper hand over the Catholic powers.

Tiapkin begged Matveev: "For pity's sake, convince the great sovereign and his privy councillors that they must send troops to attack the Crimea. This will confound and put an end to all hostile factions. If the tsar's armies fail to attack the Crimea this summer, the Muscovite realm will be subjected to abuse, insult and ignominy." Tiapkin feared an alliance between the Swedes and the Poles, and so advised that war should be declared on Sweden whilst the Swedes were still engaged in their unsuccessful war with the elector of Brandenburg. "We must drive the Swede from Livonia with a strident declaration of war. Very likely God will bless his chosen one with victory and reward him, not just with Livonia, but with the Baltic Sea itself. Now is the time utterly to crush the Swede and put a stop to his cunning intrigues with the Polish court, for the German sovereigns are giving him a good beating and he is fleeing from them like a hare from island to island. Their ambassador here proclaims: 'The privy boyars, especially Matveev, served us ill by dissuading the late tsar from making peace. But may God now safeguard the health of the patriarch of Moscow; he has given the young sovereign spiritual guidance and disposed him towards concluding a permanent truce with us.'"

In the spring the Tatars began to rampage through Volhynia, Podolia and Galicia. The king was in residence on his estate at Jaworówo, just outside Lwów, unable to go into action for lack of troops. In June 1676 his envoy Czichrowski journied to Moscow to congratulate Tsar Fedor on his accession to the throne and to deliver a demand that in August forty thousand, or at least thirty thousand Russian troops attack the Crimea. Czichrowski added that he had been authorized to extend the truce only on condition that these demands were met in full. In his reply to the king, the tsar stated that Prince Romodanovsky and Hetman Samoilovich had instructions to stand at the ready, confer with the Polish commanders, and reach an agreement on the joining of forces. An army of Kalmyks under the command of Prince K. M. Cherkassky already was advancing on the Crimea, and Table Attendant Volynsky had been sent to the Don with a large army. When Romodanovsky and Samoilovich met the Polish commanders on the Dnieper they first would discuss an extension of the truce, and only then negotiate a joint offensive. Since it was stipulated in the current treaties that neither side would make peace independently with the sultan and the khan, the Russian envoy must be present at any negotiations between the Poles and the Turks. Tiapkin wrote to Moscow: "The Tatars are said to have taken about forty thousand captives back to their country, but all the Poles can say is: 'May the vile schismatics perish.'"

In the fall of 1676, thanks to the threat of a new Turkish offensive against both Russia and Poland, peace was concluded between Poland and Turkey outside the small town of Zórawno, a measure which had long been acknowledged as inevitable. Podolia and the town of Kamieniec were ceded to the sultan, and the Ukraine was left in the hands of the cossacks, the old frontiers being retained with the exception of Belaia Tserkov and Pavoloch, which came under Polish control. Tiapkin who, according to the articles of the treaty, should have been present at the signing of the peace agreement, was not even informed of the commencement of negotiations. The Poles vindicated themselves by referring to Doroshenko's defection and the Russian occupation of towns in Right Bank Ukraine. When Tiapkin applied to Crown Treasurer Morsztyn for more information about the treaty, he received the following retort: "His majesty the tsar has seized the Ukrainian towns of Chigirin, Kanev and Cherkasy; Doroshenko has surrendered Chigirin and gone to Moscow. We are astonished that your sovereign has failed to inform ours about the capture of these towns." Tiapkin replied: "His majesty the tsar is even more astonished that your sovereign has violated the treaties and made peace with the sultan without a word to him, and even without informing me, his representative, who should have attended the negotiations." "We had no choice," the treasurer retorted. Tiapkin continued: "You should not be surprised that our sovereign consented to Doroshenko's change of allegiance and the capture of the towns. His majesty did not seize these towns and their Christian inhabitants from the king and the commonwealth. He liberated them from the Muslim yoke, to which you had condemned them, both by King Michael's treaties and by your latest truce with the Turks." "The articles of the latest truce will be put before the Sejm," said the treasurer. "God alone knows whether the Commonwealth will accept them, for we are a free people."

There were many stories circulating about the relations between former Hetman Doroshenko and the Turks and Tatars, but Tiapkin was obliged to treat them with caution, for the Poles were extremely annoyed about Doroshenko's surrender to Moscow. "There is probably nothing in these rumors," wrote Tiapkin, "but we should take every precaution and his case should be thoroughly investigated. To ensure his loyalty his wife, children, brothers, father-in-law and mother-in-law should be kept in Moscow, and he should be promised generous favors and rewards from the sovereign in return for loyal service. There are many Poles who seek his downfall, and are ready to slander him out of hatred and anger. They are afraid of him because he is a very shrewd warrior and a great expert in all military matters; he not only knows of, but has seen their wily Polish ways, and the king, senators, commanders and all the armed forces acknowledge him to be the best soldier, not only in the Ukraine, but in the whole of Poland as well."

The Sejm confirmed the Treaty of Zórawno. On March 21, 1677 the king summoned Tiapkin. He took him by the arm and led him into the garden where the following conversation took place. "Lord resident," said the king, "I simply cannot understand why we have been corresponding with his majesty the tsar for so long without being able to conclude an alliance. I do not know why the tsar and his councillors are so suspicious of me, for I have always been well-disposed towards the Muscovite realm. Many of the boyars and commanders are well aware that during the Chudnov campaign[73] I protested vehemently when our Polish troops were base enough to hand over Prince Vasily Borisovich Sheremetev to the Crimeans. Not only did I quarrel with my commanders, I even tried to go to the assistance of Prince Yury Nikitich Boriatinsky. Now that I am ruler of my country, I strive with all my heart to maintain ties of brotherly friendship with all Christian rulers, and especially with his majesty the tsar, whose well-being I value as highly as my own. Knowing that your sovereigns wish the Pope to use their full royal title in his rescripts, unbeknown to the Commonwealth I wrote to our father the Pope and requested that he address the tsar as his station demands. I had hoped that the tsar would be grateful for my intercession and be more eager to display brotherly friendship. The Pope will agree, however, only on the condition that his majesty the tsar also uses his proper titles in rescripts. Write to your sovereign and tell him exactly what I have told you. For some time now I have been trying to establish closer contact with your sovereign, but I have been hampered by the interference of various hostile nations."

Thereupon Sobieski pressed his breast and said: "Lord resident! Write down everything I have told you, for I do not wish his majesty to suspect me of any kind of treachery. I wish him to consider me his faithful brother and close friend. His majesty should take no heed of the truce we have made with the Turks, for it will be short-lived. As far as I am concerned it is an unpleasant necessity into which I have been forced by the fearsome strength of the infidels, which we were unable to overcome unaided. The heathens are now threatening Chigirin, Kiev and the Muscovite realm itself. If his majesty the tsar truly wished to strike fear into the Turks, let him send his cossacks to the Crimea and the Black Sea. You should also write and ask his majesty to allow our ambassadors and residents to confer with him without diplomatic formalities, just as you are now doing with me, free to say and learn whatever you wish, man to man. These lavish diplomatic receptions are an obstacle to closer contact and unity. It does not surprise me that you have not yet instituted the practice, for until now such major disputes between nations were unknown, as were such long and frequent negotiations and incessant embassies. But the time has come for all Christian rulers to demonstrate through their ambassadors the close and loyal friendship which they feel for one another. In the interests of security and the better organization of affairs of state we should deal directly with ambassadors and residents rather than delegating the task to privy councillors; we should personally declare our desire for brotherly co-operation. Write all this in a letter to the tsar. In order to conceal it from the senators and the Commonwealth, I shall not send a rescript."

This frank interview was to be the last. In April the Sejm was prorogued, having resolved to remain at peace with all neighboring countries, and in May Tiapkin left Warsaw for Moscow. In July 1678 the king's great and plenipotentiary ambassadors Prince Michael Czartoryski and Casimir Sapieha signed a treaty in Moscow extending the truce a further thirteen years effective from June 1680, and agreed to seek to establish a permanent truce. Under the terms of the treaty Russia also ceded the towns of Nevel, Sebezh, Velizh and their districts, and paid an additional sum of two hundred thousand rubles, all in return for Kiev!

PEACE TALKS WITH TURKEY

No price was too high to keep Kiev from the Poles, but now that Chigirin had been destroyed it was essential to defend the city against the Turks. In order to forestall a new Turkish and Tatar offensive against Kiev, in December 1678 the servitor Daudov was sent to Constantinople to deliver a letter to the sultan. The tsar proposed to restore the former friendly relations between Russia and the Porte, and also referred to the ancient claim of the Russian rulers to the whole of Little Russia. Daudov also took a letter from Patriarch Joachim to the mufti: "We trust that you, the first and foremost guardian of Islamic law, in token of your spiritual station, will employ your every effort and your erudition in seeking peace and tranquillity amongst all men, and will use every means at your disposal to stop the spread of war, and rejoice in presenting the fruit of your endeavor as a gift to God. We trust that you will intercede with his majesty the sultan to obtain well-being and peace for your people and halt the troops who are perpetrating evil for the sake of that impious lawbreaker Yury Khmelnitsky."

In Moscow the desire for peace emerged after the second Chigirin campaign brought with it the threat of a Turkish attack on Kiev in the summer, and in Constantinople too the desire for peace was equally strong, for the Turks had gained little from the war. They had suffered heavy losses at Chigirin and were not particularly eager to attack Kiev. As yet unaware of Daudov's mission, the sultan had entrusted George Duca, hospodar of Wallachia, with the task of mediating peace between Russia and the Porte. In May 1679 the Wallachian envoy Captain Jan Bilevich announced in an interview with crown secretaries that the sultan wanted peace; he required only a section of the Ukraine for Yury Khmelnitsky, as he would be ashamed to conclude peace and withdraw empty-handed after such a long struggle. The secretaries asked about the extent of the Turkish losses at Chigirin. Bilevich replied that in the first campaign eight thousand janissaries had perished, and in the second about a third of the original force of a hundred thousand had been lost. They asked about the Turks' attitude towards Yury Khmelnitsky and what they expected him to do next. "The Turks would be glad to be rid of him," answered the envoy. "He causes them nothing but trouble. He led them to expect that the cossacks would come over to him as soon as he contacted them, but nothing of the kind occurred. When I called to see him on my way here I noticed that he was in a constant state of inebriation and frenzy." The tsar informed Duka by letter that he was willing to establish friendly relations with the sultan, on condition that the Turks not invade the territory of the Dnieper cossacks.

At this time the Polish ambassadors Brostowski and Gninski arrived in Moscow with the news that their king would end his truce with the sultan were the tsar to undertake to join forces with the Poles and pay the king an annual sum of at least two hundred thousand rubles towards military costs. The Muscovite authorities firmly rejected the latter condition and all discussion was postponed until the meeting of the [Polish-Russian] commission in June 1680.

Daudov returned in the fall with a letter from the vizier demanding that the Russians send a trustworthy and skilled ambassador who would speak sincerely and truthfully, and not raise arguments about the Ukrainian cossacks. The vizier proposed that an envoy be sent to the Crimea for peace talks. Bilevich arrived for the second time and stated the conditions for a truce: the Dnieper was to constitute the boundary between the two states, for the sultan was unable to renounce the territory which had been under Doroshenko's control, as the latter had once been his subject.

The Turks refused to make peace unless the Western Ukraine was surrendered to them, but the Muscovite government was unwilling to come to a decision until they had consulted the man who called himself hetman of both sides of the Dnieper. At the end of October 1679 the tsar sent his envoy Crown Secretary Emilian Ukraintsev[74] to have secret talks with Hetman Samoilovich in Baturin. "You know of all the great sovereign's dealings with the king of Poland, the sultan of Turkey and the khan of the Crimea, and his efforts to ensure the peace and security of the Zaporozhian Host and the ordinary people of Little Russia," said the secretary. "By the sovereign's grace, nothing is concealed from you. His majesty has commanded me to tell you that the Turks are desirous of peace, but that the Polish ambassadors in Moscow are urging the great sovereign to join forces with the king's armies and make a combined attack on the sultan of Turkey's domains. Take careful consideration of these matters, hetman. Consult with your officers and give me a full written statement to convey to his majesty the tsar."

"I shall write my views on peace with Turkey and consult my officers," the hetman replied, "but I place no faith in the Polish king's desire for an alliance with his majesty the tsar. In my opinion he has his own special reasons for wanting an alliance; he wishes to increase the enmity between the great sovereign and the Turkish sultan, and to exhaust the sovereign's troops by frequent mobilizations and campaigns in different regions. What good can come of an alliance with the king of Poland? His friendship with the Turks and Tatars makes him dangerously unreliable. I bow to the great sovereign's will in all things, but I, together with the entire Zaporozhian Host, beseech the sovereign to be so gracious as to make peace with the sultan of Turkey and the khan of Crimea, for peace with the Muslims would be more advantageous than any alliance with Poland. Such an alliance is unfeasible for, in order to assist the Poles, the tsar's forces must march great distances across barren lands on the other side of the Dnieper, and the Polish troops would be unable to come to the aid of the tsar's forces for the same reason. It might be possible to make an alliance which required the tsar's forces to wage war in the Crimea whilst the Poles were invading Wallachia and the lands beyond the Danube. The sovereign should at least try to gain some advantage from such an alliance by demanding that the king of Poland sign a treaty of permanent peace; he should not be trusted unless he agrees to do so, for he is ill-disposed towards the great sovereign. The Wallachian envoy Jan Bilevich tells me that when he spoke with the king just before the fall of Chigirin the king told him that his master the hospodar should urge the sultan and the vizier to declare war on his majesty the tsar."

The hetman told Ukraintsev before his departure: "Convey a humble petition to his majesty from myself, my officers and the entire Zaporozhian Host: we beg him to make a truce with the Turkish sultan and the Crimean khan, for the cossacks and the common people of the Ukraine are weary of this war with the Muslims, and eventually they may be driven to commit some outrage. Now is the time to make peace with the sultan and the khan. So far the enemy has not engaged the tsar's troops but, once they have done so, pride will prevent them from making peace, and we also shall have our own cossacks to fear.

"There must be no alliance with the king. I hear that the Poles have been demanding the surrender of towns and payment of money from the great sovereign, and they wish both armies to advance to the Danube and the lands beyond, but this plan is quite unacceptable and unfeasible. Even if we and the Poles jointly defeat the enemy, it will be the Poles who take all credit for the victory, whereupon the headstrong people of the Zaporozhian Host might be taken in by Polish lies, and also attribute the victory to them. Should this happen, there is a danger that unruly elements, returning to Little Russia from the war, will stir up sedition. If we and the Poles engage the enemy on the steppe, the Tatars promptly will steal the horse fodder, and this will upset the unruly cossacks; the Poles then will seize the opportunity to incite them to commit all manner of crimes.

"I also fear that the Poles will disappoint the tsar's forces and the Zaporozhian Host at some moment of crisis, for they are a weak and self-willed people, quite unable to endure hardship. Even were the tsar's forces victorious, it would still be necessary to make peace with the sultan and the khan, for it is quite impossible to wage war against the enemy in his own country because of its remoteness and the intervening barren wastes. Besides, the Poles would simply be a hindrance once peace was made. The king of Poland has sent a priest from Belaia Tserkov to see Serko and foment insurrection in Zaporozhie. This priest asked my clerk Chuikevich, who was in Zaporozhie at the time, to persuade me and the Zaporozhian Host to defect to my grandfather's sovereign the king of Poland. Serko told this same Chuikevich that the time had come to unite with the Poles and Tatars and do battle with Muscovy. It is obviously the priest from Belaia Tserkov who put such ideas into Serko's head."

TRUCE WITH THE SULTAN AND THE KHAN

The hetman's view finally prevailed and negotiations were opened with the Crimea and the Porte. Late in 1679 envoys Sukhotin and Crown Secretary Mikhailov were sent to Murad Girey, the khan of the Crimea, but they were unable to reach an agreement over the frontier issue, and Mikhailov took it upon himself to leave Sukhotin and return to Moscow. For the conclusion of the talks in 1680 our old acquaintance Table Attendant Vasily Tiapkin set off for the Crimea accompanied by Crown Secretary Nikita Zotov[75] and the Ukrainian secretary, Semen Rakovich. On October 25 they reached the ambassadors' quarters on the Alma river. They were struck immediately by the squalid condition of the building, which consisted of four wretched hovels constructed of solid unhewn rock, all bedaubed with filth, devoid of ceilings, floors, benches or doors, and lit by a single window. Wrote Tiapkin: "One could truly say that the curs and swine in Muscovy enjoy more comfort than did we, his majesty's ambassadors, in that place. There were neither stables nor hitching posts for our horses, and no food was provided, either for us or our beasts. We succeeded with great difficulty in purchasing bread, barley and straw, but at exorbitant prices."

An official came to summon them to the khan, who was residing in a village some five versts from the ambassadors' quarters. On arrival the envoys were told that they were to have an audience with the khan's privy councillor, Ahmed-agi, before seeing the khan himself. The envoys objected that it was not proper for them to waste time with other officials before they had presented the tsar's rescript to his majesty the khan in person. "We shall force you to hand over the rescript," screamed the Tatars. "We shall not be parted from it," retorted the envoys. "You'll take it over our dead bodies! Your threats and abuse and any hardship to which you might care to subject us do not frighten us." The Tatars' anger subsided. They said that one envoy might remain in the forecourt with the rescript whilst the other was received by the privy councillor.

Tiapkin went to meet Ahmed-agi. He entered and greeted him. "The Tatar," he wrote, "all puffed up in his heathen pride, was seated upon a carpet and reclining on cushions of gilded velvet." He greeted Tiapkin without rising, and ordered the envoy to sit down beside him. Ahmed began by reprimanding the envoys for disobeying the khan and refusing to attend him, the privy councillor. "It has been our custom from time immemorial," he said, "that envoys are received by privy councillors before proceeding to the presence of the khan. Or have envoys more important than yourselves never visited us before?" "We set no reckoning by the importance of former envoys," replied Tiapkin. "Even if affairs always have been conducted in the manner which you describe, we still refuse to obey your orders. Our first duty is to carry out the sovereign's business. Nowhere is it customary for privy councillors to receive official rescripts from ambassadors before they are presented to the sovereign. You have a crude way of doing things in the Crimea. I have been ambassador at the courts of many rulers, and I am familiar with diplomatic protocol. I am not at all surprised that former royal ambassadors have attended privy councillors before seeing the khan, because you always subject his majesty's envoys to bondage, ill-treatment and abuse, in the hope of extracting expensive gifts from them. We are accorded the same treatment, but we have been sent to the khan to conduct important business, not to distribute gifts."

After a ceremonial reception by the khan, negotiations commenced. The captive boyar, Vasily Borisovich Sheremetev, was in attendance. Tiapkin and Zotov recommended that the frontier be marked by the rivers Ros, Tiasma and Ingul. The khan's privy councillors laughed and replied: "If that is all you can suggest, you have had a wasted journey. We have never recognized a frontier along those rivers, and never shall." The envoys' efforts to win over the councillors "by all manner of subtle persuasion," and by promising and even distributing rewards were to no avail. The Tatars remained adamant, insisting that they would agree to no other frontier but the Dnieper. According to Muslim law, once a place was traversed by the sultan's armies, it could never be relinquished.

Tiapkin tried to conciliate the khan by expounding in great detail the importance of the intermediary role which Murad Girey had assumed. He spoke of the honor and trust the tsar had shown him by sending his envoys to the Crimea instead of directly to the sultan in Constantinople. The khan was moved, but replied that he was not free, and was bound to obey the sultan. Were he an independent ruler in his own country he would consent gladly to any frontier his majesty the tsar cared to name. The envoys promised the khan ten thousand gold *chervonnye*, three thousand for the privy councillors and five thousand rubles' worth for the Turkish sultan and his vizier. The khan replied that even a hundred thousand would not secure his consent. Because of the envoys' persistence, the khan threatened to imprison them in a subterranean chamber without heating, benches, ceiling or windows. This threat was carried out, and merchants were forbidden to bring them victuals or firewood.

The envoys capitulated and presented the khan with the following terms: (1) A twenty-year truce was to be instituted, effective from January 3, 1681; the frontier was to run along the Dnieper; his majesty the khan was to receive tribute payments for the past three years, then to be paid on an annual basis according to the old registers. (2) During the twenty-year truce no towns were to be built by the sultan on the territory between the Dnieper and the Bug, nor should any of the old ruined cossack towns and settlements be restored; they were not to receive fugitives from the tsar's domains, nor were they to colonize the aforementioned cossack lands, which were to remain empty. (3) The Crimean, Ochakov and Belgorod (Akkerman) Tatars would be allowed to roam freely on both sides of the Dnieper, over the steppe and along the tributaries to collect horse fodder and on trapping expeditions; on the tsar's side, traders from the ordinary and service cossacks of the Zaporozhian Host were to be allowed to fish along the Dnieper and given access to the tributaries along both sides of the river. They should be allowed access to the Black Sea for the purpose of fishing, collecting salt and trapping. (4) Kiev, with the monasteries, towns, townships and villages of its old town district, that is to say Vasilkov, Tripolie and Staiki, with their villages to the south and the two townships of Dedovshchina and Radomyshl to the north, were to remain under the tsar's control. (5) The Zaporozhian Cossacks were to remain the subjects of his majesty the tsar. The sultan and the khan held no claim over them, and would make no attempt to take control of them. (6) His majesty the tsar was to be accorded his full titles in the form which he himself used. Boyar Sheremetev, Table Attendant Prince Fedor Romodanovsky and all other captives were to be released on payment of ransom and exchange of prisoners. (7) The sultan and the khan were not to assist the tsar's enemies.

The khan listened to the terms and declared them to be reasonable and acceptable. An emissary went to Constantinople and obtained the sultan's ratification, but when they came to take the oath Tiapkin and Zotov noticed that the charter had been altered. It had been abbreviated and whole clauses were omitted, for example those concerning Zaporozhie and navigation rights along the Dnieper. The envoys declared that they could not accept such a document. The Tatars replied with cries of "Have you come here to teach our rulers what to do, to hold to your obstinate customs and write a lot of unnecessary words? You fail to respect what the khan deigns to write and give you; every sovereign reigns supreme in his own country and does what he pleases. You have no right to lecture us and tell us what to do! If you continue with this stubbornness and refuse to accept the charters, they will be taken to your sovereign by the khan's envoys, and you, for your intransigence, will be clapped into irons and sent into eternal imprisonment." The envoys replied that they did not dare accept the charter; they would send a messenger to Moscow and await the great sovereign's instructions. The khan was informed and the answer returned that, on the sultan's orders, the envoys were to be sent to Moscow with the charters at once. To this the envoys replied that they would leave with the charters, but much against their will; the great sovereign would decide, as God dictated, whether the charters were acceptable and their contents binding as peace treaties.

On March 4, in a tent in a field near Bakhchiserai, Tiapkin and Zotov took leave of the khan. Murad Girey kissed the Quran and swore that he and the sultan would uphold the truce for a full twenty years. He presented the envoys and interpreters with kaftans of gold cloth, and the envoys gave the khan gifts in return. The khan told them that the great sovereign should send his ambassadors to obtain the sultan's ratification of the peace terms as soon as possible, and that the clauses omitted from his charter would be included in the sultan's. He had written to the sultan and would be writing again. Finally, with a beaming and joyful face, the khan said: "When you reach the capital city of Moscow and have the honor of looking upon the illustrious countenance of your great sovereign, bow to him on behalf of his majesty the khan and tell him how we mediated between him and the sultan, how zealously we conducted the peace talks, and of the love and friendship we showed to you. And may you have a safe journey!" The envoys bowed to the ground before the khan and thanked him for his good wishes. When they emerged from the tent the Tatar dignitaries—beys, karacheis and murzas—escorted them to their horses and bade them a fond farewell. At the news of the truce many Christians and Muslims crowded around the tent and accompanied the envoys with shouts of joy.

The joyful response to the conclusion of peace in the Crimea was surpassed by the delight felt in Russia, and especially in the Ukraine. In all the Ukrainian towns through which they passed the envoys were given a triumphal welcome. Clergymen bearing crosses and holy water, colonels, company commanders and lieutenants with the cavalry, standards, trumpets and kettledrums, the cossack infantry with their drums, the townspeople bearing bread, salt and beverages—all came out to greet them. Everywhere they were given a joyful and friendly reception. People wept and thanked God for the peace treaty; they gave the envoys food, drink and transport. In Baturin Hetman Ivan Samoilovich clasped the envoys in a fond paternal embrace, with tears of joy in his eyes. He thanked them for their love and advice to his secretary, Semen Rakovich, and expressed humble thanks that they had come to visit him, and in so doing honored his office as hetman of the Little Russian people.

The hetman gave a great banquet to celebrate the occasion. During the toasts cannon were fired in the courtyard of the fortress, and music was played throughout the meal. When the envoys were about to leave the hetman asked them to remind the great sovereign of the Ukrainians who had crossed from the west to the east bank of the Dnieper. They had no source of food supplies and he was feeding them from his own stores. He requested that the great sovereign order their transfer to the productive lands of the free settlements around Sumy, Krasnopol and other towns, and along the rivers and forests of the steppes. He also requested that all Ukrainians in the Belgorod military district be placed under his command and recognize him as their hetman in compensation for the loss of the west side of the Dnieper, which now had been surrendered to the Turks.

Now that a settlement had been reached in the Crimea, it remained only to obtain a charter of confirmation from the sultan. In 1681 Crown Secretary Prokofy Voznitsyn[76] was sent to Constantinople for this purpose. The Turks refused to include the clauses recognizing Zaporozhie as the property of the tsar. Voznitsyn insisted in vain that the clause be inserted, and refused to accept the charter or leave without it. Voznitsyn sought out the advice of the patriarchs of Constantinople, Jerusalem and Alexandria, who were in the capital at the time, and they advised him to accept the charter. The ambassador took their advice, but as he took the charter from the vizier, he protested: "I accept this charter unwillingly and shall submit it to the discretion of his majesty the tsar, but I do not know whether it will be approved."

DOROSHENKO BECOMES GOVERNOR OF VIATKA

His majesty the tsar deigned to accept the charter. The Muscovites were relieved to be rid of a major and dangerous war for the price of a stretch of barren steppe; that, at least, was how they viewed the surrender of the lands across the Dnieper at the time. Meanwhile Doroshenko, the man who was to blame for the devastation of the Right Bank Ukraine and its surrender to the Turks, was living quietly in Moscow.

In October 1679 Secretary Bobinin visited him with a gracious decree from the sovereign: "It has come to the attention of the sovereign that he, Peter, is suffering from a shortage of food, drink and horse fodder. The great sovereign therefore has commanded that he be appointed to the governorship of Ustiug." Doroshenko made a low bow and asked: "Is this place Ustiug far from Moscow, and what sort of town is it?" "It lies six hundred versts from Moscow and is a renowned and populous town," the secretary replied. "The great sovereign assured me of his favor," said Doroshenko. "He commanded that I live with my relatives in Sosnitsa, then he ordered me to go to Moscow for a while. Standing in his royal presence, I was given assurance of his majesty's bountiful favor. I was ordered to live in Moscow and given a home, food and drink. I shall appeal to the great sovereign and beg him not to force me to accept this governorship. When my three brothers and other relatives in Little Russia hear of this, they will conclude that I have been banished, not granted a governorship. This will be certain to lead to trouble on both sides of the Dnieper, as I can tell you from my knowledge of local habits. Yanenko [Doroshenko's father-in-law] betrayed the great sovereign and went over to Yury Khmelnitsky, and I make no secret of the fact that both these men are relatives of mine. Much of my property was left behind in Sosnitsa; much of it was taken by the hetman, and much was lost, but if his majesty appoints me to this post I shall lose all the rest as well. Even now I am very uneasy, for I have had no news from my relatives in Sosnitsa and elsewhere for the past six weeks; but if I am governor in such a remote place, they will have all the more reason to desert me, and no one will write to me when I am so far away." Doroshenko later changed his mind and took up the governorship of Viatka.

DEATH OF SERKO

Another celebrated cossack also was about to depart from the scene. In September 1680 envoys Field-Colonel Sherbinovsky and Military Secretary Bykhotsky arrived in Moscow from Zaporozhie with the news that Ivan Serko had died on August 1, and that Ivan Stiagailo had been elected in his place. In a secret interview Bykhotsky reported: "When Serko was commander-in-chief he caused nothing but trouble for the great sovereign. No one dared to confront him about this because, either by God's will or by his own ingenuity, he had made everyone mortally afraid of him and he did exactly as he pleased. Anyone who refused to obey him would be killed immediately, for each member of our cossack family enjoys complete liberty. If Serko had anything against anyone, that person would have met his death at once in the assembly without trial. Serko was ill-disposed towards the great sovereign, firstly because he had been exiled to Siberia and, secondly, because he bore a grudge against the hetman, who had subjected his wife and children to great hardship and abuse, deprived Zaporozhie of its ancient property and trade, and failed to send provisions. The king of Poland sent letters to Serko inviting him to enter his service, and the cossack began to devise a scheme for bringing bloodshed to the Ukraine. The king, hearing of his plans, sent a priest from Belaia Tserkov to see him. Serko was won over by the priest and sent his son to the king with a detachment of a hundred cossacks as a mark of loyalty. Serko's plan was that the king should direct the khan and his horde to attack the towns of Settlement Ukraine[77] and send his own troops to Zadesenie. Serko, under the king's colors, would advance simultaneously upon the Settlement towns. When the Little Russian people realized the desperateness of their position and heard that Serko was in the service of the king of Poland, they would rise in rebellion, kill the hetman and proclaim Serko as hetman, in the assurance that he would protect them from the Turks and Tatars with the king of Poland's help.

"This scheme was thwarted by God's power. Chief Justice Yakov Konstantinov and myself were obedient to God and remained loyal to the great sovereign. We foiled Serko's wicked plan and also prevented him from making a pact with the Crimea in order to gain the protection of the sultan of Turkey. Thus Serko was frustrated in his plans; he fell into despair and he began to ail. He developed a pain in his left side and grew extremely thin. During his illness he took no part in the affairs of the Host and withdrew permanently to his apiary, which is ten versts from the Zaporozhian Camp at a fortified spot on the Dnieper gulf. The cossacks began to complain, but he told them: 'Listen to me; I am an old man and an experienced soldier. I know the time and place for everything, but you lost some fine young men by sending them out into the steppe without my advice.' The king sent a Wallachian by the name of Apostolets to see Serko. This man spoke to him in private and urged him to carry out the wicked schemes

I referred to earlier. The chief justice and I learned this from Apostolets when he began telling us that we were to obey the old warrior Serko and do as he demanded. We asked Serko the reason for Apostolets's visit, but he would tell us nothing; he merely recounted his grievances and those of his Host. Shortly before his death Serko had a coffin made and lay down in it, saying that he did not expect his health to return. He died suddenly in his bee garden on August 1."

The tsar sent his envoy Berdiaev to the Zaporozhian Camp with gifts for the commander-in-chief and his officers. For the cossacks he brought five hundred gold *chervonnye*, one hundred and fifty lengths of cloth and fifty puds of both powder and lead. Berdiaev arrived at the camp in November and addressed the cossack assembly, exhorting the Zaporozhians to repent of the crimes of Serko's day and swear their allegiance to his majesty the tsar. "Why should we swear an oath?" they replied. "We have not betrayed the great sovereign, nor do we intend to. But he has sent us too little cloth; there is barely half an arshin per man. The great sovereign sends large amounts of money, cloth and grain to the Don; we are getting short measure in comparison to the Don Cossacks." The hetman's envoy, Solomakha, was present at the assembly. He told them: "The hetman promises to send you grain supplies. Just let him know how much you need each year, and he will send you money out of the fees collected from the rents.

The commander-in-chief asked: "Do you or do you not wish to swear allegiance to the great sovereign? I myself am willing because the old hostility between Ataman Ivan Serko and Hetman Ivan Samoilovich has impoverished the Host; for years we received neither the tsar's allowance nor grain supplies from the hetman." "As if we had any reason for swearing allegiance," shouted the crowd. "You officers get a big allowance from the tsar. You send petitions to Moscow about your own allowance from the tsar, but you don't complain to the tsar on the Host's behalf." The commander tried to enter the church to take the oath, but the cossacks restrained him. Most vociferous of all in his complaints was Military Secretary Peter Guk, who had received no gifts. The government had sent gifts for Secretary Bykhotsky, believing him to be the only secretary in the Zaporozhian Camp, but in fact he had been replaced by Guk some time before. The next day after matins another assembly was called. Guk had changed his mind and now began to urge the cossacks to swear allegiance, and so the people went into the church and swore a solemn oath. When Berdiaev returned to Moscow, fifty more lengths of cloth and an allowance for Guk hastily were dispatched to Zaporozhie.

SWEDISH, DANISH AND AUSTRIAN AFFAIRS

The perilous war with Turkey which occupied almost the whole of Fedor's reign obviously affected Russia's relations with other powers.[78] The old frontier disputes with Sweden continued, but Denmark's efforts to persuade the Russian government to end its truce with Sweden were unsuccessful. The menace in the south precluded any thought of war in the north. The Muscovite court rejected the Danish propositions concerning Sweden, and tried instead to deflect the might of Turkey away from Russia by setting Austria against the Porte. Boyar Buturlin went to Vienna to enjoin the emperor to break off relations with Turkey, but his proposals were turned down on the pretext of Austria's hostile relations with France and the inactivity of Poland.

KALMYKS AND COSSACKS

With the Western European powers Russia was able to deal on a diplomatic basis, but with the predatory nomadic tribes of the eastern steppes such an approach was ineffectual. The situation was aggravated by the local cossacks, who did not bother to consult the government when they felt the need to make a raid or avenge an insult. Russia's new nomadic neighbors, the Kalmyks, had been left with no choice but to recognize the great sovereign's authority and assist Russian military forces. In return the government was obliged to protect them, and in 1677 the authorities in Moscow were displeased to learn that a dispute had arisen between the Kalmyks and the Don Cossacks. It was reported from various places along the Volga that the cossacks were raiding Kalmyk settlements. Musketeer lieutenants were sent to investigate the trouble. They came across some cossacks and asked why they were attacking the Kalmyks, and on whose authority. Some of the cossacks admitted honestly that "We do not have the sovereign's permission to fight the Kalmyks, but they have offended us in so many ways that we can endure their insults no longer, so we assembled our men and attacked them, but without criminal intent." Others replied less forthrightly: "The great sovereign ordered us to attack the Kalmyk settlements. You will find the decree with our men on the Don."

There was, of course, no decree relating to the Don, but a decree was sent to Astrakhan instructing the governors there to send Zmeev, the commander of the musketeer cavalry, up the Volga to halt the cossacks and send them back to the Don. North of Cherny Yar, Zmeev came upon twenty-two boats with 245 cossacks and their ataman Ignatiev. Zmeev informed them of the great sovereign's decree; they were to halt their attacks on the Kalmyks, return to their own settlements and live in peace with the Kalmyks, who were servants of the great sovereign. The cossacks replied: "We were going up the Volga to attack the Kalmyk camps because this year Kalmyk warriors raided many of our cossack villages. They took many of our wives and children captive and drove away our livestock. We were provoked into attacking them; we want to release our wives, children and livestock. But we recovered only a hundred and fifty horses, and there was no trace of our wives and children in the settlements. We were going to make another attempt at rescuing our wives, children and the remaining livestock, but in view of the great sovereign's decree we shall turn back to our villages and shall not attack the Kalmyk camps." And return they did.

In January of the following year, 1678, the tsar's loyal servant, Prince Kaspulat Mutsalovich Cherkassky wrote to the sovereign reporting that he had made a tour of the Kalmyk settlements to call upon Aiuka and the other chieftains to fight for the great sovereign in the Crimea. Aiuka, however, had refused to fight because of the destruction wreaked upon them by the people of the Don and the Yaik Cossacks, who had killed their men and abducted their wives and children. The tsar immediately instructed Kaspulat to visit the Kalmyk camps and reconcile the Kalmyks with the Don cossacks.

The Don Cossacks on the Volga had turned back when ordered to do so by the great sovereign, but along the Yaik the spectre of Razin had again risen.[79] In July some reports reached Moscow of the capture of Guriev, a settlement on the Yaik so named after its founder Mikhail Guriev; it had been taken by rebel cossacks from the Yaik region under the command of Vaska Kasimov. They had snatched money belonging to the crown, cannon, lead and powder, and installed themselves on Kamenny Island at the mouth of the Yaik. Prince Konstantin Shcherbatov, governor of Astrakhan, sent a detachment of eight hundred musketeers in fifteen boats to attack the rebels. In Moscow, however, they were greatly troubled by memories of the Razin uprising. Boyar Peter Mikhailovich Saltykov was sent to Astrakhan with orders that suppression be carried out with the utmost energy, and with great care, for Astrakhan was sparsely populated, and there was no one to defend it against the rebels. Mamonin, commander of the Kazan musketeers, drove the rebels to the sea and defeated them. About two hundred and thirty of them, including forty wounded, managed to gain the Trukhmen shore, but the inhabitants drove them away and they ended up on the coast of Persia on the island of Sary, where Stenka Razin once had stayed. Using this island as a base, they took to piracy, but were attacked by the shah's troops and suffered yet another defeat at their hands. At the end of the year the rebels arrived at Baku in four boats, but only twenty-nine men disembarked, and they were rounded up by the local inhabitants and handed over to the khan of Shemakha.

DISTURBANCES AMONG THE BASHKIR

There had been disturbances among the Bashkir in Tsar Alexis's reign and in Fedor's reign these disturbances flared again with renewed violence as the war between Russia and Turkey had its inevitable effect upon the Muslim peoples of the steppe. At the beginning of 1679 news reached Moscow from Verkhoturie that Arapov, a peasant bailliff[80] and administrator of one of the free settlements, had gone to a Tatar village in the Kungur district to make various purchases and while there ten Bashkirs visited the Tatars to discuss how they could attack Kungur, the Siberian free settlements and outlying areas that spring. They said: "The Turks and Crimean Tatars captured Chigirin and defeated the tsar's forces. We too shall fight, because we are their kinsmen and of the same mind." Arapov reported that the Bashkirs and Tatars were feeding up their horses and making bows and arrows; they had many weapons, two or three arquebuses and muskets per man. Not long after this incident Tatars on skis appeared outside Kungur, captured the fort[81] and destroyed some villages. In the summer of 1680 it was reported that the Kalmyk chieftain Aiuka had made a truce with the khan of the Crimea and sent a thousand of his warriors to the Crimea and two thousand to the vicinity of the Russian frontier towns. It was reported also that Aiuka wished to make peace with the Ufa Bashkirs in order to stage a joint attack on the cossack settlements, Samara, and other frontier towns. In July an army of more than three thousand Tatars, Kalmyks and Circassians appeared at Penza, set fire to the outskirts and retired to the steppe. The Bashkirs also began to cross from the right to the left, Nogai, side of the Volga. In 1681 there were rumors along the Tobol that the Bashkirs had taken up arms and left their villages, leaving behind only those who were incapable of mounting a horse.

SIBERIAN PEOPLES AND THE GOVERNMENT

In the south of Siberia the battle with the Kirghiz continued. In the fall of 1679 they devastated the Tomsk district with the aid of renegade native tribute-payers. Detachments of cossack infantry and cavalry engaged the raiders, defeated them and retrieved their booty, with the loss of five men. At the same time another great band of Kirghiz marched on Krasnoiarsk and the small fortified settlements of the region. They failed to capture any of the forts, but burned sixteen hamlets. The Kirghiz were joined by the Tubin.[82] All this antagonized the junior boyars and cossacks of Krasnoiarsk; they captured some Tubin hostages, took them outside the town and shot them in full view of their relatives. When the sovereign learned of this incident he ordered that Zagriazhsky, the governor of Krasnoiarsk, be put into prison for a day for handing over the hostages to the military servitors. The servitors were told: "The worthiest men amongst you ought to be condemned to death for shooting the hostages; but in view of your service and the grievances you have suffered, we pardon you. In return for our great mercy, you should serve us loyally and take high-born hostages from amongst the Tubin princelings."

In the north the Samoyed were refusing to pay their tribute. When the tribute collectors visited the old town of Mangazeia, the Samoyed princeling Nyla came and threw a tribute of seventy-six Arctic foxes at their feet. The tribute always had been paid in sable and beaver pelts, but when the collectors ordered him to make the customary payment, Nyla responded by calling upon his kinsmen to attack them. The Samoyed rushed at the collectors brandishing knives but the collectors held them off, seized Nyla and killed him. His kinsmen fled from the town, gathered their forces and prepared to attack. The Russians kept them at bay for three days and nights, until two Samoyed princelings came to the aid of the besieged collectors, attacked their own people and drove them from the town. Another band of Samoyed besieged the settlement of Obdorsk, furious at their fellow-tribesmen who refused to join them against the Russians.

In the east either the Yakut or the Tungus were in a constant state of rebellion. News reached the governor of Yakutsk from a tribute collector in his winter quarters at Verkhneviliuisk that various tribes of tributary Tungus had been gathering around his quarters for the past month with the aim of killing the cossacks and taking the camp. In the fall of 1675 the Yakut had killed several Russian traders; their ringleader turned out to be Chief Baltuga, a Yakut from the Yaransk district. Two cossacks and several friendly Yakuts were sent to have talks with him, but one of the cossacks was brutally murdered. The governor of Yakutsk sent a detachment of Russians and friendly Yakut to attack Baltuga. After long negotiations Baltuga sent two children, his son and nephew, as hostages, and announced that he would come himself when desired. Should the Russians and Yakut attack him he vowed to kill the lot of them and keep fighting to the last babe in arms, but he would never give himself up alive. He tried to dissuade the friendly Yakut from helping the Russians and fighting against him, threatening to kill them along with the Russians if they did so. His boldness, however, was not matched by his strength. The Yakut patriot was forced to flee his enemies; he was wounded, captured and brought to Yakutsk, along with the mutilated body of the cossack killed by the Yakut.

The military servitors of Yakutsk were incensed at the sight. They submitted the following petition: "Great sovereign, we have been sent here on your service to collect your tributes and we are entrusted to pursue those who betray you. But these same traitors, both tribute-paying and non-tribute-paying natives, do us to death and commit outrages: they rip open breasts, tear out hearts, cut off hands and gouge out eyes. By God's grace the traitor Baltuga and his kinsmen were captured in battle and in the struggle they wounded many of your servitors. Gracious sovereign, command your governor to deal with these traitors under the articles of the Code of Laws."[83]

The brother of the murdered cossack lost all patience; he sought out Baltuga's brother, who was wounded and tied up, and stabbed him to death with a pike. The governor sentenced him to be flogged on trestles for wilfully killing a bound prisoner. The townspeople of all ranks then requested that he be beaten with cudgels instead of with the knout, but the servitors were outraged to see their comrade punished for killing a traitor. They submitted another petition: "We go hunting along the great Lena river, along the Vitim and their tributaries. Every tenth pelt from our bag goes to the great sovereign's treasury and we also pay monetary taxes, but now the alien Yakut and Tungus are robbing us, your orphans, setting fire to us and killing us like pigs. They have ruined us completely and put a stop to our trade. Yet we dare not defend ourselves for fear that you will punish us. We shall no longer be able to carry on trading and this will cause great losses and damage to the royal treasury."

When he received the petition the governor looked up the section on treason in the Code of Laws. On discovering that the death penalty was prescribed, he sent to Moscow for authorization. The government always sought to bring native peoples under the sovereign's rule by kindness rather than cruelty; besides, officials were well aware that the military servitors often drove the natives beyond the limits of endurance. Therefore a decree was issued announcing that, for his own abiding health and for the lasting memory of his father, the great sovereign had pardoned Baltuga; the death sentence was commuted to one of merciless flogging and he was to be released on bail. But in the second year of bail twenty tributary Yakuts submitted a complaint that Baltuga and his kinsmen were robbing their fellow Yakuts, committing acts of violence and refusing to pay their tribute.

Occasionally strong-willed chieftains emerged amongst the natives, but in general they were no match for the Russians. The tribes were too small, too widely dispersed and mutually hostile. When rebellion broke out, Russian troops would arrive to suppress it. They might number only fifteen men but they would be accompanied by a band of obedient natives, come to pacify their fellows. When the savages besieged Russian soldiers in their trading posts, other savages would flock to the aid of the Russians. The subjugation of vast tracts of Northern Asia therefore presented no great problem for the Russians. The natives' way of life was such that the tribes raised few objections when forced into paying tribute by those stronger than themselves. After all, the ancestors of the conquerors of Siberia were inherently much stronger than the Yakut, Tungus and Buriat, but in the ninth century even they, divided as they were into separate clans, paid tribute to the first man who pointed a weapon at them and demanded it. They rose in protest only when some Igor or other tried to exact twice the normal tribute, like a wolf falling upon sheep.[84] Unfortunately there were many such Igors in Siberia during this period and it was they, with their wolf-like ways, who delayed the subjugation of the natives. They fomented rebellion and raised passions, as the saying goes.

In the fall of 1677 tributary Tungus on the Urak massacred a group of cossacks on their way from Yakutsk to Okhotsk. They stole their cannon, arms and merchandise, and sent a captive cossack woman to Okhotsk to deliver the following message: "Tell the government official Peter Yaryzhkin that we massacred the cossacks to repay the ill-treatment and abuses inflicted upon us by the tribute collector Yury Kryzhanovsky. He robbed us of fine sables, lynx and reindeer skins; he took four or five sables from each man and even ordered that he be given one sable from each of the little children. He took our sables and reindeer by force and spat in our faces, saying: 'If you bring me too few, I'll come and get them myself.'"

The Tungus continued to take their revenge. The ringleader of the mutiny was our old acquaintance Zelemey,[85] who had spread the rumor among his people that all but two of the cossacks in Yakutsk were dead; since there was no one to reinforce Okhotsk, now was the time for action. Zelemey's story resulted in the gathering of a force of about a thousand Tungus, who besieged Okhotsk. Yaryzhkin sent an interpreter to speak with Zelemey: "Why have you arrived in such great numbers and surrounded the fort? Enter the town and speak with the government official. You have nothing to fear." "I shan't enter the fort," replied Zelemey. "We have no tribute with us. You can see for yourselves why we are here." The Tungus surged forward to attack. Kryzhanovsky was unable to reach the stockade in time; he was besieged by the Tungus in his own house. They broke the window and laid fires beneath the walls. They occupied some cossack houses outside the stockade and opened fire from the protection of the buildings. Arrows showered onto the stockade from all sides, like swarms of mosquitoes. Meanwhile, in answer to Kryzhanovsky's cries for help, Yaryzhkin made a sortie and rescued him. The Tungus were expelled from Okhotsk and did not repeat their attack on the fort.

Kryzhanovsky's case was tried (he was a captive Pole with a brother named Casimir, from which his origins should be clear). He was accused of keeping the registers of stores and tribute payments in his own house; the Tungus came to him by night, before paying the official tribute, and he took the best sables for himself, leaving the inferior ones for the crown. He was accused also of fornicating with the wives and children of the natives. Yaryzhkin was implicated as well in embezzling from the crown and committing acts of violence against his own men and the natives. Both were sentenced to be flogged unmercifully with the knout, exiled to the Daurian region and barred from holding office. Even so their replacement in Okhotsk, Danilo Bibikov, followed in the footsteps of his predecessors. He hanged the Tungus, flogged them, cut off their ears and noses, and during the payment of tribute he forced them to conceal the best sables in their clothing and beneath the floor in order to save them for himself. Bibikov did not survive to receive his punishment from Moscow. In 1680 he was ambushed by Tungus on the road from Okhotsk to Yakutsk and killed, together with an entire detachment of Russian troops.

In Nerchinsk it was not the natives but the Russian military servitors who rebelled against the crown official Shulgin. Shulgin accepted bribes for the release of Buriat hostages, who subsequently turned traitor and fled to Mongolia. He did not, however, release the Buriats' wives, as he had his own way of employing them. He bought grain to distill vodka and brew beer for sale, despite the fact that others had nothing to eat because of the high price of grain, and had to make do with grass and roots. He beat the servitors with knout and cudgels, ordering the use of five or six cudgels at a time. The servitors reached the end of their tether and sent petitioners to Moscow. But Moscow was distant and there was no telling how long they must wait for an official decree, and so the servitors took matters into their own hands. They removed Shulgin from the government office and chose a junior boyar and a cossack corporal to administer the affairs of the crown.

THE SILK TRADE

The Muscovite government faced many problems—a major and perilous war with Turkey, disturbances among the savage dwellers of the steppe, an underaged and sick ruler, unrest at court. It must deal with domestic affairs as best it could, and there was no time to lose.

At the very outset of Fedor's reign a perennial problem arose which had troubled both his grandfather and his father, namely the question of the rights of foreign merchants to trade in Russia and to transit the country. In Tsar Alexis's reign a treaty had been negotiated with a company of Persian Armenians who undertook to deliver all silk they acquired in Persia to Russia. The Armenians broke their contract, however. The Dutch envoy van Klenk,[86] meanwhile, proposed that Dutch merchants be allowed to trade with the Persians in Russia, and that the Persians be allowed access across Russia to deliver raw silk to Holland. As was the custom, the high merchants were summoned by the boyars. The terms of the treaties with the Armenians and translations of van Klenk's dispatches were read to them and they were asked how, in their opinion, the silk trade might best be conducted, in view of the ambassador's suggestions. The merchants replied: "The Persians and Armenians have not adhered to the treaty. They did not bring all their silk to Russia, and continue even now to send the best silk by the old routes, thereby denying us all hope of any profit from the silk trade. The Dutch ambassador asks that the Dutch be allowed to trade with the Persians in Russia and he promises that Russian trade will flourish as a result.

"If this is so, let him show us the actual fruits of this flourishing trade and immediately draw up a treaty whereby all raw silk brought from

Persia, in whatever quantity, shall be sold to the Dutch from the crown treasury and local traders in Archangel at the statutory price, in imitation of the treaties which the Dutch and other foreigners have made to regulate silk coming from Persia by way of Turkey. Any reluctance to conclude such a treaty will prove that the ambassador does not have Russian interests at heart, but intends to leave Russia with only the flower of the profits, whilst drawing off all the fruits for his own country and making the Russian merchants incur losses, for the Dutch will trade privately with the Persians and retain all the profits for themselves.

"It might be possible to allow Russian and Dutch merchants to trade in Russia with the Persians and Armenians for a period of two years; if during that time the crown treasury suffers no loss and the Russian merchants no injury, the arrangement might be made permanent. Even this has its dangers, of course, for the Dutch could deliberately refrain from wronging us during the two years in order to secure the confirmation of the treaty, immediately barring us from all trading as soon as it is ratified and monopolizing it themselves, just as they have done in the gold and silver mines and other enterprises in East India, as a result of which they have become very rich, and the local population has been reduced to penury. It would be best to adhere to the terms of our second treaty with the Armenians, whereby they trade in silk with Russian merchants at a free rate, and whatever the Russians do not buy is exchanged with the treasury for money and goods. If they reject these terms too, they should be given permission to do business with foreigners in Archangel. Russian merchants would incur some loss from this arrangement, but it would be far worse were foreigners allowed to trade amongst themselves all over Russia or allowed access to foreign lands across Russian territory."

TRADE WITH THE GREEKS

At the same time the tsar, on the advice of the patriarch, instructed the boyars, and the boyars resolved, that Tsar Alexis's decree of 1647 allowing the Greeks to trade only in Putivl be confirmed. The following reasons were given: "at one time Greek churchmen used to visit from Palestine bringing with them curative relics and miracle-working icons and their fellow-countrymen, highly distinguished Greek merchants, came with the very finest of costly merchandise. But nowadays clerics no longer come to Russia; trade is carried on by Greeks from the very lowest orders, nor is the trade direct. Even the goods offered are of poor quality; glass is substituted for diamonds and other precious gems. Many of them have turned to thieving and smuggling; others counterfeit promissory notes and trade in liquor and tobacco."

REVISION OF PENALTIES FOR CAPITAL OFFENSES

The most important of Tsar Fedor's decrees belong in the main to the latter years of his reign, when the tsar had reached maturity. By this time the Miloslavskys were gone and Yazykov, Likhachev and Golitsyn had come to power. In 1679 and 1680 punishment by mutilation was abolished. "Criminals with one or two convictions are to be tortured, punished and exiled for life to Siberia to work on the land. They are no longer to be executed or sentenced to loss of hands, feet or two fingers. Wives and children under the age of three must accompany them into exile; older children shall stay behind." In 1677 a peasant woman called Zhukova was interred in the market place in Vladimir for cutting off her husband's head with a scythe. When she had been in the ground for twenty-four hours, the local clergy requested that the miscreant be dug out and sent to a nunnery. The sovereign granted their appeal. In 1682 a similar incident occurred in Moscow: two female criminals were buried in the ground, whereupon they promised to take the veil and refrain from any further wrongdoing. The sovereign ordered that they be dug out and sent to a nunnery. In 1680 rescripts were sent to every town ruling that under no circumstances should suspects be detained for long periods in government offices or jails, but that their cases be heard promptly. In the same year the following resolution was made: "Henceforth it is an offense for jailers to take entrance payments from any new arrivals who are to be placed in jail and behind bars."[87] In 1681 the patriarch issued a memorandum: "It is forbidden for husbands to divorce their wives, or wives their husbands, by taking monastic vows. But if a wife divorces her husband in this manner, her husband should not take another wife, nor should wives remarry in such a case." In 1679 the military servitors complained that their womenfolk who had been given in marriage with landed property were being beaten and tormented by their husbands, who were trying to force them to sell their dowry estates and mortgage them in their own names. A decree was passed making it an offense for husbands to sell or mortgage their wives' estates in their wives' names.

In 1680 the corrupt form of petition "may the sovereign grant and be merciful like God" was abolished and replaced by the formula "for the festival that has come to pass and for the sovereign's abiding health." That year a decree was issued by the patriarch, ruling that confessors might be interrogated in a government department only about spoken depositions and testaments made in their presence, but not about the confession of sins.

THE SCHISM

The stringent measures instituted to prevent the spread of the schism during Tsar Alexis's reign had little effect.[88] In 1677 reports reached Moscow of monks, priests and laymen who had established hermitages in cossack settlements along the Don and Medveditsa rivers. These people disparaged the printed service books, the liturgy and icon-painting; they refused to honor the holy images and were encouraging many people from the Don settlements to join them and be re-baptized. Governor Volynsky, whose troops were stationed on the Don, sent a musketeer lieutenant named Grigorov to obtain information about the dissenters. Grigorov returned with the news that he had found no hermitage on the Medveditsa river, but had visited the Yevskaia hermitage on the Chir river, downstream from the cossack settlement of Nizhny Chir. The superior of this hermitage was a member of the black clergy[89] by the name of Job, and the brotherhood consisted of about twenty monks and thirty members of the white clergy. Job officiated from the old service books and denounced the revised books, claiming that everything in them was sinful.

On receiving this report the Muscovite authorities questioned the village ataman Pankratiev, who happened to be in the capital at the time. They asked him what he knew about the Yevskaia hermitage and the location of the Chir river. Pankratiev replied that the hermitage was remotely situated, about a day's ride from the town of Chir. It had been established about five years earlier, after the Razin rebellion. The cossacks were aware that the hermitage was inhabited by men, women, girls and boys, but they dared not make a raid upon it without the sovereign's leave. Should the sovereign order them to destroy the hermitage they would do so immediately. Pankratiev also spoke of the arrival, a year or so previously, of a member of the black clergy and two ordinary monks on the Don; they had established a hermitage in the forest on the Crimean side of the river. Then the monks quarrelled with the priest; they had come to Cherkassk [the capital of the Don Cossacks] and reported to the cossacks that the priest did not pray for the great sovereign and forbade them to do so. At this Ataman Mikhailo Samarin and the whole Host ordered the priest's arrest. He was brought to Cherkassk and burned at the stake, as cossack law prescribed. His hermitage was now deserted. Volynsky was instructed to destroy all such criminals and enemies of the church, and never again to allow them refuge with the Cossack Host. The ringleaders were to be sent to Moscow and the remainder punished under cossack law in order to stop such criminals from multiplying and bringing the Host into disrepute.

News also arrived from Siberia concerning Nikita Elizarev, the son of a Kalmyk interpreter in Tiumen. He was reported as saying that some churches which had burnt down in Tobolsk were not Orthodox churches at all, but Latin prayerhouses. He called the priests curs. At his interrogation the dissenter announced his refusal to use the accursed three-fingered sign of the cross.[90] The young dissenter's father, the interpreter, came to the government office and declared that the four-pointed cross was the seal of Antichrist.[91] Both were flogged mercilessly with the knout and released on bail.

That same year, 1677, in the cathedral at Tiumen, during the singing of the Cherubim [part of the Orthodox liturgy], three men and a nun cried out: "Orthodox Christians! Do not bow down. They are carrying a dead body, and the communion loaves are marked with the four-pointed cross, the seal of Antichrist!" The troublemakers were taken to the government office where they declared that they had come to Tiumen to revive the true faith. They were flogged mercilessly and thrown into a dungeon.

A monk named Daniel set up a hermitage in the Tobolsk district on the small Berezovka river. He built a chapel and cells, celebrated vespers, matins and the Holy Hours. He did not say prayers for the sovereign, his household, the patriarch or the metropolitan of Siberia, and referred to Orthodox Christians as heretics. In the same hermitage the nuns and girls threw themselves to the ground, shrieking that they had seen visions of the Holy Virgin and the heavens opening, and angels offering haloes to those who entered the monastery.

These rumors enticed many people of all classes to leave their homes, property and livestock and hasten to the hermitage with their wives and children to take monastic vows. The governor of Tobolsk, Boyar Peter Vasilievich Sheremetev, sent an armed detachment to arrest Daniel, but when they arrived the soldiers found the hermitage reduced to ashes. Daniel and his followers had burned themselves to death in their huts at night, and the rest had fled.

Others followed Daniel's example. In the settlement of Mekhonsk peasants, dragoons and free cossacks gathered with their wives and children at the house of the dragoon Abramov, bringing with them hemp, straw, pitch and birch bark. The chief official of the settlement would have dissuaded them from their folly had not the sexton Ivan Fedorov, a dissident priest, spoken to them and destroyed the effect of the official's words.

In 1679 in Isetsky Ostrog a peasant named Barkhatov went around preaching that people should not go to church. Barkhatov was arrested but later liberated by his brother Gavrila and twenty comrades. They rode off to the village of Mostovka, where they locked themselves into a building and declared their intention of burning themselves to death. Captain Poliakov arrived and tried to talk them out of it; the dissenters demanded time for consideration, and their request was granted. During this time they wrote a petition to the sovereign in which they explained that they had incarcerated themselves because they feared the crown officials. One crown official apparently had intercepted everyone who had come to live in Mekhonsk and made them stand all day in the freezing cold. He demanded half a ruble from everyone, but they were poor and it was beyond their means. He allowed them to return to their homes, but drove away their wives and children, and their hands and feet were chilled. "Alas, great sovereign! We have no evil intentions whatsoever. We only adhere to the old faith and refuse to acknowledge Nikon's revised books because they are completely at variance with the old ones. They force us to make the sign of the cross with three fingers, the thumb and two fingers together, and order us to abandon the true three-armed cross of Christ. O sovereign, if you will not grant us your decree, and if you allow your officials, agents and priests to ruin us poor folk and force us to accept the newly-revised faith, we wish you to know that even then we would not think of accepting the new faith and Nikon's revised books. We are all ready to meet our death, to suffer and perish in the flames as the holy monk Daniel and his followers suffered. If we are prevented from gathering together we shall suffer each in his own house, but we will not be parted from Christ."

Similar reports were received from the Ukraine, Siberia and the Don. There was even an incident in Moscow itself. In 1681, during the feast of the Epiphany, Gerasim Shapochnik scattered dissident leaflets into the crowd from the belltower of Ivan the Great.[92] After his arrest he implicated Anton Khvory, who in turn implicated Osip Sabelnik; the house of the latter had been used for singing the Holy Hours and for baking of communion bread. After the services the bread was distributed to the people, who ate it and regarded it as consecrated.

THE CHURCH COUNCIL OF 1681

In the same year, 1681, a church council was convened. The tsar read out a proclamation on those matters which required attention, firstly on the security of the Holy Church, and secondly to inform Christians about the appointment of additional prelates in the cities as a result of the increase in the number of religious dissidents, and about other matters in urgent need of revision. The tsar's first proposal stated that every metropolitan should have in his diocese a bishop subordinate to him, and his holiness the patriarch, the father of fathers, should have many such bishops under him. The council replied that the metropolitans and archbishops "humbly beseech the great sovereign that there be new prelates with their own dioceses in those distant and populous towns where they are required. But they should not be subordinated to the metropolitans lest this result in discord, feuding and tension amongst the leaders of the church, for such dissidence would have an injurious effect on the Holy Church, causing the people to be restless and reproachful."

The second proposal stated: "we have received written reports from many towns about foolish people who are deserting the Holy Church and turning their homes into prayerhouses. At their meetings they abominate Christianity and blaspheme dreadfully against the Holy Church." In its reply the council begged the sovereign to have these dissenters tried in the town courts.

The third proposal stated: "in Moscow and all the cities monasteries have been founded by the sovereign's ancestors as peaceful and silent retreats. The monks were granted many villages, hamlets and all kinds of provisions for their maintenance, so that they all had adequate food and clothing, and need concern themselves with nothing but the salvation of the soul. Hospitals were established for aged and sick monks. Nowadays, however, there is no communal life, and no hospitals are built in the monasteries, and even where such exist monks are disobedient and leave for other monasteries, abandoning the strict monastic way of life. Intoxicating liquor should also be prohibited in the monasteries."

The council replied: "We have banned inebriating beverages in all monasteries. Archimandrites, abbots and superiors[93] should live decorously and insist that the monks follow their example. They should not keep a private supply of food and drink, nor should they hold special meals for guests in their cells. They should partake of the common repast every day and not keep food and drink in their cells. Any laymen who comes to the monastery to discharge a vow of prayer should be accommodated according to monastery regulations; he should receive the same food and drink as the brethren in a guest cell, and an experienced elder should be placed in charge of these matters. Special drink should no longer be provided for guests, nor should any be accepted from them.

"Poor laymen desirous of salvation should be admitted without having to pay the usual contribution. Vows should be administered only to freemen, not to fugitives from their lawful wives and masters, which is illegal. Superiors and ordinary monks should wear the same habits, provided out of monastery funds. Superiors should stop taking money from the funds and giving it to the monks. Aged and feeble monks should be tended in the hospital, and every care should be taken that they want for neither food nor drink. Monks should not travel from one monastery to another without permission from the church authorities. They should not be allowed to leave their monastery. Recalcitrant and obstinate offenders should be dealt with under monastery regulations. Monks visiting from other monasteries should not be admitted unless they have the authorities' permission and a pass.

"Archimandrites and abbots should see to it that monks do not administer monastic vows to laymen of either sex in their own homes, even if they are on their deathbed.[94] Those brethren who refuse to honor their vows and who behave in an unseemly fashion in Moscow and other towns, frequenting pot-houses, taverns and the homes of laymen, getting blind drunk and cavorting around the streets, shall be sent to the former Piatnitsk monastery, which will be re-established for this purpose by the Trinity-St. Sergius monastery. A stout and high pallisade should be erected around it, and four cells with entrances be built to accommodate the miscreants banished from Moscow.

"As for women, there are those who have taken the veil illegally outside a nunnery, and who now frequent the houses of laymen and sit in the streets and alleyways begging for alms. For such women every prelate should establish one convent to be supported by a male monastery with hereditary estates, since there are few nunneries with hereditary lands attached, and such lands are essential for the maintenance of the inmates. Virtuous senior nuns should be selected from the convents to supervise them. Prelates should send good and experienced members of the clergy, not laymen, to the monasteries to supervise day-to-day activities and admini-stration of estates. The great sovereign should appoint worthy senior servitors to visit the nunneries endowed with property to see to the ad-ministration of their estates, in order to prevent the sisters from leaving their convents to wander around the villages and living in the homes of the laity. These servitors shall be responsible to the prelates; they are not to intervene in matters of ecclesiastical administration between the sis-ters and the agents of the church, nor wield any authority in such matters.

"Laymen should not employ widowed priests in their homes.[95] Any nobleman requiring a chaplain must make application to the church au-thorities, who will ordain an unwidowed priest for the purpose. Widowed priests and hieromonks [monks ordained as priests] should no longer be allowed to reside in the homes of laymen or to conduct services, for in recent times many priests and deacons have been living in an unseemly fashion, drinking excessively and administering the sacraments whilst inebriated."

In response to the tsar's fourth proposal, the council decreed that priests should be ordained to serve in foreign parts if the local Orthodox inhabi-tants so requested. To the fifth proposal they replied: "In the oath of service the church threatens frightful and everlasting damnation for dereliction of duty, but there are still many people who continue to transgress, especially in the collection of revenues, and thereby relinquish eternal life. Let the great sovereign impose his edict, injunction and fear upon such people and have them tried by the civil courts." To the eighth proposal they replied: "monasteries situated in close proximity to the houses of the laity should be transferred to more suitable locations."

The ninth proposal stated: "in accordance with the great sovereign's decree, consideration has been given to the problem of beggars in Moscow, and it has been ordered that they be dispersed. Vagrants and the sick should be accommodated in a special place and provided for amply from royal funds. The patriarch and prelates should also order the estab-lishment of poorhouses for beggars in the towns, but the lazy and able-bodied should be set to work." The council agreed to this proposal. In connection with this survey of beggars there are records of two almshouses being built in Fedor's reign, one in the Apparition of the Virgin (Znamensk) monastery and the other in the Granatny Courtyard behind the Nikitin gates, in order to dissuade beggars from roaming and lying around in the streets.

The tenth proposal stated: "beggars should not solicit alms in church while services are in progress, for it disturbs the Christians at their prayers." The council agreed to this. In response to the eleventh proposal, the council decreed that the clergy should not erect huts, stores and barns on church property designated as burial grounds. To the twelfth proposal they decreed that during festivals of patron saints people should be barred from bringing food and drink to the monastery and parish churches.

The thirteenth proposal stated: "many monks and nuns refuse to obey their mentors; they leave the monasteries and settle in the forests. Little by little they attract fellow rebels to join them. They build chapels and perform services and then appeal to the church authorities for charters permitting them to build churches in these places, which they call hermitages. In their hermitages they do not officiate from the revised service books, and as a result many people come to settle in the area, regarding them as sufferers for their faith. This is injurious to the Holy Church."

The council responded by appealing to the great sovereign to ban the issue of charters for rebuilding hermitages. They, the church authorities, would transfer these hermitages to the monasteries and have parish churches built on their sites. The fourteenth proposal stated: "men of all ranks have been writing out texts, allegedly copied from Holy Scripture, into notebooks, onto sheets of paper and parchment, and selling them at the Savior gates and elsewhere in Moscow. These texts are filled with errors, but simple folk, untutored in true scripture, are being deceived by them and lured into sinfulness. This is especially injurious to the Holy Church." The council replied that the sovereign should appoint a special official to stamp out this abuse; the patriarch also would appoint a member of the clergy. Anyone found distributing such works would be taken to the Patriarchal Chancellery and dealt with there. The elected officials would be assisted by musketeers. To the fifteenth proposal it was decreed that those who handed in copies of the old service books would receive free copies of the revised books in exchange.

MEASURES TO CONVERT TATARS
In the midst of the crown's efforts to protect the church from the effects of the schism news arrived that Tatar nobles holding service and hereditary estates inhabited by Christians were forcing their tenants to convert to Islam. In 1681 the following decree was issued: murzas [nobles] and

Tatars owning fiefs and patrimonial estates inhabited by Christians shall be deprived of their property and given instead estates inhabited by non-Christian Mordvinians. Murzas and Tatars who converted to Christianity might retain control of their peasants, and would receive a monetary reward. The Mordvinians were told that if they were all baptized they would receive exemption from payment of taxes for six years. In February 1682 clerks and bailliffs visited the Tatar villages proclaiming the sovereign's decree to the murzas, Tatars, their wives, widows and young men and women. They admonished them to cease their obstinacy and be baptized into the Greek Orthodox faith, and to appeal to the sovereign about their service landholdings and patrimonial estates before February 25. Those who failed to be baptized and to submit an appeal about their estates would be deprived of their lands and all other productive resources, which would be transferred to those murzas and Tatars who had been baptized or who had been converted before February 25.[96]

LOCAL GOVERNMENT MEASURES
Measures on local government also were passed. In 1679 the posts of fortification builder, crown investigator, local magistrate, postal agent, governor's assistant, artillery commander, frontier officer, granary officer and tax-collectors sent from Moscow[97] were all abolished, and their duties transferred to the governors. It was hoped thereby to relieve the townsmen and countryfolk of the burden of extra subsistence payments. The following year Tsar Alexis's decree whereby jurisdiction was transferred from one town to another in the event of the governor being under suspicion of crime was repealed because of its inconvenience.

FISCAL MEASURES
The problem of collecting revenues was as prominent as ever. Not a year went by without the towns and rural districts defaulting in their payments towards the upkeep of the musketeers, a sum of two rubles per *chetvert* of arable land, by pleading that the land was untilled. In 1679 the boyars resolved to replace musketeer money, direct, ransom and quarter post taxes, arquebus tax, small postal dues and other minor duties by a new fixed tax which was to be allotted to the upkeep of the musketeers. In the very first year of the new tax, however, payments again fell into arrears; the governors wrote that the artisans and local peasants were being flogged in an effort to extract the taxes, but even then they did not pay because

of their poverty, poor harvests, the burden of unassessed levies and the tenth and fifteenth money which had been levied to finance the war with Turkey.[98] They were migrating to the towns of Siberia. Chosen representatives were summoned to Moscow to explain why the taxes were in arrears. They replied that it was quite impossible to pay the tax in full. As a result, in 1681 it was decided to levy a new tax for the upkeep of the musketeers at a lower rate than the previous one. The musketeer taxes were to be collected by locally elected officials and their assistants and brought to Moscow by their representatives.

The crown still did not consider the problem resolved. A comprehensive and permanent solution was desired, and so in December 1681 delegates were summoned to Moscow from all of Russia, two from each town, in an attempt to confront the problem and gather the requisite information. They were told to bring the tax registers in order to ascertain the number of men of high, middle and lower rank in the towns and rural communities, and the duties and taxes that each man rendered annually. That same year the administration of inns and customs houses throughout Russia was entrusted to local sworn officials, and the monopoly franchise tax collection system was abolished.[99]

ABOLITION OF THE CODE OF PRECEDENCE

The young tsar seemed to have a premonition of his imminent death and hastened to deal with all crucial matters. Whilst fiscal reforms were in preparation Prince Vasily Golitsyn and representatives from the ranks of the military servitors were entrusted with the task of examining the question of military reform. It was obvious that any serious step in this direction was useless without first considering the abolition of the Code of Precedence.[100] For a long time now people had been obliged to attribute Russia's military defeats to the inefficiency of its army, and to contemplate reform. Foreign officers had been recruited, and a start had been made on completely restructuring and redesignating the Russian regiments. Yet, as immediately became apparent, a new coat cannot be made of old cloth.

It is small wonder that military success eluded Muscovite armies when one considers the following state of affairs: a highly qualified man might be appointed commander-in-chief and assigned equally capable assistants, but then petitions would arrive complaining that the assistants could not possibly serve under that particular commander. Two options were then open: either dismiss the commander-in-chief and replace him with someone who, although incompetent, was a boyar of ancient lineage, or dismiss the assistants and replace them with unqualified men compatible in rank with the commander. There was only one way out of this dilemma and the government had been resorting to it ever since the time of Ivan the Terrible. This was to announce before the start of a campaign that appointments would be made "without regard to precedence" and that these appointments would not be taken into account in any future disputes over precedence.

During the reigns of Michael and Alexis almost all campaigns had been conducted "without regard to precedence," and this inevitably raised the notion that sooner or later a decree would appear abolishing precedence forever and thereby obviate the necessity of repeating the formula before each campaign. A strong boost was given to publication of such a decree by the imposition of the new military formations on the old regiments of service gentry.

The authorities had been disappointed by both the conduct and the conclusion of the war with Turkey. The crown had fielded more than a hundred and fifty thousand Russian troops, but mere strength of numbers had not achieved victory. This lent further impetus to the idea of military reform. The most eminent of the boyars and the most receptive to new ideas by virtue of his education was Prince Vasily Golitsyn, who was at the same time a member of one of the most distinguished aristocratic families.[101] It was this man that the sovereign placed in charge of military affairs, in the knowledge that he would improve the administration and organization of the army. He was to be assisted by selected table attendants, generals, table attendant colonels from the cavalry and infantry, crown agents, servitors, court attendants, provincial servitors and junior boyars.

The commission, as it would be called today, was appointed because "it has come to the great sovereign's attention that in the recent hostilities the enemy displayed new military skills in their engagements with his majesty's troops, thereby hoping to inflict defeats upon the sovereign's men. The enemy's newfangled devices oblige us to review and reorganize our armies in order to provide them with more trustworthy methods of defense and protection against the enemy in time of war. Those areas of our military tactics which have proved ineffective in battle will be replaced by improved strategies, and those which have proved successful will be retained."[102]

The representatives forming the commission made the following proposals for improvements in the military system: military servitors would
be enlisted in companies, and company commanders and lieutenants
would be commissioned from among the table attendants, crown agents,
servitors and court attendants from all families and ranks from the top
downwards. They would serve without regard to precedence or discrimi-
nation in whatever rank the sovereign might confer upon them. The sovereign approved the scheme, and registers of company commanders and
lieutenants were compiled. The elected representatives then announced:
"By the sovereign's decree they, the elected representatives, their brothers, children and relatives have been registered as commanders and lieutenants, but no one has been appointed to those ranks from the Trubetskoy,
Odoevsky, Kurakin, Repnin, Shein, Troekurov, Lobanov-Rostovsky and
Romodanovsky families and others who were not commissioned because
of the short time they had served. The elected representatives feared that
they and their families later might be rebuked and reproached by the
aforementioned families and others. Therefore, in the best interests of
warfare and diplomacy and other affairs of state, and for the improvement
of military service, the great sovereign shall decree that all boyars, lords-
in-waiting, members of the council and privy councillors, and men of all
ranks serve in Moscow and in the towns, in the chancelleries and the army,
in military, diplomatic and other posts, without regard to precedence, in
whatever capacity and position the great sovereign might ordain; and
henceforth let no one take anyone to account because of rank and precedence. Disputes about rank and precedence shall be set aside and eradicated so that such conflicts never again will hamper the success of military
affairs and other affairs of state."

Golitsyn presented the representatives' petition to the sovereign. On
January 12, 1682 Fedor called an extraordinary session of the boyars. The
patriarch, the prelates and elected heads from the monasteries also were
invited to attend. First the petition of the elected representatives was read
to the assembly, and then the tsar spoke. He expatiated upon his obligation
always to follow the law and example of Christ, who preached the gospel
of love. He then passed to the matter in hand: "That crafty disseminator
of evil and common foe, the Devil, seeing how Christian people enjoyed
peace and tranquillity as a result of their glorious victories in battle, and
how the foes of Christianity were embittered and annihilated, implanted

in the mild hearts of the glorious warriors the idea of precedence. In times gone by this system brought about great misfortune in war, diplomacy and other affairs of state, and led to the disparagement of our troops by the enemy. We see that this Code of Precedence harms blessed love; it destroys peace and brotherly co-operation and united and effective resistance to the enemy; it saps zeal and it is especially loathsome and hateful to the All-seeing Eye. Therefore we, the sovereign, desire, and Divine Providence, the author of peace and earthly well-being by His Almighty will, commands that this Code of Precedence, the destroyer of love, be abolished, and hearts torn apart by this perfidy unite in peaceful and blessed love." The sovereign went on to cite the examples of his grandfather and father, who had contemplated the abolition of the Code, and also mentioned his own efforts to eradicate the evil. He concluded by asking: "Should all appointments be made without regard to precedence as proposed in the representatives' petition, or should the Code be retained?"

The patriarch replied to the question in a strongly worded invective against precedence, "from which most bitter source proceeded everything which is evil and most abominable to God and injurious to your majesty's affairs of state. It hampers every good understanding, just as the tares choked the growing wheat and prevented it from reaching its full stature and bringing forth good fruit. Not only has this Code of Precedence created lasting malice between different families, it also has created the same enmity and hatred amongst kinsmen; and if I were to tell your majesty of all these disagreeable disputes, you would grow weary of listening. I and the whole Church Council cannot find sufficient praise for your majesty's great intention and most sagacious good will."

The tsar addressed his question to the boyars, lords-in-waiting and the councillors of state. They replied that the great sovereign should act according to the wishes of his holiness the patriarch and the prelates of the church, and command them all to serve in all ranks without regard to precedence, "For in years gone by these disputes have given rise to great misfortunes, disorder and calamities in war, diplomacy and other affairs of state, bringing joy to our enemies and creating great and lasting hostility which is hateful to God."

At this reply the sovereign ordered that the registers of appointments be brought to him. He said: "Let these disputes over precedence and lists of ranks be committed to the flames and thus be eradicated completely and consigned to oblivion. Thus shall this evil perish once and for all, never again to be mentioned, and all temptation and enticement will be removed. Anyone who has registers and lists of appointments in his possession should send them to the Chancellery of Crown Service and Appointments, and we command that they all be committed to the flames. From this time on we enjoin all boyars, lords-in-waiting, crown and privy councillors and men of all ranks to serve in the Muscovite chancelleries and courts and in the military and diplomatic service and in all other capacities without regard to precedence. Henceforth no one shall dispute with anyone nor raise himself above anyone else by virtue of former position." The whole assembly replied: "May this Code of Precedence, hateful to God, creating enmity, hateful to brotherhood and destructive of love, perish in the flames and nevermore be recalled for all time!"

A bonfire was built at the entrance to the palace and the registers were burned. When it was announced to the sovereign that the registers had been destroyed, the patriarch addressed the lay members of the council: "May this thing which has been accomplished henceforth be observed strictly and irrevocable. And if anyone, now or in the future, shall contradict this decision in any way, let him fear the stern sanction of the church and the sovereign's wrath, as a flouter of the tsar's will and as a disdainer of our blessing." The whole assembly replied: "Let it be so."

The tsar, radiant with joy, praised them for their decision and announced that, as a token of remembrance for them and their descendants, geneological registers would be kept in the Chancellery for Military Affairs, and that they might also keep such books in their own homes as they always had done. In recognition of their services he ordered that missing names be added to the geneological register, and they were requested to submit lists. They were to enter into a special book before witnesses the names of all those who had not been entered in the geneological register: princely and other aristocratic families who had served as boyars, lords-in-waiting and crown councillors under his sovereign forbears and in his own reign, and other ancient families who had not served in these ranks but who had, since the reign of Ivan IV and during his own reign, held high office as commanders in the diplomatic, military and civil administration and on other important missions, and those who had been his close advisers. Those who had not served in the ranks listed above or in high office, but who had, since the reign of Michael Fedorovich and during his own reign, served as regimental commanders, ambassadors, envoys and in other worthy positions, or who were entered in the first category of the military rolls, also should have their names inscribed in a special book in the presence of witnesses. Those who had not served in the aforementioned offices, but who were recorded in the middle and lower categories of the military rolls, also were entered in a special book. The names of men of humble birth who had been registered in the Muscovite ranks for services rendered by their fathers should also be entered in a special book in columns, and all offices should be without regard to precedence.

Some may wonder how all this was accomplished so suddenly. How was a centuries-old custom abolished so easily and without resistance, indeed without the slightest opposition from those very people who had suffered prison and the knout in defense of ancestral honor? How could it have been abolished, not by an iron-willed Peter, but by the weak and mortally sick Fedor? In reply to this question we pose another: what could have been put forward to contradict the arguments of the tsar and the patriarch against the Code of Precedence? What arguments could have been found to defend the custom? Everyone *in the event of a dispute* considered himself duty-bound to defend his ancestral honor, even if it meant prison or the knout, when he knew that such a dispute could result in dishonor, disgrace and reproach. On the last occasion, for example, that the military servitors were re-registered in various ranks, they complained that members of other families had not been registered, and that it might be better to do away with precedence altogether in order to avoid future disgrace. They would all protest *in the event of a dispute*, but no one would rise up to defend the Code of Precedence as something intrinsically useful and moral. Men had risen up to defend the old service books with insuperable obstinacy because their fathers and grandfathers had worshipped by them, and the holy saints had gained their salvation through them, and because they doubted the authority of the innovators. But no one could try to vindicate the Code of Precedence by arguing that it had drawn their ancestors into enmity, which was hateful to God and a product of the Devil.

But if no justification could be found for the Code in its own right, why was it not abolished much sooner? This question is not hard to answer: everything in history has its proper time. This ancient, firmly established custom was rooted in the predominant form of individual union, the family, and was bound to survive until such time as it came into conflict with some new higher requirement of state and people, like the need for military reform, when this conflict revealed its harmfulness for all to see.

The Code of Precedence could be abolished only at a time when society was wavering and trembling on the brink of major change. At this point the roots of all ancient customs were bound to come loose, and it was an easy matter to pull them up. It would never have occurred to Golitsyn's father and grandfather that their offspring would present the tsar with the military servitors' petition on the abolition of the Code of Precedence. It is obvious that the Code tottered and collapsed as a result of the general instability of the whole ancient system and the new orientation towards the alien Western order, but it is impossible to guage the extent to which the Code's abolition was facilitated by the weakening of family ties. On the other hand, the abolition quite clearly dealt a hefty blow to family loyalties amongst the upper classes, a blow equal to that dealt by the poll tax to family ties amongst the lower orders.[103]

PROPOSED SEPARATION OF CIVIL AND MILITARY OFFICES

In epochs like the one now being examined such major measures as the abolition of the Code of Precedence cannot stand alone. Once precedence had been done away with and an obstacle to the improvement of the army and its success in battle had been elimiated, thoughts inevitably turned to the removal of the outmoded retinue or *druzhina* system.[104] Until now the service class, despite various changes of fortune, had retained the basically military role of a bodyguard in its relations to the sovereign and the country. Boyar, lord-in-waiting, councillor of state, gentleman of the bedchamber, table attendant, crown agent—all were military personnel who happened from time to time to occupy civilian posts in order, for the most part, to support themselves, but who, at the first signal, mounted their steeds and rode off to war. It is easy to see how the disadvantages of such a system were highlighted by the problem of military reform and by the urgent need for the establishment of a standing army and permanent commanders. If the best qualified men were selected to serve permanently as military commanders, then others, by the same reckoning, would have to occupy permanent civilian posts. It was during the reign of the sovereign who abolished the Code of Precedence that a scheme was drafted for separating the higher civilian ranks and duties from the military, a sure sign that Russia's social structure was becoming more sophisticated and complex.

In the new scheme the first in rank was to be a civilian official, a boyar, the marshal and supervisor of all judges in the capital city of Moscow.

Together with a committee of twelve assessors, drawn from the boyars and councillors of state, he would be accommodated permanently in chambers erected for this purpose and see that each judge carried out the will of his majesty the tsar and administered the law fairly and wisely. The second rank was occupied by a military official, a boyar and household commander who would be at the sovereign's side in time of war to protect his person and to deal with various military matters, such as the estimate of troops and the organization and preparation of arms, foodstuffs and munitions. The third in rank would be a civilian, boyar and Governor-General of Vladimir, who would be foremost among the governors-general on the council of state. The fourth rank would be a military one, boyar and commander of the Sevsk military district, who would be stationed permanently in Sevsk. He would defend the Polish or Steppe Ukraine and have under his command a large staff of officers and men on permanent alert against an enemy attack.

The fifth rank was boyar and Governor-General of Novgorod, who ranked second among the governors-general on the council of state. The sixth was boyar and commander of the Vladimir military district, permanently stationed in Vladimir with cavalry and infantry at his disposal. He would be on constant alert and ready, at the sovereign's command, to deploy his troops against the enemy wherever they might be required. The seventh rank was boyar and Governor-General of Kazan, and so on.

The reason why this project was never implemented is contained in the following interesting report: "The boyars of the palace advised the sovereign that the tsar's governors-general, high-born boyars, should be stationed permanently in Novgorod the Great, Kazan, Astrakhan, Siberia and other places throughout his royal domains, and that they should bear the titles of the regions under their command. They suggested that the metropolitans also should be addressed as metropolitan of Novgorod and All the Littoral, metropolitan of Kazan and All the Kazan region, and so on. The sovereign gave his consent and the appointments were made. A book was compiled by a crown secretary and sent to His Holiness the Patriarch to obtain his blessing for the proposal and his help in carrying it out. The supporters of the scheme at court exerted much pressure on the patriarch, but he refused to give his consent, and placed an injunction upon the scheme, for he feared that the permanently appointed high-born governors-general might in the course of a few years accrue great wealth and grow contemptuous of the autocratic power of the Muscovite tsars, declare their independence and bring autocracy to ruin."

PROJECT FOR AN ACADEMY

At the end of Fedor's reign a project for a higher school or academy was finally drawn up.[105] At first sight it seems astonishing that such a plan did not appear sooner, and was not put into effect for so long, considering the strong desire for knowledge felt by the best and most influential of seventeenth-century Russian statesmen. The failure seems less surprising when one remembers the difficulty of finding suitable teachers and especially if one bears in mind the consequences of employing foreigners during Tsar Alexis's reign. It was quite natural that concerted efforts be made to overcome these difficulties during the reign of the educated Fedor, Simeon Polotsky's pupil but in the early part of Fedor's reign education remained a minor issue, with the problems of the tsar's minority, strained relations at court and the exigencies of the war with Turkey commanding all attention.

With the breathing space provided by the opening of peace negotiations with the Crimea and Turkey, domestic issues once again came to the fore, and plans for an academy also were considered. A small school for thirty pupils had been established at the Moscow printing house, evidently as a result of the return of the monk Timothy from the East. The tsar had been moved deeply by Timothy's account of the tribulations of the Greek church and its low standard of learning, learning which was so essential for the support of Orthodoxy. Timothy was put in charge of the school, and two native teachers of Greek were sought in Moscow. Because this school was considered inadequate, the authorities continued to think about establishing an academy, and envoys were sent to the ecumenical patriarchs requesting that they send teachers well-schooled in Orthodoxy. In addition, a royal charter was drafted, the so-called Privileges, a document of great importance insofar as it clarifies both the character of the desired institution and the attitude of contemporary Russian society, and more especially of the Russian church towards education.

At the beginning of the charter the tsar declared that he, like Solomon who also came to the throne during his adolescence, was concerned above all else with wisdom, the mother of all royal duties and creator of all good things, by which God bestows His blessings on mankind. Just as Solomon founded seven schools he, Tsar Fedor, in emulation of Solomon and the Greek emperors of old, intended to found buildings for an academy at the Savior (Zaikonospassk) monastery, "and there to teach the seven wisdoms, from grammar, poetics, rhetoric, dialectics, rational, natural and legal philosophy to theology, which teaches divine knowledge and the purification of the conscience. In addition, the teaching of secular law and all other free sciences shall be included in the curriculum of the academy or school."

The following monasteries were allocated for the upkeep of the rector and teachers of the academy: the Savior monastery in the Kitai quarter of Moscow near the Neglinnye gates; the monastery of St. John the Theologian in the region of Pereiaslavl-Riazansk, for St. John drew heavenly wisdom from the fount of all wisdom; the St. Andrew monastery on the Moscow river, as it was founded by Rtishchev for the learned brethren; and the St. Daniel monastery, also situated on the Moscow river, for the accommodation of scholars from abroad, as well as four other monasteries with all their peasant and laborer households and all their productive resources.[106] In addition, the tsar made a personal endowment of the crown estate at Vyshegorodskaia and ten plots of vacant land in various places. Any individual was allowed to make a contribution towards food and clothing for the pupils. The rector and teachers were required to be pious men, born of pious parents and raised in either the Russian or the Greek Orthodox faith.

Greeks would be accepted only if they brought a valid guarantee of their firm Orthodox convictions from the ecumenical patriarchs. Once in Russia, they would be required to furnish further proof of their convictions, lest any of them follow the example of the heretic Metropolitan Isidore of Russia.[107] New converts from Catholicism, Lutheranism, Calvinism and other heresies were not eligible to apply for the posts of rector or teacher, for such men had a cunning way of secretly and insidiously instilling their heresies in their pupils. Should any scholars from Lithuania, Little Russia or such areas apply for the post of rector or teacher, their protestations of faith would not be accepted without the testimony of trustworthy, pious men. Even those who submitted a written pledge of their Orthodox convictions and denounced and disparaged the falsehoods of the Romans, Lutherans and Calvinists would not be appointed as rector or teacher for deceivers at first would feign absolute piety and claim to be staunch adherents of the faith and only then begin, little by little, to disseminate wicked lies and tear asunder the immaculate unity of the faith.

The rector and the teachers had to swear a solemn oath that they would hold firm and fast to the tenets of Orthodoxy and guard and defend it from all other beliefs and heresies. Should they break their oath, they were to be duly punished and dismissed from their post. For the crime of blasphemy against the church the penalty was death by burning, without mercy. Even if they repented, they were still to be punished and dismissed. Persons of all classes and ages were eligible to attend the academy. All disciplines not banned by the church were to be part of the curriculum. Magic was especially strictly proscribed and teachers of this art were to be burned, together with their pupils. No one was allowed to employ private foreign language tutors, but if they wished they could send their children to the academy, to the one general seat of learning. It was feared that private tutors, especially if foreign and non-Orthodox, might harm the Orthodox faith and stir up conflict.

Pupils of the academy charged debtors or accused of other similar crimes, excepting murder and other major offenses, were not to be brought to trial until they had graduated from the academy, so that their education might not be interrupted. They would be tried by the rector and teachers. In the event of criminal offenses, they would be handed over to civil courts, but only if the rector gave his permission. If the rector himself were to fall under suspicion, he would be tried by the teachers. A teacher would be tried by the rector and the other teachers. Teachers were forbidden to undertake any other duties without the consent of the rector and the other teachers. For long and diligent service, teachers would receive a pension.

All diligent youths who strove assiduously to seek out that costly treasure of wisdom in the grammatical arts and other free sciences, from writings in various languages, especially Slavonic, Greek, Polish and Latin, seeking it out like gold from the bowels of the earth, would, on the recommendation of the rector and the teachers, be rewarded for their academic success by a fitting remuneration from the great sovereign. On completion of their studies they were to be appointed to posts commensurate with their learning, and for their wisdom they would receive the tsar's bountiful favor. Apart from members of the aristocracy, no one who had not graduated in the free sciences was to be appointed to the crown offices of table attendant, crown agent and so on. Commoners might aspire to these offices solely by virtue of their education or for special services rendered in the military field or in other spheres of public activity.

All foreign scholars visiting Russia were to be subjected to the scrutiny of the academy and taken into service only with the academy's approval; if not approved they were to be expelled from the country. The academy was to ensure that the country was not harmed by conflict, quarrels and dissension stirred up by opponents of Orthodoxy. The rector must make all such opponents known to the tsar. Civil authorities were not to engage in any debates with the rector and teachers on the faith and traditions of the church. A list of all new converts to Orthodoxy must be deposited with the rector, who would supervise their behavior. Anyone who wavered in his new persuasion was to be banished to the distant regions of the Terek and Siberia.

The rector and teachers must ensure also that no members of the clergy or laity, whatever their rank, should own, use or instruct others from books and writings on magic, sorcery, fortune-telling and other blasphemous and abominable works banned by the church. Uneducated people must not be allowed to keep Polish, Latin, German, Lutheran, Calvinist and other heretical books in their homes; they were forbidden to read them because they lacked in understanding and might begin to doubt the truth of Orthodoxy. No one might at any time engage in debates about such books or make any apologies for them, for it was common for deceivers to start an argument, claiming that they were doing so purely for the sake of academic debate and not because they in any way doubted the faith and traditions of the church. Heretical books of this kind were to be burned or taken to the rector and teachers. Any foreigner or Russian accused of blaspheming against Orthodoxy must be handed over to the jurisdiction of the rector and teachers, and if found guilty the offender was to be burned. Foreign visitors who had rejected the Orthodox faith in favor of Catholicism, Lutheranism, Calvinism or any other heresy were likewise to be burned. Anyone who converted from Catholicism to Lutheranism was to be tried by the civil court and sent into exile. The royal library was to be entrusted in perpetuity to the safekeeping of the rector and teachers of the academy. The royal treasury was to bear the cost of building the institution.

This fascinating document provides some insight into prevailing contemporary attitudes towards learning and educational establishments. Education and schools were acknowledged as necessary only insofar as they corresponded with the interests of the church. A school for free sciences was to be founded as a support for Orthodoxy, which the church in the East was unable to provide for itself. Yet extreme caution must be exercised, for education, the school and its teachers might easily strike a blow against it. Thus it was deemed essential to select teachers of proven Orthodox conviction and to obtain teachers by application to the ecumenical patriarchs, the leading guardians of Orthodoxy. Even this was insufficient, for Orthodoxy was menaced from all sides; a ceaseless flow of Roman Catholics, Lutherans and Calvinists, enemies of Orthodoxy, were arriving in Moscow, many of them in the employ of the great sovereign. The dissemblers would work to undermine Orthodoxy, using whatever means they could. Orthodoxy must wage an indefatigable battle against them, and the academy was to be the chief instrument of struggle. It was fully authorized to keep watch against all hostile activities and to sound the alarm at the first sign of danger.

The Moscow academy as envisaged in Tsar Fedor's project was a citadel to be erected by the Orthodox church in preparation for its inevitable clash with the non-Orthodox West. Much more than a school, it was a frightful tribunal of inquisition. The rector and teachers merely must utter the words "Guilty of un-Orthodoxy" and the bonfire flared up to receive the offender. In Fedor's reign, as later in the reign of his brother Peter, learning was harnessed to a practical end, the difference being that in Fedor's reign it was harnessed primarily to the service of the church, in Peter's to that of the state.

DEATH OF TSARITSA AGAFIA AND TSAREVICH ILIA

None of these plans for fiscal reforms, the separation of civic and military duties or the establishment of an academy were implemented. On July 11, 1681 a son, Tsarevich Ilia, was born to Fedor, but the universal rejoicing, as it was put at the time, was short-lived: on July 14 Tsaritsa Agafia died as a result of complications following childbirth. The Polish author, whose account of the Moscow rebellion of 1682 has been cited frequently,[108] spoke very flatteringly of the late tsaritsa. According to him this woman of Polish origin exercised a beneficial influence in Muscovy by persuading her husband to do away with the shameful custom whereby troops who had fled from the battlefield must wear female robes. It was her influence which induced Muscovites to begin cutting their hair, shaving off their beards, wearing Polish sabres and coats, and founding Polish and Latin schools. At her instigation an order was given for the removal of icons which individual parishioners brought into church and considered their own property, praying and lighting candles exclusively in front of these icons and preventing others from doing so. Tsar Fedor's supporters approved these actions, writes the Polish author, but Matveev's faction was critical of them. They warned that the tsar was about to introduce the Polish faith and to comport himself like Dmitry the Pretender, who had also been married to a Polish woman, Marina Mniszech.[109]

FEDOR'S SECOND MARRIAGE AND DEATH

Tsarevich Ilia survived his mother only by six days. A second marriage was contemplated. Finally, considerably influenced by Yazykov, on February 14, 1682 the tsar was married to Martha Matveevna Apraksina, a girl of humble origin and a relative of Yazykov; but just two and a half months after this marriage, on April 27, Fedor died in the twenty-first year of his life.

DEATH OF NIKON

This period, in which the tsar reached maturity, the Miloslavskys were removed from power and Yazykov, the Likhachevs and finally the Apraksins came into fortunes, inevitably saw a change in the fate of Nikon and Matveev, those prominent figures of the previous reign. At last mention Nikon was at the monastery of St. Cyril near Beloozero, living under a much stricter regime than he had been at the Ferapont monastery. In Moscow, in the palace itself, he had a powerful protectress in the person of Tatiana Mikhailovna, the tsar's aunt and most senior member of the royal family, a devout and, moreover, influential woman. Tsarevna Tatiana always had been a devotee of Nikon and now was able to take advantage of the weakening of Miloslavsky's and Khitrovo's influence. She began to instil in her nephew the idea that he was wrong to torment and keep imprisoned a man who had rendered them all such great services at the time of the pestilence.[110]

Neither Fedor's nature nor his memory presented any obstacle to the tsarevna's plans and at her behest the sovereign began to visit the half-finished Resurrection monastery at New Jerusalem. He was captivated by its location and its grandiose and ingenious plan, and he generously provided the funds for its completion. Quite naturally the tsar found it impossible to forget Nikon in places which bore witness only to the latter's admirable qualities. He proposed to the patriarch that Nikon be transferred to the Resurrection monastery, but he met with strong opposition from Joachim. The latter was very jealous of his own power, and this had made him many enemies. He could not allow to live close to Moscow and the tsar a man who still called himself patriarch, a man who was sometimes capable of submitting when dealt a blow, but who was ever ready to raise his head as soon as the storm had passed.

It is worth recalling the rumors which circulated at the time, and which were considered far from nonsensical by people who heard them in later years. It is said that Simeon Polotsky, who was on bad terms with Joachim, wished to use Nikon as a means of removing the patriarch. He tried to persuade his royal pupil to establish four patriarchates in place of the four metropolitanates of Novgorod, Kazan, Moscow and Krutitsy. He suggested that Joachim be sent to Novgorod and Nikon be recalled to Moscow with the title of Pope. All manner of rumors were rife at the time and were given credence. Even without such rumors, Joachim had every reason to oppose Nikon's return to the Resurrection monastery. He was able to cloak his objections in very plausible terms. "It was not we who deposed Nikon but the Great Church Council and the ecumenical patriarchs. We cannot allow him to return without their consent. Nevertheless, sire, let it be as you command," he said to the tsar. A church council was summoned to examine the case, but failed to reach a decision. The chairman of the council opposed the proposal and scarcely any of the other churchmen supported Nikon. The tsar could do no more than console the prisoner with a personally written letter.

Meanwhile Nikon had fallen ill. The archimandrite of the monastery of St. Cyril sent word to the patriarch that his prisoner was close to death. He had taken the strictest vows and extreme unction had been administered. The archimandrite asked whether any special arrangements were to be made for the funeral and place of burial, and what sort of prayers should be said. Joachim ordered that Nikon receive the burial of an ordinary monk.

Yet even on his deathbed Nikon did not consider himself an ordinary monk and had no intention of renouncing his patriarchal status. In his last letter to the brethren of the Resurrection monastery he referred to himself as patriarch, telling them of the grave illness which had confined him to his bed. He wrote: "The great sovereign bestowed his favor upon me and wished to deliver me from my misfortune, as you requested in your petition. He wrote me a personal letter assuring me of his favor, but now the time has passed, and still his gracious decree has not arrived, and I could die at any moment. I beg you, my children, forget my coarseness and appeal to the great sovereign once more on my behalf. Do not let me die a wrongful death. My life is nearing its end."

The monks of the Resurrection monastery sent this letter to the sovereign, who showed it to the patriarch and the other prelates, begging them to consent to the transfer of the dying man. Finally they relented. Nikon was taken from the monastery of St. Cyril and brought with great difficulty to the Sheksna river. Here he was placed in a boat and transported along the Sheksna, then along the Volga to Yaroslavl. When they reached the Tolgsky monastery Nikon sensed that his strength was ebbing away, and told them to land on the bank, where he received the sacraments. The boat then was taken from the Volga to the Kotorost river. Here Nikon died on August 17, 1681, at the age of seventy-five. His body was taken to the Resurrection monastery, where it was solemnly interred in the presence of the sovereign.

IMPROVEMENT OF MATVEEV'S SITUATION

In 1681 the fate of the prisoners at Pustozersk took a turn for the better when they were transferred to Mezen, not, of course, as a result of Matveev's tearful appeals and adroit apologies, but because of the change of circumstances at court. To judge by Matveev's renewed complaints, the situation was not greatly improved. "You have commanded that we be transferred to Mezen from the wretched wastes of Pustozersk, from one empty sea to another,[111] where we are subjected to exactly the same hardships and confinement in dungeons," wrote Matveev to the tsar. "In Mezen, too, we have no benefactors. We were granted an allowance of a hundred and fifty rubles, which gives us three pence per day for ourselves and our dependants; we have not received your gracious clothing allowance. But those enemies of the church, Avvakum's wife and children, who were exiled to Mezen, receive an allowance of one grosha per day for each adult and three pence per child.[112] Yet we are neither enemies of the church nor of your majesty's authority. It makes me weep to see a gray-haired old man, bowed down with toil, allotted the same amount for his upkeep as a one-year-old child."

At the end of 1681 Tsar Fedor was betrothed to Apraksina, who was said to be Matveev's goddaughter. The first thing the tsar's bride did was to appeal to Fedor on behalf of her godfather. At the very beginning of January 1682 Captain Lishukov arrived in Mezen to inform Matveev and his son that his majesty the tsar had ordered their release in view of their innocence, the false accusations against them, and his pity for them. Their Moscow homes and other estates and property in the Moscow area which had not been reallocated or sold were to be restored to them, and in addition the sovereign granted them a new estate, the village of Verkhny Landekh in the Suzdal district, with eight hundred peasant households attached. He ordered that they be released from captivity in Mezen and go to the town of Lukh to await further instructions. These instructions, however, were not to come from Tsar Fedor.

II

THE MOSCOW REBELLION OF 1682

PETER AND IVAN

Fedor's young wife Martha is said to have done everything in her power to reconcile her husband with his stepmother and her children and put a stop to their intransigent and continuing disagreements. The tsaritsa succeeded in her aims and was, after much effort, equally successful in obtaining Matveev's transfer from Mezen to Lukh, though she did not secure permission for him to come to Moscow. Not only were Tsaritsa Natalia, the Naryshkins and Matveev aided by Tsaritsa Martha, they also gained the support of the Apraksins, Yazykov and the Likhachevs. The latters' change of allegiance at this late stage may seem strange, but the fact is that as long as Yazykov and the Likhachevs wielded authority they had no reason to share their power with anyone. Tsar Fedor had not yet completely succumbed to his infirmity, and there was still some prospect of his producing an heir. But then the tsaritsa and her newborn son died. The tsar remarried, but this desperate measure proved futile as Fedor daily grew weaker. Yazykov, "that expert on both relationships among courtiers and the inner workings of the palace," was obliged to make provisions for the future. Next in line to Fedor were his two brothers: Ivan, sick, blind and feeble-minded,[1] and Peter, a healthy, lively and gifted boy of ten.

There was evidently no future in supporting Ivan. It is true that Fedor had done little direct ruling, but at least he had not been in constant need of a guardian. Others would have to rule permanently on Ivan's behalf and if, as was likely, Sophia and the Miloslavskys were to assume the responsibility, Yazykov and the Likhachevs could expect a journey far beyond Pustozersk and the Urals, for the Miloslavskys would be unlikely to forget who had usurped their power. On the other hand, an alliance with the Naryshkins and Matveev was easily made by procuring their return, especially since they had no old scores to settle.

The majority of the aristocracy was bound to share this view of the succession. To support the incapacitated and no doubt short-lived Ivan would have been to court trouble for themselves and the realm, and few were prepared to obey the Miloslavskys or anyone else that Tsarevna Sophia might choose to advise her. Matveev may have come into conflict with the Miloslavskys and Khitrovo at court, but he had always respected the aristocracy. It is worth recalling that the majority of these aristocrats were either completely decrepit or quite incapable of achieving anything of distinction, and therefore only too pleased to be respected for their birthright.

Only two members of the ancient nobility—Prince Vasily Golitsyn and Prince Ivan Andreevich Khovansky—differed from their fellows by not supporting Peter. It is quite possible that by this time Prince Golitsyn had formed an amorous attachment with Tsarevna Sophia and had seen the opportunity of rising to power and playing a prominent role when she triumphed in her championship of Ivan's claim to the throne. Prince Khovansky was renowned as a military commander during Tsar Alexis's reign (although he was best known for his defeats and the complaints submitted against him).[2] He was an energetic and brave man, but lacking in good sense. He was impetuous, restless, easily carried away and aptly characterized by the popular nickname, the Braggart. Khovansky came from an aristocratic family which had not distinguished itself in service for many years; for this reason he extolled an ancestry which could be traced back to Gedimin,[3] and was more determined than others in his opposition to those "new men" who had become so prominent in recent years. A staunch adherent of the old ways, Khovansky was highly dissatisfied with this age of Nashchokins and Apraksins, and he longed for the time when all these men whom he hated so much would disappear from the scene and he would receive the recognition he deserved. He was prepared to support anyone who would offer him recognition. He considered that an alliance with the Naryshkins and Matveev could be only to his detriment and hence to the detriment of Russia, and for that reason he did not support Peter.

IVAN'S SUPPORTERS

The tsarevnas, the daughters of Miloslavskaia, and their spokeswoman Sophia could, it seemed, expect no help from the members of the boyar council. For the moment they were in a desperate position. At the beginning of Fedor's reign they had revelled in their triumph and shown no mercy to their stepmother, her relatives and guardian, and therefore could expect little joy if Tsaritsa Natalia, the Naryshkins and Matveev were now victorious. Sophia and Ivan Miloslavsky, whose interests were inextricably bound up with hers, acted from an instinct of self-preservation. They rallied the support of their relatives and young, in other words insignificant, men like the table attendants Alexander Miloslavsky and the brothers Peter and Ivan Tolstoy (Ivan Miloslavsky's nephews), two lieutenant colonels of the musketeers—the foreign officer Ivan Tsykler and Ivan Ozerov—and the musketeers' elected representatives Boris Odintsov, Abrosim Petrov and Kuzma Chermny. By distribution of money and lavish promises they succeeded in assembling a crowd of men who were willing to defend the elder tsarevich's claim to the throne.

This was the position when news broke of Fedor's death. The court dignitaries, who were firmly resolved to support Peter, knew or guessed about Miloslavsky's plans and feared that the proclamation of Peter's accession would be fiercely disputed. Tsarevich Peter's personal attendant, Prince Boris Alekseevich Golitsyn,[4] his brother Ivan and the four Dolgorukys, Yakov, Luke, Boris and Grigory, set off for the palace to attend the election with armor concealed beneath their clothing. After everyone had observed the ritual of taking leave of the deceased tsar and all had kissed the hands of his two surviving brothers Ivan and Peter, the patriarch, accompanied by the prelates of the church and court dignitaries, went out to the antechamber and asked: "Which of the two tsareviches shall be tsar?" The assembly replied that the decision must be taken by men of all ranks from the Muscovite realm, in other words from the capital city of Moscow—that is, at any rate, how the formula was understood on this occasion.[5] The patriarch, with the prelates and court dignitaries, went onto the porch and ordered men of all ranks to assemble in the square in front of the church of the Savior. He asked: "Which of the two tsareviches shall be tsar?" The crowd shouted: "Peter Alekseevich!" There were also cries of "Ivan Alekseevich!", but they were drowned. The decision had been taken by the men of all ranks. The patriarch returned to his palace and gave his blessing to Peter, the new tsar.

But who shouted for Ivan, and what induced them to do so? Contemporary accounts[6] record the name of one of them, the servitor Maksim Sumbulov. They recount the following story of a later meeting he had with Peter. Once, when the tsar was attending mass in the Miracles monastery, he noticed that one of the monks did not go up to receive the antidoron.[7] Puzzled by this, Peter asked the monk's name, and learned that it was Sumbulov. He summoned the monk and asked why he had not gone up to receive the bread. "I did not dare to walk past you and raise my eyes to you," was the reply. Peter ordered him to take the antidoron and afterwards called him back and asked: "Why did you not support me at the election?" The monk replied: "Judas sold Christ for thirty pieces of silver. He was Christ's disciple, but I, sire, was never your disciple. Can you wonder, then, that I, a petty servitor, was willing to sell you in return for the rank of boyar?"

SCENES AT TSAR FEDOR'S FUNERAL

The shouts of Sumbulov and his associates failed to uphold Ivan's claim. Peter was proclaimed tsar and the administration consequently was entrusted to his mother, Tsaritsa Natalia, a well-established custom which nobody opposed. Sophia was choked by the prospect of her hated stepmother becoming regent. She was unable to control her feelings or make any attempt at dissimulation; indeed, any pretence was now useless. On the day of Fedor's funeral she amazed everyone by following the coffin to the cathedral, quite contrary to the convention that the tsarevnas did not participate in such ceremonies.[8] In vain did people try to dissuade her, arguing that such behavior was improper and an affront to convention. Sophia paid no heed and she is said to have attracted the attention of the people by her fearful wailing.

Sophia's grief was genuine; neither did her opponents put up any pretence or try to restrain their emotions. Tsaritsa Natalia and Tsar Peter took their leave of the deceased and returned to the palace long before the service was over; they were followed by several courtiers. It is easy to believe the report that this behavior aroused deep indignation among the tsarevnas, of whom Anna and Tatiana Mikhailovna, the tsar's aunts, were the most highly respected. They sent a nun to rebuke Tsaritsa Natalia. "A fine brother! He couldn't even wait until the end of the funeral!" Tsaritsa Natalia retorted that Peter was still a child and could not endure such a long service without food. The tsaritsa's brother, Ivan Naryshkin, recently returned from exile, said: "Let the dead lie. His majesty the tsar is not dead but alive." The funeral ended and Sophia returned to the palace. It is said that as she left the cathedral, weeping bitterly, she addressed the crowd with the following words: "See how unexpectedly our brother Fedor departed this life, poisoned by his ill-wishers. Have pity on us poor orphans; we have lost our father, our mother and our brother, and our elder brother Ivan has not been chosen tsar. If you or the boyars consider that we have committed some offense, send us alive to foreign lands, to the realms of Christian rulers." These words made a deep impression upon the people.

DISTURBANCES AMONG MUSKETEERS AND SOLDIERS

Deep though the impression may have been, Sophia's faction could not count upon a peaceful, unarmed crowd. It was to the musketeers[9] that they now turned, and the latter were ready for action. In an age when strong and powerful men endeavored to maintain themselves at the expense of the weak and downtrodden and to use them for their personal ends, there was a continuous flood of complaints both from townsmen oppressed by governors and soldiers persecuted by their officers. It certainly comes as no surprise to learn that at the end of Fedor's reign both the musketeers and the soldiers were forever complaining of being mistreated by one or other of their colonels. The musketeers were especially sensitive to such abuses, for when they were not on active service they lived with their families in their own houses in special settlements and engaged in profitable trades, and their chief complaint against certain colonels was that they forced the musketeers to work for them, thereby tearing them away from their own business. At the end of Fedor's reign matters had reached a point where the colonels were displaying more license than ever before and the musketeers were becoming more and more unruly.

It would be impossible to deny that the tsar's close associates, Yazykov and the Likhachevs' were sensible and well-intentioned men if one considers the general direction of government activity. But there is no reason to suppose that these men possessed any outstanding talents or the firmness of character so essential for the maintenance of order in all spheres of administration. Even Yazykov's admirers emphasized his adroitness and cunning as a courtier, but cunning is the weapon of a weak man. In the last days of Fedor's life, when the tsar obviously was declining, Yazykov and his friends were obliged to look first of all to their own interests. The moral weakness of the other courtiers, be they boyar or table attendant, crown agent or court attendant, every one born to be a warrior and commander, was revealed clearly by their shameful behavior during the musketeers' rebellion.

The insolvency of the ancient retinue[10] system and the need for reform were vividly exposed. The musketeers were responsible for maintaining order and security in the capital, and their chancellery was directed by the old boyar, Prince Yury Dolgoruky, who had been one of Tsar Alexis's most distinguished commanders and closest associates, but he was now senile and stricken with palsy. Prince Michael, his son and assistant in the chancellery, commanded no respect whatsoever. And so the colonels went on mistreating their men and the musketeers continued to run riot, sensing that there was no authority powerful enough to check injustice and unrest.

The musketeers of the entire Pyzhov regiment had complained to the sovereign about their colonel, Bogdan Pyzhov, on grounds that he had deducted half their salaries.[11] The tsar assigned Yazykov to look into the case, but it is reported that he conducted the trial unjustly and found in favor of the colonel. It is hard to say how much credence can be given to the testimony of one man [Silvester Medvedev], whose attachment to Sophia and the Miloslavskys made him hostile to Yazykov. But it is worth noting that had Yazykov, that "expert on the inner workings of the palace," wished to expose the chaos in the Chancellery of Musketeers, he would have been obliged to discredit the director of the chancellery, that pillar of society Prince Dolgoruky! Be that as it may, the musketeer petitioners, the worthiest among them, were punished with floggings and banishment in order to dissuade them from submitting further complaints against their colonels.

The colonels breathed a sigh of relief and proceeded to mete out still worse treatment to their men. On April 23 the musketeers filed a new complaint, this time against a certain Colonel Griboedov. They were afraid that the authorities again would try to shield Dolgoruky, and so they went to headquarters and delegated one of their number to present the petition to the Chancellery of Musketeers. Dolgoruky was told that the musketeer who brought the petition was drunk and had made foul remarks about him, Dolgoruky, the boyars and others. The boyar ordered that the petitioner be arrested and flogged in front of the government office as a warning to others against further misbehavior. When the musketeer was led into the courtyard and sentence was read out to him, he appealed to his comrades. "Brothers! It was you who asked me to deliver the petition. How can you allow them to punish me so outrageously?" The musketeers were aroused; they rushed at the chancellery guards, overpowered them and released their comrade. This event sparked off disturbances in nearly all the musketeer regiments. The soldiers also filed a complaint against their general, Matvei Kravkov. The musketeers petitioned against Griboedov and were "on the verge of rebellion." The government managed to avert a rebellion by dismissing Griboedov, confiscating his hereditary estates and exiling him to Totma.

This was the state of affairs when Fedor died. On the very day of his death, when the oath of allegiance to Peter was being administered, the musketeers of the Karandeev regiment refused to swear allegiance. Lord-in-waiting Konstantin Shcherbaty, Crown Councillor Zmeev and Crown Secretary Ukraintsev were sent to deal with them and succeeded in persuading the musketeers to take the oath to Peter.

On the third day after Fedor's death a mob came to the palace on behalf of sixteen musketeer regiments and the Butyrsky infantry regiment and demanded that nine colonels be arrested and forced to repay money they had extorted from the musketeers, and also to hand over payment for work they had made the musketeers do for them. Were their demand rejected, they threatened to take matters into their own hands, kill the colonels and plunder their homes and property. "Other traitors had better watch out too!" shouted the musketeers. "Are we to endure ill-treatment from our colonels and stand by while traitors deceive his majesty the tsar?"

The reference seemed to be to Tsaritsa Natalia, for it was hard to imagine who else they meant. The authorities were alarmed and unsure how to act. They decided to arrest the colonels and place them under guard in the Chancellery of Cavalry. But this measure failed to placate the musketeers; they demanded that the colonels be handed over to them. The government refused, but promised that justice would be done. The musketeers stood their ground for a long time, but in the end they were pacified by certain court dignitaries and prelates who had influence over them. They were promised that all the money would be exacted from the old colonels, and that new officers would be appointed. According to other, maybe more reliable sources,[12] the government was so alarmed that it agreed to hand over the colonels to the musketeers. Only the patriarch realized the full horror of such a concession and hastily sent messengers to all the regiments, exhorting them to drop their demands.

The colonels nonetheless were obliged to pay the sums the musketeers demanded. As much as two thousand rubles was extracted from some of them; those who were unable to pay were flogged for two hours at a time. Others were charged with more serious crimes and were beaten with cudgels. Karandeev and Griboedov were flogged with the knout, sentence being preceded by the customary recitation of the testimonies and charges against them. Semen Griboedov heard the following: "A complaint was filed against you to the great sovereign by the sergeants, corporals and rank-and-file musketeers of your regiment. They say that you subjected them to extortion, insult and all manner of ill-treatment. You beat them savagely to extract money and labor from them. You flogged them most outrageously with cudgels, using two, three or even four cudgels at a time. You set up gardens on the musketeers' land and forced them to collect money to buy vegetable seeds for these gardens. You made the musketeers and their children work in your gardens and hamlets and forced them to carry things in their own carts. You forced them to sew colored robes, velvet hats and yellow boots. You deducted money and grain from their state allowance; you discharged them from guard duty and took money for that. Their earnings for performing sentry duty at the city walls and supplies from the palace you took for yourself. You ordered them to collect money to buy timber and other materials to build you a house and forced them to perform various tasks and to clear away the garbage. When you were on military service you also burdened them with work and made them transport your supplies in their carts. In Tsar Fedor's reign you were strictly cautioned against extorting money and forcing the musketeers to work for you, and you were even granted service tenure of a hamlet in respect of this. But, forgetful of the great sovereign's benevolence, you continued to harass the musketeers and beat them without cause."

Although the musketeers had dropped their demand that the colonels be handed over to them, they immediately swarmed onto the square where the flogging and other sentences were being carried out, and took charge of the proceedings. Whenever they yelled "Enough!", the flogging stopped. They were evidently highly displeased, not only with their own colonels, but also with all the favorites of the previous regime. In hope of placating them, the tsar withdrew his favor from Boyar Ivan Yazykov and his son, Cupbearer Semen, Gentleman of the Bedchamber Alexis Likhachev, Treasurer Michael Likhachev and personal table attendants Ivan Andreevich Yazykov and Ivan Dashkov, and banished them all from his presence. These measures had no effect.

GOVERNMENT WEAKNESS AND REBELLIOUS MUSKETEERS

Once they had got their way over the colonels the musketeers ran riot for there was no one to restrain them. Each day great mobs collected in front of their headquarters. They treated the Princes Dolgoruky with contempt, laughing at them and threatening them. Lesser-ranking officers fared even worse: they were simply driven from their offices and hailed with sticks, stones and insults. Officers who attempted to restore order and discipline met a worse fate still: they were seized, taken to the top of watch towers and hurled down to cries of "Hurrah!"

Yet the musketeers must have been well aware that it was only the utter weakness and instability of the government that allowed them to run riot. Once the government gained strength their freedom would disappear and there might be a high price to pay. How eagerly, then, must they have seized upon insinuations that the government was unworthy of respect, that they must not obey it because it was illegal! To scorn such a government and rise up against it would be not an act of rebellion but a service to their country. One contemporary witness[13] records that the news of the musketeers' activities was as great a source of joy to Sophia as the olive branch which the dove brought to Noah in the ark, just as the insinuations of the tsarevna and her supporters must have seemed like an olive branch to the musketeers.

It appears that Khovansky made the first move in approaching the musketeers. His fame as a military commander added great weight to his words. "You yourselves can see," said the Braggart, addressing each of the musketeers in turn, "you yourselves can see the heavy yoke that the boyars have placed upon you. Now that they have chosen God knows what kind of tsar[14] they will withhold your money and provisions, burden you with work, just like before, and your children will become their slaves for all time. Worse even than this—they will commit you and us to servitude under some foreign enemy. Moscow will be destroyed and the Orthodox faith eradicated."[15]

MILOSLAVSKY'S PLOT

Khovansky was not the only one to spread such ideas. Ivan Miloslavsky had taken to his bed feigning illness and was hatching a plot.[16] The musketeers' elected representatives Odintsov, Petrov and Chermny came to his house by night and discussed the musketeers' activities together with Tolstoy, Tsykler and Ozerov. The widow Rodimitsa Semenova, a former chambermaid of Tsar Fedor and a woman of Ukrainian cossack origin, went amongst the musketeers distributing money and lavish promises from Tsarevna Sophia. The unrest spread to all the regiments except the Sukharev, where the officers Burmistrov and Borisov managed to contain it. Every day groups of musketeers collected together, armed themselves without their colonel's orders, sounded the tocsin and went around the public bath-houses denouncing the government and the rule of the Naryshkins and Matveev and bragging that they would "break all their necks."

THE ARRIVAL OF MATVEEV

At this stage, words remained without deeds. It needed more than vague assurances that Tsaritsa Natalia intended only evil and Tsarevna Sophia only good. What was needed was some stronger inducement for those who were still undecided and those who were happy enough to shout but who quailed before the deed, in order to inspire them to march on the palace. The chief conspirators were keeping this prize in hand until Matveev arrived; he was to be the first victim of the musketeers' violence for he alone could bring strength to the government of the despised stepmother. It was reported earlier that Matveev had been transferred from Mezen to Lukh whilst Fedor was still alive; he had been ordered to await a further decree from the tsar. When this decree finally arrived it was in Peter's name and it instructed him to come to Moscow with all haste.

The old man set off at once. On the way he was met by seven musketeers who intercepted him with the express purpose of telling him of the unrest amongst their comrades and warning him of the danger that awaited him. The musketeers' reports speeded Matveev on his way. "I shall quell this rebellion or lay down my life for the sovereign, that my eyes should not behold yet more misfortune in my old age," he said. Matveev met with an honorable reception at the Trinity monastery and along the road to Moscow. He arrived in the capital on May 12. The next day he presented himself to the tsar and the tsaritsa; the reunion was "so rapturous that words could not fully describe it." On May 13 Matveev called on the patriarch and had a long conversation with him in his private cell. He also paid a visit to his old friend the sick Prince Yury Dolgoruky and spent a long time in conference with him. In the meantime all the aristocrats hastened to gather at the home of the man in whose hands the government would now be concentrated. Elected representatives from all musketeer regiments also arrived with gifts of bread and salt, entreating Matveev to intercede for them since he gave more recognition to their services than the other boyars. The only absentee was Ivan Miloslavsky, who excused himself on the grounds of illness.

Miloslavsky and his supporters had made their plans, and now they must act quickly. Matveev was now in Moscow and they must catch him unawares, before he could get his bearings and take up the reins of government in his experienced hands. The old enemy had lost none of his former cunning or his ability to win people over during his years of exile

Artamon Sergeevich Matveev
Portrait by an unknown master after the boyar's death

in Pustozersk and Mezen. He made a great show of giving a warm welcome to visitors. Everyone was in raptures, even those who had never held him in particularly high regard; they all hoped that Matveev would tame the musketeers and the Naryshkins, too. People had been offended by the inordinate rise of the tsaritsa's brothers, young men who had yet to give evidence of their worth. Ivan Naryshkin had been made boyar at the age of twenty-three! And now there were rumors that Boyar Artamon Sergeevich was also displeased by the swift elevation of the Naryshkins. Matveev's return was a source of general rejoicing; this is why the Miloslavskys had to act quickly.

MUSKETEERS REBEL

May 15, the fateful anniversary of the death of Tsarevich Dmitry,[17] was chosen by the conspirators as the day of the uprising. A list of the "traitors" who were to be eliminated was circulating already amongst the musketeers. In the morning Alexander Miloslavsky and Peter Tolstoy went around the musketeer regiments proclaiming the news that Tsarevich Ivan had been strangled by the Naryshkins and ordering the musketeers to report for duty in the Kremlin.[18] The musketeers sounded the alarm, beat drums and set off for the palace with their standards and guns. It was midday on a Monday and Matveev was descending the palace staircase on his way home when he met Prince Fedor Semenovich Urusov, who told him that the musketeers and soldiers had mutinied. They had entered Earthwork Town [Zemliany Gorod, a Moscow-quarter] and would soon reach White Town [Bely Gorod].[19] Matveev went back into the palace and told the tsaritsa the news. Immediately an order was issued to the lieutenant colonel of the royal bodyguard to close all the gates into the Kremlin.

But it was too late. Several boyars ran in with the news that the musketeers were approaching and shouting that the Naryshkins had killed Tsarevich Ivan and that they, the musketeers, had come to kill the traitors and destroyers of the royal line. The beating of drums resounded throughout the Kremlin. Many of the boyars' servants and their horses were killed, others were badly wounded. Matveev and the other privy councillors who had gathered round the tsaritsa sent for the patriarch, who returned with the messenger. It was proposed that the tsar and tsarevich should be presented to the musketeers in order to remove the pretext for their rebellion, and so the tsaritsa, accompanied by the patriarch and the boyars, took Peter and his brother out onto the Red Porch[20]. The mob was silenced, for they could hardly believe their eyes. Several of the musketeers mounted the staircase, climbed onto the balcony and went up to the tsarevich to ask him whether he was really Tsarevich Ivan Alekseevich and which of the boyar traitors was mistreating him. "No one is mistreating me and I have no complaints against anybody," replied Ivan.

It was a tense and critical moment for the conspirators. The musketeers had been disarmed and would leave the Kremlin in disgrace. They could hardly return a second time on the same errand and Matveev would take precautionary measures. As a last resort they tried to arouse the mob; they shouted that even though the tsarevich was still alive his ill-wishers Matveev and the Naryshkins should be handed over. They claimed that Ivan Naryshkin had tried on the royal crown and other regalia. Some of the boyars—Prince Michael Alegukovich Cherkassky, Prince Ivan Khovansky, Peter Vasilievich Sheremetev the Elder and Prince Vasily Golitsyn—went down to try and pacify the musketeers. The musketeers demanded that the great sovereign deliver over the following men: Prince Yury Dolgoruky, Prince Grigory Romodanovsky, Prince Michael Dolgoruky, Kirill Naryshkin, Artamon Matveev, Ivan Yazykov, Ivan Naryshkin, Gentleman of the Bedchamber Alexis Likhachev, Treasurer Michael Likhachev, Cupbearer Semen Yazykov, Crown Secretaries Larion Ivanov, Daniel Poliansky, Grigory Bogdanov, Alexis Kirillov and Table Attendants Afanasy, Lev, Martemian, Fedor, Vasily and Peter Naryshkin. When they were told that these men were not with the sovereign they grew agitated and Prince Cherkassky's robe was torn in the crush.

Then Matveev came down from the porch to the railings and spoke to the crowd. He reminded the musketeers of their former services, of how in the past they had helped to quell rebellion; now they were negating all their previous achievements by their own mutiny. Khovansky apparently indicated to the musketeers that they should attack Matveev, but in vain: the musketeers remained calm and immobile and begged Matveev to intercede on their behalf. Matveev was pleased by the turn of events and returned to the tsaritsa. But the conspirators were alert; when they saw that things were not going their way in front of the palace, they directed a mob of the most desperate musketeers from the entrance of the Palace of Facets to the Red Porch. Meanwhile, in front of the palace, they received help from the most unexpected quarter. Prince Michael Dolgoruky, whose job it should have been to prevent the rebellion, had not been heard of throughout the disturbances. Now that the musketeers had been placed in an embarrassing position by marching to the Kremlin palace on the basis of an absurd rumor and had been pacified by Matveev, Prince Michael suddenly took it into his head to play the officer. He began hurling abuse and threats at them, ordering them to clear out of the Kremlin immediately and return to their barracks.

The Musketeer Uprising of May 15, 1682
Miniature from Peter Krekshin's (d. 1763) *History of Peter the Great*.
Matveev's bloody death is depicted in the lower scene.

Nothing was so calculated to incense the unruly musketeers as that old imperious tone, especially when it was adopted by a man whom they neither liked nor respected, a man who always had been a laughing-stock. The musketeers were infuriated. They forced their way onto the porch, seized Dolgoruky and threw him down onto their upturned pikes then finished him off with their pole-axes. The eyes of the mob clouded over at the first sight of blood, then other musketeers came running from the entrance to the Palace of Facets and fell upon Matveev. Tsaritsa Natalia and Prince Cherkassky tried to save him, but the musketeers tore him from their grasp and cast him down into the square opposite the Annunciation cathedral, where they hacked him to pieces. There are other reports that Matveev took hold of Tsar Peter's arm in an attempt to protect himself but the musketeers wrenched him away from the tsar.[21] The patriarch was on the point of going down to the musketeers but they shouted: "We don't need any advice from anyone. It's time to find the people we're after." With that they fixed their pikes and rushed into the palace to seek out the "other traitors." Tsaritsa Natalia took her son and went off to the Palace of Facets and then everyone fled. No one knew the whereabouts of the numerous courtiers and soldiers who every day milled about on the porch and in the antechamber. They had left the palace, the Kremlin and Moscow in the hands of the frenzied musketeers whom they regarded with such disdain.

The musketeers had the free run of the palace. They ran around the tsarevnas' chambers, looked under beds, shook up feather mattresses, rummaged in store rooms, ran into the churches and up to the altars, where they groped under the communion tables and sacrificial altars, poking their pikes underneath in the hope of finding one of the Naryshkins hidden there. They met Table Attendant Fedor Petrovich Saltykov and killed him in mistake for Afanasy Naryshkin. When they realized their error they took the body to his father, Boyar Peter Mikhailovich Saltykov, and begged his forgiveness. The old man replied: "It is God's will," and commanded the murderers be treated to liquor and ale.

In Tsaritsa Natalia's room they came across a dwarf, nicknamed Hamster, and asked him where the Naryshkins were hidden. Hamster directed them to Afanasy Naryshkin's hiding place beneath the communion table in the royal chapel of the Resurrection. The musketeers dragged him onto the terrace, stabbed him and hurled him onto the square. They discovered Ivan Fomich Naryshkin in his house across the Moscow river and killed

him. They also killed Prince Grigory Romodanovsky, that famous commander of the previous two reigns, who had earned their disfavor at the
time of the Chigirin campaigns. The late Tsar Fedor's favorite, Boyar
Yazykov, tried to hide in the house of his confessor by the church of St.
Nicholas in Khlynov but he was betrayed by a slave. The musketeers took
him to the cathedral of the Archangel Michael and hacked him to pieces.
They killed Crown Secretary Larion Ivanov, the director of the Chancellery of Foreign Affairs, and several people of lesser importance.

All these murders were accompanied by cries of "Do you agree?",
which were addressed to the mob of unarmed people from whom the musketeers sought approval of their actions. The people were obliged to register their agreement by shouts of "Hurrah!" and waving their hats.
Anyone who disagreed or showed signs of regret was killed. The corpses
of the victims were dragged to the Savior or St. Nicholas gates on Red
Square. The bodies were preceded by musketeers, like a guard of honor,
crying: "Here is Boyar Artamon Sergeevich! Here is Boyar Prince Romodanovsky. Here is Dolgoruky, here goes a member of the council. Make
way!" We saw how the musketeers went to the old Boyar Saltykov to beg
forgiveness for accidentally killing his son; they now went to make their
apologies to the sick octogenarian Dolgoruky. They explained that their
tempers had got the better of them, sin had beguiled them and they had
killed his son Prince Michael. The old man listened calmly to their apologies and even brought himself to treat them to liquor and ale. But when
the musketeers had gone and his son's widow entered, loudly bewailing
her husband, Dolgoruky consoled her by saying: "Don't cry! They have
eaten the pike but the teeth remain. Their rebellion will not last long. They
soon will be hanging from the battlements of White and Earthwork
towns." A slave ran after the musketeers and told them of the old man's
threats. The musketeers returned in a frenzy, dragged the sick Dolgoruky
into the courtyard, chopped him to pieces and threw the corpse out of the
gates onto a dung-hill and covered it with salt fish.

Throughout the day of May 15 the musketeers were in complete control
of the palace and the Kremlin. At nightfall they dispersed to their settlements, posting heavy guards at all the gates into the Kremlin, Kitai Quarter and White Town. The guards were instructed to allow no one to enter
or leave the Kremlin.

On the morning of May 16 the musketeers re-appeared at the palace
to the same accompaniment of beating drums. They demanded that Ivan

Naryshkin be handed over to them, otherwise they would kill all the boyars. Despite these threats Naryshkin was not surrendered. The musketeers waited until one o'clock in the afternoon then posted sentries everywhere as before and left the Kremlin. Ivan Naryshkin, his father, brothers and other relatives and Andrei, son of the murdered Matveev, at first had hidden in the room of the little tsarevna, Natalia Alekseevna, then in the chambers of the widowed Tsaritsa Martha. Only Klushina, Martha's chambermaid, knew the whereabouts of the unfortunate men. On May 17 at dawn Klushina took them into a dark store room where they hid amongst the feather mattresses and pillows. At Matveev's suggestion the door of the room was deliberately left open in order to avert suspicion. For the third time the musketeers milled in front of the palace, crying out for Naryshkin's surrender and asserting that this time they would not leave the Kremlin without him.

There is no reason why Sophia, Miloslavsky and their supporters should have been especially alarmed by Ivan Naryshkin's remaining alive or unduly incensed by the antics of this young man who, prominent though he was in his own family, was too mediocre a personality to be a danger to them. As far as they were concerned, Matveev was dead and that was half their business accomplished. It remained only to accomplish the other half, namely to topple the stepmother from power, which would be achieved easily with the help of the musketeers, who were now sole masters of Moscow. On May 16 Khovansky had asked the musketeers whether Tsaritsa Natalia should be driven from the palace and they had responded with a resounding "Yes!"

The musketeers themselves took a different view. They had been brought to the palace by rumors of regicide. The rumors proved false but the ringleaders had tried to justify their actions by exclaiming that the crime might still be committed. There were traitors in the palace, would-be assassins, and the chief culprit was Ivan Naryshkin, who already had tried on the crown. They had killed Matveev, who had not even been accused of treason; they had killed Saltykov by mistake; they had killed the Dolgorukys but the leading traitor was still alive! They needed to justify their coming, do their duty to the royal house and perform some service to atone for the blood which had been spilt. It was quite understandable why it was not the instigators of the affair but the crowd which required Naryshkin's death: only his surrender could end the rebellion if they were unable or unwilling to end it by other means.

Tsarevna Sophia spoke sharply to Tsaritsa Natalia. "We cannot save your brother from the musketeers. Why should we all perish on his account?"[22] The terror-stricken boyars tearfully entreated the tsaritsa to give up her brother and save their lives. There was no way out: Naryshkin was brought from his hiding place and taken to the church of the Savior behind the Golden Grille. Here he made his confession, took communion and received extreme unction. On Sophia's advice they gave him an icon of the Virgin to hold in the hope that the murderers would be shamed by the sight of the holy object. There then began the dreadful leave-taking between the sister and the brother who was about to meet an agonizing death. Some of those present thought the leave-taking unduly lengthy. The terror-stricken old man, Prince Yakov Odoevsky, became impatient and chided the tsaritsa. "However much it may grieve you, my lady, you must let him go. And you, Ivan, should get out of here at once, otherwise you'll be the death of us."

Naryshkin left the church. As soon as the musketeers caught sight of their victim they flung themselves upon him with a terrible cry. They did not finish him off at once but dragged him away to the Konstantinov torture chamber for interrogation. Others had been killed in error, in the heat of the moment or for their past offenses, but Naryshkin was charged with treason and an attempt upon the tsarevich's life. The musketeers had pledged themselves to eliminate all treason from the palace and now that the traitor was in their hands he must be tortured. If he broke down and confessed, their rebellion would be fully vindicated. Naryshkin, however, disappointed the musketeers by uttering not a word under torture. They dragged him from the chamber onto Red Square and cut him to pieces.

Their last victim was the foreign doctor, Daniel von Gaden, who was charged with poisoning Tsar Fedor.[23] When Gaden learned of the fate that awaited him he managed to slip out of the Foreign Settlement disguised as a beggar. For two whole days he hid in the Marina Grove and other places in the vicinity of Moscow. Finally he was driven back to the settlement by hunger in the hope of finding refuge with a friend and getting something to eat; but he was recognized on the street, arrested and brought to the palace. The tsarevnas and Tsaritsa Martha pleaded for the doctor's life; they assured the musketeers that he was completely innocent of Tsar Fedor's death and that he always had tasted personally all drugs he prepared for the sick ruler in their presence, but their pleas were to no avail. The musketeers cried: "He didn't only do away with Tsar Fedor—he's also a practitioner of black magic. We found dried snakes in his house and that's sufficient reason for executing him." Gaden was in the same position as Naryshkin: serious charges of attempted regicide had been brought against him and he was dragged off to the same Konstantinov chamber to be tortured. Whilst the musketeers administered the torture, one of them wrote down the confession. Gaden broke down. He confessed to all manner of crimes and begged for three days' grace in which to unmask those who were more deserving of death than he. "We can't wait that long," shouted the musketeers. They tore up the record of Gaden's testimony, hauled him onto Red Square and hacked him to bits.

On the following day, May 18, elected representatives of all musketeer regiments came to the palace. They were no longer armed and they presented a petition to the great sovereign and the sovereign tsarevnas, asking the tsar to order his maternal grandfather, Boyar Kirill Poluektovich Naryshkin, to take monastic vows. This request was granted immediately. The old man became a monk under the name Kiprian and was sent to the monastery of St. Cyril near Beloozero. On May 19 the soldiers, musketeers and artillerymen presented another petition demanding back-payment of earnings since 1646. It appeared that 240,000 rubles was owing them, in addition to which they were granted a further ten rubles per man. Naturally the treasury did not have such a sum to hand and it was obliged to raise the money throughout the realm and to collect silver plate for minting of coin. Even this failed to satisfy the soldiers and musketeers, who demanded that the property of those who had perished in the rebellion he made over to them.

On May 20 yet another petition was presented, requesting that the sovereign banish the following men: Gentleman of the Bedchamber Alexis Likhachev, Treasurer Michael Likhachev, Lord-in-waiting Pavel Yazykov, Cupbearer Semen Yazykov, Crown Councillor Nikita Akinfiev, Crown Secretaries Bogdanov and Poliansky, personal attendants Lovchikov, all the Naryshkins and Andrei Matveev and Table Attendants Lopukhin, Bukhvostov and Lutokhin. Once the court was purged of the Miloslavskys' enemies[24] the musketeers' petitions about punishment and exile ceased.

The musketeers' rebellion was over but still there was no government. In the churches prayers were said for the Great Sovereign Peter Alekseevich but his "family-less" mother could not contemplate governing for lack of support. All her followers were in hiding, in fear and trembling of their lives. It was not they who would take over the government but people who were ready for action, like Sophia, her sisters and their party. The tsarevnas were governing Russia! Sophia had come to the fore by her own efforts and no one tried to stand in her way, for she was the only member of the royal family who had any desire to govern and therefore people had little choice but to turn to her. It was to her that the musketeers applied with their requests or demands and naturally Sophia did her utmost to comply. She gave them as much money as could be collected, promising them an additional payment of ten rubles per man and agreed to confer the honorary title of court infantry[25] upon them. The court infantry had lost its commander-in-chief and so Prince Khovansky took over, although it is not known who authorized his appointment. His chief assistant or henchman was Alexis Yudin, an Old Believer and an elected representative of the Vorobin regiment.

SOPHIA'S REGENCY BEGINS
Sophia was in fact the ruler but her administration was yet to be legitimized. Sophia ruled at court but in the churches prayers were offered for Great Sovereign Tsar Peter Alekseevich. On May 23 Khovansky informed the tsarevnas that the musketeers had sent delegates to announce that it was their wish and the wish of many other citizens of the Muscovite realm that the two brothers reign jointly. Were their request dismissed they threatened to take up arms again. The tsarevnas summoned the boyars, lords-in-waiting and crown councillors, but they were unwilling to take such an important decision alone. An assembly was convoked consisting of the patriarch, the prelates of the church and representatives of various classes from the Muscovite realm, or, more accurately, from the city of Moscow.

The prospect of renewed disturbances among the musketeers forced the advisers to extol the advantages of dual rule. When one tsar went to war the other would remain in Moscow to attend to domestic affairs. Neither was there a lack of historical precedents, both similar and dissimilar: they spoke of Pharaoh and Joseph, the Emperors Arcadius and Honorius and Basil and Constantine. Thus it was decided that the two brothers should rule jointly. The great bell was sounded; in the Dormition cathedral prayers were chanted and they proclaimed long life for the most pious tsars, Ivan and Peter Alekseevich.

The very wording of the proclamation gave Ivan precedence over Peter, but it was deemed necessary to express this more positively, to subordinate Peter to Ivan in order to demote Tsaritsa Natalia and rob her of the chance of taking over the government herself. Once again the musketeers' delegates came to the palace demanding that Ivan be the first tsar and Peter the second. The tsarevnas declared that their words were inspired by God and so, on May 26, the decision was ratified by the boyar council and the patriarch and prelates, and duly announced to the musketeers and the entire people. Every day the musketeers were given food in the palace, two regiments at a time. On May 29 they told the boyars that, in view of the tsars' youth, the government should be entrusted to their sister, Tsarevna Sophia. The customary formalities ensued: everyone implored Sophia to accept the regency and after refusing several times she finally consented.

THE MUSKETEERS' DILEMMA

The musketeers held a banquet in the palace. Nothing was refused them for it was they who had established and moulded the government which now enjoyed unconditional recognition. All the same, the musketeers felt slightly ill at ease. They had heard tell, or maybe simply imagined, that they were being referred to as rebels; people seemed to be looking askance at them. They had broken with the boyars and knew that the boyars would never be their friends; the boyars would remain boyars, in other words their lords, and would seek every opportunity to have their revenge. Sensing this at the time of the rebellion, the musketeers had turned to their immediate inferiors amongst the common people. They proclaimed the freedom of bondslaves and destroyed the charters of bondage in the Slavery Chancellery.[26] But to their dismay the slaves did not stage a mass uprising and did not claim their freedom. They had little reason to for many of them only recently had taken the pledge of bondage of their own free will since they found it to their advantage. The musketeers had committed many brutalities when they took the palace by storm; they had exploited the timidity of the palace guards and overwhelmed Moscow by virtue of being armed men against the unarmed populace But Moscow was only a small part of Russia. What if the entire country were to proclaim its opposition to the musketeers, what if the numerous regiments of service gentry should march on Moscow to rid it of the musketeers as once they had saved it from the Poles?[27] The ordinary peaceful people of Moscow might be frightened of the musketeers, but the musketeers themselves were terrified to death of Russia. They therefore appealed to the government which they had created and which was consequently well-disposed towards them, and asked it to protect them from Russia and absolve them from guilt by acclaiming the events of May 15, 16 and 17.

THE COLUMN ON RED SQUARE

At Alexis Yudin's suggestion the musketeers submitted a petition in which they joined with all the tax-paying people of Moscow, setting their interests against those of the aristocrats and members of the council. "This petition is submitted by the musketeers of the Moscow regiments, the infantrymen of all regiments, the artillerymen, the stockade guards, the chief merchants and tradesmen of various guilds, the artisans of the crown settlements and the post-drivers. On May 15, by the will of the Almighty God and the Immaculate Virgin, there occurred in the Muscovite realm the murder of Boyars Prince Yury and Prince Michael Dolgoruky, which was committed for the house of the Immaculate Virgin and for you, great sovereigns, because of the enslavement and brutality they inflicted upon you and the great oppression, insult and wrongs heaped upon us and for all their many crimes and boastful words. Without your leave they flogged many of our brethren and banished them to distant towns, and Prince Yury cheated us of money and provisions. We killed Crown Secretary Larion Ivanov because he was like the Dolgorukys and bragged that he would see us hanging all over Earthwork Town, although we were innocent of any crime, and snake-like reptiles were found in his possession. We killed Prince Grigory Romodanovsky for his treachery and negligence in abandoning Chigirin to the Turks and Crimean Tatars and because he corresponded with them. We killed Ivan Yazykov because he, in collusion with our colonels, subjected us to great hardship and extorted money from us. We killed Boyar Matveev and Doctor Daniel because they prepared a poisonous draught for the tsar, as Daniel confessed under torture. We killed Ivan and Afanasy Naryshkin because they tried on the royal regalia and plotted all manner of evil against Tsar Fedor Alekseevich and were exiled for it.

"We, their killers, now humbly request that a column be erected on Red Square, and that on it be carved the names of all those evil-doers and the crimes for which they perished. And let charters of privilege with red seals be granted to all of us in the musketeer and infantry regiments and artisans' settlements to ensure that no boyar, lord-in-waiting, crown councillor or any other member of your council shall ever call us mutineers or traitors or any other defamatory name, nor send us unjustly into exile or flog us or put us to death, for we have served you faithfully. As to the story that the boyars' slaves come to us to win their freedom, let it be known that we have no communication or counsel with them." Sophia granted their request. Tsykler and Ozerov undertook to meet the musketeers' demand and a column was erected hastily .

ACTIVITIES OF THE OLD BELIEVERS

Sophia had exploited the musketeers in order to save herself and her family from disaster. The hated stepmother, Natalia, had been toppled from power and Sophia herself had assumed the regency. Her brother's death had come as a great blow and the future had looked bleak; she had clutched at the musketeers' pikes in desperation, from purely selfish motives. Sophia was not the only one to find herself in a dilemma; there were others who were equally willing to utilize the musketeers in order to alleviate their problems and promote their cause. The musketeers had massacred the boyars and upheld the seniority of the elder tsarevich but they also lent their support to the Old Believers, who were being persecuted by the Nikonites.[28]

Just three days after the uprising a discussion took place in the Titov regiment about filing a petition on the Old Belief and asking the patriarch and ecclesiastical authorities to justify their abhorrence of the old books and their reverence for the new Latin-Roman faith on the basis of Holy Scripture. There was no one in the regiment capable of composing the document and debating with the authorities and so they summoned Semen Kalachnikov, an artisan from the Potters' Settlement, and asked him whether he knew of any adherent of the ancient faith amongst his fellow-artisans or others who were skilled and learned in Holy Scripture and had the ability to compose a petition and defend it against the patriarch and prelates of the church. "I have heard my brethren speak of such expounders of holy writ," replied Kalachnikov. The musketeers asked him to bring them such men and Kalachnikov promised to do so. He went back to his settlement and explained the problem to three of his fellow-artisans, Nikita Borisov, Ivan Kurbatov and Savva Romanov, former steward to Archimandrite Makary of the Yellow Water (Zheltovodsk) monastery.[29] "Let us busy ourselves," said Kalachnikov. "The musketeers have expressed a desire to fight for the Old Belief." The artisans eagerly sought out the monk Sergei, "an adherent of the ancient traditions and a staunch adamant." Sergei agreed to accompany them and all five went off to the house of Nikita Borisov, where they set about writing a petition on behalf of all the musketeers and all inhabitants of the crown settlements.

By the following day the work was finished and Kalachnikov went to the Titov regiment with the glad news that his mission had been accomplished. An officer and two musketeers went with him to his house to meet the "staunch adamant" and listen to the petition which the artisans had composed. "Take heed, brethren," said Sergei, "of all the souls which are perishing because of the new books. Do not allow us to be subjected to outrage, burning and torture as our brothers before us. We are ready to denounce the new belief." The officer replied: "We are fully prepared to die with you for the sake of the Old Belief, worthy father. We are ready to share your fate—what more can we say?" Sergei bowed low before him and ordered Savva Romanov to read the petition. The musketeers were astonished. "Never in all our lives have we heard such a work or such a description of the heresies in the new books," they said. The petition created a similar impression when Romanov read it a second time to an assembly of musketeers outside the government office. Many were in tears and when the reading was over they all shouted: "Brothers, we must fight for the Old Belief and shed our blood for Christ's light. We were prepared to lay down our lives for mortal things so why should we not die for Christ's sake?"

KHOVANSKY AND THE MUSKETEER DISSENTERS

The musketeers reported to Khovansky that they wished to submit the petition. Khovansky, a whole-hearted adherent of antiquity, also was known to favor the Old Belief; there is even a report that he had suffered for his faith.[30] Khovansky was pleased but asked: "Do you have someone, brothers, who is capable of debating with the church authorities? Religion is a serious matter—learned men are essential." "We have found a monk who is well-versed in scripture and many of the artisans are also enthusiasts," the musketeers replied. "Bring them to my house and come along yourselves" said the boyar and he fixed a time.

The dissenters were received respectfully by Khovansky's servants but their host had guests and they were kept waiting three hours until his arrival. When the boyar entered he made a low bow to the monk about whom he had heard so much and asked: "What have you come to see me about, worthy father?" Sergei replied that they had brought a petition describing the heresies in the new books. "I myself am a sinner," said Khovansky. "I heartily desire that God's churches acknowledge the old faith, with one accord and without dispute. Sinner though I am, I hold unquestioningly to the old faith, I worship from the old books and make the sign of the cross with two fingers." With that Khovansky recited the Creed, speaking of the *True* Holy Spirit as the Old Believers required.[31] He continued: "This is what I believe and profess and I pray to God that he may be merciful to Christian people and not commit Christian souls to everlasting damnation because of this new Nikonian belief."

Khovansky concluded his speech with several texts, as was the custom, "And he spake much from Holy Scripture." When he was done Sergei came to the point and asked the "royal boyar" whether it pleased him to hear the petition. The reading began and the royal boyar was astounded also by the number of heresies in the new books. He asked who had written the document. "My brethren and I labored over it," replied Sergei. The boyar, however, had not formed a very favorable opinion of the staunch adamant. "I see, father, that you are a humble, quiet and ordinary monk," he said. "How will you deal with such a great task? We need an eloquent man to debate with them." Sergei replied: "Although I am not loquacious and am unaccustomed to their artfulness and their high-flown speech, nevertheless I trust in the Son of God, who said: It is not you who will speak but the spirit of Your Father." Other dissenters intervened to assure Khovansky of the success of the venture by telling him that Nikita, the famous priest from Suzdal, would lend his support. He had denounced the schism initially but now he had returned to fight for their cause.[32]

Khovansky was encouraged by the news. He had a high opinion of Nikita and doubted the ability of the Orthodox clergy to match him in debate. "I am glad to assist you, brothers," Khovansky told the dissenters. "Rest assured that you will not be put to death, hanged and burned as of old." The dissenters urged him to arrange a meeting at the platform on the Red Square before the whole people and with the tsars in attendance. If this was impossible, they requested an assembly in the Kremlin, between the cathedrals by the Red Porch. They insisted that it be arranged for the following Friday, June 23, since Friday was traditionally the day for meetings. Khovansky replied that Friday was out of the question as the coronation was to take place on Sunday. "But we wish the sovereigns to be crowned in the true Orthodox faith, not in the new Latin heresy," said the dissenters. Khovansky swore before God that the tsars would be crowned in the ancient manner, unchanged since the reign of Ivan IV. But the dissenters were concerned with more than the antiquity of the ritual. They said: "The sovereigns will take communion during the liturgy but the patriarch will celebrate the new liturgical form and during the coronation he will admonish the sovereigns to uphold the new belief." Khovansky had no answer to this. "The patriarch can hardly force the tsars to become his bondsmen," he said. "Have it your own way. Call the meeting on Friday." The dissenters went away well satisfied.

On Friday, June 23, the musketeers' delegates visited Khovansky as arranged and asked him when he wished the fathers to attend the meeting. Khovansky told them to come in two hours and two hours later they arrived in the Kremlin. Nikita carried a cross, Sergei—the Gospels; the monk Savvaty had come from the forests of Volokolamsk to support his fellow dissenters and carried an icon of the Last Judgment. Crowds of men and women had gathered, all amazed at the strange sight. Khovansky had the dissenters admitted to the reception chamber. He came out to meet them with a retinue of secretaries, clerks and other people. He kissed the cross and the Gospels, then, feigning ignorance, he asked the purpose of the worthy fathers' visit. Nikita replied that they had come to petition about the ancient Orthodox faith; they desired that the patriarch and prelates of the church be ordered to restore the old form of service. "If the patriarch refuses, let him explain what is wrong with the old books. Why does he curse the adherents of ancient dogma and send them into exile? Why did he command that the Solovetsk monastery be destroyed and the monks put to death?[33] We shall then expose all the inventions and heresies that are contained in their new books." Khovansky gave Nikita the same reply as he had given Sergei: "I myself adhere to the old books in my prayers and the profession of my faith." He took the dissenters' petition to the sovereigns and returned with the news that they would need three weeks to consider it. He asked them to come back on Wednesday afternoon as the patriarch had asked the sovereigns to postpone the matter until then.

Nikita had not forgotten that the coronation was to take place on Sunday. He asked Khovansky: "How then, sir, are the sovereign tsars to be crowned?" "I told you that they will be crowned in the ancient manner," replied Khovansky. But Nikita persisted: "The patriarch ought to celebrate the old form of the liturgy, using seven communion loaves and they should be baked with the true cross, not the Latin one."[34] Khovansky extricated himself by replying: "See to it that loaves are baked with the old cross on them and I personally shall deliver them to the patriarch and make sure that he uses the old liturgy. Now, Father Nikita, return home."

By Sunday Father Dorofei and Father Gavril of the Volokolamsk hermitage also had arrived in Moscow. There was great rejoicing amongst the dissenters. Nikita found a skilled widow to bake the communion loaves,[35] fully convinced that the patriarch would use them during the liturgy. On Sunday he collected the loaves and set off triumphantly for the Kremlin. His triumph was short-lived. Swarms of people had crowded into the Kremlin to await the entrance of the sovereigns into the cathedral and Nikita was quite unable to force his way through. He returned with his small bundle in despair. "Forgive me, holy fathers," he said, "but the people stopped me from getting to the cathedral so I have brought the loaves back." There was nothing to be done; the loaves were blessed and distributed to the faithful.

In the meantime the dissenters' cause was meeting with little success in the musketeer regiments. By no means all regiments were in agreement with supporting the Old Belief. The dissenters blamed the patriarch who had, it seemed, summoned the musketeers' elected representatives, showered them with endearments, treated them to drinks and sent them various gifts. To further their cause, the Titov regiment decided to choose some old musketeers to visit all the regiments and persuade the people to sign the petition. Nine regiments, and a tenth regiment of gunners, signed but in the other ten regiments there was fierce debate and disagreement, with some wanting to sign and others refusing. "Why should we sign?" they protested. "We cannot dispute the petition but if we sign we shall be up against the patriarch and prelates. Will the monks be equal to facing such an assembly? They will get confused and abandon the debate. This is the patriarch's business, not ours. We are quite ready to stand up for the Orthodox faith without signing anything and we shall not allow people to be burned and tortured as previously."

In spite of the fact that the musketeers were not solidly in favor of the schism, the petition was copied onto twenty parchment rolls on behalf of all Orthodox Christians and on July 3 delegates were sent to Khovansky to find out when the fathers should attend the assembly. But rumors already had reached Khovansky of the disturbances and disagreements amongst the musketeers over the schism. He went out to the representatives and asked, in the name of the tsars: "Are all regiments united in their support of the Orthodox faith?" The delegates replied: "All the regiments and the artisans of the crown settlements are willing to stand up for the old Orthodox faith!" Khovansky repeated his question twice and both times received the reply: "We are ready to fight to the death for the Christian faith!"

Khovansky conveyed the delegates' reply to the sovereigns, in other words to the tsarevna. It was decided that he should take the delegates to see the patriarch and they were followed there by a crowd of zealots from the artisan community. Khovansky went into the patriarch's chamber, while the delegates and the artisans waited outside. The opportunity was taken of inviting the delegates into the patriarch's wine cellar and entertaining them. They emerged drunk, much to the consternation of the artisans, who realized that their support had been rendered useless.

When Khovansky finally summoned them into the patriarch's chamber, the delegates shouted to the zealot artisans: "Now we'll see how you face up to the patriarch and church authorities in debate!" The patriarch appeared and the delegates approached to receive his blessing but the zealots from among the artisans refused to budge. The patriarch asked: "Brethren, why have you come to our humble presence and what do you want of us?" Khovansky replied: "Sire, these men of all ranks have come to your holiness to complain about the revision of the Orthodox faith. They desire that the services in the cathedral again be conducted from the old books."

There was a prolonged silence. Khovansky turned to the musketeers and ordered them to speak. Alexis Yudin began: "We have come, blessed patriarch, to your holiness because we wish to know why the old books were rejected and we wish you to explain to us what heresies are to be found in them." The patriarch replied: "My children, and brethren! It does not behoove you to judge even a common man, far less a prelate of the church. You are simply military men and such matters are beyond your competence. I am a shepherd, not a hireling. I came in through the door, not by some other way.[36] I did not snatch this heavy burden of my own accord nor did I buy my way to the apostolic throne. I was elected by order of the great sovereign and with the blessing of the entire Consecrated Assembly.[37] Unworthy as I am, I am still your pastor and you must obey me. Instead you act in a contradictory and disobedient fashion, denying our faith. You call Patriarch Nikon a heretic but he was no heretic. He was deposed because of his insubordination but not for inflicting any injury upon our faith. The corrections in the books and the three-fingered sign of the cross were introduced with the consent of the ecumenical patriarchs. We did not undertake this task of our own accord but made the corrections on the basis of holy scripture."

Naturally the musketeers were unable to contradict the patriarch. Paul Danilovets, one of the artisan dissenters, took up the debate. These zealots had one very sore spot—the problem of persecution. They had dwelt upon this constantly in their meetings in the musketeers' settlements and at Khovansky's house and had demanded that all commitment for trial, burning and torture cease. Now they found themselves face to face with the patriarch and prelates, whom they considered to be their chief persecutors. "You speak the truth, your grace," said Paul. "You do indeed bear Christ's image, but Christ said: Learn of me, for I am meek and lowly of heart.[38] He did not threaten people with the stake, fire and the sword. We are told to obey our teachers but even an angel may be disobeyed if he proclaims falsehoods. Why is it heretical and blasphemous to make the sign of the cross with two fingers? Why should people be burned and tortured for it?"

The patriarch replied: "We do not burn and torture people because of the way they cross themselves or say their prayers but because they call us heretics and disobey the holy church. You may cross yourselves in whatever way you choose." There was no answer to this. The dissenters knew perfectly well that even were persecution to cease and complete freedom of worship granted them, they would still continue to oppose the church and deem it unorthodox. The dissenters were demanding that the clergy refrain from persecuting them for heresy but they themselves were not prepared to stop regarding the clergy as heretics. Paul was obliged to drop the subject of persecution and turn to the dispute about corruptions in the church books and the notorious and never-ending argument about Nikon and Arseny,[39] which continues to this day during church festivals in the Moscow Kremlin. When the debate was over, Khovansky and the musketeers' delegates went up to receive the patriarch's blessing. Paul went with them but demanded that the patriarch bless him in the old manner. The patriarch refused and so Paul went away unblessed. Khovansky kissed him on the forehead and said: "I never really knew you until now, dear fellow." A meeting was fixed for Wednesday, July 5.

Meanwhile the dissenters wasted no time and began to deliver loud sermons on the streets and squares. Crowds of ordinary folk, both men and women, gathered on Red Square to discuss the Old Belief. Nor were these people who complained of persecution and extolled Christian meekness and humility slow to manifest their own version of these qualities. When the Orthodox priest Savva, who was famed for his erudition, came out onto the square and began to furnish proof of why the sign of the cross must be made with three fingers and firmly denounced the schism, he was killed by the people he was denouncing. The monk Cheshikha also was set upon as he condemned the schism by the Moscow river (Moskvoretsk) gates.[40]

THE DISSENTERS REBEL

At daybreak on Wednesday July 5 the musketeers' delegates went to Nikita and the monks and told them that they would not report to Khovansky, to prevent the authorities asking for further time for consideration. The monks were instructed to set off as soon as the delegates sent them word. The signal was given shortly afterwards and the dissenters began to assemble. They chanted prayers and when Father Nikita had blessed them, they took up the cross, the Gospels, icons of the Virgin and the Last Judgment and the old books, lit candles and set off for the Kremlin. A great mob of people followed after them; the crush was dreadful. The crowd was heard to speak approvingly of the schismatic monks with their old-fashioned hoods pulled down over their eyes and their starved look. "They don't have fat bellies like the present-day teachers of the new testament," they shouted. The dissenters came to a halt outside the Archangel cathedral where they put up lecterns, which they covered with cloths, set up the cross, the Gospels and the icons and lit candles.

While this was happening the patriarch was conducting a service with the clergy in the Dormition cathedral. There were tears in his eyes, for the fate of Savva and Cheshikha seemed to bode ill for him. When the prayers were over the patriarch returned home but sent Archpriest Vasily from the High Savior Chapel[41] to deliver a printed denunciation to Nikita, reminding him of how he had repented of his schismatic views before the Church Council. Trembling with fear, the archpriest began to read the denunciation at the corner of the Palace of Facets but the musketeers seized him, boxed his ears and dragged him over to the dissenters. They were going to tear up his text but Sergei intervened. "Why beat him?" he asked.

"He is not here of his own accord but was sent by the patriarch. Let him finish reading." But the mob was enraged and ready to stone him to death. He could not be heard above the clamor. Sergei then asked him: "Why continue? You can see that no one is listening." The people begged Sergei to instruct them from the scriptures and explain how they might avoid Nikonian deceptions. A bench was brought; Nikita climbed up and began to read the Solovetsk texts,[42] dealing with the sign of the cross, the Latin cross, crosiers, communion bread and other points of ecclesiastical practice. The crowd listened with folded arms, breathing deeply; some were even weeping. But the monks were distressed by the people pushing them from all sides. Sergei stopped reading but the people urged him to continue: "For God's sake, tell us more from Holy Scripture lest our souls be damned." Sergei was exhausted for he had fasted for the past three days. He asked Savva Romanov to continue but the latter replied: "This is your job, not mine; it's your calling."

Curious scenes also were taking place inside the palace. When the monks had halted outside the Archangel cathedral[43] the musketeers' delegates approached Khovansky to learn the time of the meeting. Khovansky went to ask the patriarch. Joachim replied that the tsaritsa and the tsarevnas had requested that the dissenters come to the Palace of Facets since they, as women, were reluctant to appear on the square before all the people. The delegates conveyed this reply to the monks but when the crowd heard it they protested loudly: "Why can't the patriarch testify on Holy Scripture before the people? The meeting must take place here; the palace won't hold so many of us. The people are confused. Some extol the Old Belief, others the new. This doubt and confusion in Christian souls must be resolved. Don't go into the palace, holy fathers. This has nothing to do with the tsarevnas—it's the tsars who should be here."

The fathers said to the delegates: "Let the patriarch testify to the books before the whole people. We shall not enter the palace." The delegates reported back to Khovansky and he urged Sophia to defer to the people's request. Sophia, however, adamantly refused to send the patriarch and the clergy out to the square in view of the recent acts of violence. Khovansky then began to insist that no member of the royal family be present in the Palace of Facets. He feared a fresh musketeer uprising and warned that the sovereigns would be in danger of their lives if they accompanied the patriarch to the palace.

But Sophia was in communication with the musketeers and was convinced that they had no intention of rebelling. She answered Khovansky calmly: "Let it be as God wills, but I will not desert the holy church and its pastor." Having failed to intimidate Sophia, Khovansky appealed to the boyars. "For God's sake, beg the tsarevna not to go to the palace with the patriarch otherwise they will all be killed before our very eyes." The terror-stricken boyars implored Sophia not to go to the Palace of Facets but she refused to listen to them. She sent a message to the patriarch advising him and the leading clergy to go to the palace by way of the staircase of the church of the Deposition of the Robe,[44] thus avoiding the Red Porch, where they could be in danger from the fanatics. The patriarch, faced with a situation from which he did not expect to emerge alive, made for the Palace of Facets with tears in his eyes. He ordered that ancient Greek and Slavonic books be carried through the Red Porch as a display of the church's bulwarks against those who rebelled. Whilst the men were trembling at the entrance to the palace, three women—Tsaritsa Natalia and Tsarevnas Tatiana Mikhailovna and Maria Alekseevna—had volunteered to accompany Sophia. The tsarevnas, the tsaritsa and the patriarch decided that the dissenters should be summoned to the Palace of Facets simply in order to read their petition.

Khovansky personally brought the decision to the "fathers." He said a prayer before the cross, the Gospels and the icons, bowed to the "fathers" and instructed them to proceed to the palace. "You have nothing to fear," he assured them. "The tsarevnas wish to hear the petition at once but they are reluctant to be seen out here. There is no time today to hold the confrontation or the testimony on Holy Scripture. It is too late for the court to consider these serious matters. The tsarevnas and the tsaritsa will hear your petition, then you will be dismissed."

Sergei replied: "Sir, we are afraid to go into the palace because they may be plotting some trick against us, as before. The patriarch must allow everyone to witness the proceedings but there won't be enough room for them in the palace. They will let us in and keep the people outside, but we have no business there without the people." "Anyone is free to enter the palace," said Khovansky. "If, holy fathers, you ever had any trust in my sinful soul, believe me now. I solemnly swear by the cross and blood of Christ that you will come to no harm. If anything amiss should happen, then may I suffer with you." Nikita said: "Father Sergei, I believe him," and Sergei relented. Khovansky returned to the palace, warning the dissenters not to enter without his leave. Back in the palace, Khovansky tried again to intimidate Sophia into not accompanying the patriarch to the Palace of Facets, but Joachim refused to go without the sovereigns and Sophia reaffirmed her intention not to desert the patriarch. Khovansky then sent the delegates to tell the fathers to come up.

The dissenters moved off carrying the cross, Gospels, icons, lecterns and candles. Khovansky was true to his word and ordered that they all be admitted to the palace except that Orthodox priests and laymen were denied entry and some even were driven away by force. One of the dissenters [Savva Romanov] left the following account: as the dissenters mounted the Red Porch they collided with priests running in the opposite direction from the Palace of Facets. There was a scuffle; one priest grabbed Nikita by the hair and the musketeers set about the priests with their fists and sent them flying in all directions. Hearing noise and shouting, Khovansky came running. The fathers protested to him that the priests were assaulting them and they pointed out the priest who had seized Nikita by the hair. Khovansky immediately ordered that this priest be tied up and taken to the Chancellery of Musketeers. He had the others thrown out of the palace; only a few were allowed to remain at the request of the prelates. He rebuked them soundly: "The scoundrels—behaving like drunkards in a tavern!" The fathers refused to go any further, complaining that they had been treated unjustly . Then Khovansky solemnly swore that they had nothing to fear and they set off again, accompanied by a great crowd of artisans.[45]

The dissenters entered the Palace of Facets noisily and set up their lecterns and candles as they had done on the square. Despite the fact that they were there to affirm the Old Belief and denounce all "innovations," they failed to notice the unprecedented sight that greeted them in the palace—the tsar's place was occupied by women! The maiden tsarevnas were showing themselves openly to the people and one of them was in charge of the proceedings, yet the dissenters failed to see this novelty as a sign of the times. Two tsarevnas—Sophia and her aunt, Tatiana—sat on the royal thrones. Below them, in armchairs, sat Tsaritsa Natalia, Tsarevna Maria and the patriarch; to the right stood the prelates of the church, to the left the secular officials, the courtiers and the musketeers' delegates.

The patriarch addressed the fathers. "Why have you come to the royal palace and what do want of us?"[46] Nikita replied: "We have come to complain to the sovereign tsars about the revision of the Orthodox faith; we demand our rightful confrontation with you, the new law-makers, and desire that the church of God enjoy peace and unity." The patriarch responded as he had done to the dissenters in his own residence. "The correction of ecclesiastical matters is no concern of yours. You must obey Holy Mother Church and the prelates, who are working for your salvation. Grammatical revisions were made in the books from the Greek originals and our own ancient texts, but you know nothing of grammar and are ignorant of its great importance."

"We are here to speak with you about church dogma, not about grammar," protested Nikita. He immediately asked the patriarch to explain why the prelates held the cross in their left hand and the candle in their right when blessing the congregation, evidently considering this to be a question of dogma. Bishop Afanasy of Kholmogory tried to reply on behalf of the patriarch but Nikita rushed at him with his arm raised, shouting: "Would you, the foot, set yourself higher than the head? I am speaking to the patriarch, not you." The musketeers' delegates quickly dragged Nikita away from the bishop. At this point there was an outburst from Sophia. She leapt to her feet and cried: "Do you see what Nikita is doing? He attacks a prelate of the church before our very eyes and would have killed him had we not been here." The dissenters voiced their objections. "No, sovereign lady, he didn't attack him, he only pushed him away." But Sophia continued: "What right have you, Nikita, to speak with his holiness the patriarch? You are unfit for our presence. Have you forgotten how you recanted before our father and the patriarch and the whole council of the church and swore on your oath never again to petition about the faith? Now you have broken that vow."

"I don't deny it," replied Nikita. "I recanted under threat of fire and sword but not one of the prelates was able to dispute the petition I presented to the council. Simeon Polotsky composed his tract *The Scepter of Government*[47] as an attack upon me, but not one fifth of it refutes my petition. If it pleases you, I am still prepared to dispute *The Scepter*. If I am proven guilty, do with me as you will." "You are not fit to speak with us and to stand in our presence," said Sophia and ordered that the petition be read out. When they came to the place where it was claimed that the heretical monk Arseny and Nikon had perverted Tsar Alexis's soul, Sophia could bear it no longer. Her eyes brimmed with tears and she leapt up and said: "If Arseny and Patriarch Nikon were heretics, so were our father and our brother. It means that the reigning tsars are not tsars, the patriarchs are not patriarchs and the prelates are not prelates. We have no desire to listen to such blasphemy and to hear our father and brother referred to as heretics. We shall all leave the country." With these words the tsarevna left her seat and stood a little way off. Khovansky, the boyars and the delegates cried out: "What reason is there for the sovereign tsars to leave the country? We are ready to lay down our lives for them." Other musketeers muttered: "It's high time you went to a nunnery, sovereign lady; you've caused the country enough trouble. May the sovereign tsars prosper, but we'll do well enough without you."

This did nothing to diminish the impression which Sophia's words made upon the delegates. "This has come about because everyone is afraid of you," the tsarevna told them. "These ignorant schismatics would never have the insolence to come here if they didn't rely on your support. You must have been out of your minds to come here with these rebellious ignoramuses, shouting and causing us so much vexation. How can you, loyal servants of our grandfather, father and brother, sympathize with these dissenters? You say that you are our loyal servants, too. Why, then, do you tolerate these dullards? It is impossible for the tsars and us to live here any longer if we are to be treated in this appalling manner. We shall go off to some other city and tell all the people about this insubordination and chaos."

Nothing was so calculated to terrify the musketeers as this threat that the tsars might leave Moscow. They were acutely aware that their behavior on May 15 had aroused strong displeasure amongst the powerful. They knew very well that the boyars hated them and thought of them as rebels and murderers, nor would the great army of service gentry, who always had disliked them, show any mercy once the crown commanded them to attack. So far they had remained safe; they had been allowed to terrorize the peaceful population of Moscow because they enjoyed the government's protection. But what would happen were the crown to desert them and leave Moscow? The delegates replied: "We are ready to serve the great sovereigns and you, sovereign ladies, loyally. We are ready to lay down our lives for the Orthodox faith, the church and your royal majesties and to do everything you command. You can see for yourselves, sovereign lady, that the people are confused and that a great crowd has gathered outside the palace. We will be lucky to survive the day without suffering at their hands. But God forbid that the great sovereigns and you, sovereign ladies, should leave the capital. Why should you?"

Sophia returned to her seat and the reading of the petition continued. Sophia continually intervened to take up various points with the schismatic monks. When the reading was over, the patriarch took the Gospels of Metropolitan Alexis[48] in one hand and the conciliar acts of Patriarch Jeremiah,[49] which contained the same formulation of the creed as the revised books, in the other. "These are old books," said Joachim, "yet we adhere to them faithfully." Yet the greatest impact was made by a priest who stepped forward with a tome printed in the days of Patriarch Filaret.[50] "Just see what's printed in your beloved Filaret's books. Meat may be eaten on the Thursday and Saturday of Holy Week!" exclaimed the priest. Nikita, who had been silent since Sophia's outburst, was infuriated but could only curse in vexation. "They were printed by scoundrels like yourselves," he said to the priest.

When the reading was concluded the schismatics were dismissed from the Palace of Facets. They left the Kremlin and stopped at the platform on Red Square where they again began to tell the people about the numerous heresies which the Nikonites had inserted into the holy books. They boasted of how they had outargued all the prelates of the church and put them to shame. From there they went across the Yauza river. A service was held in the church of the Savior in Chigasy, accompanied by the ringing of bells, whereupon the dissenters dispersed to their homes.

MUSKETEERS DESERT THE DISSENTERS

The people had not heard the fathers debating with the prelates, and those who had not made up their minds and wanted to "know the truth" were as bewildered as ever. The musketeers' delegates, who had vowed to find out the truth, had not been enlightened by Nikita and his companions in the Palace of Facets. Their entire attention had been captured by Sophia when she threatened to leave Moscow with the sovereigns because they could no longer tolerate the dissenters' riotous conduct. All blame then would fall on the musketeers, who were considered defenders of the schism. "Do not barter us and the whole Russian land in exchange for six monks. Do not profane his holiness the patriarch and the Holy Council," said Sophia. The delegates had replied: "The Old Belief is no concern of ours. It is a matter for his holiness the patriarch and the Holy Council."

The delegates were rewarded generously and fêted for these wise utterances. The rank and file created an uproar but were powerless to resist the royal wine cellar, where every ten men were treated to a bout of drinking. They pledged never again to defend the Old Belief. They turned on the dissenters, shouting: "You trouble-makers! You have thrown the whole country into confusion!" The dissenters made their escape as best they could. The "fathers" were arrested and Nikita was beheaded, for he was the ringleader of the disturbances and had broken his oath. Khovansky was unable to save him but he did succeed in reprieving Sergei who was exiled to the Savior monastery in Yaroslavl. He also won reprieves for the gardener Nikita Borisov and his comrades, who were exiled to the Terek. They had fled to Briansk and been captured there.

THE DISTURBANCES CONTINUE

The authorities had been forced to yield to Khovansky and this made them more angry than ever with the Braggart. His dealings with the dissenters and his indulgent treatment of them had been quite open; now he was accused of trying to promote the success of the schism by exterminating the patriarch and the leading clergy. But it was impossible to get at Khovansky and remove him from his command, for he had won the affection of the court infantry. At first Khovansky pampered the musketeers and satisfied their every whim because he hoped to win prominence and power by exploiting this army, which held Moscow and the government in a grip of terror. Now that, as a result of his actions on July 5, he had broken off with the court, Khovansky was obliged to pander to the musketeers' wishes in the interests of self-preservation, for his safety now depended entirely upon them.

To the tsars and the boyars he made his behavior out to be highly prudent. "Without me, Moscow would be knee-deep in blood," he warned them. The musketeers saw that they could do whatever they liked and that everyone was afraid of them. They behaved like conquerors, taking full advantage of the conquered yet, at the same time, they knew well that they were universally hated. Ever fearful of revenge, they were in a constant state of agitation and grew excited at every rumor of imminent retribution.

There were those who willingly exploited the musketeers' nervousness. On July 12 the musketeers demanded that the tsars hand over all boyars to them because the boyars apparently were intending to kill the musketeers by various methods of execution. The source of this rumor turned out to be the baptized Tatar prince, Matvei, who claimed to have heard it at the palace. The prince was sent to the torture chamber, where he confessed that he had heard nothing from the boyars but had fabricated the whole story. He received meager rations, held a lowly station and hoped his story would stir up trouble and make him famous.

The Tatar was quartered but the disturbances continued. An artisan from Yaroslavl called Biziaev reported evidence of treason and that he had heard in the courtyard of Boyar Prince Odoevsky that the boyars were devising every devious means for putting the musketeers to death. Under torture Biziaev confessed that he had fabricated the entire story in order to foment insurrection and burn down Moscow. He was beheaded but then a bondsman of Servitor Veshniakov reported that his master and his son, a former lieutenant colonel of musketeers, were mobilizing an army to attack the musketeers, hiring twenty boyar slaves to every musketeer. The old man Veshniakov died under torture and his son barely escaped with his life. Meanwhile the musketeers tortured and quartered one of their colonels, Yanov, for various offenses. The disturbances continued throughout the summer. On August 16 Khovansky presented a petition from the musketeers to the palace asking that for each man conscripted from a royal estate that estate make a special advance payment of twenty-five rubles. The boyars opposed this illegal demand. The regent was told that Khovansky had gone out to the musketeers and said: "Children, now the boyars are even threatening me for wishing you well. There is nothing I can do—act as you wish."

Some care is needed with the choice of expression—"the regent was told that Khovansky said"—for the information is found in a work[51] which clearly aimed at establishing Khovansky's guilt. Still, it should be noted that the words are in keeping with the Braggart's character and situation. Whether Khovansky made the statement in question and the exact words he used are irrelevant. What matters is that this statement, a direct call to rebellion, was reported to the palace and the musketeers did indeed become agitated and unruly, and made outrageous demands. They held the government and the people of Muscovy in a constant state of alarm, making the position of everyone intolerable.

Sophia and Miloslavsky had used the musketeers to seize power but Khovansky had crossed them, mastered the musketeers, won their affection and was preparing to use them against Sophia and Miloslavsky. The latter knew from their own experience the full temptation of Khovansky's position and could hardly expect him to retreat or step aside to make way for them. Not surprisingly, the palace authorities believed each and every rumor about Khovansky's schemes, including the one that he intended to seize the throne on claim of his royal descent from Gedimin, and that he wished as well to forge a link with the Russian dynasty by marrying his son to Tsarevna Ekaterina Alekseevna. Miloslavsky's behavior is indicative of the credulity of the palace authorities. Fearing that he was destined to be the first victim of a musketeer uprising in support of Khovansky, just as Matveev had been the first victim of the uprising supporting him, he left Moscow and went into hiding in the vicinity of the capital, moving from one place to the next "like a mole," as one contemporary observer[52] expressed it. In an attempt to protect himself he continued to intrigue against Khovansky and urged Sophia to take decisive measures against him.

THE COURT DEPARTS MOSCOW

Sophia needed no persuasion for she was in an intolerable position, totally at the mercy of the musketeers and Khovansky. She had no choice but to carry out the threat she had used to frighten the musketeers' delegates on July 5, namely to leave Moscow and "tell the people about this insubordination and chaos." The regent was forced to act quickly by rumors about the schemes of Khovansky and the musketeers, and by the Braggart's actual behavior.

On August 19 the customary religious procession should have taken place from the Dormition cathedral in the Kremlin to the Donskoy monastery,[53] in commemoration of the salvation of the capital from a Tatar raid during Fedor Ivanovich's reign. The sovereigns were to have observed the custom of following the crosses on foot as far as the monastery, but rumors that the musketeers intended to kill them forced them to abandon the procession and the next day, August 20, the whole royal family left for Kolomenskoe.[54] The musketeers were alarmed by the tsars' departure from Moscow, fearing that they intended to mobilize the service gentry to attack them.

On August 23 all regiments sent delegates to Kolomenskoe to make the following appeal: "It has been reported to the great sovereigns that we, the court infantry, are plotting rebellion and that we harbor evil intentions against the boyars and privy councillors. It is said that the regiments secretly are devising a plan to take up arms and march once again on the Kremlin, and that this is why it pleases the great sovereigns to depart from Moscow. But none of the regiments are devising any such plot, nor do they have any intention of doing so. May it please the great sovereigns to give no credence to these false rumors and to return to Moscow."

The reply stated that: "The great sovereigns have not heard of any such plan. They deigned to leave Moscow of their own royal accord as, indeed, it has often pleased them to visit Kolomenskoe in the past." The delegates were duly dismissed. The musketeers were reassured, for the tsars observed the normal procedure and remained in Kolomenskoe, awaiting the customary time for continuing their pilgrimage.

In the meantime Khovansky, true to form, took it into his head to frighten Sophia into acknowledging how much she needed the musketeers and, consequently, him. He went to Kolomenskoe and said, in the presence of the boyars: "Some Novgorod servitors have been to see me to say that their comrades plan to come to Moscow this summer to claim their service allowances. They intend to exterminate everybody, quite indiscriminately and to the last man." "This should be made known to men of all ranks from the porch of the bedchamber in Moscow," responded Sophia, "and a rescript should be sent to Novgorod on behalf of the great sovereigns in order to obtain an accurate report."

Khovansky took fright, imploring the tsarevna not to take such measures and make trouble for him. On the elder tsar's name day, August 29, the regent wrote to Khovansky and instructed him to send the royal bodyguard to Kolomenskoe. Khovansky was afraid of this regiment because it was very loyal to the sovereigns and more subservient to the regent than others. He was afraid that by sending it to Kolomenskoe he would be delivering it into Sophia's hands and providing her with the means of influencing other regiments, and so he disobeyed the order and did not send the regiment to Kolomenskoe. Previously he had even considered sending it to Kiev without the tsars' orders! Only after the order had been repeated several times did Khovansky finally dispatch the royal bodyguard.

September 1 arrived and with it the New Year festivities,[55] when, by tradition, the tsars were expected to be present in the Kremlin. The tsars did not return to Moscow, but instructed Khovansky to attend the celebrations: Khovansky did not go. The patriarch was very angry because the occasion fell flat; only one representative of the aristocracy, a lord-in-waiting, was present. Attendance was poor even among the common people, who had been alarmed by the constant rumors that a musketeer uprising was likely to occur on this or some other feast day. Yet the unarmed people's dread of the musketeers was matched by the musketeers' own dismay at the rumors that the boyars' servants intended to seek their revenge on this or some other feast day by attacking them when they came out on guard duty, and killing their wives and children. Khovansky's carriage was constantly surrounded by about fifty musketeers and his home guarded by about a hundred.

EXECUTION OF THE KHOVANSKYS

On the next day, September 2, the tsars left Kolomenskoe for the village of Vorobievo. On September 4 they left Vorobievo for Pavlovskoe and on September 6 they went to the monastery of St. Sabbas.[56] On September 10 they celebrated the festival of St. Savva the Miracle Worker and returned to Pavlovskoe that same day. On September 12 they travelled to the village of Khliabovo and on the 13th they went to Vozdvizhenskoe to attend the local festival.[57] After mass on September 14 the sovereigns issued a decree that all boyars, lords-in-waiting, members of the council, table attendants, crown agents, Muscovite servitors and court attendants come to Vozdvizhenskoe by September 18 to attend to their business with the crown and welcome Semen, the hetman's son.[58] Semen was received by the great sovereigns on September 16. On September 17, Sophia's name day, many aristocrats and courtiers swarmed into Vozdvizhenskoe and it was reported that Khovansky and his son Andrei were also on their way from Moscow. After mass Sophia ordered that the boyars, lords-in-waiting and crown councillors be treated to vodka in celebration of her name day.

When they had drunk the vodka a serious conference took place between the tsars and their sister and the boyars. A crown secretary delivered a report: "It has come to the attention of the great sovereigns that Boyar Prince Ivan Khovansky, director of the Chancellery of the Court Infantry, and his son, Boyar Prince Andrei, from the High Court, did many things without the great sovereigns' leave, acting of their own self-will, even contrary to the great sovereigns' decree. By their insubordinate and willful acts they have brought dishonor to the great sovereigns and inflicted great damage, destruction and distress upon the state. On September 2, at the time of the great sovereigns' sojourn in Kolomenskoe, an anonymous letter was found by the front gates of the royal residence, denouncing Prince Ivan and Prince Andrei. In it a Muscovite musketeer and two artisans gave the following indictment of those scoundrels and traitors Prince Ivan and his son Andrei: 'In the past few weeks they summoned us, nine men from the Court Infantry and five artisans, to their house and told us to help them gain control of the Muscovite realm. They commanded us to persuade our comrades to destroy your royal line, to assemble a great mob to take the city by storm and to pronounce you, the sovereigns, to be the children of heretics and to kill both of you, Tsaritsa Natalia, Tsarevna Sophia, the patriarch and all prelates of the church. Prince Andrei was to marry one tsarevna and the others were to take the veil and be banished to distant nunneries. The following boyars were to be killed: the three Odoevskys, two Cherkasskys, three Golitsyns, Ivan Miloslavsky, two Sheremetevs and many other boyars who hate the Old Belief and subscribe to the new. When these evil deeds had been carried out, messengers were to be sent to all towns and villages of the Muscovite realm to spread confusion and to incite the townsmen to kill the governors and crown officials and the peasants to kill their boyar landlords and the boyars' bondslaves. And when the country was in turmoil, Prince Khovansky would be elected to the Muscovite throne and the people would choose a patriarch and ecclesiastical dignitaries who love the old books.'"[59]

When they heard this letter, the great sovereigns and their sister decreed and the boyars resolved: "On the evidence of genuine inquiry and patent testimony and actions and this letter of indictment, let them be put to death." Boyar Prince Lykov and a large detachment of courtiers immediately were sent along the road to Moscow to intercept the Khovanskys and arrest them. Lykov found the elder Khovansky in a tent by the village of Pushkino. He was swiftly arrested and taken off under guard together with several of the musketeers' delegates. Prince Andrei was arrested not far from there on his estate on the Kliazma river near Moscow.

When news of the Khovanskys' arrest reached Vozdvizhenskoe, instructions were sent to Lykov that he should stop with them at the entrance to the royal residence and read them out the death sentence. The boyars, lords-in-waiting and crown councillors came out and sat on benches in front of the gates. Crown Secretary Shaklovity[60] from the Chancellery of Crown Service and Appointments read out the charges. Khovansky was accused of distributing large sums of public money without the sovereigns' decree; he had allowed men of all ranks to enter the royal chamber, quite without awe and in a fashion which would be considered rude and arrogant even in the homes of common folk. He quite wrongfully detained many people behind bars and under guard in his chancellery and he fined many people without benefit of formal testimony or hearing. He signed a petition on behalf of conscripts for whom he demanded special advanced payments from the palace estates and when this petition was rejected he made all manner of boasts and angrily vowed that this rejection would end in bloodshed. He enumerated his services before the sovereigns and boyars with great pride, as though no one else had ever rendered such services. He said: "Without me, Moscow will be knee-deep in blood." Both father and son on numerous occasions acted contrary to the sovereigns' decree and the Code of Laws, contradicting the sovereigns rudely and noisily in their own chambers. They treated the boyars with disrespect and as inferiors, threatening many with death. Prince Ivan joined the dissenters in their struggle against Holy Church and then saved the lives of the rebels against the church's authority. He flouted the tsars' decree by failing to send the infantry regiments to attack the Kalmyks and Bashkirs. On several occasions he disobeyed the great sovereigns' orders. He slandered the Novgorod servitors by accusing them of plotting to attack Moscow. He slandered the Court Infantry by accusing them of plotting great mischief and delivered many inflammatory speeches to them. In conclusion the secretary read out the anonymous letter.

The Khovanskys did not listen to the charges in silence. They tried to vindicate themselves, tearfully begging that "their honors the boyars must take heed and learn about the real instigators of the musketeer rebellion, those who had planned the whole thing, and that their majesties the tsars should grant them a formal confrontation and not put innocent men to death so hastily." "If my son is guilty of all the charges against him, I shall consign him to perdition," said the elder Khovansky. When Miloslavsky reported all this to the tsarevna she sent back instructions that the sentence be carried out immediately. As no executioner was available, a musketeer from the royal bodyguard beheaded the Khovanskys *on the square by the great Moscow road.* This was how the tsarevna celebrated her name day!

That same day a rescript was written and dispatched to the Court Infantry in Moscow, informing them of the execution of their commander and his son. "Take heed of their patent treachery and give no credence to false and artful reports and writings. You have no need to fear our disfavor or wrath: rest assured that we are not angry with you." That day, however, Khovansky's other son, Prince Ivan, escaped from Vozdvizhenskoe. He reached Moscow that night and told the musketeers that his father had been captured in the village of Pushkino by the boyars' servants and put to death without the sovereigns' leave. It was reported in the Lopukhin regiment by Grigory Yazykov, son of Lord-in-waiting Pavel Yazykov, that the boyars Odoevsky and Golitsyn planned to mobilize a large army to overwhelm the Court Infantry. Men of all ranks and the boyars' slaves, all armed, were forming pickets along the roads and were preparing to enter Moscow, attack the musketeers and burn their homes. The Court Infantry were advised to barricade themselves in Moscow.

THE SERVICE GENTRY SUMMONED

The advice was swiftly acted upon. The most natural response to this terrible news was to take up arms and assume a defensive position, and so the musketeers occupied the Kremlin, took guns, powder and lead from the arsenal, posted guards everywhere and prepared for a siege, allowing no one to enter or leave Moscow. They called for an attack upon the boyars and thronged around the residence of the patriarch, who tried to dissuade them from their headstrong action. They threatened to kill him if he stood up for the boyars but went no further than threats and shouts. The widespread feeling of panic also gripped the soldiers of the Butyrsky regiment, who had taken part in the earlier musketeer disturbances.

On September 20 two soldiers and their horses were lost in the Marina Grove and the others, already nervous and apprehensive, removed four cannon from the arsenal. On the evening of September 24 a peasant named Voronin warned the Butyrsky regiment that an immense force of boyars' men, mounted and on foot, was advancing along the road from the Trinity monastery with weapons and cannon. They were heading for the royal village of Taininskoe and could be expected to reach the Butyrsky settlement by the night of September 25. The soldiers were horror-stricken and sent their wives and children to relatives in Moscow. News of the musketeers' disturbances had reached Vozdvizhenskoe on September 18 and the authorities had acted. Courtiers hastened to the neighboring towns to call the military servitors to arms and order them to assemble at the Trinity monastery. The court then removed itself to the monastery, which had been made ready for a siege. The regent's loyal servant Prince Vasily Golitsyn was put in charge of the operation.

On September 19 Archimandrite Adrian of the Miracles monastery arrived at the Trinity monastery with a message from the patriarch, who reported that the Court Infantry had appealed to him to beg the great sovereigns to return to Moscow and to assure them that they, the Court Infantry, were plotting no mischief. The tsars returned a rescript by special messenger calling upon the musketeers to honor their vow of service, desist from all trouble-making and stop terrorizing the capital. It stated that the Khovanskys had been executed for treason and the musketeers must not concern themselves with this matter. The great sovereigns meted out either punishment or mercy as God moved them: it did not behoove the musketeers to speak of this or even think about it. They, the musketeers, had not earned the tsars' disfavor or aroused their wrath; they should rest assured of the tsars' benevolence. Those who were assigned to serve in Kiev must demonstrate their loyalty by departing without delay. Any matters which they wished to raise should be transmitted through their elected representatives.

MUSKETEERS AND SOLDIERS BEG FORGIVENESS

The rapid convergence of bands of military servitors on the Trinity monastery allowed the regent to act more decisively. Boyar Michael Petrovich Golovin was sent to take command of the capital and to make it clear to the musketeers that they were no longer feared. This move and the news of the mobilization of the servitors at the Trinity monastery struck even more fear into the Court Infantry. The musketeers wept like children. On September 22 they appealed to Golovin to inform the tsars that they wished to submit a petition, which would be delivered by as many delegates as the authorities stipulated, for they feared to come without permission.

The reply came back immediately, summoning twenty men from each regiment. On September 24 the musketeers asked the patriarch to send a prelate of the church to accompany their delegates to the Trinity monastery as they were afraid that they would be executed if they went alone. The patriarch sent Metropolitan Ilarion of Suzdal but even this did not allay their fears completely. Some were so terrified that they fled back to Moscow; the rest were presented to Sophia on September 24. She greeted them with a stern reproval for their behavior and told them of the large army which had assembled to punish them. The musketeers presented her with a written testimony: "Our grandfathers, fathers, uncles and brothers and we ourselves have served the sovereigns and still serve them, faithfully carrying out their royal behests, and we shall be glad to serve resolutely in the future. Should we hear that one of our own men or some person of another rank is plotting against their majesties, the boyars, the crown councillors and the privy councillors, we shall seize them and detain them to await the sovereigns' decree when they return to Moscow from their pilgrimage. We have no criminal intent nor are we plotting anything. The munitions which we took—guns, powder and lead—are intact in our regiments. The men ordered to go to Kiev are ready to leave."

CONDITIONS OF PARDON

The affair did not end there. The regent agreed to pardon the musketeers and soldiers only on the following conditions:[61] (1) They were to devote their lives to atoning for their recent crimes; they were to think no evil, plot no more rebellion nor incite others to rebel; they were not to join with dissenters or other criminals; they must not gather in the city in armed bands as they had before or form assemblies in the cossack manner. (2) They were to arrest and bring to the Chancellery of the Court Infantry anyone who uttered abuse against the sovereigns, boyars and other officials, and any subversive and seditious letters they found also must be brought there. (3) They must not approach the authorities in noisy, ill-mannered mobs. (4) They were to refrain from settling their own disputes, acting in an unruly fashion and pillaging; they were to obey their officers. (5) The guns and all munitions taken on September 18 must be returned at once to their proper place. (6) They must proceed promptly to wheresoever or whomsoever they were ordered to serve. (7) They must not confiscate other people's homes nor should they provoke servants and peasants to join the infantry and seek their freedom, nor should they call them their relatives. (8) No one must be conscripted into the Butyrsky infantry regiment or into the Court Infantry without the proper authority; the children of infantrymen and musketeers below the age of seventeen whose fathers were still alive should be discharged from the infantry and musketeer regiments and considered as minors until they reached age seventeen; until then they should live with their fathers. All slaves, peasants and vagrants recruited into the infantry and Court Infantry regiments during the recent disturbances were to be discharged and given over to service and hereditary landlords under contract of bondage. Vagrants must be registered and returned to their former place of residence; they should not be allowed to remain in Moscow lest they turn to crime. (9) They must not concern themselves with the Khovansky affair.

On Sunday, October 8, the patriarch celebrated mass in the Dormition cathedral, which was packed out with musketeers. After the service two lecterns were set up in front of the altar and on one was laid the Gospels, on the other the hand of the Apostle Andrew the First-Called.[62] The patriarch came out and delivered a sermon on peace and love, then the conditions which the crown had imposed upon the Court Infantry were read out. The musketeers kissed the Gospels and the hand of the apostle and received the conditions from the patriarch. They vowed to wish the sovereigns well and to lay down their lives for them without hesitation. They handed over Ivan Khovansky to Golovin, and he was sent to the Trinity monastery. He was sentenced to death and laid upon the block but the death sentence was commuted at the last moment to one of exile.

THE MUSKETEERS ADMIT THEIR GUILT

October came to an end and the court still resided at the Trinity monastery, surrounded by the service gentry regiments. At last the musketeers decided of their own accord, or were compelled, to take the most difficult step of all, to renounce the events of May 15 and acknowledge them to have been an act of sedition and not a feat of heroism as first claimed. The musketeers presented a petition: "For our sins we inflicted a massacre upon the boyars, councillors and other officials upon Red Square and in so doing we, your slaves, enraged God and you, the great sovereigns. At the instigation of the rogue and dissenter Alesha Yudin and his friends and goaded into all manner of evil by the man we called our father, Prince Ivan Khovansky, and his son Andrei, the regiments of the Court Infantry presented a petition in which we concealed our criminal actions and entreated you, the great sovereigns, to grant us charters ensuring that no one should ever call us rogues or rebels; and these charters of privileges were granted. At the instigation of that same Yudin and Khovansky we requested that a column be set up on Red Square and inscribed with the crimes of those who had perished; and this column was erected. And now, conscious that our petition was unjustified and that column inappropriate, we implore you to hear the plea of your guilty slaves and order that the column be removed from Red Square lest the capital city of Moscow earn the contempt of other nations."[63]

The column was removed and a new charter of privileges issued to the musketeers and soldiers, declaring that the musketeers and soldiers had been made rebellious by the nefarious design of the Princes Khovansky, Alesha Yudin and their confederates and in the course of their rebellion they had killed boyars and other officials. Khovansky and Yudin had been executed for their crime on September 17 and the musketeers and soldiers had presented written confessions of their guilt. The great sovereigns, seeing their tears, had forgiven their crime, forbidding anyone to refer to them as rogues or traitors. They were to receive their full yearly allowance without deductions or formalities, and there were to be no illegal appropriations by government officials; travelling expenses were to be added and no deductions were to be made for various regimental requirements, nor were they to work for their superiors.

SHAKLOVITY COMMANDS THE MUSKETEERS

Now that the musketeers had confessed their guilt the court returned to Moscow on November 6. Their most urgent task was to find a director for the Chancellery of Musketeers (the title of Court Infantry was dropped). Lord-in-waiting Vedenikht Zmeev held this vital position temporarily, but in December a more trustworthy successor was found in Crown Secretary Fedor Leontievich Shaklovity. The new director's firmness soon was put to the test. On December 26 a band of musketeers from the Bokhin regiment was led to the chancellery by Ivan Pelepelnik and Fedor Voron. They rudely and noisily demanded that a number of their fellows be transferred to another regiment. When the musketeers learned that their petition was unnecessary as the transfer had taken place, they went away but were soon back, shouting for the handover of Brigadier Borisov and Kondratiev, the chancellery warden. They were told that this was impossible but that a royal decree for a trial would be issued. The musketeers continued their protest, shouting that they were there at the request of the whole regiment. Shaklovity had the trouble-makers arrested and detained in the chancellery. Shortly afterwards there was another disturbance in the same regiment. The musketeer Ivan Zhareny was summoned for interrogation at the chancellery but when a lieutenant arrived to arrest him, his comrades intervened to protect him. "We would sooner all be put to death than give up Ivashka!" they shouted. In the end two regiments of musketeers came and arrested Ivan, along with four of the ringleaders and put them all to death. When the musketeers of the Bokhin regiment came to beg forgiveness, they learned that as punishment for their crime they were to forfeit the right to perform guard duty in the palace and their charter of privileges was to be confiscated. Not long afterwards, however, they were given an absolute pardon.

MEASURES AGAINST REBELLION

The government took prompt measures to wipe out all traces of the rebellion. On February 13, 1683 a decree was issued: "Those slaves who were intimidated into accepting charters of manumission from the boyars during the recent troubles and then importuned other landlords with these charters and gave themselves into bondage, shall be restored to their former masters; henceforth such charters of manumission shall be deemed invalid, for they were taken out in troubled times, involuntarily and under threat of violence. When these slaves are returned they shall be punished severely and flogged mercilessly. If their former masters refuse to take them back, they shall be sent into life-long exile in Siberia and other far-off regions."

When news reached Moscow of the spread of disturbances in other provinces, the following decree was issued on May 21: "It has come to the attention of the great sovereigns that residents and travellers in the towns are speaking approvingly of the recent troubles and uttering other abuses with the aim of fomenting rebellion and subverting the people. Therefore in all town and urban districts let this strict decree be observed on pain of death, and let heralds proclaim that men of all ranks are forbidden to condone the recent uprising, to abuse the authorities and engage in subversive activities."

DISTURBANCES IN THE UKRAINE AND ON THE DON

The rebellion naturally had serious repercussions in the cossack territories of the south. The musketeers in southern Pereiaslavl revolted against their colonels. They seized the tavern and installed a rank-and-file musketeer in the government office to deal with all business. They dismissed their brigadiers and corporals and nearly killed one brigadier; they found replacements and sent twenty men to Moscow with a petition. The hetman wrote to the tsars: "I venture to inform your majesties that I have been overcome by such misfortunes that I scarcely have the strength to continue. The actions of the musketeers in Pereiaslavl are highly detrimental to our local people, amongst whom there are a number of old troublemakers."

In Konotop Afanasy Beliaev, a merchant from Putivl, reported that the tsars' troops were gathering secretly outside Putivl. They were going to convoke an assembly, invite Hetman Samoilovich to attend it or take him by force, and kill all commanding officers of the Host and the landlords.

In the summer of 1683 it was learned in Moscow that a monk called Joseph was distributing treasonous forged letters on the Don. Taras Ivanov, an interpreter from the Chancellery of Foreign Affairs, was sent at once to demand that the monk be arrested. An assembly was convened; on Ataman Frol Minaev's instructions, the lieutenants told their men that the monk and his accomplices must be discovered and delivered to the great sovereigns in Moscow. No mercy must be shown to the wrongdoers. Some of the cossacks argued that there was no point in pursuing the monk, for he was simple minded and could not have composed the letter himself. They should track down the real villains who had deceived the monk and given him the letter—Kuzemka Kosoi and the musketeer Kostka who lived at the mouth of the Medveditsa river. The monk could be found on the Northern Donets river.

Others were of a different opinion. Cossack Fomka Savostianov asked: "What's the use of tracking down these criminals? Where shall we find them?" Pashka Chekunov added: "Why send them to Moscow? Moscow has enough carnage already." The ataman and officers intervened: "Why do you stand up for these scoundrels? Why shouldn't we catch them and send them to Moscow? Or do you view the sovereigns' favor and allowance so disdainfully?"

The officers then went to see Taras Ivanov in private. "You can see what our people are like and the sort of criminals they support. Why isn't there a clause in the tsars' rescript giving us the right to track down these criminals and put them to death? We should carry out the sentence immediately. On the Don we are plagued by criminals, men who have been engaged in schismatic activities in Moscow and musketeers who have been punished for various crimes by flogging and having their feet, noses and ears cut off and then exiled to the new town of Polatov—they come to the Don and engage in villainous schemes and disturbances. Why, since your arrival seven such criminals have come from Polatov. Take Samoil Lavrentiev—he's an old cossack, but admits such criminals into his home and loans them boats and weapons. Tell Boyar Vasily Vasilievich Golitsyn that they should stop exiling these criminals to towns in the vicinity of the Don because they leave their towns of exile and come here to spread their villainy and rebelliousness. The cossack assemblies have begun to dispute the tsars' decrees and business; they treat the criminals with indulgence and protest loudly. I myself, my officers and good cossacks are unable to speak: if we did they would kill us all."

When he had spoken to the tsars' emissary the ataman ordered his lieutenants to announce that the criminals must be found: anyone who volunteered to track them down would receive a reward from the Host. Three cossacks stepped forward. "We are ready to serve God and the great sovereigns," they said. "We shall pursue the criminals—no reward is necessary." The ataman replied: "You shall have your reward. Prepare to leave. Each man will receive four rubles."

The emissary learned that the forged letter had been written in the name of Tsar Ivan Alekseevich, who commanded the cossacks to go to Moscow because his boyars were disobedient to him, their sovereign, and did not pay him proper respect. The letter contained many other quite unrepeatable utterances and a lot of abuse against the patriarch and the prelates. The seal on the letter was red, but not the royal one; very likely it came from some monastery. When the letter had been read out to the assembly, many "reckless" cossacks and exiled criminals began to clamor about going to Moscow but Minaev and the officers told them that it was a forgery and they should not be taken in by it. There was no royal seal attached, and if it had been genuine the great sovereigns would certainly have chosen some high official to deliver it, not some thieving monk. The criminals were annoyed by the words of Frol Minaev, Ivan Semenov and a number of other old cossacks and wanted to kill them. Ivan Semenov was obliged to give up his command and Minaev remained in his barracks for about two weeks for fear that the criminals might kill him.

Just before Taras's departure, Minaev and other leading cossacks told him in confidence: "Tell Prince Vasily Golitsyn that all the trouble on the Don is caused by the dissenters who live along the Khoper and Medveditsa rivers. The worst culprits are the monks Anthony and Pafnuty and the exiles who have fled to the Don from the frontier towns." On the Don only Kostka Leontiev subsequently was found guilty and sent to Moscow with the forged letters.

The activities of the dissenters were not the only thing to disturb the Don region—there were also distinct echoes of the Razin rebellion.[64] In 1683 Ataman Maksim Skalozub agreed to make a raid along the Volga with volunteer troops to root out some restive Kalmyk chieftans. But instead of attacking the Kalmyks, he attacked Tsaritsyn and was driven back after a fierce battle in which many government troops perished. Frol Minaev informed Golitsyn in secret that the Muscovite government must not make any concessions to Skalozub lest many more cossacks join him. "There are many outlaws in our area at the moment," said Minaev, "but we are unable to keep them in check, for all we officers have been overtaxed by the activities of this riff-raff. Concessions were made to the rebel Stenka Razin and he was spoiled by them, but Skalozub will find no refuge when he goes down the Volga; he will soon be done for, because he will be prevented from entering the Yaik and other places."

Skalozub's plan failed. In Moscow Shaklovity energetically hounded the musketeers. On December 30, 1683 he reported to the tsars and tsarevnas that, in order to avert another rebellion, it would be advisable to banish a number of musketeers from Moscow, especially some natives of Astrakhan. The government followed his advice.

III

THE REGENCY OF TSAREVNA SOPHIA

POLISH PLANS FOR REBELLION IN THE UKRAINE

The Moscow rebellion had its repercussions in the cossack lands to the south. The news also caused a stir abroad, giving encouragement to Russia's enemies, especially the Poles, who hoped that the uprising would provide them with an opportunity to seize the Ukraine. With this aim in mind the king instructed the Polish hetman, Stanislaw Jablonowski, to send subversive letters to Grigory Doroshenko and Solonina, the former colonel of Kiev. The letters were smuggled into the Ukraine by two monks, who had been sent there by Bishop Joseph Shumliansky of Lwów, who himself hoped to become metropolitan of Kiev in the event of the Ukraine being wrested from Muscovy. The monks had with them a list of "instructions" as a guide to the propaganda which they should disseminate in the Ukraine.

(1) They should begin their campaign in Poltava, where the local people were especially receptive to the idea of rebellion against Moscow.

(2) They were to make it known that Samoilovich[1] intended to exterminate the cossacks and had demoted the leading colonels to the ranks in order to secure his aim.

(3) Muscovy was awash in its own blood. This was God's punishment for the Russians' failure to come to the aid of the emperor, who was now being robbed of the rest of Hungary by the sultan, and for failing to help Poland. Tsar Fedor had wished to assist the Poles, but the boyars had prevented him. They had even poisoned his wife, who bore the Polish name Gruszecki, and then murdered the tsar himself and would, no doubt, have wiped out the entire royal family. For this God had wreaked a cruel vengeance upon them.

(4) An alliance between Muscovy and Poland not only would have released Christian souls from captivity and allowed the holy places to flourish again, but also might have secured the liberation of the entire Greek nation.

(5) Moscow had deceived the Poles and was responsible for the fall of Kamieniec and the loss of Podolia and the Ukraine.

(6) Both the late King Michael and the reigning King Jan of Poland[2] tried consistently to defend the Ukraine against the Turks and to safeguard the rights of the cossacks; as everyone knew, after the Truce of Zórawno Khmelnitsky had been made hetman in Nemirov, but the Muscovite boyars, alarmed by their failure to hold and defend Chigirin, ceded the whole of the Ukraine as far as the Dnieper to the Turks. The vizier had fled the city, but Romodanovsky failed to consolidate his victory by attacking him. The cession of the Ukraine to the Turks had cut off Zaporozhie; its imminent destruction was certain and the cossack reputation would perish with it.

(7) They should beware of a Russian assault on Kiev and Turkish raids on lands across the Dnieper once they got news of the rebellion in Moscow.

(8) It was bad enough that the Moscow council had refused to fight the Muslims, but they had even refused to allow the king to hire cossack mercenaries for fear that the Cossack Host and the Little Russian people might return to the sovereign of their ancestors and come to admire the freedom that the Poles enjoyed.

(9) The Host, famed throughout Christendom, should be mindful of the glory of its forefathers, follow the lead of Zaporozhie and rid itself of an

unworthy and unwarlike man. The king of Poland was wise and coura-
geous and, with God's blessing, he was well able to defend a people whom
he had loved and respected since infancy.

(10) The clergy was to be reassured that the churches in the king's domains had not been violated. The priests were treated with respect; they
had been granted exemption from taxes and transport obligations and had
been released from the jurisdiction of their landlords.

(11) The clergy was to be made aware of the advantages of having its
own leader in Kiev, just as Moscow had. The metropolitans of Moscow
now called themselves patriarchs, but it was the metropolitan of Kiev who
first ordained them. The cathedral of the Holy Wisdom in Kiev was many
centuries older than the Dormition cathedral in Moscow.[3]

(12) They should be made to see the value of having their own spiritual
and temporal authorities in Kiev, rather than truckling to Muscovite rule.

(13) The old landlords would not return to the left bank of the Dnieper;
they should have no fears on that score. None of them was left alive and
the young nobles were unfamiliar with the lands across the Dnieper and
the Seversk region.

(14) Besides, the landed estates were crown property, granted to their
owners on a conditional basis, and the Commonwealth would not restore
the former landlords.

(15) The entire cossack people must realize that God was offering them
a father, enlightening their understanding, opening their eyes, and showing them the road to freedom.

(16) It should be made known that the whole Polish army was on the
alert and ready to come to their assistance whenever the need arose.

The monks coated one set of these instructions in wax and hid it in a
tar barrel, and concealed the other in a cushion at the back of their carriage.
In addition to the items listed in the instructions, the monks had been told
to spread the word that the man who brought the people under the king's
rule would win fame and riches. The common people would receive an
annual allowance of money and cloth from the king's treasury. Polish
landlords would not be installed on Ukrainian properties and the king
planned to establish a separate Russian palatinate of Kiev.

PRINCE VASILY GOLITSYN AND HIS POLICIES

News that the Moscow rebellion had ended soon reached the Ukraine
and Poland. Despite its strange form, the new government was reported

to be quite strong, thanks to the men from whom Sophia drew her support. Shaklovity had gained a firm grip on the Moscow musketeers, but it was Prince Vasily Golitsyn, a man more distinguished than the low-born newcomer Shaklovity, who had risen to become the leading figure in the tsarevna's government.[4] On October 19, 1683 the title borne by Ordin-Nashchokin and Matveev[5] was conferred upon Golitsyn: guardian of the great royal seal and the crown's ambassadorial affairs. Golitsyn's first duty now was to defend Russia's interests in its relations with foreign powers. This was a heavy responsibility in the climate of the time, but one which Golitsyn was capable of discharging to the honor and profit of the realm. Russia had long lived in the East, but now that it was forging a new path towards the West and preparing to enter the community of European nations, a series of events was taking place in Europe destined to transform its politics and lend the new state of Russia a leading role in European affairs.

The sharpest distinction between the ancient and modern worlds is that in antiquity states lived their own separate, individual lives, without common ties or interests. This meant that when one state grew strong because conditions favored its aggrandizement or because it produced a conquering ruler of outstanding ability, such a ruler had no trouble in subjugating other states, which were weak in their isolation. It became quite feasible for many states to be absorbed by one, and for vast world-wide empires, like those of Persia, Macedonia and Rome, to be formed. In modern Christian Europe, however, a number of states emerged almost simultaneously, all equal in strength and vitality; from the beginning they shared a common existence and common interests. Conditions did not favor the expansion of one state at the expense of another and it became impossible for one nation or one ruler to indulge a lust for conquest by establishing vast, world-wide monarchies. The emergence of such ambitions in a nation or state quickly resulted in the formation of alliances between other states, which were well accustomed to co-operation, and in combination they were able to thwart the schemes of a seeker after power. This is why European governments were ever vigilant and grew immediately suspicious when they observed the expansion of any one state and therein lies the source of the balance of power system.

At the beginning of the so-called modern period of European history the house of Habsburg increased its power by a series of advantageous

marriages and began to threaten Europe through its expansionist ambitions. Marriage as a means of securing power was also a new European
phenomenon, unknown to the ancient world, which had understood only
the use of force as a means to this end. The Habsburgs' new stratagem
was destined to lead to exactly the same results as the old methods and
culminate in the formation of a vast empire which threatened the independence of the other states of Europe. France found itself in a particularly
difficult position, surrounded as it was on almost all sides by the domains
of the Habsburgs. To the south was Spain, to the north the Netherlands,
which belonged to Spain, and to the east Germany, which was ruled by
the Habsburg emperor. A large part of Italy also belonged to Spain, which
was held in awe because of its invincible armies. In such a situation France
acted from an instinct of self-preservation and used all means at its disposal to undermine the power of the Habsburgs, which was threatening to
overwhelm it. At a time when religious interests predominated, when an
embittered struggle was being waged between Catholics and Protestants,
France was the first country to cast aside religious considerations and act
primarily on a political basis. The sole aim of France was to smash the
power of the Habsburgs, and to this end Paris sought alliances with anyone,
regardless of religious differences. This was the basis of all French foreign
policy, a principle to which Francis I, Henri IV and Cardinal Richelieu
all faithfully adhered. France, a Catholic power, entered into permanent
alliance with Protestant states against the Habsburgs, and the king of
France, who bore the title "Most Christian," even formed an alliance with
the sultan of Turkey.

France achieved its goal. The might of the Habsburgs was broken in
the Thirty Years' War[6] and Europe no longer had cause to fear these rulers.
But danger soon began to threaten from another quarter, from that same
France which seemingly had rendered Europe such valuable service by
freeing it from Habsburg domination. The situation had been reversed:
whereas previously France had been almost totally encircled by the
domains of a mighty dynasty, it now was completely surrounded by weak
states, whose very weakness made them vulnerable to conquest. The
bellicose people of Gaul were not loth to play the conqueror. To the south,
as before, was Spain, but a Spain broken and paralyzed, totally incapacitated and bereft of influence in Europe. To the north of France the former
Spanish possessions had been divided into two parts: the northern region
comprised the small Dutch republic, which had grown wealthy from its

trade, but lacked the resources to wage war on land with a major state; the southern region, Belgium, remained under Spanish control, but Spain's obvious inability to defend it made it a tempting and easy prize for the French. To the east was Germany, which had been freed of religious and political oppression, but had been laid waste by the ravages of the Thirty Years' War. Germany had been much divided up among a number of petty rulers who, after the Thirty Years' War, had expanded their power because of the weakening of other sections of society, but failed in so doing to acquire any broadness of vision or dignity. They were not so much rulers as feudal landlords, concerned only with extracting the maximum income from their lands and attaching no importance to the interests of their common fatherland or to the consolidation of a series of alliances through which Germany might gain independence and the respect of its neighbors. And so France's power-seeking ambitions met with no more opposition from weak, defenseless Germany than they did from Spain.

Sweden's leading role in the Thirty Years' War had brought it territory in Germany under the articles of the Treaty of Westphalia and with it a moral obligation to protect German interests. But the Swedish crown was seduced by France into forming an alliance. Decimated Italy presented no obstacle to France and England's own internal problems prevented it from taking an active part in continental affairs, the king of England becoming the pensioner of the king of France.[7] The entire situation thus stood reversed and the spokesman of the house of Habsburg, the ruler of Austria, who bore the title Holy Roman emperor and king of Germany, was obliged to defend Germany and Spain against France under most inauspicious circumstances. Eventually he was forced to stand by whilst the king of France, the famous Louis XIV, employed every manner of pretext to seize German territory. He was condemned to this position by the struggle which had arisen in his own Hungarian domains. Hungary had never ceased to voice dissatisfaction with the Austrian government and people were heard to complain bitterly about the behavior of German garrisons in Hungarian fortresses, and the persecution of the Protestants was an especial bone of contention. The wealthiest and most eminent of the magnates formed a conspiracy and entered into negotiations with the sultan, offering to accept his sovereignty. The disturbances continued until finally in 1678 rebellions broke out under the leadership of the young Hungarian nobleman, Imre Thököly, whose cause met with early success. The situation grew even more dangerous for Austria when, in 1682, Thököly accepted Turkish sovereignty.

THE HOLY LEAGUE AGAINST TURKEY

In the second half of the seventeenth century the fortunes of Turkey, which was beginning to fall into decline, took a turn for the better. The disturbances in the borderlands of three neighboring states allowed the sultan the opportunity to make one last aggressive and triumphant assault upon the Christian world. A few years earlier in the Polish borderlands Doroshenko's dissatisfaction with Polish rule had prompted him to accept Turkish sovereignty.[8] This had culminated in the Turkish attack upon Poland, the capture of Kamieniec and the Truce of Zórawno, which had cost Poland so dearly. Having dealt with the Poles, the Turks proceeded to attack the Russian Ukraine and destroyed Chigirin, as a result of which Russia was forced into making a fairly disadvantageous truce. Now disturbances in the Austro-Hungarian borderlands and Thököly's change of allegiance were to bring the victorious Turkish armies to the gates of Vienna itself.

What would be the fate of Eastern Europe should the Turks succeed in striking this last decisive blow? Would Russia and Poland hold out, and what would become of Italy? Until now Turkey's successes could be ascribed to the fact that it had attacked neighboring states individually. Now the Porte had interfered in Hungarian affairs, armed itself against Austria and formed a truce with Russia. Eastern Europe's sole hope of averting a catastrophe was an alliance and a consolidated front against the Ottomans. Jan Sobieski, the king of Poland, realized that a Turkish victory in Austria would spell disaster for Poland, and so he entered an alliance with Emperor Leopold. Louis XIV, who rejoiced in the misfortunes of the Habsburgs and had lent his support to Thököly, tried to dissuade Sobieski from giving support to Austria. Sobieski replied that he would resign himself to Turkey's victory over Austria only were the king of France to come to Poland's assistance with all his forces when the Turks advanced on Cracow after taking Vienna. Louis would give no such undertaking and Sobieski remained firm in his intention to help Austria.

Not everyone in Poland shared his views. During the session of the Sejm in 1683 numerous publications appeared denouncing the idea of war against the Turks on Austria's behalf. "We always have refused to accept our kings from the royal house of Austria, yet now we intend to fight to keep our brothers in Hungary, Moravia, Bohemia and Croatia under the Austrian yoke. The Turks may indeed be extending their territory to the Danube, but what concern is that of ours? Did the emperor come to our aid two years ago when there were fears that the Vistula would fall to

Turkish domination? The Turks are by no means our intransigent enemies; they are more tempted by the conquest of the lands to the south than
those of Poland. Our eternal enemies are Brandenburg and Austria. That
is why our ancestors always sought the friendship of France, 'which can
always help us but never subjugate us.'"

Sobieski succeeded in overcoming the French faction.[9] The Sejm
agreed to an alliance with Austria and the treaty was signed in May 1683.[10]
The emperor undertook to bring sixty thousand troops into battle, the king
forty thousand. Both rulers pledged to come promptly to the rescue with
their full forces in the event the Turks besieged either Vienna or Cracow.
Finally, both rulers agreed to attempt to bring other rulers into the alliance
and to make special efforts to win over their highnesses the tsars of Muscovy (*Serenissimos Moschorum czaros*) to their cause.

In July Grand Vizier Kara Mustafa led two hundred thousand Turkish
soldiers across the Raabe and headed straight for Vienna. Emperor Leopold with his entire court abandoned the capital, entrusting its defense to
Baron Stahremburg. Stahremburg burnt the outlying districts, beat off all
attacks and held out for six weeks while he awaited his deliverers. Eighty-
four thousand Christian troops marched on Vienna—twenty-seven thousand Austrians under the command of the count of Lorraine, 11,400
Saxons under Elector Johann Georg, 11,300 Bavarians under their elector,
Maximillian Emmanuel, eight hundred Franconians under Prince Wald-
enski and twenty-six thousand Poles led by their king, Jan Sobieski.
Sobieski assumed command of the whole united army. On September 12
he attacked the Turks and won a resounding victory. Kara Mustafa abandoned his entire rich camp to the victors and fled back towards the Raabe.
Sobieski pursued and defeated him a second time at Parkany.

Constantinople nevertheless entertained no thought of suing for peace.
The following year Leopold and Sobieski had to make preparations for
another major engagement, and they began to seek allies. In the spring
of 1684 Venice entered a *Holy* League with Austria and Poland, and Pope
Innocent XI was proclaimed its patron. A clause was inserted in the treaty
exhorting all three powers to invite all Christian rulers to join their alliance, "and especially the tsars of Muscovy."

RUSSIA INVITED TO JOIN THE HOLY LEAGUE

Jan Sobieski had a dual task to perform and naturally he did so willingly.
Informing the tsars of his victories at Vienna and Parkany, Sobieski wrote
that the time had come to rid Europe of the foes of Christianity. The

Christian rulers promised to have troops ready by the spring and their majesties the tsars might begin action in the winter. At the beginning of 1684 the emperor's plenipotentiary ambassadors visited Moscow to try to conclude an alliance against the Turks. The Muscovite authorities were swayed by the same considerations that had influenced Sobieski in his decision to help Austria. Turkey had emerged as Russia's most dangerous enemy, an enemy which Muscovy was incapable of defeating on a one-to-one basis, as the last war had proved. Now the Russians found a real opportunity to compensate themselves for that war by joining an alliance with other Christian powers, an alliance which from the outset encountered dazzling success. Were Moscow to withhold assistance and the holy war yielded a Turkish victory, there would be constant fear of a Turkish attack on Kiev. Were Poland to make peace with Turkey to its own advantage and glory without Russia's help, it immediately would approach Russia, weapon in hand, to demand fulfillment of the terms of the Truce of Andrusovo, in other words the return of Kiev.[11] There were good reasons for entering the Holy League against the infidels, but Poland's urgent need of Moscow's assistance suggested that the Poles first could be coerced into signing a treaty of permanent peace, with the cession of Kiev to Russia. Negotiations for just such a peace began in January 1684, once again in the border village of Andrusovo. The plenipotentiary ambassadors met thirty-six times without reaching agreement, the Poles refusing to relinquish Kiev and the Russians to assist them against the Turks.[12]

In May 1684 negotiations were held in Moscow between Golitsyn and the emperor's ambassadors, Zierowski and von Blumenberg. The ambassadors conveyed the wish of his majesty the emperor that the great sovereigns assist in the struggle against the Turkish sultan by depriving him of his right arm, the Crimea. There was no need to send a large army to the Crimea; a force of Ukrainians from Ivan Samoilovich's domains supported by a few regiments of infantry would suffice. This was all the help his majesty the emperor required: he wished merely that the sultan's right arm be constrained. Golitsyn replied: "Only nine years remain to the expiry of the truce between the king of Poland and the great sovereigns. Should the great sovereigns join the emperor and the king of Poland to fight the Turkish sultan, thereby exhausting their troops and then, when the truce expires, the king declares war upon their country, what will the great sovereigns have gained? The ambassadors surely must understand

why the great sovereigns find it impossible to enter the alliance without
first concluding a treaty of permanent peace with Poland."

The ambassadors asked to know their majesties' firm outlook on the
return of Kiev to the Poles. Golitsyn replied that Kiev could not possibly
be returned to the Poles, and would never be returned, because the Poles
had suppressed the faith of the Ukrainian people and committed other offenses which had provoked insoluble disputes. The very name of Poland
was hateful to the people of Little Russia. Besides, the king of Poland had
ceded the whole of the Ukraine to the Turkish sultan under the terms of
the Truce of Zórawno and the sultan had ceded Kiev, the towns and settlements attached to it and Zaporozhie to the tsars. Golitsyn terminated
his conversation with a firm pronouncement: "Should the king of Poland
relinquish the city of Kiev to their majesties the tsars, the tsars will enter
the alliance with the king and wage war against the khan of the Crimea."

PEACE WITH POLAND AND ENTRY INTO THE HOLY LEAGUE

Meanwhile the fortunes of war, which continued to favor Austria and
Venice, deserted Sobieski. In 1684 he unsuccessfully laid siege to Kamieniec. In 1685 illness prevented him from taking personal command
of his army, and he sent Hetman Jablonowski to capture Moldavia, in the
hope of wresting Podolia from Turkish control and thereby forcing Kamieniec to surrender. Jablonowski crossed the Dniester and invaded
Moldavia, but soon was forced to retreat after suffering heavy casualties.

The king was obliged to renew his negotiations with the tsars. At the
beginning of 1686 the king's distinguished ambassadors Grzymultowski,
the governor of Poznan, and Prince Oginski, chancellor of Lithuania, arrived in Moscow. For seven weeks Golitsyn and his assistants wrangled
with them. The Polish ambassadors refused to accept the boyars' proposals; they announced that negotiations were at an end, took their leave of
the tsars, prepared to depart, and then renewed negotiations. As they said,
they were "reluctant to abandon such a glorious and profitable matter and
have all their efforts come to nought." Finally, on April 21, 1686 all disputes were resolved and a permanent peace was signed. Poland ceded Kiev
to Russia in perpetuity. The great sovereigns undertook to break their truce
with the sultan and khan, and promptly dispatch troops to the Crimean
peninsula to defend Poland against Tatar attack. The Don Cossacks were
to carry out military operations on the Black Sea, and in the following
year, 1687, all their forces were to advance on the Crimea. Both powers

pledged not to make a separate peace with the sultan. In addition, it was agreed that Russia should pay Poland an indemnity of 146,000 rubles for the loss of Kiev. Five versts would be added to those places on the right bank—Tripolie, Staiki and Vasilkov—which Russia was to retain along with Kiev. Chigirin and other ruined towns on the lower Dnieper relinquished by Russia to Turkey in the last war were not to be rebuilt. Orthodox Christians on Polish territory were not to be subjected to persecution by Catholics and Uniates. Catholics in Russia might conduct divine worship in private houses only.[13]

Boyar Boris Petrovich Sheremetev and Lord-in-waiting Ivan Chaadaev were sent to Lwów to obtain the king's endorsement of the treaty. They had to wait two months for in 1686 Sobieski had gone to Moldavia with his army and seized Jassy, but the Tatars encircled him and forced him to beat a difficult retreat with his sick and starving troops. Sobieski returned to Lwów a sad man, only to find a new grief awaiting him: he must place his signature to a treaty by which Poland renounced Kiev forever. The king took the oath with tears in his eyes.

ECCLESIASTICAL SUBORDINATION OF KIEV TO MOSCOW
Prior even to the official confirmation of the cession of Kiev to Russia the authorities in Moscow were anxious to conclude the unification of the churches of East and West Russia, an important step which came as a natural corollary to political unification. The division of the Russian church had occurred as a result of the political disunity in the fifteenth century, when the two halves of Russia were ruled by different dynasties, the Riuriks and the Gedimins.[14] The Lithuanian princes who ruled Kiev were unwilling for their Russian subjects to recognize the spiritual authority of a metropolitan residing in Moscow, and therefore insisted on the institution of a separate metropolitanate in Kiev. In the seventeenth century Kiev was reunited with Moscow and the descendants of Kalita,[15] still pursuing the old policy of gathering in the Russian lands, nullified the efforts of the princes of Lithuania and united the Russian church by subordinating the metropolitanate of Kiev to the patriarchate of Moscow. In addition, all Orthodox peoples still living on Polish territory now were placed under the spiritual authority of Moscow.

CONSULTATIONS WITH HETMAN IVAN SAMOILOVICH
For this important matter the authorities enlisted the help of Hetman Ivan Samoilovich, with whom they also had been conducting lengthy

consultations over the alliance with Poland against the Turks and Tatars. As always the idea of alliance with Poland met strong opposition in the Ukraine. Communications with the hetman had begun in May 1683. From the outset Samoilovich favored the principle of an alliance with Christian rulers, but advised that Russia first should conclude a treaty of permanent peace with Poland under the terms of which the Poles would renounce their claims to Kiev, the entire Ukraine and all cossacks of the Zaporozhian Host. It should be stipulated that Russian troops would not join forces with the Poles but would deal with the Crimean Tatars separately. He saw many obstacles to an alliance. If, as a result of their alliance with the king and emperor, the great sovereigns were to break their truce with the Turks and Tatars, the king and emperor would send the Muslims word of this. The Muslims would panic and sue for peace; the king and emperor then would make a truce with them, and Russia would bear the whole brunt of the war.

Even if they did not make peace with the Turks and the sultan launched a full-scale attack on Russia, not only would the emperor be unable to lend support because of the great distance, but the king of Poland would be of no help either. Religious differences between the Roman Catholic Poles and the Orthodox Russians also threw doubt upon the reliability of such an alliance.[16] The war fought during Tsar Alexis's reign had severely hampered relations between Russia and Poland; so far no treaties had succeeded in resolving the conflict, for the Poles were incurably hostile, especially towards the Zaporozhian Host and the Little Russian people. What faith might the latter place in such an alliance when the Poles wished the tsars' realm nothing but ill, and gladly would bring the heavens down upon Russian Christianity? Samoilovich found it suspicious that the king of Poland had not shown his original treaty with the emperor to the tsars' ambassadors and had not sent a copy to the great sovereigns. Even if the king of Poland really had made an alliance with the emperor, such an alliance was useless without the support of the king of France, who was more powerful than the emperor and the king put together, and had no quarrel with the Turks. On the contrary, the emperor was his archenemy, and he might harm the alliance.

On February 2, 1684, the feast of the Presentation of Our Lord, the people gathered at the hetman's residence after mass to watch the arrival of the tsar's emissary, Table Attendant Odintsov. Musketeers paraded before him clad in colored robes and bearing the royal allowance: silver brocade, cinnamon-colored silk cloth from Bukhara, two gerfalcons, six sturgeon, sturgeon gristle bread, a barrel of lemons, a large fresh white sturgeon, sturgeon sweet breads, three Yurloch sturgeon, fresh smelt from Beloozero, smelt from Pskov, a barrel of Rhenish wine and a barrel of vinegar.[17] The table attendant himself rode behind the gifts, seated in a carriage behind a clerk holding a rescript. The cossack officers greeted the emissary at the porch and the hetman personally came to the entrance, took the emissary respectfully by the hand and led him into the reception room by his right arm. As they entered the room the table attendant inquired after the hetman's health on behalf of the sovereigns, commended him for his services and handed him the rescript. Samoilovich took the rescript and kissed the seal; he offered humble thanks for the sovereigns' kindness and asked after their health. Then the table attendant asked after the health of the commanding officers and they also expressed their gratitude for the sovereigns' kindness. The royal allowance was presented and the hetman again gave thanks. He said: "The great sovereigns' kindness to me is great, splendid and ineffable. I give humble thanks, tenfold and a hundredfold, for their kindness, allowance and generosity and I shall not fail to serve them in the future, wish them every happiness and gladly shed my blood, even sacrifice my life in persistent toil against every foe, just as I served their royal father and brother before them." That day the table attendant and the clerk dined with the hetman. When they drank the toast to the tsars' health, musicians blew on trumpets, played pipes and beat kettledrums. The hetman was in a very jovial mood.

In spite of his joviality, the hetman was displeased. He had given his daughter in marriage to Boyar Fedor Petrovich Sheremetev. The family was distinguished, but the father of the hetman's son-in-law, Boyar Peter Vasilievich, was still alive and contributed little to his son's maintenance. Fedor also received a meager allowance from the tsars because Boyar Peter was on bad terms with Golitsyn. The hetman's daughter suffered privations, and this troubled her father greatly, her mother even more so. Samoilovich told Odintsov: "I have no quarrel with Prince Vasily Vasilievich [Golitsyn]—the boyar is not to blame, but my own misfortune. It's not as though I have not appealed to the sovereigns or have failed in my service to them. I can take no comfort in my family; my poor wife and daughter have made their eyes red with weeping. I would rather lose my life than endure such misfortune, such incessant sorrow in my own home. The great sovereign Tsar Fedor of blessed memory promised me that if I found a son-in-law, even a man of lowly birth, he would be ennobled and granted peasants. Now I have given my daughter to an aristocrat, Boyar Fedor Sheremetev, but I derive no consolation from it. All the clothes my daughter possessed have been pawned or sold to buy food. My son-in-law's father, Boyar Peter Vasilievich, treats his son unkindly; he gives him nothing, and does not teach him to live decently among good men and to respect the worthy. He who is favored by God and rewarded by the great sovereigns must be respected. It makes my poor heart ache.

"But if the great sovereigns would, in recognition of my loyal service, appoint my son-in-law to a position in Kiev, I could make him a loan and maintain him and his entire household. I would send my trusty servants to his estates and have them sow sufficient grain and plant vegetables in the gardens, thus making all necessary provisions. I beseech the great sovereigns and the sovereign lady tsarevna to regard my request favorably: let Boyar Vasily Golitsyn convey my request to them and beg them to appoint my son-in-law to the governorship of Kiev, and send Lord-in-waiting Leonty Romanovich Nepluiev to assist him. Nepluiev is a good man, familiar with our way of life, and my son-in-law could learn from him. I would be seen to enjoy the tsars' favor and the Little Russian people would take warning from the fact that I am hetman and my son-in-law the governor of Kiev. I desire this not in the hope of obtaining some special advantage for my son-in-law, but for reasons of security and as a deterrent to the Little Russian people.

"I also beseech the sovereigns to bestow their exalted favor upon me and allow my daughter to see her father, mother, brothers and sister so that we may talk together. If my son-in-law should misbehave in Kiev, I myself shall go to see him or send my son or my wife and daughter and make them persuade him to treat people decently and respectfully. I have no quarrel with Prince Vasily Vasilievich and no one has been writing to me, and I would not believe one word that my son-in-law's father wrote to me, even were he to do so, because he himself treats his son so unkindly. Let Prince Vasily Vasilievich rest assured that I am his loyal friend and servant. Simply convey my petition to his grace and beg him to take pity on my tears and the lamentations of my family, and entreat the great sovereigns and the noble sovereign lady tsarevna to post my son-in-law to Kiev in the spring."

The table attendant said to the hetman: "The great sovereigns certainly will grant your request to see your son-in-law and daughter." "But what good will that do me?" asked the hetman. "My son-in-law is a constant drain on my resources. I am always sending him money, provisions, fish and meat, but I can never send enough. The distance is too great, most of the guards are bound to be driven off and the supplies lost. But if he were in Kiev, which is close by, I would support him."

Golitsyn had told Odintsov to ask the hetman why he had failed to send Ukrainian delegates to the conference of the Russian and Polish ambassadors. Samoilovich replied: "I rely upon the sovereigns' will and also upon Prince Vasily Vasilievich in the knowledge that I shall be kept informed of what goes on and what the sovereigns ordain. There is nothing to be gained from sending bad men, and if I send good ones they will object to being pushed into the background."

The usual denunciations and complaints against the hetman continued to arrive in Moscow. One of these reports accused Samoilovich of embezzling the proceeds of the liquor franchise, which the people found so onerous. Table Attendant Almazov went to see Samoilovich in June in order to investigate the reports. Samoilovich thanked the sovereigns for their precaution. "I am amazed," he said, "and offended that such a lie should have reached the exalted ears of their majesties. Were the Zaporozhians sincere in their loyalty to the great sovereigns they would not speak of matters which do not concern them. Their commander Grishka is a real Pole at heart and he is forever goading them into sending emissaries to Poland. The commander and his supporters call the great sovereigns their patrimonial lords, and the king of Poland their father. What credence can be given to the Zaporozhians when they speak ill of my authority under the influence of hostile Polish slander?

"Neither do the tradesmen of Kiev have any particular reason to slander me, for they bear no obligations other than those which are customary in Little Russia. Very likely they are annoyed with me because I denounced and reprimanded them about the huge profits they have been making from the municipal revenues; they pay only three thousand *zolotye* into the treasury but collect more than ten thousand a year for themselves, despite the fact that the old regulations require them to pay a contribution to the governors of Kiev and maintain the troops which defend the fortress and the town. They are supposed also to provide guns and stocks of powder and lead, but they have not done so. The crafty fellows divide the profits amongst themselves but make no essential provisions for their future security. The townsmen of Kiev would be glad if all the cossacks left the city but I prefer there to be many, for their presence is essential.

"The townsmen express dissatisfaction with the tsars' governors and complain about the troops, but in my opinion they are not sincere: they want to get their own way and hate to render honor or obedience to anyone. The franchise was inaugurated in the following manner: during Tsar Fedor's reign we reported to the sovereign's illustrious throne that our city regiments were in need of cavalry and infantry volunteers but we had no means of paying them. The great sovereign kindly made us a grant from his treasury but bade us procure the money here in future. To carry out the monarch's behest, the cossack officers, colonels and men of all ranks, at the time of their conference in Baturin, deliberated as to how this money was to be raised and the troops maintained. It was decreed unanimously that a franchise should be introduced since neither the cossacks nor the common people were deriving any profit from the sale of liquor, whilst the tavern keepers were making a fortune. The introduction of a franchise was not a new idea but a revival of old practice: in Bogdan Khmelnitsky's time[18] a permanent franchise was levied on both sides of the Dnieper. In those days one or two regiments yielded as much revenue to the treasury as is yielded by the whole region today, but even so Khmelnitsky received no complaints and no one took offense. I am not personally responsible for collecting the franchise duties—there are especially appointed sworn officials. I should be only too glad were the great sovereigns to send their own representatives to relieve me of the franchise receipts. No one has ever told me that they find the tax over-burdensome.

"It was the monarch who commanded me to maintain the volunteers for whom the franchise was instituted. Indeed, their presence here is essential, as was shown at the time of the Moscow rebellion [of 1682] when I deployed these troops to check the faint-heartedness of unruly elements, who might otherwise have succumbed to Polish intrigue and stirred up trouble. I humbly await the royal decision: should the franchise be abolished, or retained to finance the troops? If it is abolished the troops have to be disbanded, and if this happens they will defect to the Polish side, and the Poles will rejoice. If the troops are not disbanded after the abolition of the franchise, the crown will have to provide an annual donation for their upkeep.

"As far as my relatives are concerned, I have nothing of which to be ashamed. None of them are colonels except my son Semen and my nephew Mikhail Vasiliev, and I keep them in these positions on the understanding that they will not mistreat their soldiers. If I receive any complaints about them I shall dismiss them and provide for them myself, which I am well able to do. It seems that the authorities have considered the case of my son-in-law Fedor Sheremetev, and have decided to appoint him, not to the governorship of Kiev, but to some other position. I am most aggrieved at this reversal, for I shall be put to shame and disgraced if my son-in-law is not made governor of Kiev after all the rumors which have been circulating about me."

In November [1683] Crown Secretary Emilian Ignatievich Ukraintsev,[19] one of Moscow's most active agents, visited the hetman in Baturin to speak with him about two very important matters: the old problem of the alliance with Poland against the Turks and Tatars and the new issue of the election of the metropolitan of Kiev. Samoilovich was more strongly opposed than ever to an alliance with the Poles. "What is the use of breaking our truce with the Turks and Tatars and declaring war on them?" he asked. "If the Holy Roman emperor and the king of Poland send envoys to the great sovereigns and try to drag them into this war of theirs, the great sovereigns always can refuse on the grounds that they made their truce with the Tatars quite independently and have no reason to declare war on them now. The emperor and the king have not divulged their own reasons for fighting the Turks, nor did they invite the great sovereigns to join their alliance in the first place."

The secretary retorted: "It would be wrong to refuse to help the Holy Roman emperor and the king of Poland; many Christian rulers are fighting on their side."

The hetman continued to insist that numerous good reasons could be found for refusing. "Russia has a truce with the Turks and Tatars; when it was at war with them nobody came to Moscow's assistance. They shamelessly refused on the grounds that it would be a breach of their truce. And what assistance could we give them, anyway? It would be unthinkable and quite without precedent to send troops to assist the emperor, just as it would be to send troops to the king of Poland for an assault on Kamieniec, to the Danube and beyond. If we send troops to the Crimea, what assurance will the emperor and the king give that they will not betray the great sovereigns and make a separate truce? Could their assurances be trusted? Any pledge they gave would not be binding, because the Pope can absolve them from it. The Crimea will never be conquered in one campaign: we shall take a few villages, and the Turks will come and recapture them. It would be difficult to maintain a defensive force there in winter; if the troops were not withdrawn many would die of starvation and local epidemics or catch scurvy. But my main objection," the hetman concluded, "is that I do not trust the Poles. They are a deceitful and unreliable crowd, inveterate enemies of the Muscovite and cossack peoples."

"In what way in particular, then, has the king of Poland displayed his ill-will towards us?" asked the secretary.

"I am astonished that you need ask." replied the hetman. "The king was overjoyed when rebellion broke out amongst the troops in Moscow. In the hope of aggravating the situation, he sent in spies with subversive leaflets to incite the people here by deriding the boyars and members of the council. He tried to persuade the sultan and the khan to declare war on the sovereigns. Recently he enlisted the support of the Don Cossacks and the Kalmyks, quite unbeknown to the tsars, and he has persuaded many of them to remain in his service. Constantly he is seeking some means of poisoning, stabbing or shooting me. I have to take stringent precautions; I employ no one from Poland or Lithuania in my own house and I have given orders that nobody from these countries be admitted to the towns along the Dnieper, monks included. Had I once relaxed my guard I should have been eliminated long ago and these vagrants would have caused a great rebellion in the Ukraine. You have no idea how many subversive letters they distributed on this side of the Dnieper and in Zaporozhie at the time of the uprising. I am still being tormented by them; they were snatched up and kept by unreliable people and I cannot rid myself of their influence however hard I try."

"The desire to lend assistance to the emperor and the king of Poland is not the great sovereigns' only motive for joining this venture," said Ukraintsev. "If the Turks and Tatars, those eternal enemies of God's church, defeat the emperor and the king and force them into a truce, they will wage war on us. We cannot rely on our truce with them because they always violate truces. Then they will be joined by the king of Poland, who will be aided by his present allies, the emperor, the Pope and the Venetian republic."

"As it pleases the great sovereigns," replied the hetman, "but I see no point in ending the truce with the sultan and the khan. This truce was achieved by the ceaseless wise endeavor and assiduous efforts of the great sovereign Tsar Fedor Alekseevich of blessed memory after a major and terrible war. I too gave my unremitting support to the cause. To end this truce now strikes me as unseemly and fruitless. May the sacred and wise judgement of the tsars and their sister the sovereign lady tsarevna and the sound advice of their illustrious council prevail, but you will not quickly find peace if you seek it by declaring war. The king of Poland will start a quarrel with the aim of draining the royal treasury and having our troops perish in battle. Neither we nor our children should be under the illusion that the Poles ever will cease to be our enemies. To my mind it would be best to maintain the truce, keep a wary eye upon the Poles and treat the Turks and Tatars judiciously. What have we to gain by declaring war? The realm will enjoy neither profit nor territorial expansion because the land on this side of the Danube is all wilderness, and the other side of the Danube is too remote. The Wallachians may have come to grief, but they are unreliable people who will accept anyone's authority. Maybe the king of Poland will rule them, but why should we worry? We have enough trouble with the old disputes without starting a quarrel over them! There is no way in which the Crimea can be conquered and held. It is certainly a great and sacred undertaking to fight for the church of God, but one fraught with difficulty. The Greek church is being persecuted and will remain so until God wills otherwise, but the king of Poland is persecuting the church of God close to the great sovereigns' borders. He has destroyed Orthodoxy in Poland and Lithuania in spite of his treaties with the great sovereigns."

"The Turks and the Tatars are inveterate enemies of Christianity," Ukraintsev repeated. "They are forced to keep their truce with us because they are at war with the Poles and Germans. Now is the time to attack them. All rulers have taken up arms against them and if we do not join their alliance we shall be derided and hated by all Christians. It will be thought that we are closer to the Muslims than the Christians."

"No one will despise or deride us," replied the hetman. "Everyone is free to look to his own safety and advantage. It is more despicable and shameful to have peace and then to lose it for no reason whatsoever. The Poles are lying when they claim that all Christian rulers are sympathetic to their cause. Should they make peace with the Turks now and turn their attack upon us, we can persuade the Tatars to attack them. If it pleases the great sovereigns, I shall certainly see to it that the Tatars remain on our side."

"The great sovereigns would not wish to hire Muslims and have them spill Christian blood," said Ukraintsev.

"What is so sinful about enlisting Tatar aid?" asked the hetman. "Why did the kings of Poland use them in their war against the Muscovite realm?

"What is so sinful about enlisting Tatar aid?" asked the hetman. "Why did the kings of Poland use them in their war against the Muscovite realm? The Tatars can be compared to a sharp sword or a fortified town: even Christians carry a sword to defeat their enemies and defend themselves. It does not matter who a man is, as long as he is my friend and helper in time of need."

"Their royal majesties' domains are extensive and populous," said Ukraintsev. "Many people now seek some form of employment; they are unaccustomed to living without war and have no means of earning their living. The Don Cossacks are forever complaining to the great sovereigns that their valley is becoming depopulated. The cossacks think continually of war because without it they have no livelihood. If we don't send them to war we have to provide them with a large subsidy. With no opportunity for service there is a danger that with such overpopulation the troops and the Don Cossacks will start some venture of their own. There are also a great many people in the volunteer and city regiments of the Ukraine all seeking employment. You should watch out that they don't rebel and do you some mischief!"

"I have my safeguards everywhere," replied the hetman. "I am surrounded by loyal colonels and reliable troops. Should the common people turn against me, I have about four thousand volunteer foot and cavalry at the ready, as well as the Muscovite musketeers. It will be much more dangerous when the Muscovite and Little Russian troops are united for war; there is every likelihood that they will kill the boyars, commanders and even me, no doubt with Polish connivance. When I was serving with Prince Romodanovsky I observed on many occasions how the boyar would command a regiment to take up position where it was needed and the colonels would respond with the most indescribable clamor and insubordination. Our soldiers are different. They may be unruly, but if I command them to go, they obey unquestioningly. It is wrong that so many troops are stationed in Moscow, they should be distributed around the border towns and employed in building fortifications. One or two regiments of loyal hired men should be retained in Moscow. As for the problem of the Don Cossacks, it could be solved by sending them to fight the Circassians or the Kumyks."

The crown secretary's arguments were to no avail. The hetman remained firm in his opinion that it would be wrong to exchange "a golden

Chetvertinsky, the bishop of Luck,[20] was residing at the Krupets monastery in Baturin, whither he had fled from his bishopric to escape Catholic persecution. The crown secretary had questioned the bishop about the plans and activities of the King of Poland, attempting to discover why the bishop had come to the Ukraine, how long he had held office and who had consecrated him.

Gedeon answered that: "On many occasions I heard the king and the senators say that they intended to declare war on the great sovereigns when the time was right. But I have no knowledge of their current plans and activities. I came here because the king was making my life a misery with his persecution. He was forever trying to force me to accept the Catholic faith or become a Uniate. Then, when he was about to depart for the war, the king and the queen personally told me that if I had not become a Catholic or Uniate by the time the king returned I would be sent to Marienburg and imprisoned for life. I took fright and escaped here, wishing to end my days in piety. Whilst I held office there were many men who still kept to their faith, but now I am gone the king certainly will make them convert to Catholicism. He is determined to eliminate the true faith from Poland and Lithuania. I was consecrated by Metropolitan Dionisius Balaban of Kiev."

After he had seen the bishop, Ukraintsev spoke with the hetman about the election of the metropolitan of Kiev. "It has always been by desire," said Samoilovich, "to see a Little Russian pastor installed upon the throne of Kiev and I have always tried to accomplish this aim. Now the Holy Spirit has prevailed upon the hearts of the great sovereigns and their sister and they have sent you with their decree. I shall make every effort to organize this election and shall consult the clergy and laity, but I imagine that it will not be to the liking of a number of Little Russian churchmen. I humbly beseech the great sovereigns to send an envoy to his holiness the patriarch of Constantinople and obtain his dispensation for the Little Russian clergy to be placed under the authority of the patriarch of Moscow. And may the great sovereigns bestow their favor upon me and the Little Russian people and command that henceforth we elect our own metropolitans by a free vote and according to our own regulations. I know as a certainty that this will not please Archbishop Lazar Baranovich of Chernigov. He is annoyed also that the bishop of Luck has come to Little Russia and asks "Could it be that they will make him metropolitan of Kiev? There is no other position for him." But the bishop is a good and humble man and has no desire for power.

"If the archbishop of Chernigov hates the bishop of Luck, you would be well advised not to allow the bishop to go to Moscow until the clergy and laity have elected a Kievan metropolitan," said Ukraintsev.

As he was taking leave of Ukraintsev the hetman made a new proposal. "Let the great sovereigns order five or six thousand Russian troops and their wives and children be transferred permanently to Kiev, Pereiaslavl and Chernigov. This would give the Little Russian people assurance that the sovereigns have no intention of abandoning the Ukraine and it would drive the Poles to despair."

Samoilovich was not content with the arguments he had put to Ukraintsev against the alliance with Poland. He gave him a long letter to take to Moscow listing his reasons for considering an alliance with the king of Poland to be dangerous. "Wallachians, Moldavians, Bulgarians, Serbs and a great number of Greeks, all of them Orthodox Christians, are living under Turkish domination; their only protection and refuge from the rule of the papacy are the Russian tsars, who one day, they hope, will bring them peace. It is well known that the papists are doing their utmost to gain possession of the Sepulchre of Our Lord in Jerusalem. It would be an inextinguishable sorrow for all Orthodox people if the tsars' entry into this alliance allowed the Holy Roman emperor and the king of Poland to seize Turkish territory, force the local population into Uniate church, erect a Roman Catholic church in Jerusalem itself and reduce Orthodoxy to ruin.

"Therefore the great sovereigns must take pains to safeguard the interests of Orthodoxy before entering into any alliance, for they will gain nothing from an alliance which denies them the opportunity of protecting and extending Orthodoxy and expanding their own frontiers to the Dniester and the Sluch. Even if the Poles agreed to these boundaries and undertook not to violate Orthodoxy, they would never honor their undertaking, for the Pope could release them from their oath. The Poles are enticing away the tsar's subjects, Kalmyks, Don and Zaporozhian cossacks, by means of secret messages and subversion. This all goes to prove that the Poles are enemies of the glorious Russian realm: all Orthodox Christians must fight them for the sake of our Graeco-Russian faith which they are destroying and annihilating. If the great sovereigns are absolutely determined to enter the alliance, could they not at least postpone it in order to allow the troops to rest and the frontiers to be fortified?"

In January 1685 the senior clerk Vasily Kochubei visited Moscow with a proposal from the hetman that the Sozh river should be defended and

Zaporozhie made the exclusive property of the great sovereigns. "And since all lands on the other side of the Dnieper—Podolia, Volhynia, Podgorie, Podliasie and all of Red Ruthenia[21]—have belonged always to the Russian monarchy since time immemorial, we would be quite justified in taking back that which is rightfully ours when opportunity presents itself, even if we have to do it on the sly." Kochubei handed over a letter which had been intercepted from the king to the archpriest from Belaia Tserkov, exhorting him to urge the Ukrainians to unite with Poland. "I would pay any price and go to any expense to raise the cossack army and the whole Russian people," wrote Sobieski.

The hetman had informed the leading clergy about the impending election of the metropolitan of Kiev, and Kochubei had brought the written reply to Samoilovich of the archbishop of Chernigov, Archimandrite Varlaam Yasinsky of the Kiev monastery of the Caves[22] and the abbots of the other monasteries in Kiev. They all gave their blessing to the great sovereigns' proposal of installing a prelate in the foremost Russian metropolitanate. Kochubei reported that Bishop Gedeon of Luck had been gravely ill and close to death. His sickness had been precipitated by a letter from the tsars, delivered to him by one of his priests, in which he, the bishop, was not addressed as prince, contrary to the practice of the king of Poland, who always had used the title in his letters. The bishop was a mistrustful man, and felt that the tsars must be angry with him. If the bishop died there would be great rejoicing in Poland: it would be insinuated that God had chastised him for deserting his diocese. The hetman told Kochubei to ask Prince Golitsyn's permission for the bishop to travel to Moscow for an audience with the tsars.

The tsars replied that the truce with Poland could not be broken. The hetman and the Host knew very well how many years remained until it expired. God would take revenge upon the Poles for their persecution of the Orthodox faith when the time came. This was the tsars' most fervent desire, and one which they would continue to cherish. The great sovereigns praised the hetman most graciously for his efforts concerning the election of a metropolitan, and bade him complete the proceedings as soon as possible.

The hetman asked whether he should put any explicit proposal before the clergy to guide them in their choice. Lord-in-waiting Nepluiev brought the tsars' answer to Baturin in April: "After consultation with the clergy of all the towns in Little Russia, with the cossack high leadership and all the colonels, you should elect a man who is well-versed in Holy Writ, peaceful and judicious, chosen from among the inhabitants of these parts, but not a foreigner. The metropolitan should apply to Moscow for instructions on his behavior, the obedience he should render His Holiness Patriarch Joachim of Moscow and All Russia and his successors, how to pass judgement, the reasons why he must reject the authority of the patriarch of Constantinople, the respect he should afford the hetman, officers and Zaporozhian Host, and for advice on all ecclesiastical matters. But he should have no communication whatever with his holiness the patriarch of Constantinople, either by letter or by messengers; he should show him no special deference and he should renounce his authority and withdraw from his flock because of the remoteness of his see. For Constantinople has been wont to mete out excommunication or blessing on the basis of envy and hostility, especially in recent times through the influence of the apostate Uniate Bishop Joseph Shumliansky of Lwów and others like him. This has led to the corruption of the church of God, to much discord and the downfall of the church in Red Ruthenia, Volhynia and elsewhere. The metropolitan of Kiev shall have jurisdiction over all the clergy of Little Russia. The metropolitan of Kiev shall rank first amongst the Russian metropolitans. All these articles should be incorporated carefully into a charter signed by the metropolitan and the entire Holy Synod, together with the hetman, officers, the colonels, lieutenants and company commanders, and it shall be confirmed with seals. The newly-elected metropolitan shall come to Moscow to be consecrated by his chief pastor."

In addition to requesting instructions about the election of the metropolitan, the hetman asked why the Don Cossack delegations should not be received in Kursk, as always had been the custom, instead of in Moscow. Nepluiev was obliged to reply that the Don Cossacks were required to conduct their business with the Chancellery of Foreign Affairs in Moscow. Besides, it would be inadvisable for the Don Cossacks to go to Kursk, thereby familiarizing themselves with the Ukraine and gaining the opportunity to make agreements and take counsel there. The hetman knew very well that the Don Cossacks were not to be trusted, and had committed many misdemeanors. Nepluiev finally informed the hetman that the sovereigns had granted him hereditary possession of fifty-two peasant households in the Pronsk district, and had sent him the gift of a polar bear for his amusement.

The hetman replied that he had sent Chief Lieutenant Ivan Mazepa[23] and four colonels to Kiev to attend the election of the metropolitan, and that the clergy would raise no objection to the subordination of the metropolitan to the patriarch of Moscow. But he, the hetman, together with the Host and the Little Russian people, humbly besought the great sovereigns to send a communication to the patriarch of Constantinople without delay, for he was afraid that the patriarch might consign the hetman, the metropolitan and all electoral delegates to perdition. "The Greek ecclesiastical authorities are known to withhold their dispensation at the slightest provocation." He begged the tsars to act quickly before the clergy of the Polish-held regions had a chance to persuade the patriarch of Constantinople to withhold his blessing. The hetman also took advantage of a rescript issued by Patriarch Parthenius of Constantinople approving the installation of a metropolitan in Kiev by the patriarch of Moscow. The hetman wrote that the monarchs' kindness had brought him consolation in the midst of profound sorrow; his daughter, Boyarina Sheremetev, had died in March, shortly after he finally had succeeded in procuring the appointment of her husband to the governorship of Kiev, and in June his elder son Semen, colonel of Starodub, had died—"My beloved son, my first-born and the hope of my old age," the old man wrote. The tsar's emissary Nepluiev, "being of sound mind and reason, spoke words of solace to the hetman in his cruel hour of grief," and was a great help to him. He accompanied the old man the thirty versts from Baturin to the Makoshinsk monastery where he took leave of his son, whose body had been brought from Kiev for interment.

Samoilovich wrote to Golitsyn that he had sent Mazepa and his comrades to Kiev with strict instructions that they were not to divulge his preference; they were to respect the clergy's choice and not tamper with the election, whatever that choice might be. No hint was needed from Mazepa, for it was widely known that the hetman would like to see Gedeon Chetversintsky as metropolitan rather than Lazar Baranovich, with whom he had had several misunderstandings. The fact that Lazar himself did not attend the election or send any of his leading clergy to represent him in Kiev posed an initial impediment to the proceedings. Matters also were complicated by the new conditions under which the election was being conducted, namely the transfer of authority from the patriarch of Constantinople to the patriarch of Moscow. Samoilovich remarked that this caused many "to be sorely troubled in their minds." The delegates were disturbed also by rumors from the Belgorod diocese, where the metropol-

caused many "to be sorely troubled in their minds." The delegates were disturbed also by rumors from the Belgorod diocese, where the metropolitan's agents were said to be oppressing the non-monastic clergy with their requisitions, flogging the priests to extract debt payments, meting out corporal punishment and introducing new Muscovite practices such as baptism by complete immersion instead of by pouring water, which had resulted in a number of infants being drowned by inexperienced priests.

CHETVERTINSKY BECOMES METROPOLITAN OF KIEV

All these obstacles eventually were overcome and on July 8, 1685 Prince Gedeon Sviatopolk Chetvertinsky was elected unanimously . The hetman informed the tsars of this happy event, and made the following requests: (1) All ancient rights and liberties of the Ukrainian clergy should remain inviolable. (2) The metropolitan of Kiev should rank first among the metropolitans of Russia. (3) The patriarch of Constantinople must be urged to relinquish his authority over the metropolitanate of Kiev to the patriarch of Moscow. (4) The metropolitan of Kiev should retain the status of exarch[24] of the patriarchate of Constantinople, otherwise the Orthodox bishops of Polish territory might elect a separate metropolitan and force the entire people to recognize the authority of this new metropolitan. (5) The patriarch of Moscow shall ordain and consecrate the metropolitan of Kiev, but should not interfere in his jurisdiction, just as the patriarch of Constantinople had never done. (6) The metropolitan of Kiev should wear a mitre with an upright cross and in his diocese a cross shall be carried before him. (7) Books shall continue to be printed at the Kiev monastery of the Caves, and the Bratsk monastery continue to provide instruction in the free sciences in Latin and Greek. (8) The conventions and relations of the ecclesiastical authorities with respect to the metropolitan should be preserved and on the death of the metropolitan his successor should be elected freely.

The Moscow authorities conceded all these points but one, rejecting the proposal that the metropolitan of Kiev bear the title exarch of the patriarchate of Constantinople, as it seemed glaringly incongruous for the metropolitan to be subordinated to one patriarch while simultaneously calling himself the deputy of another! In the fall of that year the newly-elected metropolitan went to Moscow where he was consecrated by Patriarch Joachim on November 8.

CONSULATIONS WITH THE EASTERN PATRIARCHS
There were still many people who considered the business to be unfinished, Hetman Samoilovich among them. He was afraid that the patriarch of Constantinople would curse him and all Ukrainians for leaving his authority, and he repeatedly begged the tsars to obtain Constantinople's dispensation for the change. At the end of 1684 the Greek Zakhary Sofir had been sent to Patriarch Jacob in Constantinople for just this purpose, but the patriarch had told him that the troubled situation in the country, with the vizier on his deathbed, prevented him from taking any action for the time being.

Naturally the illness of the grand vizier could not be allowed to delay the unification of the Russian church. At the end of 1685, after Gedeon's consecration in Moscow, the clerk, Nikita Alekseev and the hetman's envoy, Lisitsa, travelled to Turkey to complain to the sultan about the enlistment of troops from the east side of the Dnieper to the west, and to speak to the patriarch about the metropolitan of Kiev. In Adrianople, where the sultan was then in residence, a Greek called Yury Metsevit visited Alekseev and said: "When the Greek Sofir came here to deliver the great sovereign's rescript about the metropolitan of Kiev, I told his holiness the patriarch that he should issue a charter authorizing the transfer of the metropolitanate of Kiev to the patriarchate of Moscow. The patriarch replied: 'I am powerless to act without first consulting the other patriarchs and convoking the metropolitans of my diocese and, besides, I am afraid of the vizier. If I summon the metropolitans, and the vizier finds out and asks why, I shall have no choice but to tell him. And if I take the decision alone, my authorization will be invalid. Furthermore, if the vizier hears of it, he will have my head cut off. I cannot deal with this matter without the vizier's permission.'" Yury continued: "I wrote to Prince Vasily Golitsyn about this. If you have a decree from the tsars, try to persuade the vizier to order the patriarch to deal with this matter."

"The patriarch does not need the vizier's permission," replied Alekseev. "There is no need for the vizier to know anything about it; the patriarch will not receive his injunction." "No, that is out of the question," Yury replied. "The metropolitans must be summoned and some are the patriarch's friends, others his enemies. If the patriarch acts without the vizier's permission, some of the metropolitans may report that the patriarch is in communication with Moscow and he will be put to death immediately."

that he could not receive the envoy before he had seen the grand vizier. Alekseev saw the vizier, then paid a visit to the patriarch. Dositheus said at once that he would not advise the patriarch of Constantinople to renounce his authority over the metropolitan of Kiev in favor of the patriarch of Moscow, for such actions were proscribed in the rules of the Church Fathers. "We shall not give our blessing, for the metropolitans of Kiev have always come to Constantinople to be consecrated. Had it pleased the great sovereigns to write to us about the installation of a metropolitan in Kiev, we should have given our permission for the patriarch of Moscow to consecrate him, but would not have agreed to his assuming authority over the diocese indefinitely. Now they are requesting our dispensation after he has already been consecrated! A division has occurred in the Eastern church. I shall not consult the patriarch of Constantinople about this, nor shall I give my blessing."

To Lisitsa, Dositheus gave a sharp rebuke: "The hetman, the Zaporozhian Host and the Ukrainian people are the subjects of the great sovereigns. Now the sultan also wishes the clergy to recognize the ecclesiastical authority of the patriarch of Moscow. The step has been taken, and so it must remain." Alekseev spoke gently and kindly to Dositheus to win him over. He argued that it was impossible for the Ukrainians to communicate with the patriarch of Constantinople because of the great distance involved, Muslim persecution and military considerations, and he promised him a great reward from the treasury. Dositheus replied: "I want no part in this affair. Let the patriarch of Constantinople do as he wishes, but no sum of money would induce me to take such action and the patriarch of Constantinople can do nothing without the vizier's permission." "Their holinesses the patriarchs would be better advised to settle this matter without divulging it to infidels," said Alekseev. But Dositheus stood firm.

Alekseev learned that he did not need to visit Constantinople for an audience with the patriarch. The former patriarch, Dionisius, had been reelected to the patriarchal throne, and this had brought him to Adrianople. Alekseev visited the vizier and told him of the tsars' desires concerning the problem of the metropolitanate of Kiev. The vizier promised to summon the patriarch and enjoin him to meet the tsars' request. When Alekseev went to Dositheus with the news, he found that he had undergone a complete change of heart. "I have consulted the regulations," said the patriarch, "and I find that any prelate of the church is at liberty to transfer his jurisdiction to another. I shall speak to Patriarch Dionisius and urge

patriarch, "and I find that any prelate of the church is at liberty to transfer his jurisdiction to another. I shall speak to Patriarch Dionisius and urge him to meet the tsars' request. I shall write personally to the great sovereigns and to Patriarch Joachim and send my separate blessing, independently of Dionisius."

Dionisius did not raise the least objection. He promised to comply with the tsars' request as soon as he returned to Constantinople and consulted the metropolitans. The time was propitious, for the Turks, threatened by war on three fronts, were anxious to maintain their truce with Moscow, and hastened to consent to the tsars' demands. The vizier promised Alekseev that the sultan would forbid the enlistment of men from the east to the west bank of the Dnieper and the building of towns there. Russian prisoners were released.

The vizier said to Alekseev: "I know very well that the Polish ambassadors have been trying to solicit the tsars' assistance in attacking us, and that they have conceded a large area of land, but your rulers replied that their truce with his majesty the sultan had not yet expired. When you return to Moscow, ask the great sovereigns not to inflict any injury on his majesty the sultan; tell them that their mutual love and friendship will continue to grow. We know that the great sovereigns of Moscow are glorious and powerful: there is no ruler to match them in the whole of Christendom." Alekseev's request for the restoration of the church of St. John the Baptist in Constantinople, which had been destroyed by fire, was granted. Alekseev travelled from Adrianople to Constantinople, where he obtained written confirmation of Patriarch Dionisius's decision in the Kiev affair. Dionisius was given two hundred *zolotye* and three bags each containing forty sables; Patriarch Dositheus of Jerusalem also received two hundred *zolotye*. Dionisius asked the sovereigns to send emoluments to all prelates who had signed the charter for the metroplitanate of Kiev, just as Tsar Fedor Ivanovich had rewarded all prelates who signed the charter for the establishment of the Moscow patriarchate.[26]

The rapid settlement of the dispute over the metropolitanate of Kiev was facilitated by the Turkish government's desire to appease the tsars and thus avert their alliance with Poland and Austria. But the grand vizier's conciliatory gestures and compliments did not blind the Muscovite government to the fact that the Turks would soon change their tune once the war was over. The signing of the truce during Tsar Fedor's reign had not ended Turkish harrassment of Russia. In 1680 Yury Khmelnitsky[27] had

eastern territory. Wallachians settled in Chigirin; Peter Umanets was installed as colonel, and in 1683 he hired eight incendiaries and sent them over to the Left Bank, which was soon ablaze. The incendiaries were caught, and when questioned admitted that these acts of arson were aimed at forcing the inhabitants of the east bank to migrate to the west. The incendiaries reported that a Greek called Mitrofan had been corresponding with Yury Khmelnitsky from Nezhin; he was gathering information in Moscow and in towns along the border and in the Ukraine, and was sending off detailed reports. As it happened, the Muscovite government was preparing for war, not with the Turks themselves, but with the Tatar raiders of the Crimea. Moscow's growing sensitivity about its national pride and ever-increasing intercourse with civilized countries made the old relations with the Tatars more and more intolerable.

In 1682 the tsar's emissary, Tarakanov, reported from the Crimea that the official receiver of gifts[28] had placed him under arrest, had him taken to his stable and beaten with the butt of a weapon and subjected to torture by fire and other torments. Tarakanov refused to give more than the stipulated number of gifts. They had released him at the ambassadors' quarters on the Alma river, having robbed him of everything he possessed. This incident prompted the regent to inform the khan that in future all necessary negotiations and the presentation of gifts must take place at the border. The tsars also demanded that the khan cease hostilities with Poland, to which the khan responded by inviting the Russians to join the Tatars in attacking the Poles. The Muscovite government, however, impatiently sought a suitable opportunity of freeing itself from its humiliating relations with the Crimea, and this made Hetman Samoilovich's insistence on continued peace with the sultan and the khan especially exasperating.

In the end, Lord-in-waiting Nepluiev was instructed to reprimand Samoilovich for his resistance. The hetman took fright and sent a letter begging the tsars' forgivenness and promising "to prepare for war with the Muslims, not regretfully, but joyfully." In October 1686 the great sovereigns sent to inform him that his transgression graciously had been pardoned and committed to eternal oblivion; he was advised to carry out their royal behest with a joyful heart. Golitsyn assured Samoilovich, "his most amiable brother and friend," that the great sovereigns always would regard him favorably, and that their favor would never diminish. But resistance was encountered from another quarter: Patriarch Dionisius of Constantinople entreated the tsars not to declare war on the Turks lest they vent their

was encountered from another quarter: Patriarch Dionisius of Constantinople entreated the tsars not to declare war on the Turks lest they vent their fury upon the Russians' fellow Orthodox Christians. "I beg and entreat your royal majesty,"[29] wrote Dionisius in January 1687, "not to be responsible for the shedding of much Christian blood; do not destroy your fellow Orthodox Christians in your efforts to help the French. It will not be pleasing to God, neither will men praise you for it."

FIRST CRIMEAN CAMPAIGN

The letter arrived too late. In the fall of 1686 a proclamation of the impending Crimean campaign had been distributed to the troops. It was announced that the campaign was undertaken with the aim of ridding the Russian realm of intolerable affronts and degradation. The Tatars took more prisoners from Russia than from any other country; they sold Christians like cattle and abused the Orthodox faith. In addition, the Russian crown paid the Muslims an annual tribute, a source of shame and degradation in the eyes of neighbors. Payment of this tribute did nothing to safeguard Muscovy's borders; the khan took the money yet continued to abuse Russian emissaries and devastate Russian towns, and the Turkish sultan did nothing to restrain him.

Prince Vasily Golitsyn, now "household commander of the great regiment, guardian of the great royal seal and the crown's ambassadorial affairs", and Governor General of Novgorod, was appointed commander-in-chief of an army of a hundred thousand. Golitsyn naturally was reluctant to surrender the honor of conquering the Crimea to another, but he and the regent must have been anxious at the possibility of defeat. There were reports that Golitsyn assumed command of the army unwillingly, goaded into it by hostile boyars who knew the difficulties he would encounter.[30]

As usual, the mobilization of troops proceeded slowly. The customary strong inducements were employed, but even so, many landowners failed to report for duty. As soon as the guardian left Moscow for the south his enemies, chief amongst whom was Prince Michael Alegukovich Cherkassky, began to harrass him. "I had many friends and enemies," wrote Golitsyn later. In Moscow he still had a loyal friend in Shaklovity, who was bound to him by common interest. It was to Shaklovity that the guardian applied during the campaign, continually exhorting him to pursue his enemies doggedly, keep them from consolidating their position, and to bring the weight of Golitsyn's, in other words Sophia's, power to bear upon them. Golitsyn was fully aware that this power had no legal basis, and therefore he was eager to legalize his position and forced by his sensitivity to public opinion to be ever vigilant and on the alert.

On one occasion during the campaign Golitsyn gave a banquet attended by over fifty soldiers. After the meal the host proposed a toast to the sovereigns and took the step of adding the name of Tsarevna Sophia to those of her brothers.[31] Golitsyn immediately wrote to Shaklovity, asking him to find out whether his decision had caused any reaction in Moscow. The news from the capital offered him little comfort; it was reported that Cherkassky was gaining in influence and was about to replace Boyar Rodion Streshnev.[32] "What a lot of sorrow and how little joy we have," wrote Golitsyn to Shaklovity, "whilst there are some people who always seem to enjoy good fortune and accomplish their desires. I have complete faith in you; you are my only hope. I beg of you, write to me and tell me what diabolical schemes they are devising. For God's sake, keep an ever watchful eye on Cherkassky, and do not allow him to succeed to Streshnev's position, even if you have to enlist the help of the patriarch and the elder tsarevnas to prevent it."

In his letter Golitsyn suggested that Shaklovity enlist the patriarch's help, but he learned from Moscow that the patriarch, far from being one of his supporters, also was opposed to him. He had ordered the removal of vestments and robes which Golitsyn had donated to a church in Barashy and forbidden that they be used in services. "I marvel at the patriarch's audacity," wrote Golitsyn to Shaklovity. "Tell me, what is wrong with these vestments? He is acting arbitrarily; the less access he has to the palace the better."

The commander-in-chief also experienced an unpleasant incident among his own troops. Two table attendants, Prince Boris Dolgoruky and Yury Shcherbatov, appeared on parade dressed in black; their soldiers also wore black and the horses were draped in black cloth. Considering how superstitious people were at the time, it is easy to imagine the strong impression this performance must have made on the troops.[33] Golitsyn wrote to Shaklovity demanding that some penalty be devised for the offenders in order to make an example of them: "The whole regiment was astonished; they said that everyone will follow their example if the culprits are not punished. I beg of you, see to it that the authorities prepare a stern decree for these rebels. This prophesying is an act of defiance against the sovereigns. You could send an official rescript, warning them that the sovereigns have been informed of their action, which was quite blatant and witnessed by everybody. If no decree is issued it will be impossible to deal with them. Such behavior must not be tolerated; they should be ruined, forced to take monastic vows and their estates should immediately be transferred to needy individuals. In this way an example will be made which will cause everyone to tremble."

Golitsyn's demand was carried out. When Dolgoruky, Shcherbatov and Mosalsky and Dmitriev, two other miscreants about whom the commander also had complained, heard of the terrible decree being prepared for them in Moscow, they were alarmed and came to Golitsyn in tears, begging his forgivenness and swearing that they would not misbehave again. Golitsyn "was swayed by their tears" and ordered the decree be rescinded. He sent a letter to Shaklovity in which he begged the sovereigns to pardon the offenders. As he said, it would be inappropriate to punish the penitents at this time.

In May the troops were at last drawn up on the banks of the Merlo river and Golitsyn set off in the direction of Konskie Vody.[34] At the Samara river he was joined by Hetman Samoilovich with a force of fifty thousand cossacks. The united army continued its march towards Konskie Vody and on July 13 they crossed the river and reached the natural boundary of Bolshoy Lug. There was no sign whatsoever of the Tatars, but they were greeted by a yet more fearful enemy against which they were quite powerless—fire on the steppe. Golitsyn took counsel and decided to carry on, but they covered no more than twelve versts in forty-eight hours. The horses could barely move from exhaustion and lack of sustenance, for there was neither grass nor water. The men were weakened by the heat and the terrible sooty haze which impeded their vision. Some water was provided by heavy rain showers which flooded the dried-out river beds, but there was still no grass. Golitsyn stopped for further consultations on the banks of the Karachakrak. It was decided to turn back and to send a detachment of thirty thousand men, half Russian and half Ukrainian, to the lower reaches of the Dnieper. Lord-in-waiting Nepluiev was put in command of the Muscovite regiments, the hetman's son Grigory of the cossacks.

The main army turned back and stopped to rest at Konskie Vody, where there was woodland and grass in plenty. In his report to the regent Golitsyn did his best to conceal the fact that the campaign had been a failure.

in the camp at Konskie Vody had another theory, however. Patrick Gordon recounts the rumor that it was the cossacks themselves who set fire to the steppe, either on instructions from or certainly with the permission of the hetman, in order to prevent the Russians from invading the Crimea, which raised mutual distrust between the Russians and cossacks.[35] This was certainly the more plausible explanation, for the cossacks had everything to lose if the Russians laid waste and subjugated the Crimea. Then there would be nothing to prevent the Muscovite government from infringing their rights and liberties.

SOPHIA SENDS SHAKLOVITY TO VISIT THE TROOPS

The regent was extremely alarmed by the failure of the campaign and the exultations of Golitsyn's opponents. She began to devise a way of setting the failure to rights so that the guardian would not return to Moscow in disgrace. Her anxiety increased when she learned that it was not the Tatars but the cossacks who had set fire to the steppe. Sophia decided to send Shaklovity to military headquarters to put the following proposal to Golitsyn: "If it is at all possible, make ready the horse fodder and lay in provisions and make a military expedition into the Crimea. Send word to the Don Cossacks that they should harrass the Crimea and carry out whatever military operations they can. If this is presently impossible, have boats made ready and launched from some place upriver. Capture the settlements of Kazykermen as a base from which Lord-in-waiting Nepluiev and the hetman's son and their men can stage an attack upon the Crimea by water. You should at the same time send your officers into battle with supply trains, accompanied by a guard of prudent cavalrymen, and as many foot soldiers, guns and shells as possible. The provisions, guns and fodder for the cavalry should be carried on oxen and it should be ensured that both forces arrive in the Crimea at the same time. If this is impossible, then build fortifications on the Samara and the Orel and leave heavy equipment, supplies and troops to guard them, thus providing our men with a reliable refuge for the future and striking fear into the enemy."

Shaklovity was instructed to convey the sovereigns' gratitude to the troops in effusive terms and to praise Samoilovich for his efforts, telling him in Golitsyn's presence that "the great sovereigns have heard that on the steppe, to the rear and on the flanks of your supply trains, natives of Little Russia who were riding behind the train with the victuals set fire to the horse fodder. You, hetman, must investigate this act of arson very thoroughly and punish the culprits without delay, for it would be a most serious matter if the Little Russian people were to be blamed for the misdemeanors of a few impudent and intrepid criminals."

OVERTHROW OF SAMOILOVICH AND ELECTION OF MAZEPA

Even before Shaklovity's arrival men who hated Samoilovich—and there were many of them in the Ukraine—snatched the opportunity of ensuring that the hetman took all the blame. The Ukrainian chronicler[36] provides an explanation of why Samoilovich was so hated: "This son of a priest was at first very humble and treated the people kindly, but when he became rich he began to act arrogantly, both to the cossacks and the clergy. The cossack officers must remain standing in his presence; no one dared to sit or enter his residence carrying a staff. Even the most eminent churchmen were obliged to stand with their heads bare. He never went to church to receive the sacraments, but had the priest bring them to him. His sons acted in the same way. If he went out, hunting, for example, he believed that an encounter with a priest meant bad luck, even though he himself was a priest's son! He rode surrounded by a huge retinue, and both he and his sons always rode in a carriage, and he accompanied the troops in a carriage. He was far prouder than any senator. Both the hetman and his sons, who were colonels, devised all manner of means for extracting as much money as possible from the people. He increased his own power and that of his sons by paying the troops very little. His sons were called not colonels but lords. They had no intention of relinquishing their authority, which was based upon hired troops and large sums of money. They regarded the cossacks with contempt and did not admit them to their homes, which were guarded by hired infantry, who received a yearly salary. A priest might wait in vain for several days to gain admittance to the hetman's house, even if his business was very urgent. In general they regarded all men with contempt, forgetful of their own lowly origins."

At first Samoilovich gave little cause for complaint because he treated people well, no doubt mindful of the danger from his rival Doroshenko. Samoilovich's selfless performance of his duty to the tsars had prevented his enemies from denouncing him to Moscow. But after Doroshenko's removal from the Ukraine, Samoilovich and his sons gave free range to their activity. Dissatisfaction grew amongst the officers, clergy and cossacks, and then the hetman had his disagreement with the government over the alliance with Poland. He already had received one reprimand for his "resistance," and now it was possible to use the fire on the steppe as a pretext for accusing him of treason and demanding that the government replace him. Having no special reason to take the hetman's part, the government was sure to comply.

Moreover, it was known that Samoilovich had had his disagreements with Golitsyn. During Golitsyn's quarrel with Romodanovsky in 1677 Samoilovich had supported the latter. But Gordon, who was an eyewitness to the events and whose testimony is to be trusted, insists that the chief reason for Samoilovich's downfall was the universal loathing with which he was regarded in the Ukraine. The Ukrainian chronicler confirms Gordon's opinion. And so the question of the attitude of the government and Golitsyn towards Samoilovich loses its relevance: the main point is that Samoilovich was a bad ruler and was universally hated, and so it was impossible for the government to take his part.

On July 7 the high command of the Zaporozhian Host, Quartermaster Vasily Burkovsky, Chief Justice Mikhailo Voekheevich, Chief Secretary Savva Prokopov, Vasily Kochubei, Lieutenant Ivan Mazepa and Colonels Konstantin Solonina, Yakov Lizogub, Stepan Zabela and Grigory Gamaleia came to Golitsyn's headquarters to present him with a denunciation of Samoilovich. "The hetman tried to prevent the truce with the Poles; when he heard that an agreement had been reached, he was very distressed, and told Lord-in-waiting Nepluiev: 'Just you wait, not everyone in Moscow will be grateful that you have been taken in by the Poles and broken your truce with Turkey and the Crimea.' In the presence of the officers he was heard to say: 'Moscow has brought itself nothing but trouble with the money given the Poles. You'll soon see what they gain from this truce with Poland, and what success they will have against the khan. Because they begrudged paying a small tribute to the Tatars, they'll have to hand over a fortune as soon as the Tatars demand.' The hetman forbade any prayers of thanksgiving be said in church. He refused to listen to news of the allies' victories, but rejoiced at their defeats. The hetman's wife once said to the officers' wives: 'My Ivan is very angry and reproachful against Moscow. He will very likely do the same as Briukhovetsky.'[37] When the king of Poland had to retreat from Wallachia last year, the standardbearer reported after a private conversation with the hetman: 'Our master the hetman would be glad if the Poles were forced to make peace with the Tatars in Wallachia; then Moscow would have to accord us recognition and respect for our firm friendship with the Crito make peace with the Tatars in Wallachia; then Moscow would have to accord us recognition and respect for our firm friendship with the Crimean state.' He advised the tsar's forces to embark upon their campaign at an unpropitious time. During the campaign he made no attempt to take prisoners or to extinguish the fire on the steppe; from this many people have deduced, and we are certain, that it was he who gave the order for the steppe to be fired. Once during the campaign, when he was suffering from sunstroke, he said: 'Look what damage this foolhardy Muscovite war is doing us. It has robbed me of my health. Why doesn't Moscow stay at home and guard its frontiers instead of waging this unnecessary war with the Crimea?'

"Wishing to bring the Muscovite and cossack forces into disrepute, he advised them to turn back, but when they had done so, he said: 'Didn't I tell you that Moscow would have no success against the Crimea? I have been proved right and now we shall have to defend ourselves from the Crimea.' He laughs about the failure of the campaign, and is in excellent spirits. He said in the presence of one leading churchman: 'When, by God's grace, my son returns from the lower Dnieper in good health and comes to Baturin, I know what I shall do.'

"Let it also be made known to the great sovereigns," the indictment continued, "that the hetman rules despotically and plans to take over Little Russia. He seizes the monarchs' rescripts at will and transfers the properties that have been granted others to himself and his children. He does not allow laymen or clergymen to go to Moscow. He speaks of the towns of Little Russia as though they were not crown property but his own, and he enjoins the soldiers to render loyal service, not to the monarchs but to him. He said: 'When we return from the Crimean campaign we shall strive to bring order to Little Russia but we shall pay no attention to the old statutes.' His son Grigory abused the mayor and townsmen of Chernigov, threatening to put them to death because they wished to set up a double-headed eagle[38] over the town hall to signify that the town of Chernigov was the hereditary property of their majesties the tsars. Grigory told the mayor and the townsmen: 'Woe betide you, you scoundrels, if you try to flout the authority of my father and become subjects of Moscow.' He strictly forbade them to set up the eagle.

"On many occasions the hetman said to the officers: 'Foolish Moscow has not heeded my advice and has been reconciled with the Poles. The time is not far off when they will again beg me to mediate between them

me and we shall teach them to respect us.' He ridiculed the royal coinage. He was in communication with the king of Poland and offered to enter his service. He left the tsars' troops only two bridges to cross by. He claimed to have knowledge of the khan's movements and said that the khan would give the Poles a good thrashing. 'And it's no use the boyars, those sons of unnatural mothers, rushing to the Poles' assistance—they're sure to come to grief.' This same day the mayor of Pereiaslavl came to tell him that Moscow was complaining about the high rate of mortality and sickness among the government troops. The hetman replied: 'It wouldn't bother me if they all died.' Once the hetman was dining with Muscovite colonels and the cossack officers in the quartermaster's residence. After dinner Colonel Peter Borisov had an argument with Gamaleia. The latter, no doubt counting on the hetman's support, said to the colonel: 'Mind how you speak to me, colonel. You didn't capture us with the sword, you know.' The hetman heard this but said nothing. He simply laughed and very likely approved Gamaleia's words.

"He spoke harshly about the lands to the west of the Dnieper. 'We shall take no account of the articles of the treaties between the Muscovites and the Poles. We shall act according to our own needs.' He does everything independently and takes advice from no one. He dismisses people from their positions in the heat of anger without adequate grounds. He punishes and abuses at will, without bringing the accused to trial or allowing them to defend their case. He hands out commissions in return for large bribes and turns a blind eye to oppression, something which never happened under previous hetmans. He devises ways of ill-treating men who have given many years of military service and speaks only ill of them, yet he patronizes other petty, undeserving men and raises them to high positions, just to prove that he can do as he pleases.

"The cossacks, however eminent or deserving they may be, have no control over their own mills; he just takes what he wants. If somebody else's property takes his fancy he appropriates it, and his children take the leftovers. He is accessible only to those who offer him bribes; anyone who fails to do so is thrown out, even if he has a genuine case. The commanding officers do not enjoy the respect and security they deserve. There are more who die as a result of his anger and threats than live in peace. The office of chief justice has been vacant for four years because he considers nobody good enough to occupy it, but he would be willing to sell the office for a large sum of money. He took the tsars' allowance of sables and silk, meant for two people, for himself. In the absence of judges, the rule of law has been extinguished and many people are suffering because it is impossible for the injured to obtain redress.

"For the reasons stated above, and because of his incompetence, the Zaporozhian Host cannot possibly discharge its duty to the monarchs honorably. The entire Host desires and tearfully implores the Lord God that it may please the great sovereigns to act in the best interests of their royal affairs and for the alleviation of many sorrows: let him be dismissed from the hetmanship and let some zealous man, both more trustworthy and more righteous, be elected to the office by a free vote as the regulations of the Host stipulate. Let it be a man who at all times will serve the great sovereigns enthusiastically and loyally in this war. When the new hetman has been elected it will be possible to cut off the Crimea and quickly conquer it with the combined forces of the crown and the Zaporozhian Host. If Samoilovich remains in office the monarchs can expect nothing but misfortune; they cannot hope for glory. He will drive everyone away with his ill-treatment or good men will be corrupted, from which God preserve us. The entire Zaporozhian Host humbly beseeches that after his dismissal he should not be allowed to remain in the Ukraine, but should be sent to Moscow with his whole household, and there be put to death for his palpable treason against their majesties the tsars and the Zaporozhian Host. His other wicked deeds are too numerous to mention: we fall before the exalted throne and beg that the hetman be replaced. If their majesties withhold their consent, the Zaporozhian Host, from the lower ranks upwards, will simply lose all patience with this patent wrongdoer. As loyal servants of the great sovereigns they will feel obliged to deal with him quickly according to their own laws and conventions. If this should happen, we beg their majesties' indulgence."

After the signatures came the following postscript: "Let it also be taken into consideration that he has such a high opinion of himself that he deems no one in Little Russia to be his equal, despite the fact that he himself is of humble birth, and equally he despises all Orthodox Russians, regardless of their rank. That is why he refused to give his daughter to any of them, but chose instead a foreigner, Prince Yury Chetvertinsky,[39] most likely with the intention of establishing his own independent domain in the Ukraine. This is obviously why he did not return Yury Khmelnitsky's seal to the great sovereigns but retained possession of it."

Golitsyn sent the indictment to Moscow, for he was naturally unable to act either in the hetman's favor or against him without instructions from

Golitsyn sent the indictment to Moscow, for he was naturally unable to act either in the hetman's favor or against him without instructions from the tsars. The army continued to retreat, losing many officers and men on the way. On July 12, when the army was crossing the Orel river, Shaklovity arrived to commend the troops for their services and asked after the health of all, from the lowest to the highest. On July 14 a council of war was held in order to decide the measures to be taken to prevent a Tatar invasion of Poland or the Ukraine. Shaklovity put forward the last proposal of his instructions, namely that fortifications be built on the Samara; Golitsyn probably had convinced him that the first proposals were quite impracticable, especially now that the problem of the hetman had arisen. When the council of war ended Shaklovity asked the hetman why he had allowed the burning of the steppe. Samoilovich replied that he knew nothing about the fire. No more was said, and after the council the officers went to dine with the hetman, and after dinner the guests observed the custom of presenting a gift to their host.

Shaklovity left on July 16 and on July 21 the troops crossed the Kolomak river not far from Poltava and set up camp. Here a messenger from Moscow arrived with instructions that Golitsyn summon the cossack officers and tell them that "the great sovereigns, having read your indictment of Ivan Samoilovich and having learned that he is unacceptable to the commanding officers and the entire Little Russian Host, order that he be dismissed from office. The great sovereigns' standard and mace and all insignia shall be taken from him, and he shall be brought to Russia under heavy guard. Let him be replaced by a new hetman, a man acceptable to the commanding officers and the entire Little Russian Host. The noble boyar shall proclaim this decree, then arrange for the hetman to be dispatched to some Russian town and see to the matter of his children and relatives until a new hetman is elected. Let him deal with this affair as God instructs and admonishes him." It is clear from this decree that the authorities in Moscow regarded the problem of Samoilovich as a purely local, Ukrainian affair; they were far from convinced by the accusations of treason against him, but they were reluctant to allow a man who had aroused general dissatisfaction to remain in office. They were afraid that "confusion, rebellion and bloodshed might result throughout Little Russia, from which God preserve us," as it was expressed in the same document.

When he had read the decree Golitsyn summoned the Russian colonels who were attached permanently to the hetman's staff and ordered them to move up transport to surround Samoilovich's headquarters. He warned

hetman. The boyar told the colonels to inform the cossack officers that a decree had arrived ordering the dismissal of the hetman and the election of a replacement. He asked them to let him know when everything was ready. That evening the colonels began quietly to move up transport, but they were unable to conceal the operation from the hetman's servants, who immediately told Samoilovich what was happening.

Samoilovich guessed that something was amiss. He feared some violence from the cossacks, and that night he wrote a letter to the colonels enumerating his services to the government, protesting his innocence and demanding a proper hearing. There was no reply. At midnight General Secretary Kochubei reported to Golitsyn that all necessary precautions had been taken, and requested permission to arrest the hetman. The boyar ordered that the hetman and his son be seized at dawn and brought to him, and the hetman's close associates be taken into custody also. Finally, he ordered that guards be posted on all roads leading out of camp to deter anyone from escaping and bringing word of the hetman's fate to his son Grigory, or fomenting rebellion in the towns and countryside. The orders were carried out.

When they went to arrest him at dawn, Samoilovich was not in his tent but in the church, praying fervently. When the service was over and the hetman left the church, Dmitry Raicha, the retired colonel of Pereiaslavl, went up to him, took him by the arm, and said, "Come with me." The hetman looked round and demanded permission to speak with the Russian colonels. The colonels were not long in arriving, bringing with them the hetman's son, Yakov, whom they had arrested. They seated the hetman in a dirty cart and his son on the back of an old nag, and took them under musketeer escort to Golitsyn in the main camp. The commanders, generals and colonels were sitting in the open air; the cossack officers arrived and delivered a short speech describing how they had long witnessed the hetman's misdeeds and how lately he had also committed acts of treason which they felt it their duty to report to their majesties the tsars. Now that the hetman had been arrested and brought to the camp they demanded that he be tried under the regulations of the Host.

Golitsyn asked whether they might not be prosecuting the hetman from motives of revenge and personal animosity, and whether their displeasure might not be appeased by some other means. The officers replied: "The humiliations the hetman has inflicted upon the people and upon many of us are great indeed, but it is because treason is involved that we have decided to deal with him in this manner, for our oath of allegiance prevents us from remaining silent. Besides, we would be hard pressed to stop the people tearing the hetman to pieces, so universally hated has he become."

At this point the old hetman entered, leaning on a cane with a silver handle. His head was wrapped in a wet cloth to relieve the pains he had long suffered in the eyes and head. Golitsyn briefly read out the charges; the hetman denied them all and tried to exonerate himself. An argument flared between him and the three colonels, Raicha, Solonina and Gamaleia. Golitsyn ordered Samoilovich removed. The cossacks tried to lay hands upon him, but Golitsyn restrained them and placed the hetman and his son under the protection of the musketeer colonels. After this the cossacks began to discuss the election of a new hetman.

It was thought necessary to summon the clergy and leading cossacks from the neighboring regiments, but that same evening and the following day it became evident that they could delay no longer. Cossacks from the Gadiach regiment had mutinied and killed their colonel and various other people. Golitsyn was forced to send in Russian cavalry to supervise the cossack camp. The cossacks had begun to leave the camp in great numbers, and so the election could not be postponed.

On July 24 the cossack officers assembled to hear Golitsyn read out the conditions under which the former hetmans had taken the oath. It was proposed that the Glukhov articles[40] be accepted, with the following additions: (1) A regiment of Muscovite musketeers was to be maintained in Baturin for the hetman's safety and protection. (2) The hetman and his commanding officers, as servants of the great sovereigns, must do their utmost to unite the Ukrainian with the Russian people. They must work for the establishment of firm and indivisible agreement, by encouraging marriages and by other means, so that the two peoples might live as one under the rule of their majesties the tsars, just as they both professed a single Christian faith. No one might dare suggest that the Ukraine was the hetman's domain, and the hetman, commanding officers and the Ukrainian people, at one with the Russian people, must proclaim unanimously the autocratic rule of their majesties and that the inhabitants of the Ukraine enjoy free access to the towns of Russia.

After the terms had been discussed, conversation turned to the former hetman's property. Golitsyn said: "Although the law stipulates that the possessions of a traitor revert to the crown, I shall, at the peril of earning the tsars' disfavor, take it upon myself to allot half the property to the

Zaporozhian Host and half to the royal treasury." Everyone was satisfied and the leading cossacks began to make discreet inquiries about Golitsyn's preference for hetman. Golitsyn hinted that he favored Mazepa, and that same evening the officers decided to lend their support to Mazepa and proposed that all Samoilovich's minions be dismissed and their posts reallocated to members of the new Mazepa party.

On July 25 the select regiments and the musketeers gathered round the mobile chapel which had been erected in a field beside the cossack camp. At ten in the morning Golitsyn arrived with the commanding officers and ordered the cossacks, eight hundred horse and twelve hundred foot, to join the assembly. The leading cossacks accompanied the boyar into the chapel, preceded by the hetman's insignia of office. After prayers had been said they left the chapel. A small table had been set up outside and covered with a rich carpet upon which the mace and other insignia were spread. Golitsyn stood on a bench and told the cossacks that their majesties the tsars had granted them leave to elect a new hetman according to their ancient practice and that everyone was free to cast his vote, so let them make their choice. For a moment there was silence, then several voices near at hand pronounced the name Mazepa, others joined in and soon the entire assembly was chanting "Mazepa for hetman!" The name Burkovsky was also heard, but was drowned in the clamor. Golitsyn repeated his question and asked the leading cossacks whom they favored. They replied unanimously, "Mazepa." The new hetman took his oath and signed the conditions, then received the mace, staff and banner from Golitsyn. Golitsyn's indication that Mazepa was acceptable to him and hence to the government must have influenced the outcome considerably, and Mazepa was obliged to give more than verbal expression of gratitude by making the boyar a gift of ten thousand rubles.

The crisis in the Ukraine had been settled, but Golitsyn was as anxious as ever to keep in touch with the Moscow gossip and the machinations of his ill-wishers. He wrote to Shaklovity: "Please write truthfully what they are saying about the hetman." Shaklovity told him that there was speculation about why Samoilovich had been overthrown without a formal hearing. Golitsyn replied: "I made full reports on the hetman affair in my dispatches and rescripts and you can draw your conclusions from them. The affair could not have been conducted in a more proper fashion.

It would have been without precedent to give him a formal trial, as you will discover if you consult former cases. If anyone voices a formal objection, I leave it to God to decide. He can judge who is right. We should have expected people to praise God and be grateful to us for the fact that this whole affair was conducted without resistance, bloodshed or confusion. If they are still unable to make up their minds, let them consider the action of the Turkish sultan two years ago, when in the space of one summer he replaced two khans at the request of the Tatars without having a formal trial. He was simply thankful that they had remained obedient to him and had not risen in rebellion. We would have been most foolish not to have replaced Samoilovich; there is no telling what might have happened."

LAZAR BARANOVICH

Despite the adverse comment in Moscow, Golitsyn was welcomed and rewarded as a victor. The guardian was especially commended for handling the affair on the Kolomak. On his return from the campaign Golitsyn was as powerful as ever, and anyone with a request to the government applied first to him and his son Alexis.

One such application he received from the veteran Lazar Baranovich. Reluctant to let slip the opportunity afforded by Samoilovich's downfall, Baranovich filed a complaint against Metropolitan Chetvertinsky, who was a friend of the despised hetman. On March 30, 1688 Archdeacon Anthony of Chernigov brought the complaint to the tsars. "I was forgotten as surely as if I were dead," wrote the old man, "I was helpless, I lived as though I were already in the grave. I, who humbly pray for you, in my old age and enfeeblement of my powers was loathed by the former hetman, oppressed by his many insults, weighed down by innumerable griefs and unutterable sorrow. I was not simply oppressed but forgotten, like a dead man, buried in the earth while still living. The hetman even added to my burdens by forbidding me to send letters or petitions to your throne to invoke your royal grace and favor. He wished me to be quite without succor, a free man imprisoned amongst the dead. But God, Who vivifies the dead, has provided me this opportunity that I might indeed say: now is the acceptable time, now is the day of salvation.[41] I have come forth from the oblivion of the tomb and approach your exalted throne with my humble petition: do not repudiate me in my old age, look with charity upon my cruel fate.

"When His Eminence Father Gedeon Sviatopolk ascended the throne of Kiev, I, disdaining my old age, met his grace in Baturin and bowed my weak knees before him, in the hope that he would act charitably towards me in view of the thirty years I had spent toiling as a prelate of the church. I asked him to confirm the charter for the installment of seven archpriests which was granted to me by Metropolitan Dionisius Balaban. I also asked to see the charter which your majesties had granted him on his appointment as metropolitan of Kiev. But his eminence the metropolitan insulted my gray hairs. First he demoted me from archbishop to bishop, even though I was raised to the office by your father Tsar Alexis of blessed memory with the blessing of three of the ecumenical patriarchs. Then he took away three archpriests. In a resentful letter to a priest from Voronezh in the deanery of Glukhov he called me a bad pastor and accused me of stealing several parishes which he claimed belonged to him. I fall therefore before your royal majesties' throne: grant my petition and allow me and my whole diocese to be placed directly under the authority of his holiness the patriarch of Moscow on an equal footing with the Russian prelates, and grant that my successors be consecrated not in Kiev, but in Moscow."

The archdeacon also delivered a letter from the hetman. "I most humbly beseech your illustrious majesties," wrote Mazepa, "to listen favorably to the archbishop's petitions and requests and to grant them out of kindness and charity." Lazar and Mazepa also sent letters of petition to Prince Golitsyn and his son Alexis. The petitions and requests were granted.

TURKISH CHRISTIANS URGE RUSSIA TO WAR

The guardian began to prepare for a second campaign against the Crimea, made all the more urgent by the fact that the khan was taking revenge for the first campaign by making raids on the Ukraine, and the Christians on Turkish territory were appealing to the Russian armies to come to the rescue of Orthodoxy. In the latter event it was not the Turks who were the villains. At the time the Russians had been forced to return in failure from the burnt steppe and the Poles were besieging Kamieniec unsuccessfully, the other allies, the Austrians and Venetians, had been winning victories over the Turks in Hungary, Dalmatia and Morea. Turkey's defeats at the hands of the Christians were aggravated by a mutiny in the sultan's own army. Sultan Mahomet IV was overthrown and replaced by his brother Suleiman II. Turkey had never known such dire straits and the sultan's Christian subjects naturally began to cherish the hope that Muslim rule was coming to an end.

In September 1688 Archimandrite Isaiah of the St. Paul monastery in Athos came to Moscow with a letter from former Patriarch Dionisius of Constantinople who had been deposed, so he claimed, for yielding to the tsar's demands concerning the Kievan metropolitanate. Dionisius told the tsars that now was an opportune moment for saving Christianity from the Turks. "All the states and pious kings and princes of the Orthodox world have risen as one against Antichrist; they are fighting him on land and sea, but your realm slumbers. All pious men—Serbs, Bulgarians, Moldavians and Wallachians—await your holy tsardom. Arise from your slumber, come and save us!" Isaiah further brought a letter from the hospodar of Wallachia, Serban Cantacuzene, who also wrote that the Orthodox peoples awaited their deliverance from the grip of a veritable Pharaoh by the Russian tsars. There was a third letter along similar lines from Arsenius, the so-called patriarch of Serbia. Isaiah announced that he had been sent by all Greeks and Slavs to beg the great tsars not to let slip this opportune moment for attacking the Turks. Such action was essential were the Orthodox peoples not to be delivered from Muslim bondage into a yet more dreadful servitude. The papists hated the Greek Orthodox church and therefore in all the towns in Hungary and Morea which the Austrians and Venetians had won from the Turks the papists had begun to force the Orthodox churches into the Uniate church and transform others into Catholic chapels. Were the Romans to prosper, were they successful in capturing Orthodox Christian lands and perhaps even Constantinople itself, Orthodox Christians would be overtaken by even greater misfortune, and the Orthodox faith would disappear. All Orthodox Christians awaited the arrival of the tsars' armies, and even the Turkish inhabitants of these lands preferred the rule of the great sovereigns to that of the Austrians because they were born among Serbs, Bulgarians and other Orthodox peoples.

On behalf of Serban, Isaiah advised the great sovereigns to send an army to attack the Belgorod [Akkerman] Tatars in Bessarabia, sending word by boat along the Danube to the hospodar, who would march on Bessarabia with a force of seventy thousand men to assist the Russians. Part of the army must be stationed in Zaporozhie to keep the Crimeans at bay, but the hospodar did not expect the Belgorod horde to hold out against the tsars' forces. The region was well-watered and there was no shortage of provisions. Once the tsars' troops joined the hospodar's men at Belgorod they would be joined by the Serbs, Bulgarians and Moldavians. Constantinople itself would be within their grasp, for the Belgorod area was populated by Christians and no fortresses guarded the route to Constantinople. Christians joyfully awaited the arrival of the tsars' forces; about three hundred thousand Serbs and Bulgars had assembled, and all local Christians would rise in rebellion.

The people held the Austrians in no high regard and would not help them unless forced to. The commanding hospodar and his troops were gathered in the city of Bucharest and supported neither Turk nor Austrian; the hospodar defended his country from Turks, Tatars and Germans alike. Although he had received many letters from the emperor of Austria urging him to rebel against the Turks, and had not refused outright to accept Austrian sovereignty, he had made no firm promises, telling the emperor only that he would recognize his authority when the Austrians had crushed the Turks. The hospodar explained that he deceived the emperor for religious reasons, for he had no wish to be ruled under a different faith, and much preferred the sovereignty of Orthodox rulers. The Turks and Tatars had not devastated the country because he offered them no open resistance and gave them all the supplies he could. He was provisioning the Austrian armies in order to avert an attack.

In their replies to Dionisius and Serban the tsars assured them of their unfailing solicitude for all Orthodox Christians living under the infidel yoke. It was this which had prompted them to send their commanders with a large army to attack the settlements of the Crimea, the troops setting off in the early spring. The devastation of the Crimea would allow them to cross the Dnieper and attack the Belgorod horde and the lands beyond the Danube. They advised the hospodar of Wallachia to stage an attack upon the Turkish settlements along the Dnieper.

A Greek named Fomin carried this reply to Wallachia and, when he discovered on arrival that the hospodar had died, he gave the letter to his nephew, Constantine. The latter told Fomin that he was quite willing to become the subject of the great sovereigns, but the current crisis made this an inauspicious moment to write to them. Many must be informed and once the news spread the Austrians would hear of it and destroy them all. He asked the great sovereigns about the conditions under which he might accept their sovereignty, whereupon he would draw up a charter of allegiance for everyone to sign. He and his troops would march to join the tsars' commanders the moment he received confirmation of the march of the tsars' soldiers to the Crimea.

SECOND CRIMEAN CAMPAIGN

In September 1688 plans for a new campaign to the Crimea were announced to the troops. The proclamations stated: "Their holinesses the ecumenical patriarchs, his majesty the Holy Roman emperor, his majesty the king of Poland and the Venetian republic have written to the great sovereigns. All are agreed that the Lord God is inflicting punishment upon the Turkish state, and Muslim rule is about to meet its doom. The Turks have been rendered weak and powerless by the Christian rulers and internecine strife, never before have they suffered such ruin and destruction, never was there such confusion. They themselves say that all Muslims face total destruction and they place their last hope in the Crimean khan and his hordes. In their despair these Muslims have massacred three hundred thousand Orthodox Christians, men, women and innocent babes, by fire and sword, in Greece, Rumelia, Morea, Serbia and Bulgaria, putting them to death after subjecting them to all manner of torments and foul abuse. And they have taken countless numbers of Christian women and children into Muslim servitude and carried them off across the sea."

Taking warning from his earlier experiences of water and grass shortages and fire on the steppe, Golitsyn decided to launch the campaign early in spring. The troops were ordered to mobilize not later than February 1689. On November 8 a levy of tenth money[42] was imposed upon the artisan and merchant communities. It was essential for Golitsyn to conquer the Tatars if he wished to overcome his adversaries at home, who continued to harrass him. It is related that an assassin attacked him in his sledge and was only narrowly restrained by the prince's servants. The assassin was executed in prison after undergoing torture, but the incident was not publicized. Shortly before Golitsyn set off on campaign a coffin was found outside the gates of his residence with an inscription which intimated that if the second campaign was as unsuccessful as the first, the commander-in-chief knew what to expect.[43] Another interesting story survives. A certain Ivan Bunakov was tortured after he had taken a cast of Golitsyn's footprint. Bunakov explained: "I took the earth and wrapped it in a cloth because I had an attack of lumbago; it has always been my custom to gather some earth from the spot where the pain strikes me."[44]

These acts of hostility against the guardian were accompanied by intrigue against his protégé, the new hetman of the Ukraine. Certain good-for-nothings, as Mazepa put it, spread the rumor around Kiev that the hetman was in league with the Poles and was buying up estates in Poland. Governor Buturlin of Kiev sent the scandalmongers to Moscow, and from there they were sent back to Mazepa in Baturin. This prompted Mazepa to write to Golitsyn: "I humbly beg to remind my gracious benefactor and patron that when I was raised to the rank of hetman by your hand you promised in a kind and fatherly fashion to be my patron and defender against misfortune, for you knew the simplicity of my heart and soul. May it please you now to keep your beneficent word and take my part and defend me against such perils. The accusations that I tried to buy property in Poland are quite unfounded; no such thought ever entered my head."

Mazepa asked Golitsyn's permission to torture the men who had spread these rumors. The hetman suspected that Metropolitan Gedeon of Kiev, who had been on cordial terms with Samoilovich, was unfriendly towards him. He knew that the metropolitan's son, Prince Yury Chetvertinsky, the fiancé of Samoilovich's daughter, was living in Moscow and was anxious to have him expelled from the capital by making the authorities suspicious of him. "It is with some regret," wrote Mazepa, "that I hear that Prince Chetvertinsky is living in Moscow and making offensive statements. He disparages their majesties' senate and considers no one his better or even his equal, and he curses them most foully. He also expresses his intention of restoring Samoilovich to his former office and taking revenge against their mutual enemies. And he writes to his former sweetheart here in Little Russia. The metropolitan is a mistrustful man; he obviously is annoyed with me since he thinks that it was I who had his son sent to Moscow in disgrace. Governor Buturlin of Kiev shares the metropolitan's animosity; he never writes to me and has failed to reply to two of my letters. If such disputes are to be avoided Chetvertinsky must be expelled from Moscow." Mazepa also requested that "in the interests of security and as a warning to the lawless" the sovereigns should give him leave to maintain a bodyguard of hired cossack infantry and dragoons.

And so it was that the second Crimean campaign began at a time when both commanders-in-chief were experiencing personal difficulties. In February 1689 one hundred and twelve thousand troops marched into the steppe under the guardian's command. On March 20 Golitsyn wrote to the tsars from Akhtyrka: "Our progress is being hampered by severe cold and heavy snows; and the regimental allowance has not yet arrived, so we have nothing to give the troops, cavalry and infantry." The cold and snow did not impede Mazepa's progress. As soon as he met Golitsyn he submitted a petition to the tsars begging the great sovereigns to reward him, the hetman, and all the Little Russian Host by ordering installation of the royal coat of arms over the towers and town halls of the Ukraine. Golitsyn naturally assured Mazepa that the great sovereigns would grant his request. In the middle of April it was reported that there were no fires on the steppe, but that the khan planned to set the grass alight as soon as Golitsyn drew near to Perekop. When this report reached Moscow a letter was dispatched to Golitsyn instructing him to collaborate with the hetman in sending competent men across the Samara river to burn the grass as far as Perekop and the Turkish settlements on the Dnieper. New grass would have sprung up by the time the Russian army reached the area. Golitsyn set out for Perekop and in the middle of May he met the khan and his hordes. The barbarians swooped down on the Russians in their customary headlong fashion but were repelled by a barrage of artillery fire. They made no further attacks, but groups of them could be seen on the horizon, moving back and forth like clouds. The beasts were encircling their prey, the Scythians were luring the enemy into their boundless steppes.

Golitsyn had repulsed the khan and he was quick to send news of his triumph to Moscow. He wrote to the regent, asking her to pray for his safe return. Sophia wrote back: "Light of my life, my dear Vasenka, may you have long life and prosperity! You have fully earned prosperity since, by the grace of God and the Blessed Virgin and by your own wisdom and good fortune, you have triumphed over the Hagarenes![45] May the Lord grant you further victories over your foes! I cannot believe, light of my life, that you will ever return to us. I shall believe it only when I see you and hold you in my embrace. Why, my light, do you ask me to pray for you? Am I not truly sinful and unworthy in the eyes of God? And yet, sinner that I am, I dare to trust in His merciful goodness. In truth I always ask Him to send joy to my light. And so may you prosper for countless ages."[46]

On May 20 the army approached the renowned Perekop, the fortress castle guarding the channel which intersects the isthmus. Beyond Perekop lay their goal, the cherished Crimea. But what sort of place was the Crimea? Distinguished and highly experienced men such as Gordon long held the theory that the Crimea was not in itself invincible: it was the route across the steppe which presented certain difficulties. Golitsyn had experienced these difficulties in the first campaign and avoided them in the second, but he now reached the Crimea only to find that the most important question was still unanswered: what sort of place was the Crimea, and how should they set about conquering it? It had been thought that they merely need invade the Crimea with a large army in order to alarm the Tatars and force them into submission. It simply had not occurred to them that the arid steppelands which lay beyond Perekop were identical to those on the way to the peninsula, and that the Tatars were perfectly capable of laying waste the countryside and wearing down their adversary by hunger and thirst.

Golitsyn now stood at the approach to Perekop. The fortress must be captured, but the armies had been without water for two whole days. They had hurried to Perekop in the belief that once there all hardships would be over, but what a sight met their eyes: on one side the Black Sea, the Sivash lagoon on the other, nothing but salt water and not a spring in sight. The horses were dying and in a few days' time they would be hard-pressed to make a retreat, with no transport for the guns. Golitsyn was reluctant to go back empty-handed and so he initiated negotiations with the khan in the hope that he would grant concessions to Russia in order to avert an invasion. But the talks dragged on, and Golitsyn could delay no longer; he was forced to turn back without making a truce. Their one consolation was that the Tatars did not add to their sufferings in the fierce heat of the steppe and the tormenting pangs of thirst by making a concerted pursuit. Some two years later Poplonsky, a nobleman from Smolensk, recounted on his release from captivity by the Tatars that "when the tsars' envoy came to Perekop, Nuradin Sultan asked his father why he refused to attack the Russians from Perekop. He said that if his father was reluctant he should command his son to stage the attack. The khan explained that he was holding off his attacks because Prince Golitsyn had sent to him to sue for peace. If negotiations came to nothing and the Russians attacked, they would allow Prince Golitsyn and his whole army to enter Perekop and finish them off without a battle, but both they, the Tatars, and the enemy would perish because there were only three fresh-water springs in Perekop."

On hearing of his retreat from Perekop, Sophia sent Golitsyn the following letter: "My light, my dear and my hope, may you have long life and prosperity! Joyful indeed is this day on which the Lord God has glorified His holy name and the name of His mother, the Blessed Virgin, through you. The like of His divine mercy has not been heard of throughout the centuries, nor have our forefathers related it. God has delivered you, my dear, as once He delivered the Israelites from the land of Egypt through His saint Moses. Praise be to God, Who has chosen you to be the instrument of His mercy! My dear, how can I ever repay you for your innumerable labors? My joy, light of my eyes! I cannot believe that I shall ever see you again, dear heart. Great indeed will be the day when you are with me again, my dear. If only it were possible, I should have you beside me every single day. Your letters, in God's safekeeping, have all reached me. Five dispatches arrived from Perekop on the 11th. I was walking in the vicinity of Vozdvizhenskoe and had just reached the monastery of St. Sergius the Miracle Worker, when at the main gates I received the war dispatches. I cannot remember how I entered; I read as I walked along! How can I ever express my thanks to God and His blessed mother and St. Sergius the gracious worker of miracles for their mercy? I have carried out all your instructions about visiting monasteries and have been to them all on foot. And your zeal, my dear, has been amply demonstrated.

"You write, my dear, that I should pray for you. God knows I long to see you, my love, and I trust in His mercy. Carry out the military operations just as you have written in your letters. I, my lord, am well, thanks to your prayers; we are all well. When, God willing, I see you, my light, I shall tell you everything that has happened. As for you, my light, do not tarry, continue your march gradually. You have put yourself to so much trouble. How can I ever repay you for your great service, for labors greater than all the rest, my light? If you had not taken such pains, no one else would have done so."[47]

An official letter on behalf of the tsars also was sent to Golitsyn. "We, the great sovereigns, give you our most gracious thanks, our own boyar and guardian, for your great and zealous service. By your efforts those savage and inveterate foes of the holy cross and all Christianity have been crushed, defeated and scattered by our royal army in their infidel abode, an event far from fortuitous and quite unprecedented. They destroyed their own dwellings, their customary savage impudence deserted them, they were seized with terror and despair and set fire to the suburbs, villages and hamlets of Perekop. They did not come out of Perekop with their infidel hordes to meet you in battle, and did not engage you as you retreated. And now you have returned in safety to our frontiers with all the troops after winning the aforementioned victories, famed throughout all the world."

Sophia was blinded by passion, delighted that "her light" had escaped from danger and returned in safety from the campaign on the steppe, where he might easily have perished together with his entire army. She saw Golitsyn as a second Moses, leading his people across the sea bed, she thought only of his labors and the dangers he had faced, and saw the repulse of the khan as a feat of heroism and a great victory. There were many others, however, who quite justifiably saw things differently and were offended by all the adulation and rewards for a campaign that had failed to achieve its aim even at the second attempt. Golitsyn's contemporaries were unable to take such a lenient view of his campaigns as can we, separated from the events by more than a hundred and fifty years.

Such was Russia's role in the Holy League against the Turks. In relation to the number of troops, the preparations and the expense involved, the Russian army produced negligible results; it would, however, be wrong to write off the campaign completely, for it did divert the khan's attention and prevented him from assisting the Turks elsewhere.

RELATIONS WITH EUROPE AND ASIA

The crown authorities channelled their main efforts to the south, where Russia was striving to consolidate its hold over the Ukraine by means of Kiev and to win liberation from the humiliation of paying tribute to the Tatars. With these two aims to the fore, they were naturally eager to keep the peace with Sweden, and in January 1683 the terms of the Treaty of Kardis[48] were renewed. Relations with Prussia are also worthy of mention. In 1688 free trading rights in Archangel were conferred upon citizens of Brandenburg. The following year the Brandenburg emissary Czaplitz secured an agreement with the Prussian court establishing free trade between the two countries. The same Czaplitz was also influential in issuance of a royal decree allowing French emigrants of the Evangelical faith, forced to leave their native land by the revocation of the Edict of Nantes, to settle in Russia.[49] The decree stated: "Czaplitz has revealed that his majesty the king of France has begun to persecute those close to him and other adherents of the Evangelical faith. He has tormented many into leaving the country. He has employed sundry cruelties in order to force them to convert to Catholicism against their will, and many have been put to death. He has separated husbands from their wives and children by imprisoning them. Others have managed to obtain their freedom by fleeing to neighboring countries. A great number of these exiles have fled into the domains of his highness the elector of Brandenburg, who expects the arrival of many more of these fugitives from France. There are also some who wish to come to our country, where they hope to find refuge from persecution and secure themselves a livelihood; we have heard their appeal, and regard it with favor."

The favorable response to the appeal was not unconnected with the fact that, in 1687, during a mission to France, the Russian ambassadors Prince Yakov Dolgoruky and Prince Yakov Myshetsky had received a not very courteous reception. The king of France had been displeased by their representations, which served formal notice of the tsars' entry into the Holy League against the Turks, and invited the king to join the allies. In Dunkirk a steward arrived to question them on behalf of the king: "Is the purpose of your mission to offer resistance and to raise issues which will be disagreeable to the king?" The ambassadors replied: "We are truly astonished by this strange question. Our mission is a friendly one; we are not here to start a quarrel. Previous envoys never were asked such extraordinary questions." After some talks with the minister of foreign affairs[50] Louis sent word to the ambassadors that further negotiations were unnecessary. The king was fully aware of the issues and would send a formal reply direct to the ambassadors without further ceremony. Dolgoruky protested that this was quite improper; it was customary for rulers to hand their rescripts to the ambassadors in person. They, the tsars' ambassadors, would accept the letter only from the king's own hand. In his reply the king expressed his extreme displeasure; he vowed to disgrace the ambassadors and ordered that they be returned to the town of Dunkirk on the French border. Dolgoruky replied that he cared nothing for the king's anger; even the threat of death would not induce him to receive the rescript in his own residence.

Louis sent them gifts, but the ambassadors refused them. The master of ceremonies warned the ambassadors that if they persisted in their refusal, the king had ordered the gifts to be placed forcibly in their carriages. The ambassadors replied that they would have nothing to do either with the gifts or the carriages. "Were we guilty of some crime, we should fear the king's anger," said Dolgoruky, "but we are not afraid because we are innocent. Our first duty is to carry out our sovereigns' behests." The French relented. They informed the ambassadors that the minister of foreign affairs would renew his talks with them in Saint-Denis, not in Paris, after which the king would receive them at Versailles. The ambassadors went to Saint-Denis and on August 22 had an interview with the minister. The ambassadors proposed that the king of France join the alliance against the Turks for, as the Savior Himself had said, "For where two or three are gathered in My name, there am I in the midst of them" [Matth. 18:2].

The minister replied: "My sovereign desires to be on friendly and amicable terms with their majesties the tsars. He gives thanks for the alliance against the enemy of the holy cross, and wishes the Christian allies every success. But the king wishes to make it known that he cannot possibly enter into alliance with the Christian rulers at this juncture, for he has learned from the gazettes that the Christian armies have won a victory over the enemy, and if the king were to enter the alliance now and send an army to attack the Turks, he would be the last to win glory. Our great sovereign monarch seeks his own personal glory for his crown; he is sole commander of his forces and will not transfer them to another's command.

"There are other reasons, too, why the king cannot join the alliance. In the past he has sent his armies to aid the emperor against the Turks, but his troops were treated badly by the emperor's men. His army was given the worst positions on the battlefield, where poultry and bread were unobtainable, and where they were in the front line of the enemy's attack. The French armies suffered terrible casualties, yet won no glory. The laurels went to the emperor, who gave us no compensation. When the Turks were approaching Vienna the king offered to send auxiliary troops, but for some reason the emperor spurned his offer. The king sent eight thousand men to help the Venetians in their struggle in Candia and Morea, but the Venetians surrendered these men in battle, and again the king won no glory. The Poles have a small army and they lost many troops in their last war against the Turks; but the king has a large army and is quite capable of winning an independent victory over the Turks. Our country and yours are very far apart; the king cannot possibly send auxiliary troops, besides which the tsars are capable of winning a victory unaided."

The minister finally spoke frankly: "The king cannot enter the alliance because of the inveterate and continuing enmity between him and the emperor and his long-standing truce and firm friendship with the sultan. The king's merchants have important trading links with the Turks; if we break with the Turks, France will be ruined. The world would see little wisdom or glory in the king's action if he helped an enemy fight a friend. This the king will never do."

"How can you prefer a truce with the Muslims to an alliance with Christians?" the ambassador retorted. "The king's merchants will not be ruined by a war with the Turks because most of the merchants on Turkish territory are not Muslims but Orthodox Christians. The Turks will be put to flight by an alliance of Christian rulers, thus liberating the Christians from their yoke; they then will have control of their own trading enterprises and this will provide the French with a better source of profit than their present trade with the Muslims."

"My sovereign has served his country for many years and brought us glory by his wise deeds. But it would be most foolish of him to break his truce with the Turks for no reason whatsoever and assist a man from whom he can expect nothing but ill-will." The ambassadors suggested that the king might at least undertake not to hinder the allies, even if he refused to join their alliance. The minister agreed to this.

After the talks the ambassadors went to Versailles to take leave of the king, but here a new problem arose; in the king's rescript to the tsars the words "great sovereigns" had been omitted. The ambassadors demanded that the rescript be rewritten, but they were refused on the grounds that the king referred to nobody, not even himself, by this title. The ambassadors refused to accept either the rescript or the king's gifts. The master of ceremonies told them that the king had never been so vexed by anybody. The steward and the king's officials left the ambassadors' residence. The ambassadors stayed in Saint-Denis at their own expense, bought horses and prepared to depart for Spain as instructed. When they applied to the minister for a permit to travel through France, however, they received the following reply: "The king will permit you to travel to Le Havre at your own expense, and from there you will be taken by naval vessel to San Sebastian, but he will not permit you to travel overland." When the ambassadors arrived in Le Havre they discovered why they had been assigned this particular route: it was proposed that they either accept the king's gifts, in which case they would be taken to Spain, or remain stranded in Le Havre. The ambassadors accepted the gifts.

It is easy to imagine what effect Dolgoruky's report had at court in Moscow. Not long afterwards two French Jesuits, Avril and Beauvollais, came to Moscow with a letter from Louis XIV, in which he asked the Most Exalted, Sovereign and Magnanimous Princes Ivan and Peter Alekseevich to grant the Jesuits transit through Russia to China. Golitsyn gave the Jesuits a warm welcome and made it be known that, had it depended upon him, the king's request would have been granted, however.... On January 31, 1689[51] the Jesuits were summoned to the Chancellery of Foreign Affairs and informed of the great sovereigns' decision: "his majesty the king of France, in the letter which you presented, wrote in a disagreeable and irregular manner; therefore the great sovereigns have decreed that your letter is unacceptable and that you shall not be permitted to travel to China through the towns of the Great Russian realm. They decree that your letter be returned to you and that you be sent back to your country on the road by which you came. The great sovereigns also have withheld their permission because of your sovereign's rude behavior towards their ambassadors at the time of their mission to France. Their majesties consider this to have been a slight upon their honor."[52]

Dolgoruky was given an honorable reception in Spain and assurance that the king had a permanent alliance with the emperor and assisted him with funds and troops. The Muscovite authorities were so poorly informed of the situation in Europe and the relations between the various powers that the ambassadors had been instructed to ask the king of France to join an alliance with the emperor against the Turks and to ask the king of Spain for a loan of two or three million thalers! The Spaniards replied that they were unable to oblige because their own treasury had been depleted by over-expenditure.

THE TREATY OF NERCHINSK

Whilst Russia was drawing closer to Europe and entering the Holy League of Christian powers to fight the infidels in the hope of shaking off once and for all the shameful vestiges of the Tatar yoke, Moscow was also anxious to put to an end to conflicts in the Far East. Russia and China had clashed over the cossack occupation of the Amur region, to which the emperor of China laid claim. It was essential to end the dispute because Russia was quite unable to send large forces to the unknown lands beyond the Urals, and the cossack detachments, who were perfectly capable of exacting tribute from the small scattered tribes of Siberian natives, proved ineffectual against the manifold armed forces of the Middle Kingdom.

The Albazin Cossacks founded settlements along the Amur, engaged in hunting and trading, enslaved the Chinese subject peoples and exacted tribute from them. The Chinese wrote to Alexis Tolbuzin, the military governor of Albazin, telling him to leave the area and return to Nerchinsk in his own country. They told the Russians to trap sables and other game in their own lands around Nerchinsk, not on the Amur. Tolbuzin naturally ignored this warning. On July 12, 1685 a large force of Chinese appeared and staged an attack on Albazin and captured the town. A treaty was made, under the terms of which Tolbuzin and his men were released. The Chinese left without harvesting the grain, and the governor of Nerchinsk, Vlasov, sent Tolbuzin and his men back to Albazin to gather in the harvest. They were instructed to build a small stronghold in a suitable spot and to harvest the crop from the protection of this stronghold. When they had completed the task they were to erect a new fort or town at a suitable spot below the former site of Albazin in order to concede nothing to the enemy. Tolbuzin harvested the grain and set about rebuilding Albazin.

In June 1686 the town was completed, but in July the Chinese attacked again, about five thousand of them with forty guns. There were less than a thousand defenders. Governor Tolbuzin was wounded fatally by a cannon shot. At this time Lord-in-waiting Fedor Golovin[53] was on his way from Moscow with an army in the capacity of plenipotentiary ambassador. Messengers were sent to Peking to inform the Chinese of Golovin's arrival. When the emperor heard the news he sent an order to his commanders to call off their assault on Albazin. In the spring of 1687 the Chinese, alarmed by the approach of Golovin's army, withdrew to a position some five versts down the Amur from Albazin. This allowed the besieged men in Albazin, who since Tolbuzin's death had been commanded by the cossack captain, Afanasy Baiton, to move upriver. On August 30 the Chinese made a complete withdrawal from Albazin and headed for the mouth of the Ziia river.

On October 10 Golovin received instructions from Moscow listing the terms on which he was to base his negotiations with the Chinese.

(1) The Amur was to be proposed as the boundary between Russian and Chinese territory. If the Chinese rejected this proposal he was to suggest a compromise boundary along the Amur as far as the Bystraia or Ziia river.

(2) If this proposal also was rejected, every effort should be made to designate Albazin as the border.

(3) If this too was turned down, then both the Russians and the Chinese should undertake not to maintain a fort or allow any settlement in Albazin. The present buildings should be demolished and the garrison withdrawn in order to prevent further conflict between the inhabitants of Albazin and the subjects of the emperor. But Russian traders and military servitors must have liberty to operate in the Albazin region along the Bystraia and Ziia rivers. Golovin was urged to press for the inclusion of this clause and, if necessary, to give the Chinese plenipotentiaries a reward

from the sovereigns, which should be presented with all due secrecy and discretion in order to avoid bringing the great sovereigns into disrepute.

(4) If the Chinese still refused to yield, the conclusion of peace terms should be postponed till some later date. Russians should be at liberty to ply their trades in the designated areas until final agreement was reached.

(5) He must employ all his powers of eloquence and friendly persuasion to induce the Chinese plenipotentiaries to consent to a treaty under the terms of the first clause, proposing the second if absolutely necessary and the third only as a last resort. War and bloodshed must be avoided at all costs unless the Chinese offered open hostility or made a surprise attack.

(6) He should find out as much as possible about Chinese methods of warfare: what kind of troops they had, how they fought, their numbers, their battle array and formation, whether they waged war in the field or by water or by raiding and beleaguering towns and fortresses, which methods they appeared to favor and which people they resembled most in military practices.

Golovin did not reach Nerchinsk until August 9, 1689, where he found the Chinese ambassadors waiting for him outside the town. Tents had been pitched in a field for the ambassadors' meetings by Junior Boyar Demian Mnogogreshny, former hetman of the Zaporozhian Host.[54] The Chinese sent two envoys to Golovin to discuss the arrangements for the meetings. They were dressed in Chinese fashion, with Chinese hats, shaved heads and pigtails; they bowed in the Chinese manner, and then requested the presence of a Latin interpreter, as they wished to converse in that language. An interpreter was found. The envoys turned out to be Jesuit priests, a Spaniard by the name of Pereira and a Frenchman named Gerbillon.[55] They apologized to Golovin for having bowed in the Chinese manner and not after the fashion of Christian peoples but said they had no alternative; they were employed by the Chinese and had been accompanied by a Chinese, and a European-style bow would only have aroused suspicion.

Golovin rode up to the tents exactly at the same time as the Chinese ambassadors, and entered at the same moment as they did. The Russians sat in armchairs, while the Chinese sat cross-legged on a wide bench covered with felt and the Jesuits sat a little way off on a smaller bench. The talks were conducted in Latin.

Golovin began by complaining that the Chinese government had opened hostilities without giving prior warning. He demanded that they settle their differences and that all captured territory be returned. The

Chinese replied that the Russian cossack Khabarov and his comrades had come to China, built Albazin and for many years treated the Chinese tributary peoples with unendurable brutality.[56] The emperor had sent an army to capture Albazin, but Governor Tolbuzin had been released on the understanding that he would not return, rebuild the town or cause any quarrels or provocation. He broke his promise, and the emperor again sent his troops to attack Albazin, ordering his army to withdraw as soon as he learned of the arrival of the great ambassador for peace talks. But the territory on which Albazin was built and all the Daurian lands belonged to China.

Golovin retorted that if the Russians had given cause for complaint, the emperor should have reported their offenses to the great sovereigns, as was the universal practice, instead of immediately opening hostilities. The region in which Nerchinsk, Albazin and other forts were situated had never belonged to the emperor; the natives of the region paid tribute to their majesties the tsars. If in the distant past they had ever paid tribute to the emperor they had done so under duress, because the area was remote from the nearest Russian towns; but when the Russians built Nerchinsk, Albazin and other small strongholds in the area the Daurian peoples had resumed their tribute payments to the tsar.

The Chinese ambassadors asserted that the Russians had never ruled the lands of the Amur basin and that all territory to the east of Lake Baikal belonged to the emperor, since it belonged to the Mongol khan who long had been a subject of the emperor. Finally, they came to the problem of defining the border. Golovin declared that the boundary should run the full length of the Amur as far as the sea. The left bank would come under the authority of their majesties the tsars, the right bank under the emperor. The Chinese argued that the Amur river had been ruled by the emperor since the days of Alexander the Great. Golovin replied that it would take too long to confirm this by consulting the relevant chronicles, but that after the time of Alexander many lands had been divided under a number of different rulers. The Chinese abandoned this line of argument and proposed that the border run through Lake Baikal. They clung stubbornly to this proposal, threatening to send more troops to attack Albazin. Golovin reminded them that it was not customary to threaten war during diplomatic conferences; if what they really wanted was war, they should admit it frankly. He asked that this be translated into Mongolian, for he suspected the Jesuits of making their own additions in their translation from Latin into Chinese. This suspicion was confirmed when the Chinese replied that they had instructed the Jesuits to speak only about the frontier but had made no mention of war. Even in Mongolian the Chinese stuck firmly to their proposal of a border through Lake Baikal. Golovin was obliged to present them with his second proposal, of a border along the Bystraia river. The Chinese proposed that the border be at Nerchinsk: the left side, down the Shilka river to Nerchinsk, to go to Russia, the right side as far as the Onon river and the Onon river itself as far as the Ingoda river to go to China. The Chinese had no further proposals, and began to speak of ending the talks.

Golovin then suggested the Ziia river as the border. The Chinese laughed, saying that they could not accept such a boundary. After two sessions of negotiations the Chinese ordered their tents to be removed from the meeting place; they announced that they would not be attending any further meetings since they had no more concessions to make. This was merely a threat. The Jesuits came to Nerchinsk to learn which new concessions Golovin was prepared to make. Golovin replied that he had none. The Jesuits told the interpreter Andrei Belobodsky in secret that Golovin should make his final offer quickly: "We are doing all we can to win over the Chinese, but they are unfamiliar with the practices of political nations, and have a great propensity for war. They will never agree to the Ziia river boundary." Belobodsky replied, on Golovin's instructions, that the great sovereigns would be grateful for their efforts, but that the Russians were not afraid of war.

Golovin now learned that the Chinese ambassadors were in communication with neighboring tribesmen and that the latter intended to betray the great sovereigns by abetting the Chinese in an attack upon Nerchinsk. The Jesuits returned to announce that the Chinese ambassadors were willing to concede a border along the Shilka river as far as the Chernaia river: the right side to remain in the possession of the Chinese, the left of the Russians; it was some seven days' march from Nerchinsk to the Chernaia. Golovin replied that there were small Russian trading posts along both banks of the Shilka below the Chernaia, which he refused to reliquish. Albazin was situated to the south of the Chernaia, and was also seven or more days' marching distance from that river. The Jesuits replied that the emperor had given his ambassadors strict instructions not to abandon Albazin to the Russians; they were adamant on this point. There was also the fort at Argun, but it had such a small population that the Russians could easily cede it to the emperor. Golovin gave Belobodsky a map to deliver to the Chinese ambassadors with a request that they mark upon it any border but the Chernaia river. The Chinese retorted that the Chernaia river was the only border to which they would agree. On his return Belobodsky reported to Golovin that the Chinese were transferring from their waggons into boats. Then the Jesuits brought a new proposal: the frontier should run along the Gorbitsa river, which was located between Nerchinsk and Albazin. The Jesuits told him in confidence that this was to be the very last offer.

Soon afterwards Golovin heard that the tributary Buriat and Onkot were in constant communication with the Chinese ambassadors and had announced their desire to become subjects of the emperor. The Chinese ambassadors had instructed them to drive herds of horses and cattle away from Nerchinsk when the Chinese crossed the Shilka on their way to the town. "In view of the Chinese ambassadors' collusion with the renegades and their great obstinacy over the fixing of the border and for fear that the Chinese might declare war and take all the tributary peoples into their possession and lay waste the Daurian lands," Golovin once more sent Belobodsky to the Chinese with the proposal that the border should be at Albazin, and that both sides should enjoy trading rights in the region of the Ziia river. The Chinese rejected this and suggested instead that the Argun river be taken as the frontier. They insisted that Albazin be ceded to the Chinese but were willing to allow the garrison to withdraw with its armaments and supplies. Golovin was told that a number of boats had left the Chinese camp and were assembling at the rapids below Nerchinsk.

Golovin realized that the Chinese were preparing for war. He was afraid that they and the renegades would devastate the Nerchinsk area and take control of the tribute-paying Tungus, who had about four hundred camps up along the Nercha river. He therefore again sent Belobodsky to inform the Chinese that he would agree to fix the border at the site of Albazin; neither side should allow any settlers in the town, the buildings should be demolished and the garrison withdrawn. The Chinese rejected this proposal on the grounds that Russian outlaws might gather and build other fortresses in the vicinity of Albazin and return to their old crimes. They pointed out that Albazin had been built illegally in the first place, without the tsar's authorization. When Belobodsky demanded that the ambassadors refrain from inciting the tribute-paying natives to betrayal, the Chinese laughed and said that they were not responsible. They invited

Golovin to deal with the matter personally and send in troops to quell the renegades. The Chinese laughed because they realized that Golovin was short of men and that the Russians were far outnumbered by the natives.

The Chinese ambassadors took to their boats and sailed down the Shilka. About three thousand Chinese warriors appeared in the hills around Nerchinsk. They set up their standards opposite Nerchinsk and in the hills about half a verst from the town, pitched their tents and posted sentries around the camp. Golovin sent Belobodsky to find out what the Chinese were up to. He himself left the town with the musketeer regiments in anticipation of a battle. It was impossible for them to entrench themselves in Nerchinsk; the fort could not be defended against an enemy attack, for it was small and ramshackle, and many of the logs had rotted away. Belobodsky returned with the final Chinese offer: the Gorbitsa river, which flows into the Shilka not far from the Chernaia, should constitute the border on one side, and on the other the boundary should run along the Argun river upstream to the Big Godzimur river, which flows into it from the left. The fort at Argun be demolished and no fortresses or settlements should be built along the Argun. Albazin must be destroyed, and the Chinese undertook not to allow any settlement there. Belobodsky told Golovin that he had seen many renegade Buriat and Onkot, armed and doing sentry duty alongside the Chinese.

The Buriat and Onkot continued to cross the river to join the Chinese. Junior Boyar Demian Mnogogreshny was sent out with a detachment to try to persuade them to remain loyal to the tsars, but they refused to enter into negotiation and opened fire. Demian skirmished with them and took a number of prisoners, but lack of men precluded a large-scale engagement with the renegades. In the meantime some two thousand insurgent warriors had positioned themselves up the Nercha river about one and a half versts from the town alongside the Chinese patrols, and their numbers were increasing all the time. The Chinese ambassadors insisted that the patrols were there as a safety measure, not as an obstruction to the diplomatic negotiations. They said that the renegades were no concern of theirs, and that Golovin could deal with them as he wished; they laughed as they repeated this last statement.

On August 23 Golovin sent Belobodsky with an answer to the Chinese proposal. He was influenced by "the Chinese ambassadors' great obstinacy and the treachery of the Buriat and Onkot, and he feared lest the Tungus follow their example and, with the connivance of the Chinese, devastate the Daurian lands and enlist all the nomadic tribesmen of the Lake Baikal region. He had observed the Chinese ambassadors' inclination for war, and had learned from the fur traders and military servitors of the small Daurian settlements that there were few areas suited to colonization between Albazin and the Gorbitsa river, and there had never been any trapping of sables and other fur-bearing animals in the area. He recognized the desirability of retaining control over the mine where silver ore had been discovered, as well as the salt lake and the extensive arable lands on this side of the Argun." He agreed therefore to establish the border area along the Gorbitsa river and to the total destruction of Albazin, with the proviso that neither Russia nor China would allow colonization there. Of the region to the right of the Shilka river, from the mouth of the Argun up to its source, the right side should go to the tsars and the left to the emperor of China.

The Chinese agreed and sent the Jesuits to Golovin for final negotiations, but fresh difficulties arose. Golovin had proposed that the boundary run from the source of the Gorbitsa river to the sea by way of the mountain range which lay alongside the Amur. The rivers which flowed from this range into the Amur were to belong to the emperor and the rivers to the north of this same range were to go to the tsars. The Jesuits said that the Chinese ambassadors were sure to reject this. As they were leaving, the Jesuits secretly handed Belobodsky a letter written in French, in which they asked Golovin to send them sables, ermines and dark brown foxes to make hats, some good liquor, chickens and butter. Golovin sent them forty sables to the value of eighty rubles, a hundred ermines to the sum of ten rubles and a dark brown fox worth ten rubles from the crown treasury, and on his own behalf he sent them a black fox worth fifteen rubles, forty ermines worth four rubles, half a pud of butter, fifteen chickens and a bucket of vodka. In return the Jesuits presented him with two cases each containing a knife, scissors and a rule, worth ten altyns, two paper portraits of the king of France and a printed book on the king's palace at Versailles.

Golovin insisted that the border be defined as previously agreed and that the disputed areas near the sea at the mouth of the Amur as far as the Ud river remain neutral for the time being, as he was unfamiliar with the region around the Amur estuary. The Chinese insisted that the border must run from the source of the Gorbitsa straight along the mountain range to a place on the coast called Sviatoi Nos. They also claimed that

the provision against erection of buildings in Albazin was of little importance and refused to include it in the treaty. Finally the Chinese conceded
the first point, and the Russians the second. A treaty was drawn up defining
the border as follows: the river called the Gorbitsa which flows into the
Shilka river from the left side near the Chernaia river shall constitute the
border between the two states; likewise from its source the boundary shall
run along the stone mountain chain which begins at that river's source
and along the ridge of these mountains to the sea, thus dividing the realms
of both states. All rivers both great and small which flow into the Amur
river from the south side of these mountains shall belong to China, and
all rivers which flow from the other side shall belong to their majesties
the tsars of Russia. Other rivers which lie between the Ud river, which
belongs to the Russian crown, and the border mountains which are located
near the Amur in the domains of China and flow into the sea, and all the
lands between the aforementioned Ud river and the mountains which form
the frontier shall remain undemarcated for the time being, for since the
great and plenipotentiary ambassadors do not have the tsars' authorization
for the demarcation of this area, they will leave it undesignated until some
more suitable time.... Likewise the river called Argun, which flows into
the Amur river, shall form the boundary, so that all the lands situated to
the left of the river as far as its source will go to the emperor of China,
and the lands on the right side to their majesties the tsars of Russia, and
all buildings on the south bank of the Argun river will be transferred to
the other side. The town of Albazin, which was built by the subjects of
the tsars of Russia, shall be razed to the ground, and the inhabitants shall
return to the tsars' territory with all their munitions and other supplies.[57]

DOMESTIC AFFAIRS

At home the major reforms planned in Tsar Fedor's reign had been delayed by the rebellion which broke out immediately after his death. It will
be recalled that at the end of Fedor's reign two delegates had been summoned to Moscow from every town in the country to assist in the task of
regulating and standardizing all forms of service and taxation. When Fedor died these "dual delegates" were sent home and rescripts, in Peter's
name, were sent to all the governors: "We have decreed that the dual delegates be dismissed and sent home; when they return to their cities, suburbs,
urban districts, free settlements, rural communities and villages, they shall
consult with the district elders and fellow citizens of other ranks and see

to the election of officers and sworn fiscal assistants to administer the customs houses, liquor stores and other department of the crown treasury; they shall choose the best and most honest men from among those who made these collections in the past and do so now. And you, governor, shall give them every assistance in these elections, but on no account should you personally participate in the elections or hamper them in any way."

It is not known whether the summoning of the dual delegates produced any results or whether they took home any special instructions. It is worth noting that the rescript warned the governors against intervening in the elections or doing anything to obstruct them, but in fact the governors long had been forbidden participation in elections. The reiteration of the injunction suggests that they had been ignoring this ruling. The inhabitants of the rural district of Viatka had petitioned Tsar Alexis for the right to choose their town clerks by local election, but in June 1682 they filed the following complaint: "Despite the tsar's decree clerks are being employed without local elections; they burden and oppress us by charging for their signatures and taking bribes; they charge exorbitant fees for writing documents. Their extortions and surcharges have ruined us completely and the Viatka region is being depopulated." The sovereigns naturally decreed that clerks be employed only on the basis of local elections.

The problem of peasants, household serfs and debtors who took up trades in the cities dragged on. The Code of Laws of 1649 had enacted that such people be attached to the urban communities and assessed on the same basis as artisans. Since the publication of the Code of Laws, people had been breaking their contracts of bondage, leaving their hereditary and service landlords, and moving to the towns, where they took up trades and paid taxes along with the artisans. A new clash of interests arose: the landlords demanded the return of the fugitives, while the artisans appealed to the sovereign, begging that the fugitives not be handed back as they would then have difficulty in meeting their financial obligations and their taxes would fall into arrears. This posed a grave threat to the government, which reacted by releasing the fugitives from their bondage obligations.[58]

In 1655 Tsar Alexis issued a decree forbidding the restoration of fugitives to their former owners. On December 17, 1684 Tsarevna Sophia decreed that "those people who resided in the artisans' districts and free settlements by virtue of their engagement in trades and handicrafts, or by marriage to tax-paying widows and maidens from the artisan community, or who lived in artisans' districts and towns, both those who were registered in the census of 1678 or were not registered because they were absent on business and others who arrived after the registration—these newcomers, too, shall enjoy the immutable right of residence in the artisans' districts, and shall pay their taxes and render service on the same basis as the artisans. Neither their landlords, either hereditary or by contract, nor any other person shall compel them to become serfs or bondslaves, whereas any peasants who arrive after the decree of December 17, 1684 shall be liable to prosecution."

The countryside was still suffering from depopulation. It was reported to Moscow that "a great number of fugitive peasants with their wives and children from the towns of Russia and the Far North have passed through the settlements of Verkhoturie and the districts of Verkhoturie and Tobolsk." A peasant would flee beyond the Urals to escape his pursuers, for flight was his only salvation from the brutality of the oppressor. When a man assumed the status of serf he took out a contract which enumerated all his obligations but offered him no safeguard against his master's abuse: "I, Ivan Kondratiev, son of Bolshakov, undertake by this bond to discharge my debt to Table Attendant Ivan Grigory Neronov: I, Ivan, received from him a loan of ten rubles in exchange for which I undertake to perform agricultural labor and reside wherever he, my master, shall command. But should I leave my place of residence or fail to perform my duties, or flee his authority, he may exact this debt by committing me to permanent bondage, and he shall be at liberty to sell, mortgage or retain possession of me."

There were certain reprobates who took advantage of the gullibility of the peasants by inciting them to rebel against serfdom. In September 1682 the peasants of the village of Novaia Slobodka and its inhabitants, which belonged to the metropolitan of Belgorod, banded together and sounded the tocsin to call for rebellion. They gathered in mobs and attacked the bailliff of Belgorod, who had been sent to deal with them, tying him up and seizing his memorandum of instructions. They went to the metropolitan's residence and tried to kill the metropolitan's steward and domestic servants. A detachment of musketeers was sent from Belgorod to put down the rebellion, but the rebels refused to surrender. Five of the peasants went to Moscow to appeal for their release from the metropolitan's service; they were arrested and sent to Kursk for trial. It appeared that Fedor Ozerov from Belgorod had come from Moscow and urged the peasants to ask for their freedom. In return he had demanded twenty rubles, arguing that it would cost each household no more than one grivna, and assuring them that now was an auspicious moment to go to Moscow and obtain their release from serfdom. He said that his uncle, Anisim Ozerov, was a secretary in the patriarch's office in Moscow, and would present their petition to the tsars and deal with their case. Ozerov and the metropolitan's peasant, Troshka Chepurny, the ringleaders of the rebellion, were hanged; the other rebels, twenty-seven in all, were mercilessly flogged lying down and standing up, and returned to the metropolitan's custody.

There is a sad old saying that when the wolves fought, the wool flew from the sheep. Boyar Peter Vasilievich Sheremetev was on bad terms with Prince Vasily Golitsyn, and in consequence the officials of the palace took every liberty with Shermetev's peasants. Shishkin, the manager of the crown estate of Dunilovo, the director of the customs and liquor houses and all the peasants and soldiers armed themselves with pole-axes, hatchets, truncheons and pikes, and broke into Sheremetev's village at Goritsa, where a pilgrims' fair was being held on the feast of the Nativity of the Virgin. They pillaged the boyar's house and carried off all his valuables; they beat and injured his peasants and robbed them of their money and every last stitch of clothing. The peasants of Goritsa naturally filed a complaint against their assailants, but in Russia there was another popular saying: "In Moscow they don't do anything for nothing."

In 1683 a laybrother from the Prilutsk monastery came to the Chancellery of Musketeers in Moscow on business and compiled a list of expenses; the secretary received ten rubles, a pie, a loaf of sugar, a salmon, a carved comb, half a pud of poppy-seed candles, two buckets of mushrooms, and his assistants received two altyns. The senior clerk received twenty-eight rubles, a pie and a bucket of mushrooms, and his assistants four dengas. The junior clerk received three rubles, and he and the secretary's nephew drank church wine in the cellar to the sum of seven altyns. In the Treasury the senior clerk received a pie and a salmon for signing a document which went to the Chancellery of Musketeers. The junior clerk received ten dengas for copying this document.

Relations between the weak and the strong are typified by the contract of bondage. An orphan girl lives with her married sister; an extra mouth to feed is a burden, and so the elder sister and her husband place the girl in the employment of a stranger. A contract is drawn up, in which the solicitous and tender relatives stipulate that, not only must the stranger support the girl in return for her labors, but also decide her future with her consent: "I, so-and-so and my wife, have contracted this our kins-woman, her sister and my sister-in-law, to live in the house of so-and-so until she comes of age; and when she comes of age, he shall provide her with a dowry in accordance with his means and give her in marriage to a free man or to the man of her choice. Whilst she is resident in his house, she shall be obedient and respectful, perform various domestic duties and behave herself well; and he shall feed her and provide her with clothing and footwear." She was to behave herself well, and he in return was to provide her with clothing and footwear; it was not deemed necessary to make any stipulation about his behavior towards her.

The picture is unchanging—that of a young society which was yet to impose restraints upon the strong. The strong lived separate, untrammelled lives and waged war among themselves. The government conducted a bloody battle against them, but the hydra thrives in adversity, the sword grows dull, and new methods must be found.

Martha Kishkina, the wife of a service landowner, came to the gover-nor's office in Kaluga with the corpse of her husband. She filed the fol-lowing complaint: "My neighbor Ivan Kondyrev came to the orchard in my village at Chuvasheva with his servants and peasants, all armed, and proceeded to break down our fence and set fire to it. When my husband came out and tried to stop them, Ivan killed him." The corpse was in-spected, and a record made of the case. The governor ordered the murder-er to come to Kaluga, but Kondyrev did not appear, and the governor was powerless to deal with a strong man. When the widow realized that she would get no satisfaction in Kaluga, she took the body to the Chancellery of Investigations in Moscow, where another inspection was made, a record taken and sentence pronounced. Witnesses testified that Kishkin had been killed, not by Kondyrev himself, but by his servants. Kondyrev was given a merciless flogging and exiled to Siberia with his wife, his children remaining behind. One of his estates was transferred to Kishkin's widow, the others left to the offender's children.

A similar incident is also recorded. Levashov and Pushchin, two ser-vice landowners, had a territorial dispute; Pushchin set fire to Levashov's rye- and haystacks, and the enraged Levashov sent his son and peasants to kill Pushchin, which they did. The offender was beheaded. If landown-ers killed each other over land disputes it is not surprising that they tried to keep out land surveyors when they suspected that the measurements might be to their disadavantage. In 1686 the land surveyors complained that junior boyars, cossacks and landowners' servants were assembling in riotous mobs, assaulting them with various weapons, driving them off the land and preventing them from carrying out their work; they took their tapes and destroyed them, and some surveyors, their clerks and their assistants had even been killed. The governor sent honest servitors to conduct an investigation. The culprits were sentenced to be flogged without mercy on the trestles and standing up. Sentence had been passed after a formal investigation, but still the land surveyors continued to complain of abuses.

As always, priests were especially vulnerable to the abuses of the strong. In 1684 Metropolitan Kornily of Novgorod received the following complaint from landowners in the parish of Elijah the Prophet in the Novotorzhok district against Sverchkov, a parishioner of the same church, and his son and kinsmen: "He, Sverchkov, his son and kinsmen drove our priest Vasiliev from the house of God; his kinsmen beat our priest until the blood flowed and, as a result, for a long time there were no services conducted in the church of Elijah the Prophet. And the son of this Sverchkov took the priest out onto the porch, twice forced him to undress and tried to beat him with lashes; at the same time he also lashed the sexton and the reader to within an inch of their lives without any cause whatsoever."

In 1688 the priest Yakov from the district of Arzamas reported that Ivan Rzhevsky had invited him to his home to conduct prayers and dine there with his wife. Peter Shadrin was also there. After dinner the priest's wife went home and Shadrin's servants, on their master's instructions, waylaid her on the street, assaulted her and left her for dead. Yakov came out to collect his wife, and he too was set upon and injured. When they reached home the priest's wife was on the point of expiring as a result of her dreadful injuries. The priest sent his son to Michael Argamakov's estate to fetch the priest Varfolomei to hear his wife's confession and administer the last rites. When Varfolomei arrived, Yakov was not at home, having gone to Peter Shadrin's house. When he left there to set off home, Ivan Rzhevsky's son Afanasy rushed out of Shadrin's house with his servants, beat him up and made for his house. They were followed by Peter Shadrin and his servants. They found Varfolomei hearing the wife's confession in her chamber; Afanasy Rzhevsky seized the priest by his stole, dragged him from the room and began, with the help of his own and Shadrin's servants, to beat him within an inch of his life. Rzhevsky spilled the Holy Sacrament beneath his feet and trampled it, exclaiming as he struck Varfolomei:

"You are Michael Argamakov's priest, so why do you come to our parish with your sacraments? Peter Argamakov and his son will get the same treatment as you."

Brigandage had long been rife in Russia, for circumstances favored its growth. It was reported earlier how the superior of a monastery turned robber and now the period under consideration provides us with another remarkable incident. In 1688 Prince Yakov Lobanov-Rostovsky and Ivan Mikulin staged a hold-up on the Trinity road in the hope of intercepting the sovereigns' guards with money from the royal treasury. They waylaid the guards and stole the money, killing two men in the process. The robbers were put on trial and, on the findings of the court, Prince Yakov was brought from his residence to the Red Porch in a common sledge and there sentenced to be flogged in the attendants' cellar at the request of the lady-in-waiting and nurse, Princess Anna Nikiforovna Lobanova: he was also irrevocably dispossessed of four hundred peasant households, and his Kalmyk servant and treasurer were hanged for their part in the robbery. Mikulin was flogged without mercy on the square, exiled to Siberia, and irrevocably deprived of his service and hereditary estates.

There are many records to crimes committed by members of the nobility. In 1684 Peter Vasilievich Kikin was sentenced to be flogged in front of the Chancellery for Musketeers for seducing a young girl. This same man once had been tortured in Viatka for attempting to forge the signature of a crown secretary. In 1685 Khvoshchinsky, a servitor, was flogged for trying to forge a document on an empty roll of parchment. Prince Peter Kropotkin was flogged for erasing a signature and inserting his own. Kutuzov and Naryshkin, both servitors, were beaten with rods for standing surety for a servant of the tsarevich of Kasimov.[59]

It is interesting to observe the legislation approved at this time.[60] At the beginning of Sophia's regency it was enacted that a man who had committed robbery or theft without murder or arson, was to be flogged, deprived of his left ear and two fingers from his left hand, and banished to Siberia with his wife and any dependent children. Two crimes earned the penalty prescribed in the Code of Laws of 1649, three the death sentence. The following year, however, it was resolved that criminals should have their ears cut off instead of their fingers; at the same time the prescription of the death penalty for seditious utterings was commuted to flogging and banishment to various locations. At the beginning of 1689 it was enacted that wives who murdered their husbands were to be decapitated instead of being buried alive, as formerly had been the practice.

Private contracts contained no provision for the good behavior of a master towards those who entered his service, nor were such safeguards deemed necessary; but the government did make some attempt to protect unfortunate debtors from ill-treatment by their creditors, to whom they had been bound over to work off their debts. In 1688 it was decreed that male debtors and their wives and female debtors and their husbands discharge their debts to the sum of five rubles per year for men and two and a half rubles per year for women. The creditors to whom they were entrusted were required to provide written guarantees that they would not kill or injure the debtors. The same year it was decreed that widows and children must not be held liable for the payment of debts if their relatives died leaving no property.

Some of the decrees issued at the beginning of Sophia's regency provide a sharp and fascinating insight into the social mores of the period. There are certain phenomena which, despite their apparent triviality, can give a true measure of social development. One would certainly consider, for example, a place where a man meets an acquaintance on a busy street and quite calmly stops to talk to him in the middle of the road as socially underdeveloped, as one would a place where people do not keep to the right or drive at full speed along the busy streets of large cities. Phenomena such as these smack of the steppe, they indicate that people are accustomed to leading their own untramelled lives, just as their Dregovich or Viatich[61] ancestors did; they reveal ignorance of the fact that in society no one can do anything without first considering the effect his action might have upon others. In view of the many antisocial acts committed in our own time, it is no surprise to come across decrees forbidding people to drive horses in the streets with long whips and inadvertently striking passers-by, or bans on shooting firearms indoors, or depositing dung, carrion and other foul excrement on the streets. One decree states: "Table attendants, crown agents, Muscovite servitors and court attendants! Your servants indiscriminately have been leaving their horses in unauthorized places in the Kremlin; they make a din with their shouting and engage in fist fights; they obstruct passers-by, shoving them, tripping them up and whistling at them. And when the captains of the guards and the musketeers try to move them from the unauthorized places and dissuade them from their shouting and misbehaving, your servants insult the captains and musketeers and threaten to assault them." This decree concerned servants, but it also was found necessary to curb the unruly behavior of their masters in the palace itself.

No one dared openly to insist upon the right of precedence, in other words to refuse to accept an appointment on the grounds that they found it impossible to serve alongside some individual,[62] but there were instances of people finding pretexts for avoiding appointments they deemed unsuitable on these grounds. In 1686, for example, Boyar Prince Vladimir Dmitrievich Dolgoruky refused to send his sons to serve as palace bodyguards alongside the Golitsyns, claiming that they were sick and had gone off to pray at the St. Nicholas monastery at Ugresha. The regent ordered that Boyar Prince Vladimir be stripped of his rank, and that his sons, Princes Boris and Luke, be registered as provincial servitors; in addition Boris and Luke were dispossessed of their service and ancestral estates. Boris and Luke tearfully begged for mercy, claiming that it was not their unwillingness to serve with the Golitsyns that had kept them from attending court, but the fear that they somehow had aroused the sovereigns' wrath and displeasure. All the Dolgorukys were pardoned.

Whilst the crown was doing battle with the raiders of the steppe in order to end the humiliating payment of tribute, and fighting at home against the antisocial behavior displayed everywhere in the community, the church too had a dual battle to wage. The victory over the dissenters in Moscow after July 5, 1682 had not put an end to the schism, which continued to flourish in the provinces. The victors grew increasingly more exasperated and were forced to take even stronger measures against their stubborn opponents. In November 1682 official letters were sent to all prelates of the church instructing them to conduct exhaustive investigations and bring dissenters to trial. In 1683, in the Pskov Caves monastery,[63] Ulian Ivanov, a laborer from the monastery's artisan quarter, submitted a complaint to the archimandrite, steward and brethren: he reported that unknown dissenters had corrupted his wife Ekaterina and led her astray from the true church; they had talked her into running away somewhere. They were living in the monastery artisans' quarter in the house of the widow Agafitsa, and were teaching people schismatic beliefs. The priest Ivan Andreev was sent to arrest the newcomers together with the widow Agafitsa, and bring them to the Caves monastery.

At the interrogation one of the dissenters said that he was a Russian by birth and that his name was Martynka Kuzmin; he had lived as a laborer in his own house in Pskov, but the house had been destroyed by fire and the site taken for the building of a church and since then he had lived as best he could. He had come to the Caves monastery for the feast of the

Dormition, and had put up in the artisans' quarter with his sister, the widow Agafitsa. But he had not come to church to celebrate the festival because they used the new form of singing and liturgy, and the mass was celebrated, not with properly consecrated bread, but with small round loaves.[64] He had been to confession about ten years ago, and as he was receiving the sacrament of modern bread, serpents appeared from the bread and began to writhe and wave about. Since then he had neither been to confession nor received communion.

When he entered the treasury cell where the investigation was being conducted, Martynka did not make obeiance to the holy icons. When questioned on this, he replied: "Those icons are not holy; the Christian faith has dried up, and the icons are no longer sanctified. Today they even celebrate the liturgy in the Roman manner with small unleavened loaves; the communion bread is imprinted, not with the true cross, but with a Latin one, and the true life-giving cross of Christ has been put to death all around us. All the priests," Martynka continued, "are forerunners of Antichrist. The Antichrist has been in the world for two years—I saw him in the Caves monastery: he is Metropolitan Markell of Pskov. Tsar Alexis had the monks of the Solovetsk monastery put to death for their faith, and on the third day the tsar died.[65] I have been sent from God to teach and preach the Christian faith. The heavenly apostles Peter and Paul are my kin. Christians should cross themselves with two fingers, not three. Old Nick the Devil and all the powers of darkness are seated in that cross. When Antichrist appeared, the altars in the church of the Life-giving Trinity in Pskov and in the Caves monastery fell to the ground; and the Holy Trinity and the Blessed Virgin are now in the heavens, not in the church."

Martynka revealed under torture that everything he said in the interrogation he had learned at the Solovetsk monastery. He also added that when Michael Fedorovich was tsar, it was in reality the Archangel Michael who reigned. After enduring harsh torture by fire, tongs and the rack, Martynka made a full confession, declaring that he would obey the Holy Church in all things. Martynka's mentor was found to be his friend Ivashka Merkuliev, who had been arrested with him and also crossed himself in the old manner and professed the Old Belief. The boyars sentenced Merkuliev to be burnt at the stake and ordered that his ashes be collected and trampled underfoot. Martynka and Agafitsa were given over to the metropolitan's custody.

In the reign of Fedor the monk Daniel had led a hermitage on the Berezovka river in the Tobolsk region, and burned himself to death with his devotees when he heard that government troops were approaching.[66] In 1682 the government received reports that people of all ranks were leaving the towns and free settlements, abandoning their homes, property, livestock and crops and making for the Utiatsk settlement on the Tobol, where the settlement elder, Fedor Inozemtsev, led a hermitage very similar to the one on the Berezovka. The government posted armed detachments to prevent people from entering the settlement. In 1685 it was decreed that anyone who tricked ordinary folk and their wives and children into burning themselves to death themselves would be burnt at the stake. A response to this measure was not slow in coming: that same year about thirty dissenters burned themselves to death in a barn in the hamlet of Ostrovo, which belonged to the Khutynsk monastery. Another group barricaded themselves in the Paleostrovsk monastery[67] and burned themselves to death in the church when they heard that Colonel Mishevsky was on his way there. The ringleader, Emilian Ivanov, who had incited them to self-immolation, survived; he robbed the monastery treasury, made his escape and again began to attract crowds of followers. In 1689 once more he ensconced himself and his comrades in the Paleostrovsk monastery. The detachment sent to arrest the dissenters tracked down three refuges in the impenetrable forest and burned them, but on their way back they had to fight off a dissenter attack for two nights. The dissenters who had barricaded themselves in the Paleostrovsk monastery set fire to the buildings and perished in the flames.

The dissenters fled across the Swedish and Polish borders and into the cossack steppes in order to escape persecution. Already they had gained a foothold on the Don, where their numbers were still growing. In 1683 the cossacks had identified one Kuzma Kosoi as the ringleader, but he remained at liberty. In 1686 about seven hundred dissenters suddenly swarmed into Cherkassk, urging the cossacks to support the Old Belief. The Orthodox believers drove off their uninvited guests after an armed tussle. In November of that year Loban, a Ukrainian cossack, arrived in Ostorozhok from the Don and reported that he had been forced to leave the town of Kagalnik, where he had lived for the past thirty years, by the many dissenters who had come to the cossack towns along the Medveditsa and Chir and other small rivers of the steppe. The dissenters were plotting to go to Moscow to kill the patriarch, boyars and prelates of the church, who had all deserted the faith. Loban asked to be sent to Moscow, where he would divulge some "secret" information. In Moscow he revealed that a priest called Kuzemka (Kuzma Kosoi) was living on the Medveditsa river, where he was fomenting disorder and calling himself the pope.

The "pope" and his followers had established a community on the Medveditsa, named Kuzmin after its founder, and from here the dissenters had launched their offensive against other settlements.

At the end of September 1688 the Don Cossacks sent a detachment under the command of Ataman Kuteinikov to attack the settlement. On arrival at Kuzmin, Kuteinikov erected a stockade with a platform and "did battle with the dissenters with excavations and wooden storming equipment," but to no avail. The cossacks next tried to storm the settlement using a wooden rampart, which they spent a whole day constructing. Behind this rampart they built another platform from which they taunted the dissenters with their pikes and hurled bricks; but the cossacks were forced to retreat when the besieged dissenters succeeded in setting fire to the rampart. On February 1, 1689 another ataman, Averkiev, was sent to Kuzmin to relieve Kuteinikov. Averkiev beleaguered the settlement until May, when he at last managed to capture and destroy it and kill the dissenters.

Apart from Kosoi, the leading dissenters on the Don were the three priests Dosifei, Pafnuty and Feodosy. In 1688 the arrival of a cossack detachment forced them and their followers to flee across the border into the territory of Shavkal Tarkovsky, and they settled on the Argakhan river.

In the village of Repnoe in the district of Voronezh there appeared an itinerant called Vasily Zheltovsky. This man refused to receive the priest's benediction or make the three-fingered sign of the cross; he blasphemed against the churches, the Orthodox faith and the priesthood. "Can these be churches and priests?" he asked. "Our God is in heaven, but there is no god on earth." Then he would cross himself and exclaim, looking up at the sun: "My God, why have You punished me alone?" When he was brought to the ecclesiastical office in Voronezh, the devil constrained him to remain silent. A monk called Sergei from the metropolitan's residence reported that he had seen Vasily in the cossack settlement of Ilovlia, where he had spoken of the churches as mosques, and had belittled the body and blood of Christ. He had claimed that the sovereigns were not in Moscow, and called them Antichrists, the patriarch their agent, and the priests their envoys.

Under torture Zheltovsky confessed to nothing, simply stating that his father and brother were on the Don. Zheltovsky was banished to the Svirsk monastery, and Sergei to the Siisk monastery.[68] Whilst the cossacks were doing battle with the dissenters, in Moscow the monks Savvaty and Gavril started a quarrel about certain incidents in Cherkassk itself. Savvaty reported that services in Cherkassk first were conducted from the revised service books, but when Gavril began to officiate in the cathedral he went to the cossack assembly and insisted that the four-armed cross was Latin. The Host heeded this warning and ordered that the communion loaves be baked according to his specifications and stamped with an eight-armed cross, and that services be conducted from the old books. Gavril was tortured, but denied being a dissenter or having committed any crime beyond officiating in the Don cathedral from the old service books.

The schism was causing great problems on the Don, as were certain cossack claims which the Muscovite authorities felt bound to reject. In 1685 the Don Cossack Host submitted the following petition to the tsars: Abbess Uliana and the nuns of the Intercession convent in Voronezh had complained to the cossack assembly that people from Korotiak were damaging and destroying their estate at Farasan, and that there was nobody to protect the interests of their peasants. The cossacks therefore begged the great sovereigns to favor them by granting them possession of the estate at Farasan and awarding the sisters an emolument. The nuns were brought to Moscow, and the abbess banished to a convent in the north, despite her protestations that she herself had not visited the cossacks; she had sent two nuns to beg for alms, but had not instructed them to appeal to the cossacks. A rescript was sent to the cossacks warning them not to interfere in matters which did not concern them.

This incident was not unique. Dosifei, the treasurer of the Trinity Borshchov monastery in Voronezh, and eight monks drew up a complaint against Abbot Kornily on behalf of themselves and the monastery workers and sent it to the Don Cossacks. The monks were brought to Moscow, where they tried to exculpate themselves by claiming that the cossacks had come to the monastery and compelled them with threats to write the complaint against their abbot. Bishop Mitrofan of Voronezh complained that the Don Cossacks were undermining his authority over the brethren and peasants of the Borshchov monastery; the cossacks were refusing to hand over accused persons to the bishop's court.

In Siberia and the Novgorod region, along the Don and in Moscow, the dissenters continued to spread the rumor that the patriarch was false because he had been infected with the Latin heresy. Patriarch Joachim was obliged to write to the tsars and Tsarevna Sophia and beg them to defend the church against its detractors: "Do not allow the honor of the prelates and the entire priesthood to be defiled by these ignorant and troublesome people; rid us of this corruption and these numerous affronts."

The patriarch was locked also in an intractable and hazardous battle with men whom he himself accused of disseminating Latin innovations and heresy. During the reigns of Tsar Alexis and Tsar Fedor, Latin and Polish influences had penetrated into Russia, together with the Latin and Polish languages, which had gained wide currency at court and among the aristocracy. The chief propagator of this influence had been Simeon Polotsky, the tsarevich's tutor, who very soon came into conflict with the old teachers and the patriarch himself.[69] Simeon refused to yield to the dignitaries of the Russian church, whom he considered to be more ignorant than himself, and the Russian clergy naturally were offended by his attitude; they detected a disparity between Simeon's views and those sanctified by antiquity, and took great pleasure in offering this as evidence of the troublesome newcomer's dissidence. They chose as their spokesman Epifany Slavinetsky,[70] a monk who had been summoned to Moscow from Kiev, and who was famed for his extensive erudition. He was, however, something of a scholarly recluse, temperamentally unsuited to acting as a leader and inspiring others to action.

The following contemporary account provides an excellent illustration of how Patriarch Joachim and his supporters felt about Polotsky, and how they tried to play Slavinetsky off against him. "A certain hieromonk called Epifany Slavinetsky was summoned from Kiev to Moscow by Tsar Alexis Mikhailovich to instruct the children of the Slavonic Russian people in the Hellenic arts. He was very learned, not only in grammar and rhetoric, but also in philosophy; he was a renowned investigator of theology, a highly skilled debater and a meticulous translator of Greek, Latin, Slavonic and Polish." There was also another hieremonk, Simeon Polotsky, and he was also a learned man, but not as erudite as Slavinetsky; he knew Latin and Polish, but had no knowledge of Greek. Once Patriarch Pitirim invited both Epifany and Simeon to his residence. They began to converse, and Simeon asked Epifany: "What, father, does your reverence believe

about transubstantiation?" Epifany replied that transubstantiation occurred after the priest's prayer inviting the descent of the Holy Spirit.[71]
To which Simeon replied: "In Kiev there are learned men who profess
and believe that the sacraments are transformed by the repetition of
Christ's words of institution: Take, eat." Epifany replied:"Our Kievan
scholars have studied and still study only in Latin; they have read only
Latin books. They do not know the truth because they have no knowledge
of Greek." Patriarch Joachim said of Polotsky: "Although he was a learned
and virtuous man, he had been trained by the Jesuits and subverted by
them, and that is why he only read Latin books." The patriarch called
Polotsky's *Crown of Faith* "a plaited crown of thorns, grown in the west."
His *Spiritual Repast* was full of hidden snares for the spirit.[72]

Two learned monks, summoned to Moscow to teach the children of
the Slavonic Russian people, were raising the notorious dispute over the
exact moment of transubstantiation. Polotsky's words implied the heresy
of artolatry;[73] he suggested that the bread must be worshipped by asserting that transubstantiation takes place when the priest pronounces Christ's
words of institution, that is to say, before the accepted time. Polotsky was
not the only disseminator of this heresy; Patriarch Joachim attested that
the heresy came to Moscow with Russian youths who had studied Latin
in Poland. On their return these young men transmitted the Latin practice
to leading clergymen of their acquaintance and to nobles holding high
office at court. They came to believe that the mystery really did occur when
Christ's words were pronounced.

It was essential for Russians to know when the great mysterious transformation took place, and to make their prayers conform with it, but the
argument was not easily resolved. When Polotsky died he left behind a
Russian disciple who was prepared to fight for his teacher's opinions and
was perfectly capable of doing so. Semen Petrovich Medvedev had been
a clerk in the Privy Chancellery in Tsar Alexis's reign, and had been
friendly with a colleague by the name of Fedor Shaklovity.[74] Medvedev's
ability soon attracted the attention of the authorities and he was sent to
study Latin under Simeon Polotsky. He studied for three years and when
Ordin-Nashchokin was sent on his mission to Courland, Medvedev and
his colleagues were ordered to accompany him "for educational pur-
poses."[75] The learned clerk did not wish to remain at the chancellery and
in 1674 he took monastic vows under the name Silvester. His reputation
as a monk of great intelligence and scholarly acumen earned him the post
of superior of the Savior (Zaikonospassk) monastery in Moscow.

Medvedev became a fervent advocate of Polotsky's views, including the heresy of artolatry, but his friendship with Shaklovity assured his position at the regent's court. Then the learned Medvedev began to speak disparagingly of Patriarch Joachim's abilities, and personal enmity flared up alongside the dispute over the time of transubstantiation and other of Polotsky's teachings and Latin innovations. Medvedev's most powerful opponents in the debate were the corrector Evfimy and the sacristan Akinf who, Polotsky claimed, were subverting the patriarch's soul. Evfimy and Akinf found powerful allies. In 1682 Karion Istomin,[76] archdeacon of the Miracles monastery, had presented some verses to Tsarevna Sophia, admonishing her to bring the plans of her brother Fedor to fruition:

> Therefore entreat our present autocrats
> That they the sovereigns command,
> That they our common masters decree
> That learning be instituted
> And teachers be appointed.

Teachers were appointed and arrived in 1685, two Greek scholars, the brothers Ioanniky and Sofrony Likhud,[77] who in the same year introduced courses for pupils of the former Printing House school and for people of various professions and ages, including priests, monks, sons of princes and table attendants. Learning was instituted: the Likhuds taught grammar, rhetoric, poetics, logic and physics; grammar and poetics were taught in Greek, rhetoric and physics in Greek and Latin.

The Greek scholars provided Joachim with powerful support in his struggle against the views of Polotsky. A polemic arose between them and Medvedev. Medvedev wrote a work entitled *Manna*, in which he tried to prove that transubstantiation occurred when the Words of Institution were uttered. The Likhuds set about refuting this in their book *Akos*, or an antidote to the poisonous bite of the serpent. Deacon Afanasy wrote a refutation of *Akos*, subtitled "A Polemic against Ioanniky and Sofrony Likhud." The Likhuds replied with their *Dialogues* between a Greek teacher and a Jesuit. The controversy did not confine itself to scholars, but became a general topic of interest. Not only priests but laymen too, even women, were arguing about the time of transubstantiation wherever they met. Not all prelates shared the patriarch's opinion. In a letter of instruction from Metropolitan Paul of Riazan to the clergy of his diocese we read: "You must be firm in your convictions about the blessed liturgy. When the words *Take, eat and drink* are pronounced, concentrate your whole mind on these words, if the bread is to become Christ's body and the wine His blood; as they are spoken, think this and nothing else. Take heed, O priest! For if at that moment your mind is resolute, you will perform the holy liturgy correctly but if, as your lips pronounce the words, your mind thinks differently, you are committing a mortal sin."

Poles and Jesuits then visiting Moscow intervened in the debate. Polish books, full of Latin sophisms, were passed from hand to hand, and people were heard to say that the Latins had overcome the Greeks at the Council of Florence.[78] Very little was known about the Council of Florence and the authorities had difficulty in obtaining works which could help them refute their opponents. Joachim wrote to Metropolitan Gedeon of Kiev: "The serpent of hell is breathing its vengeance upon our flock because we have sinned; some accept the Council of Florence and praise it, others reject its decision. The matter is being hotly debated, but neither side can produce written evidence for lack of references in our own books. Perhaps you, my son, can endeavor to enlighten us and explain why the council was convoked, how it began and whether its decisions were accepted by all four patriarchs. We hope to be able to obtain information from your books because you have more manuscripts and printed books on the topic than us." Gedeon sent an explanation and referred to printed works which contained reports of the Council of Florence, including one published in Moscow in 1648, *The Book of the One True and Orthodox Faith and of the Holy Eastern Church*. At the end of his letter Gedeon wrote: "I confess to your holiness, my father, chief pastor and superior, that I do not accept the Council of Florence; indeed, I denounce it as foul heresy."

The matter might have rested there, but Medvedev's supporters produced a book printed in the Ukraine, *An Exposition of the Holy Church and the Divine Liturgy*, in the hope of substantiating their views. Joachim again applied to Metropolitan Gedeon, to Archimandrite Varlaam Yasinsky of the Kiev Caves monastery and to Lazar Baranovich in Chernigov. He referred them to the authority of the fathers of the Eastern church and denounced the new books printed by Mohila[79] (the great prayer book and service book, the *Exegesis* of Silvester Kossov, the *Book of the Seven Sacraments* and the *Lifos*) on grounds that they were at odds with Orthodox teaching. But there was no reply from Kiev. The patriarch was insistent that the Ukrainian clergy voice their agreement with the Muscovite definition of the time of transubstantiation, threatening to complain to the four patriarchs if they failed to do so and demanding that they send "a man of humility and understanding, a true son of the Eastern church, well-versed in the writings of the holy fathers but not practised in syllogisms and scholastic arguments."

The Kievan churchmen's silence was due to the fact that they were at the time engaged in another correspondence with Moscow. Copies of Medvedev's *Manna* and the works of the Likhuds had been sent to Hetman Mazepa and leading churchmen in Kiev. They had written a denunciation of the latter and given it to Prince Vasily Golitsyn to send back to Moscow when he was waging his second campaign in the Crimea.

The Medvedev party had strong backing at court; *Manna* was actually commissioned by Tsarevna Sophia. Golitsyn sent on the denunciation of the Likhuds which had been written in Kiev. He had, after all, been responsible for the arrival of the Jesuits in Moscow. A French Jesuit, in Moscow for permission to travel to China across Siberia, gave the following estimation of Golitsyn: "The first minister, who is descended from the noble family of Jagiello, was without doubt the most worthy and enlightened of the magnates at the Muscovite court. He liked foreigners, especially the French, for he observed that they possessed the same noble propensities as himself: that is why he was reproached for having a heart as French as his name [Gaul]. Had it depended on him alone, all our requests most certainly would have been granted. Had he been sole master in his realm, had his relations with the other boyars not obliged him to act circumspectly, he gladly would have permitted us to travel through Siberia and would have facilitated our access to China, for he had great respect for King Louis, whom he admired passionately. I was assured that his son wore a portrait of his majesty in the form of a Maltese cross, which his father deemed a great token of respect."[80]

Another envoy who was also in Russia at the time referred to Golitsyn as a great man. Here he describes his first audience with the first minister of state: "I thought myself to be in the court of some Italian ruler. Our conversation was conducted in Latin and we discussed all the more important current events in Europe. Golitsyn wished to know my opinion of the war which the emperor and so many other rulers are waging against France, and was especially eager to hear about the English revolution. He had me accept vodkas and spirits of various sorts, but advised me not to drink any of them. Golitsyn wanted to colonize the desert, enrich beggars, make savages into men, turn cowards into heroes and herdsmen's huts into stone palaces. Golitsyn's house was one of the most magnificent in Europe."[81]

A detailed description of this magnificent house has survived, written by order of the authorities after Golitsyn's downfall.[82] "In the main hall there is a vaulted ceiling, with a canvas covering; in the middle of the ceiling is a sun with rays, gilded with gold leaf. Around the sun are painted the heavenly constellations with the signs of the Zodiac and the planets; from the sun is suspended a white ivory chandelier on three iron bars; it has five sides with eight candleholders on each; the value of the chandelier is a hundred rubles. To one side of the sun is a silver moon with rays; around the ceiling gods and goddesses are depicted in twenty carved and gilded panels. Four German prints in four carved frames, each worth five rubles." Golitsyn had portraits of Grand Prince Vladimir of Kiev, Tsars Ivan IV, Fedor Ivanovich, Michael Fedorovich, Alexis, Fedor, Ivan and Peter and four portraits of [Polish] kings. On the walls of the room were five mirrors, one in a tortoiseshell frame. In the same room there were forty-six windows with glass panes; the glass was decorated with pictures of men and beasts. In the bedroom there were maps printed on canvas in Germany, hung in gilded wooden frames, four mirrors, two stone busts of negroes, and a German bed of carved walnut, decorated all over with human heads, birds and plants. This bed has a carved wooden head with a mirror in the middle, and is worth a hundred and fifty rubles.[83] There were nine chairs upholstered in gilded velvet, a number of chiming and table clocks in tortoiseshell cases, covered with whalebone and red leather, a German mounted on a horse containing a clock, fascinating cupboards with a large number of drawers, amber inkstands, and three German figurines in walnut, holding glass trumpets, each bearing a brass medallion with German inscriptions and beneath the trumpets mercury in glass bowls.

The first minister had many books: *A Euology to the Pious Sovereigns*, composed by Hieromonk Anthony Rusakovsky. A printed book of thanks to the great sovereigns. A manuscript of the charter to the Academy. A book in manuscript on civic life or the good organization of all matters pertaining to the life of the community.[84] The testament of Emperor Basil to his son Leo the Philosopher. How Empress Olunda gave birth to twins and how her mother tried to murder them.[85] A printed grammar. A book in Polish. A manuscript of Hiob Ludolph.[86] A manuscript of Deacon Meletius's translation from the ecumenical patriarchs.[87] A translation from Polish of a book called the Quran of Mahomet. A translation from Polish of the tale of Magielone Krolewnie.[88] A book on diplomacy, with instructions on the protocol of various states. Four books in German. Four manuscripts on the staging of comedies.[89] Eight calendars for various years. A manuscript of the law or military regulations of Holland. A songbook in German. A Polish-Latin grammar. A history in Polish in manuscript. A medical primer for horses. A book in German with illustrations of various fishes and animals. The Code of Laws. A genealogy. A list of regulations. A manuscript of Yury the Serb.[90] The Kievan Chronicler. The Solovetsk petition. A book on the art of warfare.[91] A German book on land surveying.[92]

In [July] 1689 these magnificent rooms saw the sad return of their owner from his unsuccessful campaign. Once again people began to flock into the lavishly decorated chamber to seek the favorite's mediation; they admired the sun and moon on the ceiling, spoke of the success of the campaign and congratulated him on the favors the tsars had bestowed upon him. But Golitsyn realized that many people were displeased by these favors, considering them to be undeserved. The regent gave Golitsyn her full support, extolling his heroic feats, but the crown itself was in need of support, and Golitsyn was unable to provide it. He had failed to enhance his reputation as a military commander by crushing the settlements of the heathen Tatars, and in so failing had forfeited the people's love, which would have allowed him to shield Sophia and keep her enemies respectfully at bay. The failure of the Crimean campaign had robbed them of all moral means of salvation. Now only Shaklovity was in a position to support Sophia by methods of which Golitsyn was incapable. The guardian was in a dilemma: he disapproved of Shaklovity's methods, but he was obliged to suppress his distaste and timidly wish success to the only man who could save him. The time for procrastination was past. Matters were fast coming to a head.[93]

NOTES

Additional information on personalities and topics found in the text and notes is available in Joseph L. Wieczynski, ed., *The Modern Encyclopedia of Russian and Soviet History* (MERSH); Harry B. Weber, ed., *The Modern Encyclopedia of Russian and Soviet Literatures (Including Non-Russian and Emigre Literatures)* (MERSL); Paul D. Steeves, ed., *The Modern Encyclopedia of Religions in Russia and the Soviet Union* (MERRSU); and David R. Jones, ed., *The Military-Naval Encyclopedia of Russia and the Soviet Union* (MNERSU), all published by Academic International Press.

A comprehensive account of the period immediately preceding the era covered in this volume, with illustrations, an extensive bibliography and background information, is Joseph T. Fuhrmann, *Tsar Alexis. His Reign and His Russia* (Gulf Breeze, Fla., Academic International Press, 1978).

CHAPTER I

1. Soloviev uses the adjective Western Russian (zapadnorusskii) to refer to inhabitants of the areas now termed Ukraine and Belorussia. In the seventeenth century part of these regions, whose population was largely Orthodox and whose language was closely related to Russian, was still ruled by Poland. The historical terminology for these areas is a highly controversial matter. See F. E. Sysin, *Between Poland and the Ukraine. The Dilemma of Adam Kysil, 1600-1653* (Cambridge, Mass., 1985), pp. 26-28. I use a literal rendition of Soloviev's term. Many scholars now favor the term "Ruthenian" to refer to the language and peoples of seventeenth-century Ukraine and Belorussia.

2. In the seventeenth century the modern Russian term for "German" (nemets, nemetskii) was used to refer to natives of the Protestant countries of northern Europe (sometimes with their country of origin added, e.g. Danish Germans, English Germans), or sometimes more widely as a term for "West European." Hence the German Settlement or Foreign Quarter in Moscow (see below, Note 17), where such foreigners resided.

3. Soloviev takes the boyars' designation of themselves as "slaves" quite literally, but recent studies have argued that such practices were part of the "facade of autocracy" by which harmony and unanimity were maintained. See N. Shields Kollman, *Kinship and Politics. The Making of the Muscovite Political System, 1345-1547* (Stanford, 1987).

4. The reign of Tsar Alexis (1645-1676) is the subject of volumes 10, 11, 12 and Chapter I of volume 13 of Soloviev's *History*. See S. M. Soloviev, *History of Russia From Earliest Times*, Volume 24, *The Character of Old Russia*, edited,

translated and with an Introduction by A. V. Muller (Academic International Press, 1980). Philip Longworth, *Alexis, Tsar of all the Russias* (London, 1984) and Joseph T. Fuhrmann, *Tsar Alexis, His Reign and His Russia* (Academic International Press, 1981) are the standard works in English on the reign.

5. The Polish Commonwealth, created in 1569 by the union of the kingdom of Poland and the grand principality of Lithuania, was an elective monarchy, which meant that after the death of a king numerous candidates, often foreigners, and their sponsors vied for the throne. Unsuccessful Russian candidates included Ivan IV in 1573 and his son Fedor in 1586. Tsar Alexis on several occasions thought of uniting the crowns of Poland and Muscovy, through his son Alexis after the abdication of King Casimir in 1668, and after the death of King Michael in 1673, when a proposal was received from Poland that Fedor be king, but on the condition that he convert to Catholicism. Alexis's counterproposal of his own candidacy was unsuccessful, and Jan Sobieski, who features prominently in the present volume, was elected.

6. See L. A. J. Hughes, "Miloslavskaia, Maria Il'inichna," in *The Modern Encyclopedia of Russian and Soviet History* (hereafter MERSH) Vol. 22, p. 135. Her thirteen children were as follows: Dmitry (1648-1650), Evdokia (1650-1712), Martha (1652-1707), Alexis (1654-1670), Anna (1655-1659), Sophia (1657-1704), Ekaterina (1658-1718), Maria (1660-1723), Fedor (1661-1682), Feodosia (1662-1713), Simeon (1665-1669), Ivan (1666-1696) and Evdokia (1669).

7. Soloviev does not name this enemy who was, in fact, Andrei Artamonovich Matveev (1666-1728), son of Tsar Alexis's favorite. See below, Chapter II, Note 6. On Sophia Alekseevna, see L. A. J. Hughes, "Sophia, Regent of Russia," *History Today* (July 1982), pp. 10-15, and "Sophia Alekseevna (1657-1704)" in MERSH, Vol. 36, pp. 165-172.

8. Soloviev uses the term *bogatyr*, denoting a legendary hero of formidable strength, to refer to both Peter and Sophia. I have adopted the terms "Hercules" and "Amazon" respectively, whilst acknowledging that the reference to Russian folklore is thus lost.

9. Natalia Naryshkina (1651-1694) was married to Tsar Alexis on January 22, 1671. Their first child, Peter, was born on May 30, 1672. Her father, Kirill Poluektovich, had served in Smolensk as a captain in the musketeers, where his daughter lived with him. This is why one source (see below, Note 25) calls him the "captain from Smolensk," and why Shaklovity later told Tsarevna Sophia: "Remember, my lady, what she was like in Smolensk; she wore baste shoes." (Soloviev's note) See also E. V. Leonard, "Naryshkin Family," MERSH, Vol. 24, pp. 71-73.

10. On Fedor, see the Introduction to this volume, and my entry in MERSH, Vol. 11, pp. 77-79. The author of a dissertation (sadly unpublished) on the period believes that "given half a chance" Fedor "would have been a strong and perhaps even a great ruler." Consult H. E. Ellersieck, *Russia Under Aleksei Mikhailovich and Fedor Alekseevich, 1645-1682. The Scandinavian Sources* (University of California, Los Angeles, 1955), p. 275.

11. Samuel Piotrowski Sitnianowicz (his name in Polish orthography, with the additional patronymic Hawrilowicz in some sources, 1628/29-1680) was born in Polotsk, in present-day Belorussia. He took monastic vows and the name Simeon in 1656, having studied at the Kiev Mohyla Academy from about 1642 to 1653, and possibly at the Jesuit College in Wilno, both of which cities were then under Polish rule. He first visited Moscow in 1660, when he was invited to read his verses to the royal family. In 1663 or 1664 he settled permanently in Moscow, where he served as tutor to Tsar Alexis's children (notably Alexis, Fedor and Sophia) and as court poet. His literary output included theological works, epigrams, occasional and narrative verse and sermons. He also ran a school for government clerks. A. Hippisley, *The Poetic Style of Simeon Polotsky* (Birmingham, 1985), has some biographical data and much on Polish influence. See also L. A. J. Hughes in MERSH, Vol. 29, pp. 8-11.

12. Lazar Baranovich (Lazarz Baranowicz, c.1620-1693) was the author of many literary and theological works. He was professor and rector of the Kiev Mohyla Academy from 1650 to 1657, when he became archbishop of Chernigov.

13. The following information comes from an unpublished note of the historian Tatishchev (1686-1750): "During his father's reign the sovereign was taught Latin by the monk Simeon Polotsky. Although he was not as accomplished at the language as his elder brother, the Tsarevich Alexis, his teacher testified that he showed great skill in poetry and composed very elegant verses. At his majesty's request Polotsky transposed the Psalter into verse and it is said that his majesty himself transposed a number of the verses, in particular Psalms 132 and 145. This work was always sung when he was in church, for his majesty was a great lover of singing. During his reign the first part-singing was introduced, and four-part and Kievan singing in five-stave notation; Greek singing continued to follow the old notation." (Soloviev's note) I have found no reference in recent Soviet studies of Polotsky to Fedor's supposed authorship. *The Psalter in Verse* (Psaltyr rifmotvornaia) is a landmark in Russian publishing history, the first work of poetry to be published in a separate edition. It remained popular well into the eighteenth century.

14. The Slavic-Greek-Latin Academy, Russia's first seat of higher learning, was founded in 1687, although the charter Soloviev discusses below dates from Fedor's reign. See Hugh F. Graham, MERSH, Vol. 35, pp. 208-211.

15. Silvester Medvedev (religious name of Simeon Agafonnikovich Medvedev, 1641-1691) came to Moscow from Kursk in 1665 and entered Simeon Polotsky's school for government clerks. He subsequently became Polotsky's disciple and successor as court poet. He took monastic vows some time between 1673 and 1675. After Polotsky's death in 1680 he assumed some of his master's pedagogical and publishing activities, but he clashed with the church authorities, notably Patriarch Joachim, because of his alleged Catholic tendencies. He was charged with aiding Tsarevna Sophia in a bid to take power in 1689, and was executed in 1691. See L. A. J. Hughes, MERSH, Vol. 21, pp. 180-182.

16. Two Jesuits were allowed to reside in Moscow to officiate for the small foreign Catholic community there, as a result of an agreement between Russia and Austria in 1684. Georgius David and Tobias Tichavsky were expelled in October 1689.

17. The Foreign Quarter (nemetskaia sloboda) was founded in 1652 on a site by the Yauza river on the outskirts of Moscow. Non-Orthodox foreigners from Western Europe (hence the designation "German") were obliged to reside in the settlement, which quickly became "a small corner of Western Europe." By Tsar Fedor's reign the population numbered about a thousand, mainly Protestant military personnel, merchants and craftsmen. It was to such foreigners that Peter applied for advice and friendship in his youth. See Samuel H. Baron, "The origins of 17th-Century Moscow's Nemeckaja sloboda," *California Slavic Studies*, Vol. 5 (1970), pp. 1-18, and L. A. J. Hughes, "Foreign Settlement," MERSH, Vol. 11, pp. 216-218.

18. Stefan Yavorsky (1658-1722) was acting patriarch from 1700 and president of the Holy Synod (founded 1721).

19. Artamon Sergeevich Matveev (1625-1682) generally has been numbered by historians amongst a small group of seventeenth-century Russian "Westernizers." He was a career official with a long record of military and government service by the time he entered the boyar council in 1670. His real rise to power coincided with the marriage of his ward, Natalia Naryshkina, to Tsar Alexis in 1671. From 1671 to 1676 he directed the Chancellery of Foreign Affairs. His subsequent fall from favor and death at the hands of the musketeers in May 1682 are charted by Soloviev below. See L. A. J. Hughes, MERSH, Vol. 21, pp. 142-144.

20. Soloviev's statement is incorrect. During the reign of Ivan III (1462-1505) there was a dispute over the rival claims of his son Vasily, by his second wife Sophia, and his grandson Dmitry, the heir of the eldest son Ivan (d. 1490) by Ivan's first marriage to Maria of Tver. Dmitry's claim was supported by his mother, Elena of Moldavia, hence there was "dissension between the offspring of different mothers," even though the two boys were of different generations. See N. Shields Kollmann, "Consensus politics. The Dynastic Crisis of the 1490s Reconsidered," *Russian Review*, Vol. 45 (1986), pp. 235-267.

21. In pre-Petrine Russia the women of the aristocracy were confined by custom to special chambers, hidden away from the male gaze. The daughters of the tsars — the *tsarevny* — were especially closely guarded in the upper chamber (terem) of the palace. Generally they only came to public attention through ceremonials for their births, deaths and namedays. Marriage was denied them, not only because of the lack of suitable candidates (marriage to foreign princes being fraught with religious difficulties) but also because of the need to limit the spread of patronage networks that would have arisen from such marriages, and perhaps also to enhance an air of exclusiveness. Soloviev does not make it clear that the relaxation of restrictions and an increase in the number of out-of-town outings and entertainments coincided with the arrival of Natalia Naryshkina in the palace in

1671. On related matters, see N. Shields Kollmann, "On the Seclusion of Elite Muscovite Women," *Russian History*, Vol. 10 (1983), pp. 170-187.

22. For a detailed study of alliances and networks at court, see R. O. Crummey, *Aristocrats and Servitors. The Boyar Elite 1613-1689* (Princeton, N.J., 1983).

23. The musketeers (streltsy) came into being in the middle of the sixteenth century as the first regular troops in Muscovy. By the seventeenth century service was hereditary. The musketeers lived in special settlements, received grants of money, provisions and land from the government, and in peacetime engaged in small-scale trades and handicrafts. A special crown department, the Chancellery of Musketeers' (Streletskii prikaz), administered the corps. See L. A. J. Hughes, "Strel'tsy," MERSH, Vol. 37, pp. 205-210; also John H. L. Keep, *Soldiers of the Tsar* (Oxford, 1985), pp. 60-73.

24. Prince Yury Alekseevich Dolgoruky (? - 1682) was a close friend of Tsar Alexis and enjoyed a distinguished career in the military and civil service. Altogether he acted as the head of ten different chancelleries, the last of which was the Chancellery of Musketeers.

25. This story comes from the account of an anonymous Polish author, first published in 1901 under the title *Diariusz zabojstwa tyranskiego senatorów Moskiewskich w stolicy roku 1682 y o obraniu dwóch carów Ioanna y Piotra* (Diary of the Barbaric Massacre of the Moscow Boyars in the Capital in 1682 and the Election of the Two Tsars Ivan and Peter). Soloviev consulted and quoted from the manuscript in the Imperial Library. Internal evidence suggests that the account was written in the spring of 1683 and that the author may have arrived in Moscow *after* the 1682 rebellion on which his account centers. Soloviev is right to give little credence to this version of events in 1676, which is based on hearsay. A member of the delegation of the Dutch ambassador, Koenraad van Klenk, who was actually in Moscow when Alexis died and had access to his foreign doctors, makes no mention of any "plot" by Matveev. The *Diary* is one of Soloviev's main sources for his account of the 1682 rebellion, below.

26. She had been Fedor's wet-nurse.

27. Ivan Mikhailovich Miloslavsky (?-1685) was a kinsman of Tsar Alexis's first wife. He first entered the boyar council with the rank of lord-in-waiting in 1660 and attained the rank of boyar in June 1676. He was later to earn notoriety for his part in the rebellion of 1682, dealt with by Soloviev in Chapter II of this volume, but his reputation as an unscrupulous schemer was derived largely from the memoirs of A. S. Matveev's son Andrei (see below, Chapter II, Note 6). Very little is known about him. See L.A.J. Hughes, MERSH, Vol. 22, p. 136. On the Miloslavsky clan, see N. Tolstoy, *The Tolstoys. Twenty-four Generations of Russian History, 1353-1983* (London, 1983).

28. Bogdan Matveevich Khitrovo (1615-1680) first entered the boyar council in 1647, probably as a result of the patronage of Tsar Alexis's favorite, B. I. Morozov (see Note 29, below). Early in his career he undertook a number of

military missions, but after 1660 was based at court in chancellery posts. He headed the Chancellery of the Royal Household (Prikaz bolshogo dvortsa), which supervised the numerous royal palaces and estates, from 1663, and from 1661 until his death was director of the Armory (Oruzheinii prikaz), the royal workshop which produced icons, church furnishings, carriages and miscellaneous decorative objects as well as small arms. See L.A.J. Hughes, "The Moscow Armoury and Innovations in 17th-century Muscovite Art," *Canadian-American Slavic Studies,* XIII (1979), pp. 204-223.

29. Boris Ivanovich Morozov (1590-1661) was one of the leading figures of the earlier part of Tsar Alexis's reign. A wealthy landowner, he was raised to the rank of boyar in 1634, a year after being appointed as tutor to the future tsar. When Alexis came to the throne in 1645 Morozov was the leader of his inner circle and accumulated a number of chancellery posts. In 1648 he consolidated his power still further by marrying the sister of Alexis's new wife Maria. During the Moscow rebellion of 1648 he was accused of bribery and corruption, but weathered the criticisms with the tsar's support. See L.A.J. Hughes, MERSH, Vol. 23, pp. 71-73.

30. Afanasy Lavrentievich Ordin-Nashchokin (1605?-1680) was one of the outstanding statesmen and diplomats of Tsar Alexis's reign. He was well educated for his time, with a knowledge of foreign languages and mathematics, and an expert on foreign affairs. He held a number of government offices during his career, but his most notable period of service was as head of the Chancellery of Foreign Affairs from 1667 to 1671. Thereafter he retired from service and took monastic vows. Ordin-Nashchokin was a keen proponent of a firm alliance with Poland and joint action against the Swedes. His major diplomatic achievement was the Truce of Andrusovo (see Note 57, below). He was also in favor of military and economic reform. See E. Chistiakova, MERSH, Vol. 26, pp. 72-73.

31. Much of Soloviev's information on Matveev's exile in derived from the account of Matveev's son Andrei, published by N. I. Novikov in 1785 under the title *History of the Wrongful Imprisonment of the Boyar Artamon Sergeevich Matveev.* Andrei, who was banished with his father, was aged about ten at the commencement of his exile. For more on him and his writings, see Chapter II, Note 6.

32. There was no official exchange of permanent ambassadors between Russia and foreign powers until Peter I's reign, but from the 1660s several countries (Sweden, Denmark, Poland and Holland) maintained accredited agents, termed *rezidenty* (residents), in Russia. Russia's major permanent representative abroad was the resident in Poland. Business with other countries was conducted by means of *ad hoc* missions.

33. Nikolai Gavrilovich Spafarius (Milescu) (1636?-1708) was a native of Moldavia who had studied in the West after falling into disfavor at home, and in 1671 settled permanently in Russia. He became one of the leading specialists in the Chancellery of Foreign Affairs, undertaking a mission to China in 1675-1678,

collaborating with Prince V. V. Golitsyn in the 1680s, and advising Peter I on eastern affairs during the latter part of his career. See entry by C. M. Foust, MERSH, Vol. 37, pp. 20-24.

34. The settlement of Pustozersk (which roughly translated means "barren lake") was situated on the estuary of the Pechora river where it enters the White Sea opposite Novaia Zemlia. Founded in 1499, its remoteness and the harshness of its climate made it an ideal location for a penal colony. Apart from Matveev, its most renowned inmate was the religious dissenter Avvakum, who arrived in 1667 and was burned at the stake there in 1682. Later in the narrative Matveev mentions a meeting with Avvakum's family.

35. Matveev refers to the lavishly illustrated manuscript books produced by the Chancellery workshop. The best known of these, the *Book of Titles* (Tituliar-nik, 1672), contained stylized portraits of all Russian rulers from Riurik to Alexis, the patriarchs of Moscow and a selection of foreign rulers, together with coats of arms and insignia. The Chancellery library also had a good collection of foreign printed books and maps, as did Matveev himself.

36. This refers to an incident during the Russo-Polish war of 1654-1667 when, in the summer of 1655, Russian and Ukrainian troops retreated from Lwów under attack from the Poles and Crimean Tatars.

37. Another incident from the 1654-67 war. In the summer of 1658 the Ukrai-nian town of Konotop was beseiged unsuccessfully by the Russians under their commander Prince A.N. Trubetskoy, one of the major figures in the army. On him, see L.A.J. Hughes in MERSH, Vol. 39, pp. 238-240.

38. Stepan (Stenka) Razin, a Don Cossack, was the leader of a major rebellion in 1670-1671. Before declaring war on the Moscow authorities and the landown-ers, Razin earned notoriety for his daring raids on merchants along the lower Volga and on the Caspian Sea. In August 1669 (the incident to which Matveev probably refers here) Razin went to the city of Astrakhan to negotiate with the authorities. No agreement was reached and he was allowed to leave. Six months later rebellion broke out in the lower Volga region. Astrakhan itself was captured by Razin's men in June 1670. See P. Avrich, *Russian Rebels* (New York, 1972); P. Longworth, *The Cossacks* (London, 1969), pp. 124-153.

39. Little Russia (Malorossiia) is the old name for the Ukraine. The old-fashioned term has been retained where it appears in seventeenth-century docu-ments quoted by Soloviev.

40. *Chetvert*—a standard dry measure for grain, equivalent to 126.39 lbs (3.5 Russian puds). Subsequent references to Russian weights, measures and monetary units may be checked in the table on p. vii.

41. Tsar Alexis's reign was beset with financial problems. In 1654-1656 sil-ver coinage was replaced by copper, but the measure was highly unpopular and the "Copper Coin Riot" of 1662 obliged the government to re-introduce silver. It is worth noting, Matveev's mention of minting notwithstanding, that no silver was mined locally. Metal was obtained by melting down or overstamping foreign coins or plate.

42. Kukui was a popular name for the Foreign Quarter. See above, Note 17.

43. Peter Marselis (?-1672) was one of the many "Germans" who entered Muscovite service. A merchant from Hamburg, he was associated with the organization of iron works in Russia during the 1630s-1640s; he set up a postal service between Moscow and Wilno and performed various missions abroad.

44. Vorobievo, situated south of the Kremlin on the Sparrow (present-day Lenin) Hills, was one of several royal estates in the vicinity of the capital.

45. The name Orel means "eagle" in Russian. The "young eagle" (a reference to the tsarist coat of arms) is Tsar Fedor.

46. Ivan Andreevich Savelov (1620-1690) took monastic vows in 1655 under the name Joachim (Ioakhim). In 1657 he was taken into the entourage of Patriarch Nikon (see below, Note 47) and quickly rose to prominence, despite the fact that he was apparently only semi-literate. In 1664 he became superior of the important Miracles (Chudov) monastery in the Kremlin, and in 1674 he ascended the patriarchal throne. Joachim was, by all accounts, a narrow-minded conservative. He did constant battle with foreign influences, deplored the role of "Germans" in the Russian army, the building of Protestant churches on "Holy Russian soil" and the penetration of "Latinist" tendencies into the church itself. He also wielded some political influence, engineering the election of Peter in 1682 and implementing anti-foreign measures after the overthrow of Sophia in 1689.

47. Nikon (1605-1681) was born Nikita Minich Minin. He became patriarch of Moscow and All Russia in 1652, thanks to his close relations with Tsar Alexis, and immediately set about reforming the service books and ritual of the church. Although his reforms were concerned not with dogma but with corruptions in spelling and ceremonial, many of the Orthodox faithful were outraged at the discarding of ancient tradition (see below on Old Believers, Note 88). Although Nikon's reforms were confirmed, the patriarch himself was deposed by the Church Council of 1666-1667 for his attempts to raise the power of the church above that of the crown. He was banished to the Ferapont monastery, situated to the east of Beloozero in the Novgorod region. On Nikon's quarrel with Alexis, see W. Palmer, *The Patriarch and the Tsar* (6 vols., London, 1871-1876), the relevant passages in P. Longworth, *Alexis, Tsar of All the Russias* (London, 1984), and the related chapters in Fuhrmann, *Tsar Alexis. His Reign and His Russia* (Gulf Breeze, Fla., Academic International Press, 1981). On Nikon's career, see G. E. Orchard in MERSH, Vol. 25, pp. 4-10.

48. In Soloviev's text this portion of Jonas' testimony is placed in the footnotes, no doubt because of the unseemly nature of the monk's accusations. There would seem to be little reason for shielding the offending passage from the eyes of the modern reader.

49. Ivan Afanasievich Zheliabuzhsky (1639-?1709) had an active and varied career in government service. Before he was entrusted with Nikon's case in 1676 he had served with embassies abroad (Brandenburg, Courland, England, Florence and Venice in 1661-1662; Vienna in 1667) and on missions to the Ukraine. He

became a member of the boyar council in 1676. During Sophia's regency he served in the Ukraine (as military governor for Chernigov from 1683). Virtually nothing is known about his career under Peter I's regime. He was the author of an important memoir covering the period 1682-1709 and composed in the Old Russian annalistic style. Soloviev draws on this source later in his narrative. See entry by G. E. Orchard, MERSH, Vol. 46, pp. 37-38, and H. J. Torke, introduction to *Zapiski russkikh liudei* (St. Petersburg, 1841) (Russian Memoir Series, No. 27, Newtonville, 1980), pp. 6-7.

50. The monastery of St. Cyril (Kirillo-Beloozerskii monastyr) was founded in 1397 on the shore of Lake Sivensky in Novgorod province. By the seventeenth century it was one of the richest and most powerful of Russian monasteries, a place of pilgrimage and of detention.

51. The Resurrection (Voskresensk) monastery at New Jerusalem was founded by Nikon in 1656 as a personal residence. This grandiose project, with buildings named after the Holy Places in Jerusalem, was part of Nikon's scheme for raising the power and prestige of the patriarchate. The monastery is situated about 60 kilometers northwest of Moscow near the present town of Istra.

52. The gentleman of the bedchamber (postelnichii) was responsible for the management of the sovereign's clothing, linen and toilet. He frequently assumed the role of "personal secretary". Alexis Fedorovich Adashev (?-1561) held the position in Ivan IV's reign (1533-1584). Fedor Mikhailovich Rtishchev (1636-1673) was gentleman of the bedchamber to Tsar Alexis from 1650, as well as occupying posts in the Chancellery of the Royal Household (Prikaz bolshogo dvortsa) and interesting himself in foreign affairs. He was a pioneer of Russian education, in 1648 sponsoring a school in the monastery of St. Andrew in Moscow, and in 1664 he was appointed tutor to Tsarevich Alexis Alekseevich. See L.A.J. Hughes in MERSH, Vol. 31, pp. 223-227.

53. In other words, Yazykov rose through the hierarchy of ranks and government service. With the title of conciliar gentlemen of the bedchamber (dumnyi postelnichii) he gained access to the boyar council. The rank of lord-in-waiting (okolnichii) was second only to that of boyar (boiarin) within the council. Yazykov became a boyar in May 1681. The armorer (oruzheinichii) directed the royal Armory (see above, Note 28). On promotions to the council during Fedor's reign, see the listing in Crummey, *Boyar Elite*, op. cit, pp. 198-203.

54. Prince Vasily Vasilievich Golitsyn (1643-1714) was one of the most remarkable statesmen in seventeenth-century Russia. He was unusually well educated, with a knowledge of Latin and a taste for Western books and culture. A member of one of Russia's leading families, he served at court during his adolescence, becoming a boyar in 1676 and serving Tsar Fedor as Russia's representative in the Ukraine and in court and chancellery posts. He headed the commission, examined later in this volume, that recommended the abolition of the Code of Precedence. His subsequent career during Sophia's regency is charted by Soloviev below, and in the next volume in this series. Golitsyn was exiled by Peter in 1689 for his part in the unsuccessful Crimean campaigns and for abetting Sophia in her

bid to extend her power. He lived the rest of his life in the far north of Russia. See L. A. J. Hughes, *Russia and the West. The Life of a Seventeeth-century Westernizer, Prince V. V. Golitsyn, 1643-1714* (Newtonville, 1984) and entry in MERSH, Vol. 13, pp. 6-10.

55. The earlier Vasily Vasilievich Golitsyn (dates of birth and death unknown) was a prominent soldier and courtier during the reigns of Fedor Ivanovich (1584-1598) and Boris Godunov (1598-1605), and especially during the Time of Troubles, which culminated in 1613, when he was one of a number of candidates for the Russian throne. He died in captivity in Poland some time before 1619. See G. E. Orchard, MERSH, Vol. 48, pp. 166-167.

56. Peter Dorofeevich Doroshenko (1627-98) was hetman, or supreme military and civil commander, of the Right Bank (Polish) Ukraine from 1665 to 1676. He refused to recognize Polish rule after the Truce of Andrusovo of 1667 (see the following note), but agreed to submit to Moscow were he be made hetman of the entire Ukraine. In his capital, Chigirin, Doroshenko was an embarrassment to both Moscow and Warsaw because of his frequent avowals of allegiance to the Turkish sultan. After his removal from power, described later by Soloviev, he was governor of Viatka from 1679 to 1682, and ended his life in "honorable exile" in Moscow.

57. The Truce of Andrusovo (1667) ended the Russo-Polish war that had begun in 1654 over the secession of the Ukraine. Negotiated by A. Ordin-Nashchokin, the truce was to last thirteen and a half years, and confirmed Russia's possession of Smolensk, part of Belorussia, and the Left Bank Ukraine (the territories east of the Dnieper river). The Right Bank went to Poland but Kiev, also on the Right Bank, was to be leased to Russia for a two-year period. In fact, Russia retained Kiev, and gained permanent possession by the treaty of 1686, examined by Soloviev below. There were also articles on religious toleration, on the Zaporozhian Camp (to become a joint protectorate) and on combined action against the Tatars. See Note 62, below. See C. B. O'Brien, *Muscovy and the Ukraine From the Pereiaslavl Agreement to the Truce of Andrusovo, 1654-1667* (Berkeley, 1963).

58. Prince Grigory Grigorievich Romodanovsky (?-1682) was one of Russia's leading military commanders during the war of 1654-1667. He led a series of campaigns against the Poles in the Ukraine, as well as dealing with local disputes among the cossacks. He seems to have been a typical representative of the upper service class, except that he spent unusually little time in the capital during his long service career. He became a boyar in 1665. See L.A.J. Hughes in MERSH, Vol. 31, pp. 156-158.

59. The Zaporozhian Cossack army (Voisko zaporozhskoe), was the official title of the Ukrainian cossack army. Not to be confused with the Zaporozhian Camp (Sech) a geographical location (see below, Note 62).

60. The mace (bulava) was one of the insignia of office of the Ukrainian hetmans. The others were the horsetail standard (bunchuk), the banner and the seal.

61. Ivan Samoilovich (?-1690), the son of a priest (hence the occasional nickname Popovich) became hetman of the Left Bank Ukraine in 1672, in place

of the unreliable Demian Mnogogreshny, and with the strong support of G. G. Romodanovsky. From 1674 to 1681, with the strong backing of Moscow, he assumed the title hetman of Both Sides of the Dnieper, hence his dispute with Doroshenko. Soloviev's is still one of the fullest portraits of the hetman. See also L.A.J. Hughes in MERSH, Vol. 33, pp. 76-79.

62. Ivan Dmitrievich Serko (?-1680) was elected commander of the Zaporozhian Camp (*Sech*) in 1663. The Zaporozhian Camp was a cossack stronghold situated on islands in the Dnieper river below the present town of Zaporozhie. The cossacks of the Zaporozhian Camp clung fiercely to their independence and democratic traditions. A significant factor in Moscow's fight against the Poles and Turks, they were treated circumspectly by the Muscovite government. Under the Truce of Andrusovo the Camp came under Muscovite protectorship but, as Soloviev's account shows, Serko's allegiance was variable. The Camp was abolished by Catherine II in 1775.

63. Mikhail Khanenko was recognized by the Poles as hetman of Right Bank Ukraine in 1670. He was ousted by Doroshenko and went to the Left Bank in 1674, having renounced his claim to the hetmanship.

64. *Sanjak* generally refers to one of the administrative districts of a Turkish province. In this case, it appears to refer to a local ruler.

65. Yury Khmelnitsky (Chmielnicki) (1641-1685), son of the famous Bogdan, hetman of the Ukraine (see below, Chapter III, Note 18), was himself hetman from 1659 to 1663. In 1663 he took monastic vows, was imprisoned by the Poles from 1664 to 1667, and in 1672 was captured by the Tatars and sent to Constantinople. In 1676, after Doroshenko's surrender to Moscow, Khmelnitsky was backed by the Turks as the new hetman. He was executed by them in 1685.

66. On the Dnieper north of the Zaporozhian Camp settlement.

67. Ivan Stepanovich Mazepa (1639?-1709) is one of the best known characters in Ukrainian history, and one who has been both vilified and worshipped. He was educated in the West (Germany, Italy and France), returning to the Ukraine in 1663 to enter the service of Doroshenko. In 1674 he transferred his allegiance to Ivan Samoilovich. After the latter's fall from favor in 1687, described below, he became hetman with Moscow's backing. By 1708 he was virtually a sovereign ruler. In that year he openly rebelled and joined Charles XII of Sweden in his campaign against Peter I. After Peter's victory at Poltava in 1709 he fled to Moldavia, where he died. See entry by J. Cracraft, MERSH, Vol. 21, pp. 150-154.

68. The Code of Precedence (mestnichestvo) regulated military and civil appointments on the basis of a candidate's pedigree and family service record. See Soloviev's account of its abolition, pp. 83-89, and Note 100.

69. Jan (John) Sobieski (1629-1696) ascended the elective throne of Poland in 1674. Previously he had held commands in the Polish army—grand marshal (1665), field commander (1666) and in 1668 the supreme post of grand hetman of the crown. He was by all accounts a remarkable figure, perhaps the outstanding military man of his generation. See J. B. Morton, *Sobieski. King of Poland* (London, 1932), and N. Davies, *God's Playground. A History of Poland*, Vol. I, (Oxford, 1981), pp. 472-491.

70. Michael Wiśniowiecki was king of Poland from 1669 to 1673. Described by a recent historian as a "royal mouse," he became king "virtually by mistake" and died from a surfeit of gherkins. See N. Davies (Note 69), pp. 470-472.

71. The town of Marienburg (Malbork) on the Vistula delta was the site of a fortified estate founded by the Teutonic Knights and once the seat of their grand master. The fortress was one of the most powerful in Europe and after the town's inclusion in Poland in 1457 often was used as a place of detention.

72. The "French faction" refers to those nobles who favored a league between Poland and France once peace had been made with Turkey. Sobieski himself was associated with the French party at court by his marriage to Marie-Casimire de la Grange d'Arquien in 1665. In 1675 a treaty was signed between France and Poland at Jaworówo, providing a French subsidy in return for Polish action against Prussia, but the agreement was short-lived.

73. The battle of Chudnov took place in 1660 near the Teterev river. The Russians under Prince V. B. Sheremetev were besieged by the Poles.

74. Emilian Ignatievich Ukraintsev (1641-1708), described later by Soloviev as "one of Moscow's most active agents," was one of a growing band of diplomatic specialists who worked his way into the boyar council from fairly humble beginnings. Most of his career was spent in the Chancellery of Foreign Affairs, and he became its director from 1689 to 1699. During his career he visited Poland, Sweden, Denmark, Holland and Turkey. He was a leading participant in the negotiation of a number of important treaties, including the "permanent peace" of 1686 and the 1700 truce with Turkey. See L.A.J. Hughes in MERSH, Vol. 40, pp. 174-177.

75. Nikita Moiseevich Zotov (1644-1717) is better known as one of Peter I's tutors, a post he assumed in 1677, and as "archbishop of Pressburg and patriarch of all the Yauza and Kukui" of Peter's All-Drunken Assembly. He also served as privy councillor and president of the Personal Chancellery. See L.A.J. Hughes in MERSH, Vol. 46, pp. 128-30.

76. Prokofy Bogdanovich Voznitsyn (?-1702) began his career in the diplomatic service in the 1660s, but did not enter the boyar duma until 1690. He was third ambassador in Peter's Grand Embassy of 1696-1697, and Russia's representative at the Congress of Karlowitz in 1699.

77. Settlement Ukraine (Slobodskaia Ukraina), comprising the territory of Kharkov province and parts of Voronezh and Kursk, was an area of free settlements offering arable land and tax exemptions to fugitives from the Polish Ukraine.

78. Soloviev's section on relations with the West is negligible here. A useful overview may be found in J. L. Black, "Russia's Rise as a European Power, 1650-1750," *History Today* (August 1986), pp. 21-28.

79. On the "spectre" of Stenka Razin, see Note 38, above.

80. *Sadchik*, responsible for the conscription and settlement of immigrants.

81. The wooden *ostrog* (fort or fortified settlement) were the basic outposts of Russia's colonization of Siberia. Each provided a base for both trade and military operations, and for collection of tribute in furs (yasak) from the local

tribesmen. See G. V. Lantzeff, *Siberia in the Seventeenth century. A Study of Colonial Administration* (Berkeley, 1945).

82. The Tubin (tubintsy) were a Turkic people based in the lower reaches of the Tuba river.

83. The Code of Laws (Sobornoe ulozhenie) of 1649 replaced the Statute (sudebnik) of Ivan IV, issued in 1550. The Code consisted of 967 articles in 25 chapters. It included confirmation of the enserfment of the Russian peasantry. The underlying premise of the code was the primacy of God and the sovereign tsar. The next recodification of the laws did not take place until the 1830s. See R. Hellie's entry in MERSH, Vol. 40, pp. 192-198, and idem. transl. and ed., *The Russian Law Code (Ulozhenie) of 1649*, 2 vols., (Irvine, Cal., 1984-1985).

84. Igor was prince of Kiev from 912 to 945, and renowned for his expeditions against the Byzantines. He was notorious also for asserting his authority over subject peoples and imposing heavy tribute. He was murdered by members of one such tribe, the Drevliane, after making demands for additional payments.

85. Zelemey was already known to the authorities. In an earlier section Soloviev records that in 1665 Zelemey informed Fedor Pushchin, the crown's representative in Okhotsk, that rebel Tungus were planning to ambush Muscovite troops. The report was a trap. Fifty soldiers sent by Pushchin on a reconnaissance mission were killed by Zelemey and his men.

86. The Dutch ambassador Koenraad van Klenk came to Moscow in 1675. He was in Moscow at the time of Tsar Alexis's death in January 1676. The account of the mission by a member of his retinue, published in Dutch in Amsterdam in 1677, is a useful source for the period.

87. It was customary for jailors to demand a subsistence payment (vlaznoe) from new prisoners.

88. The schism (raskol) originated in the protest against Patriarch Nikon's (see Note 47, above) reform of Orthodox church rituals and service books, introduced in the 1650s to bring the Russian practice in line with the Greek. It was argued that errors and corruptions had crept into Russian texts and ceremonial, and revisions were made with the help of scholars from Greece and the Ukraine. Initially, objections were raised by members of the Russian non-monastic clergy, for example by Archpriest Avvakum (see Note 112, below), who regarded the reforms as an arbitrary and foreign-influenced violation of cherished traditions, and resented Nikon's high-handed and despotic behavior. But, as Soloviev makes clear in this section, by the time of Fedor's reign the protest movement had spread to laymen. The dissenters or schismatics (raskolniki), also referred to as Old Believers (starovery) and in later literature as Old Ritualists (staroobriadtsy), were anathematized by the Church Council of 1666-1667, which approved Nikon's reforms whilst deposing the patriarch himself. Dissenters associated the reforms, specific examples of which are referred to in Soloviev's text, with the coming of Antichrist. In the words of Michael Cherniavsky: "There was only one general conclusion possible: if Moscow, the Third Rome, had instituted religious changes

which required the condemnation of itself and its own past, then Moscow had accepted heresy—and the end was at hand." ('The Old Believers and the New Religion," *Slavic Review*, Vol. 25 (1966), pp. 1-39). The violence of the dissenters' reaction, as described by Soloviev here and below, should be seen in this context. See also N. Lupinin, *Religious Revolt in the Seventeenth Century. The Schism of the Russian Church*, (Berkeley, 1984).

89. The Russian Orthodox clergy was divided into two categories: the black, or celibate, monastic clergy (cherntsy), and the white or secular, non-monastic, married clergy (beltsy), who formed the mass of parish priests. The terms derive from the color of their habits. The prelates of the church were drawn exclusively from the black clergy.

90. See Note 88, above. Because of the frequency with which the sign of the cross must be made by the Orthodox faithful in both public and private worship, the substitution of the Greek practice of using the thumb and two fingers in place of the "two-fingered" sign made with finger and thumb, was one of the most bitterly opposed of Nikon's reforms, and became a symbol of the schism.

91. The four-pointed crucifix of the Roman Catholic church (crux immissa) differed from the traditional Orthodox depiction, in which extra bars below the head and above the foot of the upright produce an eight-pointed design.

92. The belltower of Ivan the Great in the Kremlin was built by Italian architects at the end of the reign of Ivan III (the Great, 1462-1505). It was raised to its present height of 81 meters in 1600 in the reign of Boris Godunov. It was the tallest building in Moscow until the early eighteenth century.

93. There were three ranks of monastic hierarchs in the Orthodox church: archimandrite (arkhimandrit), abbot (igumen) and superior (stroitel), in descending order of importance.

94. It was fairly common practice for members of the boyar elite to take monastic vows on their deathbed or, in a smaller number of cases, to enter a monastery in old age. Robert Crummey calculates that something like one in ten may have ended their lives as monks (*Aristocrats and Servitors*, p. 152).

95. In Orthodox practice the parish or "white" clergy were obliged to marry. In the event of a priest's wife predeceasing him, canon law required that he either take monastic vows or stop officiating as a priest.

96. Of Patriarch Joachim's enactments, the following is worthy of mention: in 1677 the patriarch sent two prelates, Metropolitan Joseph of Riazan and Archbishop Simon of Tver to Kashin to inspect the relics of Princess Anna, wife of St. Michael of Tver. The relics were discovered by Archbishop Jonas of Tver in the time of Tsar Alexis and Patriarch Joseph. When the prelates returned, Joachim reported: "On the basis of their report and the evidence of the *Life* of the pious Princess Anna and her miracles, and the chronicles, it transpires that the *Life* and the chronicles are at variance. (1) In the *Life*, Anna is referred to as the daughter of a boyar from Kashin, in the chronicles as a daughter of Prince Dmitry Borisovich of Rostov. (2) In the *Life*, it says that Michael's son *Dmitry* was with him in the

Horde, in the chronicles, *Konstantin*. (3) In the *Life* it is said that he was cut in half with a sword, in the chronicles that he was stabbed in the ribs with a knife, and so on. At three points in the *Life* it is stated that the relics were not subject to corruption, but on inspection they were found to have rotted and decayed in several places. The *Life* states that not only the relics but also the garments were intact, but the inspection revealed that they were completely decayed. This matter will be referred to the great Church Council, when God's verdict will be proclaimed and confirmed. In the meantime the tomb shall be sealed; no special festivals or prayers shall be celebrated, only the offices for the dead; and the icons shall be brought to Moscow." (Soloviev's note).

97. For a discussion of taxation in this period and in Sophia's regency, see C. B. O'Brien, *Russia Under Two Tsars* (Berkeley, 1952), pp. 66ff.

98. Tenth and fifteenth money (desiataia and piatnadtsataia denga) were a tax of tenth and fifteenth of income respectively, exacted as required to meet the cost of military campaigns.

99. Under the franchise system (otkup) individuals paid the government a fixed sum of money for a monopoly on the sale of liquor or the collection of customs dues in a given area. Under the new system (vernaia sluzhba) sworn officials collected these revenues for the crown.

100. The Code of Precedence or "place system" (mestnichestvo) regulated military, civil and court appointments, and on occasions even social rankings, such as seating at banquets, among the upper service class on the basis of the genealogical and service record of the candidate's family. It was considered a serious slight to family honor to accept a place below someone who was socially inferior according to the computations of the Code, and anyone thus slighted was obliged to lodge a complaint. See entry by Hugh F. Graham in MERSH, Vol. 22, pp. 8-13 and N. Shields Kollmann, "Ritual and Social Drama at the Muscovite Court," *Slavic Review*, Vol. 45 (1986), pp. 486-502.

101. On Prince V. V. Golitsyn, see Note 54, above.

102. For a detailed account of the restructuring of the Muscovite military practice in the seventeenth century, including deployment of new-formation troops and the decline of the old cavalry, see R. Hellie, *Enserfment and Military Change in Muscovy* (Chicago, 1971).

103. The poll or head tax (podushnyi oklad) was a levy on individual males of the lower social orders, introduced by Peter I in 1722, to replace the less lucrative collective tax on households. The tax, finally abolished in 1883, was bitterly resented, particularly as the nobles were exempted from it.

104. The *druzhina* (from *drug*, friend) of Kievan Russia comprised the prince's immediate retinue, who served as personal bodyguards and advisers, as well as leaders in the administration and army.

105 On the Slavic-Greek-Latin Academy, which was not established until Sophia's regency, see Note 14, above. The so-called "Privileges" or "Charter" to the Academy, formulated in Fedor's reign, were published in the 1780s by Nikolai Novikov. This is the text which Soloviev draws upon.

106. Of the three Moscow monasteries mentioned in this passage, it was the monastery of the Savior "beyond the icon painters' row" (Zaikonospassky), situated on present-day 25 October Street in the former commercial quarter and visible from the Revolution Square by the Hotel Metropol, that actually became the Academy premises in 1687. Formerly it had housed a school run by Simeon Polotsky and later by Silvester Medvedev. The monastery of St. Andrew, situated by the Moscow river near the present-day Andreev railway bridge, was founded in 1648 and associated with Fedor Rtishchev, an early pioneer of Russian education (see above, Note 52). The ancient monastery of St. Daniel (Danilov) was founded in 1271, on present-day Danilovsky Val, not far from the Tula metro station. It survived into recent times as the premises of a factory, but now has been restored as the new residence of the patriarch of Moscow.

107. Metropolitan Isidore of Moscow, a Greek, represented Russia at the Council of Florence in 1439 (see below, Chapter III, Note 78). Isidore was condemned in Moscow for accepting the council's recognition of papal supremacy, and was deposed formally in 1443 after escaping abroad.

108. On the Polish author, see Note 25, above.

109. Dmitry the Pretender, or False Dmitry I, ruled Russia 1605-1606. Claiming to be the son of Ivan IV (see below, Chapter II, Note 17), he gained sufficient popular and aristocratic backing in face of the unpopularity of Tsar Boris Godunov to bring him to the throne, but he was later deposed and murdered by the boyars. Although Dmitry did not honor an undertaking to introduce Catholicism into Russia, he antagonized the Muscovites by his neglect of Orthodoxy, his Polish retinue and his marriage, in May 1606, to Marina Mniszech, the daughter of a Polish magnate. The subsequent invasion of Russia and the occupation of the Kremlin by the Poles, and the series of wars with Poland during the reigns of Michael and Alexis, strengthened hostility to the Catholic Poles. Thus Fedor's marriage to a woman with Polish "connections" was sure to have political repercussions, and to rouse the suspicions of conservative elements, especially amongst the church hierarchy.

110. This is a reference to the great plague of 1654-1655, which broke out when Tsar Alexis was away on military campaign. In July 1654 Nikon took Alexis's pregnant wife and the rest of the royal family to the comparative safety of the Trinity-St. Sergius monastery, then further north to the Koliazin monastery. At the time Nikon was criticized for abandoning his flock in Moscow, but the tsar endorsed his action, including his issuing of orders to deal with the pestilence in the name of Tsaritsa Maria.

111. Matveev makes a play on words; the word "Pustozersk" comprises *pustoi*—"empty", "barren", and *ozero*—"lake".

112. Archpriest Avvakum (1620-1682), the leader of the schismatics or Old Believers, was exiled in 1653 for his opposition to Nikon's reforms. In the intervening years he travelled through Siberia to the Far East as chaplain to an expedition, was recalled to Moscow by Tsar Alexis in 1662 in an attempt at reconciliation, but banished again in 1664, to Mezen on the White Sea. In 1666 Avvakum and

other dissenters were anathematized "for schism, sedition and false teaching" by the Church Council that also approved Nikon's reforms, and he was sent to Pustozersk, where he was burned at the stake (according to Old Believer tradition) in April 1682. For an English translation of his autobiography, one of the landmarks of seventeenth-century Russian literature, see *The Life of Archpriest Avvakum by Himself*, transl. J. Harrison and H. Mirrlees (London, 1924). See also entry by J. T. Fuhrmann in MERSH, Vol. 2, pp. 193-197.

CHAPTER II

1. Ivan Alekseevich, born 1666, reigned as Ivan V from 1682 to 1696, was the last son of Tsar Alexis's marriage to Maria Miloslavskaia. Copious evidence of his physical and mental disabilities, which included partial sight, a disease that limited his mobility (he had to be held up and prompted by attendants during receptions) and slow wittedness, is found in contemporary foreign accounts, for example those of Heinrich Butenant, the Habsburg envoy Johann Hövel, the German traveller Engelbert Kämpfer and others. Official sources drew a discreet veil over his handicaps, even maintaining the fiction that he might "rule at home" while Peter went to war. Ivan's main contribution to Russian history was as father of the future Empress Anna (reigned 1730-1740) and great-grandfather of the ill-fated Ivan VI (1740-1741). He was married to Praskovia Fedorovna Saltykova in January 1684, an event which many contemporaries interpreted as a bid by Sophia to secure the Miloslavsky line; but the marriage produced only daughters.

2. Prince Ivan Andreevich Khovansky (?-1682) began his career in the reign of Tsar Michael on service in wars with Sweden and Poland. He acted as military governor in a number of towns (Tula, Viazma, Mogilev, Pskov, Novgorod and Smolensk) and participated in the suppression of the Moscow rebellion of 1662. His defeats in the Russo-Polish war of 1654-1667 included battles in 1660 against the Polish generals Sapieha and Carnecki, and in 1661, when he lost a division of twenty thousand men. His role in the troubles of 1682 (sometimes referred to inaccurately as the *Khovanshchina*), his relationship with the musketeers and, in particular, his connection with Sophia's party (he had been absent from Moscow for most of his career up to 1680) require further elucidation.

3. Gedimin (Gediminas), grand prince of Lithuania from 1316 to 1341, is traditionally viewed as the founder of the Lithuanian state and of its capital Wilno (Vilnius, Vilna).

4. Prince Boris Alekseevich Golitsyn (1654-1714) was to become one of Peter I's closest advisers and played a prominent role in the events leading to Sophia's overthrow in 1689. He acted as the tsar's attendant (diadka), was director of the Chancellery for Kazan from 1687 to 1713 and was one of the three officials left in charge of the country during Peter's visit to the West in 1697-1698. He fell from royal favor around 1705. He was a cousin of Prince Vasily Vasilievich Golitsyn.

5. This hastily convoked gathering (a similar one was called on May 23, 1682 to ratify the creation of a dual monarchy) is regarded by some historians as a late example of the Assembly of the Land (Zemskii sobor), the first of which dates from the reign of Ivan IV (1533-1584). Assemblies of the Land, composed of representatives of the boyars, military servitors, church hierarchs and townsmen, and convoked on issues of national importance, had been a regular feature of the reign of Tsar Michael (1613-1645) and the early years of Tsar Alexis's reign. The fact that the last recorded assembly had been called in 1653 and that the 1682 convocations were drawn from the immediate vicinity of the Kremlin rather than from the "whole land," casts doubt upon the status of the latter.

6. In addition to drawing on official documents, for example the records of the Chancellery of Crown Service and Appointments (razriad), Soloviev makes use of four main contemporary witnesses for his account of the 1682 rebellion. (1) The memoir of Andrei Artamonovich Matveev (1666-1728) entitled *Description... of the Troubled Times Arising from the Rebellion of the Former Moscow Musketeers...* (Opisanie ... o smutnom vremeni, prikliuchivshemsia ot vozmushcheniia byvshikh moskovskikh streltsov...). Andrei was the son of Tsar Alexis's former favorite Artamon Matveev (see Chapter I, Note 19, above) and was bitterly hostile to the Miloslavsky party on account of his father's exile at the beginning of Fedor's reign (see pp. 12 ff.,above) and his murder by the musketeers in May 1682. He was to become a close associate of Peter I, serving on missions to Holland, France, England and Austria, and later in the Naval Academy and Senate. His memoir (which centers on 1682 but makes reference to events up to 1699) probably was written in the 1720s, certainly not before 1716 and very likely after Peter's death. It is colored by Matveev's reverent attitude towards Peter and his hatred of the Miloslavsky clan. The account was first published in 1787, and again in 1841. Soloviev used these two published versions.

(2) In contrast, the notes of Silvester Medvedev (1641-1691), *A Short Account of the Years 1682 to 1684* (Sozertsanie kratkoe let 7190, 91 i 92), were written during or shortly after the events described, and include valuable documentary material. Unlike Matveev, Medvedev was an adherent of Sophia, and was executed soon after her downfall. The *Short Account* was published in an incomplete version in 1787, in full only in 1894. Soloviev used a manuscript copy. On Medvedev's career, see Chapter I, Note 15, above.

(3) The *Diary* of the anonymous Polish author, probably written in 1683, has been referred to already (see Chapter I, Note 25). It was not published until 1901. Soloviev worked from the manuscript.

(4) The memoir of the Danish commercial agent, the Hamburg merchant Heinrich Butenant (?-1702), *Eigentlicher Bericht wegen des in der Stadt Moskau... entstandenen greulichen Tumults und grausahmen Massacre* (True Account of the Tragic and Terrible Massacre which Occurred in the Town of Moscow on Monday, Tuesday and Wednesday 15, 16 and 17 of May of the Present Year 1682), appeared in Hamburg in 1682. Butenant (who later added "von Rosenbusch" to his name) was involved involuntarily in the rebellion and recorded his impressions

in its immediate aftermath. For an edited translation of the memoir, see J. Keep, "Mutiny in Moscow, 1682," *Canadian Slavonic Papers*, XXIII (1981), pp. 401-442.

For a discussion of these and other sources, see L. Hughes, "Sofiya Alekseyevna and the Moscow Rebellion of 1682," *Slavonic and East European Review*, LXIII (1985), pp. 518-539, and "Sophia Alekseevna in Foreigners' Accounts," *Oxford Slavonic Papers*, XXI (1988), pp. 65-89.

7. The antidoron is the bread, blessed but not consecrated, which is distributed at the end of the Orthodox liturgy.

8. The anonymous Polish *Diary* is the only source for Sophia's activity at Fedor's funeral. It forms the basis of Soloviev's account of this entire incident. None of the other sources, including the hostile Matveev, record her attendance at the funeral, and the Soviet historian V. I. Buganov doubts whether she was even present.

9. On the musketeers, see Chapter I, Note 23.

10. On the retinue (druzhina), see Chapter I, Note 104.

11. The disturbances in the Pyzhov regiment, in February 1682, are recorded by Medvedev.

12. Medvedev had no reason to praise Patriarch Joachim (who was his enemy), therefore his information is more reliable than that of Butenant, who reported that the government intended merely to dismiss the officers, having forced them to pay up.

13. Andrei Matveev.

14. Khovansky here refers to the origins of Tsaritsa Natalia, who was the daughter of a musketeer colonel who had served in Smolensk. See Chapter I, Note 9.

15. Khovansky's speech is taken from the Polish *Diary*, the only known source.

16. The notion of a "plot" masterminded by Ivan Miloslavsky is most fully treated in Andrei Matveev's memoir (see Note 6, above). Matveev, as we know, was extremely hostile to the Miloslavskys. The Polish author also presumes pre-planning on Sophia's part. Needless to say, no such "plot' is indicated in Medvedev's account, nor indeed in the more neutral account of Butenant, both of which are consistent with the escalation of musketeer complaints about grievances pre-dating Fedor's death. V. I. Buganov rejects the existence of a plot, arguing that Sophia and her party were able to take advantage of anti-Naryshkin feeling at a later stage.

17. Tsarevich Dmitry (born 1582) was Ivan IV's son by his seventh wife, Maria Nagaia. He died in Uglich on May 15, 1591, having stabbed himself during a fit or, as rumor would have it, murdered on the orders of the regent, Boris Godunov, who wished to clear his own path to the throne of Muscovy. Whatever the truth of the matter (modern historians tend to absolve Boris of guilt), the circumstances of Dmitry's death paved the way for the appearance of a number of False Dmitrys during the Time of Troubles (see Chapter I, Note 109). Dmitry

was canonized in 1607 by order of Tsar Vasily Shuisky in order to discourage further pretenders, and he became something of a cult object. It was customary, for example, for the sovereign to make obeisance at his tomb during coronation ceremonies.

18. Butenant ascribed the spreading of the rumor to "the musketeers who guarded the tsar's chambers."

19. By the sixteenth century Moscow was divided into several walled districts, with the Kremlin at the center skirted to the east by the Kitai Quarter (Kitai Gorod), the commercial district. To the north, east and west, in a horseshoe shape, lay White Town (Bely Gorod). Earthwork Town (Zemliany Gorod) formed the outer belt to the city, and was the abode of artisans and musketeers. Leading boyars lived in the immediate vicinity of the Kremlin. For example, Prince Vasily Golitsyn had his house on the now demolished Hunters Row (Okhotnyi Riad), near present-day Marx Prospekt.

20. The Red Porch or staircase (krasnoe kryltso) once ran along the south wall of the Palace of Facets (granovitaia palata), the royal audience chamber dating from 1487. The stairs led down from the ceremonial rooms on the first floor. They were demolished in the 1930s.

21. The report of Matveev taking Peter's arm appears in the Polish Diary.

22. This interpretation of Sophia's betrayal of Ivan Naryshkin comes from Matveev. Butenant records that she, together with Natalia Naryshkina and Martha Apraksina, fell on her knees and pleaded for Naryshkin's life.

23. Doctor Daniel von Gaden (in some accounts Haden) was a converted Jew from Poland, who came to Moscow in 1657.

24. An analysis of the careers and family background of those murdered and exiled during the rebellion (e.g. in Crummey, Aristocrats and Servitors, pp. 88-97) indicates that by no means all victims were the "Miloslavskys' enemies" or members of a "Naryshkin faction." Clearly many suffered because they had offended the musketeers, regardless of their affiliation at court.

25. Nadvornaia pekhota.

26. In seventeenth-century Muscovy the status of slave (kholop) was distinct from that of serf. Large numbers of men and women entered into "limited service contracts" in lieu of paying off a monetary loan, and most remained enslaved, or indentured, until their owner's death, performing servile labor in the latter's home, acting as baggage handlers and fighters on military campaigns, working on estates, and so on. Richard Hellie in Slavery in Russia, 1450-1725 (Chicago, 1983) calculates that up to ten percent of the population may have been included in this and other classes of slavery. Chapter 20 of the 1649 Code of Laws (see Chapter I, Note 83) was devoted to questions relating to slavery (kholopstvo).

27. Soloviev refers to the eviction of the Polish occupying force from the Kremlin in 1612.

28. See Chapter I, Notes 47 and 88. The dissenters used the word Nikonites (nikoniantsy) as a term of abuse for supporters of the patriarch's reforms.

29. Soloviev draws extensively upon Savva Romanov's account for this section, using a manuscript from his own library. The work was published in 1863 under the title "History of the Faith and Petition of the Musketeers" (*Istoriia o vere i chelovitnaia o streltsakh*). The other major source is Medvedev, who as a clergyman and theologian, as well as an adherent of Sophia, had a personal interest in the crisis.

30. According to a reference in Avvakum's autobiography (see Chapter I, Note 112), "Dear Prince Ivan Khovansky was beaten with rods," but there is no evidence to confirm this claim or, indeed, that it is the elder Khovansky who is referred to. Khovansky had encountered Nikita Pustosviat (see Note 32, below) and other leading schismatics while he was governor of Novgorod in 1680-1681, visiting their homes and discussing matters of faith with them.

31. The alteration of the description of the Holy Spirit in the Creed was one of Nikon's many reforms. The new Creed omitted the epithet "true" (istinnyi) as an "uncanonical accretion." This was one of the dissenters' greatest objections. Avvakum wrote: "It were better in the Creed not to pronounce the word Lord, which is an accidental name, than to delete "True," for in that word is contained the essence of God."

32. Nikita Dobrynin "Pustosviat" (?-1682), one of the leading dissenters, had been a parish priest in Suzdal. Between 1658 and 1665 he composed his long "Petition" on the Old Belief, which contained a list of the heresies in the reformed religion. The work was condemned by Simeon Polotsky in his tract *The Scepter of Government* (Zhezl pravleniia). Polotsky's views were upheld by the Church Council of 1666, and Nikita was defrocked and imprisoned. He recanted, but subsequently reconfirmed his adherence to the old faith.

33. The rich and influential Solovetsk monastery, founded in about 1430 on an island in the White Sea, was one of the main centers of Old Believer resistance. The monastery was besieged by government troops for seven years, falling to the attackers just a few days before Tsar Alexis's death in January 1676. The monks were executed or exiled. See G. E. Orchard, "Solovetskii Uprising of 1668-1676," MERSH, Vol. 36, pp. 141-144.

34. As a result of Nikon's reforms the number of communion loaves (prosviry) used in the liturgy was reduced from seven to five. On the controversy over the crucifix, see above, Chapter I, Note 91.

35. In Russian Orthodox tradition the communion loaves were baked by a proskuritsa, generally a middle-aged widow.

36. In his speech the patriarch draws upon the Gospel according to St. John, Chapter 10.

37. The Consecrated Assembly or Council (osviashchennyi sobor) comprised the hierarchy of the Orthodox church: the patriarch, four metropolitans, archbishops, bishops and abbots of leading monasteries. It was replaced by Peter I in 1718 by the Ecclesiastical College (dukhovnaia kollegiia), later called the Holy Governing Synod.

38. Matthew, ch. 11, verse 29.

39. Soloviev refers to Arseny Sukhanov (?-1668), superior of the Moscow Epiphany monastery, who travelled to the east in 1649 and 1651 to investigate the situation of the Greek church and to examine discrepancies between the Russian and Greek rites and service books. His travels took him to Moldavia, Wallachia, Constantinople, Alexandria, Cairo and Jerusalem. In 1653 Patriarch Nikon commissioned him to bring manuscripts from Mount Athos as an aid to revisions. From 1661 to 1664 he directed the Moscow printing house, and thus was directly associated with the production of the "new books."

40. Savva Romanov reports that the people's actions struck fear into the prelates. Some of them even reverted to the old form of blessing: "And the pious Tsaritsa Natalia sent a message to the believers, asking that the meeting take place at the platform on the Red Square, and that the sovereign tsars be present, and I too was invited to attend. But she begged us not to go into the cathedral, however much they pleaded with us. She sent this message three times, asking us not to enter the cathedral or the Palace of Facets." (Soloviev's note)

41. The High Savior cathedral (Verkhospasskii sobor), sometimes referred to as the cathedral of the Savior "behind the Golden Grille" on account of the ornate railings at its entrance, was the domestic church of the royal family, one of several chapels incorporated into the upper stories of the Kremlin palace. It was built in the 1630s at the same time as the palace itself. The cupolas, still visible from the small square of the Palace of Facets and the church of the Deposition of the Robe (see below, Note 44), date from the 1680s. Access was strictly forbidden to all but the royal family and its immediate circle.

42. See Note 33, above.

43. The cathedral of the Archangel Michael (Arkhangelskii sobor) was built in 1505-1508 by the Italian architect Alevisio Novi, who incorporated Renaissance details into its largely conventional design. It served as the burial place of the Muscovite rulers from Ivan Kalita (1325-1340) to Ivan Alekseevich (1682-1696).

44. The church of the Deposition of the Robe (Rizhpolozheniia) on the northwest corner of Cathedral Square adjacent to the Palace of Facets, was built in 1484-1486 (replacing the earlier church of the same name). It once served as the private chapel of the patriarchs of Moscow, but when Nikon built a new patriarchal palace and cathedral nearby in 1650s it reverted to the royal family. It was linked with the royal palace and the nearby Dormition cathedral by covered passageways.

45. But why did the priests collide with the dissenters? They could not have been intending to start a fight as royal permission for the admittance of the dissenters had been given. Medvedev provides an explanation: he reports that Khovansky had stopped the priests from entering and they collided with the dissenters on their way out. (Soloviev's note)

46. Here we follow Savva Romanov's account, as he had no reason to conceal the fact that Sophia reprimanded the dissenters. Later he describes with hatred her interference in the debate and how she silenced Nikita. Medvedev's aim is equally clear: to keep Sophia constantly in the foreground. (Soloviev's note)

47. Polotsky's *Scepter of Government* was a refutation of the teachings of the Old Believers, including Nikita, commissioned by the Church Council of 1666 and published in 1667. The work later was denounced as heretical by Patriarch Joachim in the controversy over Polotsky's alleged Catholic tendencies. See Note 32, above.

48. Alexis (?-1378) was metropolitan of Moscow from 1354. He was one of the major ecclesiastical and political figures during the period of the rise of Muscovy. In 1355 he translated the New Testament from Greek. In 1449 he was canonized.

49. Soloviev probably refers to Patriarch Jeremiah of Constantinople (held office 1572-1579, 1580-1584, 1586-1594), who came to Moscow in 1589 to consecrate Job, the first Russian patriarch.

50. Filaret, in secular life the nobleman Fedor Nikitich Romanov (?1553-1633), was the father of Tsar Michael (1613-1645) and patriarch of Moscow from 1619 to 1633. Acting as virtual co-ruler with his son, he introduced a number of reforms into ecclesiastical practice. See entry by G. E. Orchard, MERSH, Vol. 11, pp. 126-130.

51. Medvedev.

52. Matveev.

53. The Donskoi monastery, dedicated to the highly venerated icon of Our Lady of the Don, was founded in 1593 to the south of the Kremlin (near present-day Leninsky Prospekt) to commemorate the defeat of the Tatar khan, Kazy Girey, in 1591, near this spot and apparently through the intervention of the same icon. It was patronized by Tsars Michael and Alexis, and also by the latter's children. Tsarevna Ekaterina provided funds for the construction of the new cathedral and walls, started in 1684. Because of its association with victory over the Tatars, the monastery was much frequented by Sophia during her regency.

54. The royal estate at Kolomenskoe, situated on the Moscow river some six miles southeast of the Kremlin, became the main summer residence of the tsars in the sixteenth century. In the 1660s Tsar Alexis constructed an exotic wooden palace and the adjacent church of Our Lady of Kazan. The withdrawal of the royal family to the estate during the summer months was a regular event. The trip was not the first in the summer of 1682, however. Other sources show that between July 13 and 29 the royal party visited estates and monasteries to the north of Moscow, a fact not recorded by Soloviev.

55. Until 1700, when Peter I reformed the calendar, the Russian New Year began on September 1 and the number of the year itself was computed, not from the birth of Christ, but from the notional date of the creation of the world. Hence September 1, 1682 marked the beginning of the Russian year 7191.

56. The official account [used by Soloviev for this section] makes no mention of a rescript referred to in Matveev and printed in Medvedev, which was supposed to have been sent from the St. Sabbas monastery to summon service gentry from the vicinity to protect the tsars from Khovansky and the musketeers. Evidently a rescript was prepared, but it was decided not to send it, otherwise Khovansky would certainly have known about it. It was decided to maintain secrecy and to pass off the expedition as a normal pilgrimage in order to trap Khovansky. (Soloviev's note)

        This draft document, printed in a recent Soviet anthology, signalled a change of tone in reference to Khovansky, who so far had not been accused of any crimes in royal missives. It referred, among other things, to the "many offenses, unlawful and gross actions and violations committed by criminals and traitors!"

57. The route described here took the royal family northwest from Kolomenskoe to Vorobievo on the Sparrow Hills to the south of the Kremlin (see Chapter I, Note 44), thence west to Pavlovskoe and to the important St. Sabbas (Savva) monastery at Zvenigorod, some 32 miles west of Moscow. St. Sabbas had been venerated by Tsar Alexis, who believed in his miracle-working powers. The tsar made many benefactions to the monastery (his favorite) and visited it regularly, as did his children. Continuing the journey, they returned to Pavlovskoe and struck northeast to reach the royal village of Vozdvizhenskoe to the north of Moscow for the festival of the Elevation of the Cross of Our Lord (Vozdvizhenie kresta Gospodnia) in the church of the same name. Later the royal party was to move to the great Trinity-St. Sergius monastery (Troitse-Sergieva Lavra), 45 miles to the northeast of the capital, in the present town of Zagorsk. The monastery, founded in 1345 by St. Sergius of Radonezh, one of the great Russian saints was, and remains, a major place of pilgrimage. The tsars customarily visited the monastery for the feast of St. Sergius on September 25.

58. Simeon (not Semen, as Soloviev writes) Ivanovich Samoilovich, the colonel of Starodub, was the son of the hetman of the Ukraine, and had come to Moscow to swear allegiance to the new tsars. His visit was used as a pretext for summoning the service gentry to avert the threat from Khovansky and the musketeers.

59. Soloviev quotes only part of the letter of denunciation, which goes on to list rewards allegedly promised by Khovansky to the conspirators, and explained that those who had betrayed the conspiracy were in hiding. It concluded: "To be handed to Tsarevna Sophia Alekseevna without making a copy." In the opinion of most specialists on the period, this letter was a forgery, prepared by the government to aid their case against the Khovanskys.

60. Fedor Leontievich Shaklovity (?-1689), soon to be appointed director of the Chancellery of Musketeers and to become a leading figure in Sophia's regime, was one of a small but growing band of bureaucratic specialists, mostly of humble origin, who formed the professional backbone of the government chancelleries.

He began his career in the 1670s in Tsar Alexis's Privy Chancellery, and from 1676 worked in the Chancellery of Crown Service and Appointments (razriad). He entered the boyar council in July 1682 with the rank of crown secretary (dumnyi diak). In September 1689 he was accused of masterminding a plot to extend Sophia's power by murdering the tsars, members of their family and inner circle. He was executed on September 12. See L.A.J. Hughes in MERSH, Vol. 34, pp. 146-148.

61. Soloviev provides a condensed version of this eleven-point document, issued on October 3. The omitted clauses (10) and (11) include generalizations about "loyal service" and threats of execution for violations of the articles.

62. St. Andrew, the "first-called" apostle, was the patron saint of Russia. His hand allegedly was discovered by Patriarch Joachim earlier in 1682, locked into the reformed three-fingered sign of the cross!

63. The petitions for the removal of the column were dated October 28 and 29.

64. On the Razin rebellion, see Chapter I, Note 38.

CHAPTER III

1. On Hetman Ivan Samoilovich, see Chapter I, Note 61.

2. On King Michael and King Jan Sobieski of Poland, see Chapter I, Notes 69 and 70 respectively.

3. The cathedral of the Holy Wisdom (Sofiiskii Sobor) was founded about 1018-1037 by Prince Yaroslav the Wise of Kiev. It was based on the model of the eponymous cathedral in Constantinople. The Dormition cathedral (Uspenskii Sobor) in the Moscow Kremlin was commissioned by Ivan III of Moscow and designed and built by the Italian architect Aristotele Fioraventi in 1475-1479. It was the chief church of all Russia, the venue for the coronation of tsars, and major national festivals and services of thanksgiving.

4. On Vasily Golitsyn, see Chapter I, Note 54.

5. On A. L. Ordin-Nashchokin and A. S. Matveev, see Chapter I, Notes 19 and 30 respectively.

6. The Thirty Years' War (1618-1648) was ended by the Treaty of Westphalia, which irrevocably changed the balance of power in Europe. Ranging over vast territories and involving many issues, the war centered on the German towns and principalities and on the conflict between the Holy Roman empire and the Protestant rulers. It culminated with the emergence of France as the principal power of Europe, Swedish control of the Baltic, and the sovereignty of the states of the Holy Roman empire. Russia was involved peripherally through its conflicts with Sweden and Poland.

7. By the Treaty of Dover (1670) Charles II of England agreed to support French policy in Europe, particularly with regard to the Dutch, in return for a

payment of three hundred thousand pounds per annum, hence Soloviev's reference to him as the "pensioner" of the French king.

8. See above, Chapter I.

9. On the "French faction", see Chapter I, Note 71.

10. N. Davies, *God's Playground. A History of Poland*, I (Oxford, 1981, p. 481), gives April 1 (backdated to March 31) as the date of the treaty of mutual assistance. On the war with Turkey, see ibid., Chapter 16, and J. Stoye, *The Siege of Vienna* (London, 1965).

11. On the Truce of Andrusovo (1667), see Chapter I, Note 57.

12. On the negotiations leading to the Treaty of Moscow of 1686 and its implications, see L. Lewitter, "The Russo-Polish Treaty of 1686 and its Antecedents," *Polish Review*, IX (1964), No. 3, pp. 5-29 and No. 4, pp. 21-37.

13. Unlike Lutherans and Calvinists, who had four or five churches in the Foreign Quarter (see Chapter I, note 17) during the period in question, and were allowed to replace wooden with stone structures, the much smaller foreign Catholic community did not receive permission to build its own church until 1695. Before then, as indicated here, services had to take place in private accommodation.

14. According to the Russian Primary Chronicle, Riurik was one of the three Varangian or Norsemen brothers who in AD 862 came "from across the sea" by invitation to rule Russia. He was regarded by tradition as the founder of the Muscovite ruling dynasty of Riurikids, which ended with the death of Tsar Fedor Ivanovich in 1598. On Gedimin, founder of Lithuania, see Chapter II, Note 3.

15. Ivan Kalita ("Money Bags"), grand prince of Moscow, 1325-1340, was one of the early "gatherers of the Russian lands." Pursuing shrewd policies aimed at maintaining the clan's power by acting as tax collector to the Mongol overlords and extending the boundaries of his Moscow principality by conquest and purchase, he contributed to the unification of Russia under the leadership of the Muscovite dynasty. For a recent assessment, see R. O. Crummey, *The Formation of Muscovy, 1304-1613* (London, 1987), pp. 39-41. It was Ivan's son, Simeon, who first began to call himself prince of "All Russia".

16. The Thirteen Years' War (1654-1667) between Poland and Russia was precipitated by Moscow's assuming protectorship of the Dnieper cossacks and the annexation of the Ukraine in 1654. Fighting ranged over Polish-held territories long claimed as their patrimony by the princes and tsars of Moscow, in the Ukraine, Belorussia and Lithuania, as well as in the Baltic. The war was ended by the Truce of Andrusovo (see Chapter I, Note 57). For an account of the war and assessment of its significance for Russia's relations with the rest of Europe, see P. Longworth, "Tsar Alexis Goes to War," *History Today* (January 1981), pp. 14-18.

17. The cinnamon-colored cloth from Bukhara was known as *bai-berek*. *Viaziga* is a foodstuff made from sturgeon gristle, and *tesha* a foodstuff made from the abdomen of fish. It is uncertain whether the adjective *yurlochnye* is a biological or geographical term.

18. Bogdan Khmelnitsky (Chmielnicki) (c. 1595-1657) was hetman of the Ukraine from 1648 to 1657. It was he who led the cossacks of Polish Ukraine in their so-called "War of Liberation" which culminated in the Union of Ukraine and Muscovy under the terms of the Treaty of Pereiaslavl in 1654, and precipitated the Thirteen Years' War. See Note 16.

19. On E. I. Ukraintsev, see Chapter I, Note 74.

20. Prince Gedeon Sviatopolk-Chetvertinsky (?-1690), religious name Gedeon, became Orthodox bishop of Luck and Ostrog in the Polish Ukraine in 1659, but was forced to flee to Muscovy after being urged by Polish authorities to convert to the Uniate (Catholic of the Byzantine rite) faith. He arrived in Baturin in 1684. As Soloviev indicates, Gedeon's elevation to the metropolitanate of Kiev was due partly to the support of Hetman Samoilovich. When the latter was deposed in 1687 Gedeon suffered a diminution of power, including withdrawal of the right to the title metropolitan of All Russia.

21. The regions referred to in this passage were "threshold provinces" of the Polish Commonwealth in the south and east of the country. Red Ruthenia (Rus Czerwona) included the city of Lwów. To the north lay Volhynia (Wołyń), to the south Podolia (with the town of Kamieniec). Podliasie lay to the north of Volhynia. The significant point about these provinces is that they had a largely Ruthenian (Russian-speaking Orthodox) population, even though most of the nobles were Catholic or Uniate and Polish-speaking.

22. The Kiev monastery of the Caves (Kievo-Pecherskaia Lavra), founded in 1051, was the first monastic establishment in Russia, and one of the most famous and influential, a seat of chronicle writing and Orthodox theology. The monks lived in caves excavated into the hillside above the Dnieper river, hence the name.

23. On Mazepa, see Chapter I, Note 67.

24. The term exarch refers to a delegate or subordinate of a higher ecclesiastical dignitary, appointed to rule in his name.

25. Dositheus, patriarch of Jerusalem 1669-1707, was one of the leading Orthodox churchmen of his era. His *Confession* (1672) has been described as "a document of primary importance in the history of modern Orthodox theology," and his influence was of particular significance in a period when Orthodox scholarship had fallen into decline. As a subject of the Turkish sultan, of course, Dositheus was in a delicate political situation.

26. In 1589 the metropolitan of Moscow was raised to the status of patriarch, fifth after the patriarchs of Constantinople, Alexandria, Antioch and Jerusalem. Ironically, the fifth-ranking patriarchate was the only one located in an independent country ruled by an Orthodox sovereign.

27. On Yury Khmelnitsky, see Chapter I, Note 65.

28. The term *nuradin*, which Soloviev applies to this official, usually refers to a Tatar prince, member of the ruling dynasty, often second heir to the throne.

29. The singular is used in the actual text.

30. This report is taken from F. de la Neuville, *Relation curieuse et nouvelle de Moscovie* (The Hague, 1699), p. 65 (First edition: Paris, 1698). In some respects this account, published eight years after its author's visit to Moscow, is unreliable, but there is strong evidence that Neuville met Golitsyn, whom he admired greatly, and had conversations with some of his close associates in the Chancellery of Foreign Affairs, who were able to supply information on Golitsyn's problems at court two years before the Frenchman's visit.

31. On Sophia's controversial adoption of royal titles, including that of autocrat (samoderzhitsa), see L.A.J. Hughes, "Sophia, 'Autocrat of All the Russias,'" *Canadian Slavonic Papers*, XXVII (1986), pp. 266-286.

32. Rodion Matveevich Streshnev (?-1687) first appears in records for 1634, serving at the court of Tsar Michael as table attendant. He entered the boyar council in 1656. From 1663 to 1680 he was director of the Chancellery for Siberia and, thanks to his marriage links with the royal family, figured prominently at ceremonial occasions, carrying the crown at Fedor's coronation and attending Peter at his in June 1682. From 1679 he was one of Peter's personal attendants (diadka) and it was no doubt Cherkassky's acquisition of this influential post that Golitsyn feared when Streshnev died in July 1687. Prince Michael Alegukovich Cherkassky (?- ca. 1713) became one of Peter's closest associates. It was he who tried to protect Artamon Matveev and the Naryshkins from musketeer violence in May 1682. Later, he was one of the few nobles allowed to keep their beards when Peter issued his orders on shaving in 1698.

33. This incident was, despite the abolition of the code in 1682, primarily a dispute over precedence. The protesters considered that family honor had been slighted by the new allocation of commands and revised deployment of troops for the 1687 campaign.

34. Soloviev bases the account which follows on a number of contemporary sources, including Golitsyn's dispatches and his letters to Fedor Shaklovity, records of the trial of the latter and his associates in 1689, and the diary of Patrick Gordon. See the following note.

35. Patrick Gordon (1635-1699) was perhaps the most eminent of the numerous mercenaries who served the Romanovs in the latter half of the seventeenth century. A Scottish Catholic from Aberdeen, he entered the tsar's service in 1661 and remained in Moscow, with the exception of a few brief trips home, for 38 years. In the 1690s he was one of Peter's closest advisers and friends. Gordon was a prolific correspondent, and kept a detailed diary which is an invaluable source, not only for Muscovite military affairs, but also for the life of the foreign community and the court. Soloviev consulted a German translation, *Tagebuch des Generalen Patrick Gordon während seiner Kriegsdienste unter den Schweden und Polen vom Jahre 1655 bis 1661 und seines Aufenthaltes in Russland vom Jahre 1661 bis 1699* (St. Petersburg, 1851). The original journal survives in the Military Historical Archive in Moscow. Only sections of it have been published in English. See *Passages from the Diary of General Patrick Gordon of Auchleuchries*

in the Years 1635-1699 (London, 1859). On Gordon, see P. Dukes, "How the Eighteenth Century Began for Russia and the West," *Russia and the West in the Eighteenth Century* (Newtonville, 1983), pp. 2-19.

36. The chronicler is the anonymous "eyewitness" (*samovidets*). He began his service in the hetman's chancellery about 1654 and died about 1702. His lively account of events in the Ukraine was first published in Moscow in 1846.

37. Ivan Martynovich Briukhovetsky (?-1668) was hetman of the Left Bank Ukraine from 1663 to 1668. In February 1668 he led a rebellion against Moscow, with the aid of the Tatars, intending to place the Ukraine under Turkish rule. He was killed by the cossacks.

38. The double-headed eagle was the insignia of the Muscovite ruling house, adopted in the reign of Ivan III (1462-1505) following Byzantine and Habsburg models.

39. Prince Yury Chetvertinsky was the son of Metropolitan Gedeon of Kiev. See above, Note 20.

40. The Glukhov articles, adopted in 1669 on the election of Demian Mnogogreshny as hetman, redefined the relationship between the Ukraine and Muscovy originally formulated in the Treaty of Pereiaslavl in 1654. It was agreed to limit the stationing of Russian military governors and troops to five towns, and that the cossack high command retain jurisdiction over internal affairs and the right to hire troops to deal with local disturbances. Cossack rights over estates and peasants were confirmed. In the event, these articles concentrated too much power in the hands of the hetman and his inner circle.

41. II Corinthians, 6:2. Baranovich's speech is full of biblical references, including the raising from the dead of his namesake Lazarus.

42. Tenth money (*desiatinnaia denga*) was a levy of one tenth of income on townsmen and merchants to finance military campaigns.

43. This incident is taken from the account of the Jesuit Philippe Avril. See below, Note 52.

44. Taken from the memoir of I. A. Zheliabuzhsky. See Chapter I, Note 49. The practice of taking a sample of earth from a footprint was linked with black magic. Golitsyn is reported to have been very superstitious.

45. The term Hagarenes (*agariane*) refers to the reputed descendants of Hagar, the concubine of Abraham. Here, an abusive term for Muslims.

46. This is an extract from a letter in cipher, first transcribed and published by N. G. Ustrialov in his *History of the Reign of Peter the Great* in 1858, and still preserved in Moscow. A second letter is quoted below. These represent almost the sole documentary evidence for an amorous relationship between Sophia and Vasily Golitsyn, although there was much rumor and speculation, particularly in the works of foreigners. The conventional terms of endearment employed, for example *batiushka* (literally "little father") and *moi svet* (literally "my light"), require fuller elucidation before one can state with certainty that these are "love letters" in the modern sense.

47. See previous note.

48. The peace treaty of Kardis (1661) settled the Russo-Swedish war of 1656-1658, restoring the border fixed by the Treaty of Stolbovo (1617) and obliging Russia to return lands conquered in Estonia and Livonia. Criticized by some as a cowardly concession to the Swedes, the treaty allowed Russia to concentrate efforts on the war with Poland, concluded in 1667.

49. By the abrogation of the Edict of Nantes in 1685 Louis XIV revoked the 1598 charter granting Huguenots freedom of worship and civil rights, thus precipitating a large-scale emigration of French Protestants to Holland, Prussia and England.

50. The minister was Colbert de Croissy.

51. Soloviev gives the erroneous date 1688. Although Avril's account (see following note) fails to state the date clearly, his visit in January 1689 is well documented in other sources.

52. Philippe Avril (1654-1698) first visited Moscow in 1685. His account of this visit and his ill-fated 1689 trip first appeared in Paris in 1691 under the title *Voyage en divers états d'Europe et d'Asie entrepris pour découvrir un nouveau chemin à la Chine*. Soloviev used the 1693 edition. The English translation is entitled *Travels in diverse parts of Europe and Asia... to discover a new Way by Land into China*.

53. Fedor Alekseevich Golovin (1650-1706) later became one of Peter I's closest associates. He was second ambassador on the Grand Embassy of 1697-1698, helped to create the Russian fleet as head of the War and Naval Chancellery and directed the Chancellery of Foreign Affairs from 1700. In 1715 his work *Globus nebesnyi* (The Celestial Globe) was published in Amsterdam.

54. Demian Ignatievich Mnogogreshny (?- c. 1696) was hetman of the Left Bank Ukraine from 1668 to 1672, when he was charged with conducting secret negotiations with the Turks and exiled to Irkutsk.

55. Fr. Jean François Gerbillon and Fr. Thomas Pereira both left accounts of their experiences: "The Second Journey of PP. Gerbillon and Pereyra in Tatary in 1698," in Jean Baptiste du Halde, *A Description of the Empire of China and Chinese Tatary*, Vol. 2 (London, 1741), pp. 301-333, and J. Sebes, *The Jesuits and the Sino-Russian Treaty of Nerchinsk (1689). The Diary of Thomas Pereira, S. J.* (Rome, 1961).

56. Erofei Pavlovich Khabarov was a pioneer of Russian exploration in Siberia. In 1649-1651 he led an expedition of trappers along the Amur to the Sea of Okhotsk and conquered the Daurian region.

57. On the Treaty of Nerchinsk, which governed Sino-Russian relations for the next 38 years, see M. Mancall, *Russia and China. Their Diplomatic Relations to 1728*. (Cambridge, Mass., 1971), with an English translation of the text, and Clifford M. Foust, MERSH, Vol. 25, pp. 156-160.

58. The communal obligation (tiaglo) system of taxation imposed a joint burden upon the listed members of rural and urban communities; that is, payment was

a collective, not an individual responsibility. If the fugitives registered in towns were returned to their villages, the remaining taxpayers would have to pay a larger share until the lists were redrawn.

59. The Kasimov princes were a group of Tatar rulers who served Moscow in the 15th-17th centuries. The khanate of Kasimov, on the Oka river, was founded in 1452 or 1453. In the 1680s their duties were mainly of a ceremonial nature, attendance at court functions, for example. This particular incident is taken from Zheliabuzhsky's memoir (see Chapter I, Note 49). No explanatory information is supplied.

60. Soloviev's source for this section is the *Complete Collection of Laws of the Russian Empire*, Vol. 2 (St. Petersburg, 1830).

61. The Dregovichi and Viatichi were ancient Slavic tribes.

62. On the Code of Precedence, see Chapter I, Note 100.

63. The Caves monastery in Pechora, Pskov province, was founded in the mid-15th century, serving as a major religious centre and a defensive outpost on the Lithuanian border. The caves, which initially housed hermits, were used as a cemetery.

64. The bread used in the Orthodox liturgy differs from the unleavened wafers (here referred to as *kolobki*) of the Catholic mass. On the form of crosses imprinted on loaves, see Chapter I, Note 91.

65. See above, Chapter II, Note 33.

66. On Daniel, see Chapter I, pp.76-7.

67. The Paleostrovsk monastery was on Lake Onega in the north of Russia.

68. The monastery of the Savior on the Svir river and the St. Anthony monastery on the Siia river, both in the Onega region.

69. On Polotsky see Chapter I, Note 11.

70. The monk Epifany Slavinetsky (?-1676) was summoned to Moscow from Kiev in 1649 to teach school in the Miracles monastery in the Kremlin, and to translate and correct Russian religious texts from the Greek originals. In 1674 he directed the translation of the Bible from Greek into Slavonic. He also translated a number of secular works, including extracts from Copernicus and lexicons. He was associated with Nikon's "Graecophile" school.

71. The belief of the Orthodox church is that the moment of consecration does not occur until after the Epiclesis—the priest's invocation of the Spirit on the holy gifts—which comes towards the end of the liturgy. As Timothy Ware points out in *The Orthodox Church* (Harmondsworth, 1963, pp. 289-290), this is not a rigid point of dogma. The Roman Catholics believe that the consecration is effected by the earlier Words of Institution: "This is my Body...". (Matthew 26:26-27). On this and related matters, see the introduction to Georgius David, *Status modernus magnae Russiae seu Moscoviae*, ed. A. V. Florovskij (The Hague, 1965), pp. 27 ff.

72. Polotsky's *Crown of Faith* (*Venets very kafolicheskoi* (1670) aroused displeasure in conservative circles by its references to western writers and its use

of the Apostolic rather than the Eastern Nicene Creed. Polotsky is believed to have studied in the Jesuit College in Wilno.

73. Artolatry means "bread worship."

74. On Medvedev, see Chapter I, Note 15. On Shaklovity, see Chapter II, Note 60.

75. Medvedev's fellow pupils were Vasily Repsky, a chorister who had come to Kiev with Bishop Methodius, and Semen and Ilia Kazantev. (Soloviev's note)

76. Karion Istomin (late 1640s-1717), a pupil of Simeon Polotsky, was employed in the Moscow Printing House from 1672 as scribe and clerk, serving as its director from 1698 to 1701. He was a prominent publicist, poet and educationalist, the author of several reading primers. In 1682 he presented a book of verse dedicated to Tsarevna Sophia, containing a plea for the establishment of an academy in Moscow.

77. Ioanniky (1643-1717) and Sofrony (1652-1730) Likhud arrived in Moscow in 1685, having studied in Cephalonia, Venice and Padua. The Moscow Academy, where they taught grammar, rhetoric, dialectics and physics, was opened in 1687. In 1688-1691 Ioanniky served as Russian ambassador to Venice. In 1694 the brothers fell into disfavor amongst ultra-conservative, mainly anti-Latinist groups in Moscow, and were demoted, but they continued their teaching activities elsewhere in Russia. They were the authors of numerous works and translations. Their careers still await thorough investigation. See MERSH, Vol. 20, pp. 44-45.

78. The Council of Florence (1438-9) established a union between the Eastern Orthodox and Roman Catholic churches, based on unanimity in matters of doctrine and respect for the rites and traditions of each church. Only one Orthodox prelate refused to sign the agreement, but the Union was never accepted by the Orthodox church as a whole, and many of the signatories later revoked their decision. Constantinople abandoned the Union in 1453. See also Chapter I, Note 107.

79. Peter Simeonovich Mogila (Mohila) (c.1596-1647), abbot of the Kiev Caves monastery, and metropolitan of Kiev from 1633 to 1647, in 1632 founded the Kiev Academy, which was to become a bulwark in the struggle of the Ukrainian Orthodox church in Poland against Catholic and Uniate domination and the model for the Moscow Academy. Mogila was the author of a number of influential theological works. See Hugh F. Graham, "Peter Mogila—Metropolitan of Kiev," *Russian Review*, XIV (1950), pp. 345-356, and MERSH, Vol. 23, pp. 9-12.

80. On Avril, see above, Note 52.

81. The envoy was Foy de la Neuville. See above, Note 30.

82. The contents of Golitsyn's houses and estates, including his new mansion on Hunters Row (Okhotny Riad) in the center of Moscow, were described and valued meticulously by government officials after his downfall. The documents were published in 1884, together with other materials relating to the trials of Fedor Shaklovity and his "accomplices." See L. A. J. Hughes, *Russia and the West*, pp. 94-96.

83. This was probably the gilded painted bed presented to Golitsyn by Sophia in 1687.

84. *Commentarorium de republica emendanda*, by Andrzej Frycz Modrzewski (c.1503- c.1572).

85. This is the popular tale of Ottone, emperor of Rome, which tells the story of Empress Olunda, wrongfully banished with her twin sons. A Polish version of the tale, *Historya piknaikrotochwilna o Ottonie cesarzu rzymskim* (1569), was translated into Russian in 1677. Many such tales reached Russia in the late seventeenth century, often through the medium of Polish and Czech.

86. In 1684 the Saxon envoy Dr. Laurent Rinhuber presented Golitsyn with a copy of Hiob Ludolf's *Historia habissinica* (Historia Aethiopica, 1681?).

87. A work by Melety Smotritsky?

88. The story of Brave Knight Peter and the Golden Keys (*Romant de Pierre de Provence et de la belle Maguellone de Naples*), a romantic tale popular throughout Europe. The Polish version, *Historya o Magielone Krolewnie Neapolitanskiey*, was translated into Russian in 1680.

89. The first theatrical performance in Russia took place at the court of Tsar Alexis in 1672. The plays presented included a number of "comedies" on biblical and classical themes, adapted from western originals. Simeon Polotsky wrote two "comedies" in the 1670s, and it is perhaps these which Golitsyn had in his library.

90. Yury Krizhanich (Juraj Križanič) (1618-1683), a Croatian priest, scholar, linguist and philosopher, lived in Russia from 1659 to 1679. Exiled to Siberia in 1661, he wrote a number of works analyzing the roots of Russian "backwardness," expounding the ideal of Slavic unity and advocating the conversion of Russia to Catholicism. The work in Golitsyn's library is presumably the *Discourses on Government or Politika* (1663). See *Russian Statecraft. The Politika of Iurii Krizhanich*, ed. and transl. J. M. Letiche and B. Dmytryshyn (London, 1985).

91. A book on the art of artillery by J.-J. von Wallhausen, translated from the German and published in Moscow in 1649 under the title *Uchenie i khitrost ratnogo stroeniia*.

92. For more on Golitsyn's books (a total of 216, printed and in manuscript, was discovered on his estates), see L. A. J. Hughes, *Russia and the West*, pp. 87-99. Golitsyn also had access to libraries of foreign works in the Chancellery of Foreign Affairs and other government departments. On his use of architectural books, see my "Western European Graphic Material as a Source of Moscow Baroque Architecture," *Slavonic and East European Review*, LV (1977), pp. 433-443.

93. In September 1689 Sophia was removed from power and placed under house arrest in the New Virgin convent. Golitsyn was stripped of rank and property and exiled to the Far North, where he remained until his death in 1714. See Volume 26 in the Soloviev series.

INDEX

Abramov, dragoon, 77.
Academy (see also Slavic-Greek-Latin), xv, 91-5, 229, 265.
Adadurov, jailor, 19.
Adamovich (Adamov), Simeon, priest, xxvii, 28, 29-34, 37; condemned, 38.
Adashev, Alexis, 22, 242.
Adrian, archimandrite, 142.
Adrian, patriarch, 5.
Afanasy, archbishop of Kholmogory, 132.
Afanasy, deacon, 229.
Agafia, tsaritsa, (see Grushetskaia).
Agafitsa, widow, 222-3.
Ahmed-agi, 57.
Aiuka, Kalmyk chieftain, 66, 67.
Akhtyrka, 29, 198.
Akinf, sacristan, 229.
Akinfiev, Nikita Ivanovich, 117.
Albazin, 206-14.
Alekseev, Nikita, emissary, 176-8.
Alexander II, tsar, xii.
Alexandria, patriarch of, 61.
Alexis Alekseevich, tsarevich, 4, 235, 242.
Alexis Mikhailovich, tsar, xv, xvii, xviii, 2, 31, 73, 75, 84, 91, 104, 132, 194, 215, 223, 227, 232, 234, 235, 236, 239, 240, 241, 249, 251, 254, 259; second marriage, 6, 235; death, 5, 8-9, 16; funeral, 17.
Alexis, metropolitan of Moscow, 134, 256.
Almazov, Semen Erofeevich, 29, 31, 34, 35, 43, 164.
Andreev, Ivan, priest, 222.
Andrew, apostle, 145, 258.
Andrusovo, Truce of, (1667), xx, 24, 45, 47, 158, 239, 243, 244, 259.
Anna Mikhailovna, tsarevna, 102.
Anthony, archdeacon, 193.
Anthony, dissident monk, 149.
Apostolets, Wallachian, 63-4.
Apraksin, clan, 96, 99-100.
Apraksina, Martha Matveevna, tsaritsa, 96, 98, 99, 115, 116.

Arapov, bailliff, 67.
Archangel, 73.
Argamakov, Michael, 219-20.
Argamakov, Peter, 219.
Aristov, N., xxxi.
Arsenius, patriarch of Serbia, 195.
Arseny the Greek, (Sukhanov), 127, 132, 255.
Astrakhan, 10, 14, 65, 90.
Austria, xxii, 155ff., 196. See also Holy League, Leopold I.
Averkiev, ataman, 225.
Avril, Philippe, Jesuit, 205, 231, 262, 263, 265.
Avvakum, archpriest, xxvii, 98, 240, 246, 249-50, 254.

Baiton, Afanasy, cossack captain, 207.
Bakhchiserai, Treaty of, (1681), 60.
Baltuga, Yakut chieftain, xxiv, 68-70.
Baranovich, Lazar, archbishop of Chernigov, xxvii, 4, 28, 29, 33, 170-2, 174, 193-4, 230, 236, 262.
Barkhatov, Gavrila, 77.
Barsuk, colonel, 38.
Bashkirs, 67, 141.
Bashkovsky, Ignaty, 18.
Baturin, 24, 30, 37, 40, 43, 55.
Beauvollais, Jesuit, 205.
Belgorod, xxv, 175, 216.
Beliaev, Afanasy, merchant, 148.
Belobodsky, Andrei, interpreter, 210-12.
Berdiaev, envoy, 64.
Berkh, V.N., xiv.
Berlov, David, apothecary, 12-13, 16.
Bessarabia, xxiii, 195.
Bezobrazov, P.V., xiii.
Bibikov, Danilo, 71.
Bilevich, Jan, Wallachian envoy, 54-5.
Biziaev, artisan, 136.
Bobinin, secretary, 62.
Bogdanov, A.P., xxxi.
Bogdanov, Grigory, 111, 117.

THE EDITOR AND TRANSLATOR

Lindsey Hughes was born in England in 1949. Her love affair with the Russian language began in 1965 when the subject was introduced into her school as an experiment, and she went on to study it for her bachelor's degree, graduating with First Class honors from the University of Sussex in 1971. As an undergraduate she made an eleven-month study visit to Moscow, where she worked for Progress Publishers and wrote a dissertation on seventeenth-century Moscow churches, which later grew into her doctorate on Moscow Baroque architecture, received from the University of Cambridge in 1976. Whilst at Cambridge she again visited the USSR on a British Council studentship to the Moscow Architectural Institute. In 1974 she went to lecture in Russian at Queen's University, Belfast, moving in 1977 to the University of Reading, where she taught courses covering all of Russian history. Since 1987 she has been senior lecturer in Russian history at the School of Slavonic and East European Studies, University of London. She is the author of two books, on Prince Vasily Vasilievich Golitsyn (Newtonville, 1984) and on the life and times of Sophia Alekseevna (forthcoming), over thirty articles and many more reviews, mostly on early modern Russian history and culture. She is a contributor to *The Modern Encyclopedia of Russian and Soviet History* and compiler of an annual bibliography covering eighteenth-century Russia for the *Year's Work in Modern Language Studies*. She regularly visits the United States and the Soviet Union, and lives in London with two cats, Sophia and Catherine.

FROM ACADEMIC INTERNATIONAL PRESS*